CRITICAL INSIGHTS

John Steinbeck

CRITICAL INSIGHTS

John Steinbeck

Editor
Don Noble
University of Alabama

Salem Press
Pasadena, California   Hackensack, New Jersey

Library of Congress Cataloging-in-Publication Data
John Steinbeck / editor, Don Noble.
    p. cm. — (Critical insights)
Includes bibliographical references and index.
ISBN 978-1-58765-703-0 (v. 1 : alk. paper)
    1. Steinbeck, John, 1902-1968—Criticism and interpretation. I. Noble, Donald R.
PS3537.T3234Z715466 2011
813'.52—dc22

2010030193

PRINTED IN CANADA

Contents_____

Resources

About This Volume

Don Noble

As Matthew J. Bolton reminds us in his essay in this collection, John Steinbeck wrote more than thirty prose works over the course of his career. He wrote short stories and linked-story collections as well as novellas and novels; he wrote journalism, essays, reportage, and even what might be considered scientific writing. He also wrote plays, several of which were enormously successful.

The issues with which Steinbeck concerned himself—and which critics, friendly and not so friendly, have addressed—are also numerous: the dignity of all people, in every social and economic stratum; workers' rights and capitalism; the need to nurture the spirit of brotherhood in mankind; the fight against fascism; the relationship of the human species to the rest of creation; the meaning and use of myth and archetype in understanding everyday human behavior. The list goes on and on and could itself make up a book. It would be impossible, then, to have in one volume an essay devoted to each discrete subject of interest or Steinbeck title, but in this collection the major works and issues receive individual treatment and no title or important concern goes unmentioned.

Hua Hsu, writing for *The Paris Review*, begins his brief essay with a reference to Preston Sturges's 1941 film *Sullivan's Travels*, which satirizes Steinbeck, Upton Sinclair, and Sinclair Lewis together and thus shows the linkage of these three novelists/social critics, at least in Sturges's mind. Hsu also reminds readers that Steinbeck was never better than when writing of California, his home state, and, as Faulkner put it when talking about his own home in Mississippi, his "little postage stamp of soil." Hsu judges that while Steinbeck may not be admired for his prose style, which is "spare and workmanlike," he can be praised for his optimism in "celebrating the democratic resolve of the masses."

In the first essay in the volume's "Critical Contexts" section, Bolton delivers a quick biographical sketch of Steinbeck's childhood in California and the importance of hands-on, physical labor in developing his outlook and psyche. As a laborer, Steinbeck got to know work and the workers in the fields in ways that his peers William Faulkner, Ernest Hemingway, and F. Scott Fitzgerald did not. Bolton's main task, however, is to trace the responses to Steinbeck's published works as his career moved through its forty-year arc, as well as the development of his reputation over the forty-two years since his death.

Two patterns emerge. First, Steinbeck rarely followed up a successful book with another in the same vein. After only modest success with the "swashbuckling adventure novel" *Cup of Gold* (1929), the linked stories *The Pastures of Heaven* (1932), and the mythological and archetype-inspired *To a God Unknown* (1933), Steinbeck broke out with *Tortilla Flat* in 1935. This comic, picaresque novel of the colorful Monterey *paisanos* brought him fame and fortune. But instead of cashing in by immediately writing another picaresque, he moved next to his most controversial work, the social protest novel *In Dubious Battle* (1936).

He followed this book with *Of Mice and Men* (1937), which was a best seller but widely rejected by reviewers. This novel, too, was proletarian in theme, but, at a time when psychological realism was in ascendancy, Steinbeck had made another excursion into myth, fable, and parable. The characters, especially the mentally slow Lennie Small, were deemed subhuman, and the novel, though violent in parts and found obscene by many, was labeled sentimental. These contradictions would follow Steinbeck throughout his career. The public would always hugely admire Steinbeck's work; the reviewers would rarely be more than lukewarm. In 1937 and 1938, Steinbeck returned to pastoral stories in *The Red Pony* and *The Long Valley*. Readers loved them; reviewers "roundly criticized" them.

Bolton appropriately spends the most time on *The Grapes of Wrath* (1939), which brought Steinbeck "adulation," the Pulitzer Prize, and much criticism—from the Left for being inadequately radical and from the Right for supposedly sympathizing with socialism and criticizing wealthy California landowners. So Steinbeck chose next to go on a marine biological expedition, which resulted in *Sea of Cortez* (1941), followed by his Mexican film documentary text *The Forgotten Village* (1941). During World War II Steinbeck produced, as his contribution to the war effort, a small shelf of books, including *The Moon Is Down* and *Bombs Away* (both 1942). *The Moon Is Down*, as novel and play, received fierce criticism—reviewers accused it of being far too kind in its treatment of the obviously Nazi invaders of a country much like Norway—but time would prove that the Norwegians and other occupied European countries loved the work and thought it captured the tone of foreign occupation just fine.

For the rest of his career, Steinbeck would enjoy great popularity and sales and, with the exception of *Cannery Row* (1945), little admiration from reviewers. *The Wayward Bus* (1947) sold well and was "savaged"; *The Pearl* (1947) was regarded as evidence of "deterioration." *Burning Bright* (1951) and *Pipe Dream* (1955) failed on the stage, and it was not until *East of Eden* (1952) that Steinbeck received again kind, though well-qualified, words from reviewers. *Sweet Thursday* (1954) was panned and *The Short Reign of Pippin IV* (1957) was poorly received, as was *The Winter of Our Discontent* (1961)—although, again, the European audience admired it, enough to make it the catalyst for Steinbeck's receipt of the Nobel Prize in 1962.

Steinbeck had a last popular success with *Travels with Charley: In Search of America* (1962), and even the usually harsh critics grudgingly enjoyed Steinbeck's trip around America with his poodle. Posthumous Steinbeck publications—fiction such as *The Acts of King Arthur and His Noble Knights* (1976) and the author's journals and letters—have aided scholars in understanding his methods and intentions but have not enhanced his critical reputation very much. Such publications rarely do, as Hemingway admirers have complained with the appearance of *Islands in the Stream* (1970), *The Garden of Eden* (1986), and other posthumous works.

Nevertheless, as scholarly interest in Steinbeck rises and the political controversies around his work subside, his place in the canon seems to be buttressed, even enhanced. Both Jackson J. Benson and Jay Parini have published authoritative biographies that help us understand this largely silent and largely misunderstood author, and Steinbeck's early interest in ecology—the interrelatedness of all life on the planet—now seems prescient. Scholarly and critical examinations of Steinbeck are now coming at a faster pace than ever, and this author who has always been loved and read by millions seems to be on the brink of winning the academic respect he deserves.

Jennifer Banach's essay, "'Roar Like a Lion,'" examines the historical and cultural contexts of Steinbeck's works, looking at Steinbeck's career from a different angle. Banach begins by reminding readers of Steinbeck's great pride in his profession and the importance he placed on writers, who, he believed, might just save humankind from destroying itself in this nuclear age. Because literature matters, he believed, writers have a grave responsibility. Banach summarizes Steinbeck's childhood and then moves, book by book, through his career, pointing out the various biographical strands.

The political currents of Steinbeck's time perhaps had the greatest influence on his work, particularly as he wrote *In Dubious Battle*. This novel of a labor strike is sympathetic to the strikers but also shows the pragmatic cynicism of the union leaders. Yet the *In Dubious Battle* controversy was dwarfed by the uproar over *The Grapes of Wrath*. Steinbeck had researched this novel extensively and was sure of his ground, but the California response was ferocious. Although he was never a socialist or a communist, this work prompted the Federal Bureau of Investigation to open a file on him in 1943 and prevent him from receiving a commission in the U.S. Army.

The Pearl, which, Banach explains, demonstrates the corruptive potential of great wealth on the soul, was seen by many as contemptuous of American capitalism. *The Wayward Bus*, a kind of *Ship of Fools* novel, was seen by some as an attack on the moral character of postwar America in general, especially the ethics of the business community. In the 1950s, Banach writes, Steinbeck was still seen as a leftist. He was antagonistic toward the House Un-American Activities Committee, a supporter of Adlai Stevenson, and a worker for improved relations between the peoples of the United States and the Soviet Union. Ironically, Steinbeck's friendship with Lyndon B. Johnson and his support of the war in Vietnam made him persona non grata to the American literary Left.

Never has a writer been attacked so steadily, over decades, from both political sides. Yet there is no doubt that Steinbeck was a writer in touch always with the political and cultural currents around him. He must have been doing something right, because, politically, he pleased almost no one.

Aside from politics, Steinbeck was also deeply interested in myth, mysticism, and the natural world. His use of myth is especially evident in *To a God Unknown*, and it was perhaps strengthened by his friendship with Joseph Campbell and influenced by Ralph Waldo Emerson's essays, such as "Nature." Steinbeck's interest in nature is evident in almost all of his work, and one of the most debated issues around his philosophy is the extent to which he is a literary naturalist. Naturalists, simply put, believe that man has little or no free will and is the pawn of his genetic inheritance as well as social, economic, and other environmental forces. Gurdip Panesar explores this issue, on which Banach touches, by comparing Steinbeck to Frank Norris, author of the naturalistic novels *McTeague*, *The Octopus*, and *The Pit*.

The two authors have a great deal in common. Both were highly critical of the social conditions endured by the poor and powerless. Both wrote of California and of individuals, usually simple people, struggling against powerful, crushing forces. Both authors infuse their fiction with mythical and allegorical dimensions. Both have been accused of sentimentality, melodrama, and sensationalism and of being anticapitalist. Both demonstrate the working out of natural laws, though, as Panesar notes, Steinbeck's natural laws are nonteleological—that is, not predetermined. Of the two, Norris is the far more doctrinaire naturalist, while Steinbeck focuses more on the human, individual level, not the abstractions of naturalistic theory.

As was natural with the rise of feminist criticism, a good deal of attention has been given to Steinbeck's female characters. In her essay on the short-story collection *The Long Valley*, Cynthia A. Bily focuses on Steinbeck's women, a concern that she joins with the author's concern for the environment and the earth. The two subjects dovetail nicely. Citing Mimi Gladstein, Bily reminds us that Steinbeck's few female characters are usually "from the lower classes, uneducated and domestic" and usually found at home or in brothels. Yet, as Bily argues, the women in this collection are not unimportant or uninteresting; rather, it is the men who, largely uninterested in women, do not understand their powers. Citing Lorelei Cederstrom, Bily argues that it is the female characters that Steinbeck draws as representatives of the archetypal feminine, who are in touch with the natural world and have the correct balanced and nurturing relationship to the earth. The men, often as not, seek to conquer the earth, dominate it (her), and wrest production from it. This masculine attitude can—and occasionally, as with the Dust Bowl that was in part caused by deep plowing, does—bring devastation and sterility to the earth.

The flowers in "The Chrysanthemums," then, are obviously symbolic. Elisa Allen has a rich relationship to the earth that neither her husband nor the heartless traveling tinker can understand. Steinbeck's polarities are not absolute, however, as we see Peter in "The Harness" take enormous pleasure from the flowering, the colors, and the aroma of his sweet-pea crop. Their market value is, at least for a while, secondary for him.

Not surprisingly, the quintessential symbol of female nurturing is the breast, and feminist critics tend to see Rose of Sharon's breast-feeding of the starving stranger as a powerful representation of the earth mother, the nurturer. Similarly, the women in *The Long Valley* are often seen preparing and offering food. Bily extends this metaphor with a closing discussion of the role of sexuality in Steinbeck's male and female characters' lives. The men crave intimacy and love—a craving that they feel as a "hunger"—but find it difficult to connect. Women, too, crave intimacy, but their needs are seldom met. Bily concludes that, in *The Long Valley*, neither men nor their sometimes domineering women find intimacy or satisfaction. Because the sexes tend to be separate from each other, both "go hungry."

The "Critical Readings" section of this volume begins with Jackson J. Benson's "John Steinbeck: The Favorite Author We Love to Hate." Benson not only recites the critical establishment's pillories of Steinbeck but also explains why, unfairly or not, these censures have been heaped on him. Benson begins by underlining Steinbeck's popularity. In a single year, his books sell one million copies—*The Grapes of Wrath* alone sells two hundred thousand copies, and *Of Mice and Men* and *The Red Pony*, which are required reading in many secondary schools, sell several times more. All of Steinbeck's many books are in print, and he is a popular favorite in Europe and, especially, Japan. There is a Steinbeck Library and a Steinbeck Society, and in 1984 the National Endowment for the Humanities ranked him eighth among the top thirty authors a high school graduate should have read. No other twentieth-century writer made the top ten.

Yet, even though he won the Nobel Prize, Steinbeck's critical reception has often been lukewarm to cool and he is not taught much in universities today. Why? Benson suggests a series of reasons. Steinbeck was a western writer, and the American literary establishment, located in the East, has tended to believe there is no real cultural or historical life in California to write about. Steinbeck was hugely popular and thus, like a Stephen King, an object of critical suspicion: if too many people like it, it can't be much good. He sometimes wrote comedy, which is never as revered as serious writing. He was accused of sentimentality (an issue John Seelye examines at length elsewhere in this volume), which is a cardinal literary sin. And as both Banach and Benson remark, Steinbeck's politics were highly controversial throughout his career—too far to the left in the 1930s, too conservative in the 1960s.

Benson dwells at some length on the political attacks because they have been particularly vicious and ill grounded. Steinbeck often asserted that he was apolitical and that the stories—happy or catastrophic—are in fact accounts of "something that happened." Although he would criticize meanness and greed, he was a politically detached writer and was never a Marxist or even a socialist. More recently, he has again been attacked as "immoral" because of his books' crude language and casual sex, although there is actually little of either to object to.

After this introduction to Steinbeck's critical fortunes, the volume turns to some of Steinbeck's most popular novels. *Tortilla Flat*, a picaresque novel about a group of *paisanos* in Monterey, was his first big hit in 1935. Joseph Fontenrose explicates several of the themes in *Tortilla Flat* that lift it above a simple comedy about a group of shiftless drunks. First, Steinbeck explores the idea of group as single organism. Danny and his friends and the house are one; they share a nervous system, their emotions, and a destiny. The *paisanos* also live in ecological harmony with the land around them; the relationship is somewhat parasitical, true, but besides pilfering, they take up the extra that would go to waste, and they certainly do not dominate or rape the land. Second, the novel is underwritten, as many have noted, by the structure of Sir Thomas Mallory's *Le Morte d'Arthur*, and Fontenrose demonstrates how Danny and his friends, however unwashed, have a lot in common with the Knights of the Round Table.

Readers would have welcomed another picaresque novel, but instead Steinbeck published his first novel about unions, strikes, and protests, the highly controversial *In Dubious Battle*. Thomas M. Tammaro, agreeing with Warren G. French, believes *In Dubious Battle* to be the "best novel about a strike ever written." He begins by reminding the reader that there is in fact very little working-class literature included in the American canon, making it "near[ly] invisible." The lives of businessmen and other white-collar citizens—or, sometimes, as in southern literature, the lives of sharecroppers or slaves—are represented, but there is not much blue-collar fiction. Tammaro finds the merits of *In Dubious Battle* to be numerous, but most important is the work's balanced treatment of workers, unions, and union organizers. Tammaro insists that Steinbeck "avoids polemic and propaganda." Furthermore, Tammaro maintains, the novel is not dated. The wages and working conditions of migrant agricultural workers are as unresolved and important today as they were in the 1930s.

Of Mice and Men is perhaps more often read (and seen on stage) today than *The Grapes of Wrath*. Since it concerns the private lives of only a small number of individuals, and since the issues it handles are not obviously political, the novel has been less controversial. That the migrant workers in *Of Mice and Men* are almost all men excludes from the novel issues raised by other Steinbeck works such as marriage, family, and the pathetic suffering of children. On this isolated ranch Steinbeck creates, with just a few characters, a narrative that approaches the inevitable and the tragic.

George and Lennie are, just the two of them, a family, and, as a kind of "couple," they share a dream, the American Dream of owning a place of their own. The novel's setting, the wheat ranch, is lovely and idyllic. Likewise, the little place George and Lennie dream of buying is nothing less than Edenic. But this is a fallen world, by definition an imperfect place, and Edens are not available. By killing Curley's wife, however "accidentally," Lennie also kills the pair's hope for a home. The novel ends with George compassionately killing Lennie to save him from a lynch mob.

Anne Loftis, in her "Historical Introduction," sketches the novel's background and guides the reader through the various forms the work took—from novel to stage play to film—as well as through the changes Steinbeck thought necessary for each form. Louis Owens's approach is from a slightly different point of view. Owens reviews a number of critics' opinions of the novel's themes of paradise and, more particularly, loneliness. Owens also focuses on George and Lennie's commitment to their impossible dream and, more important, to each other.

Owens ends by suggesting that Steinbeck's emphasis on the importance of people's commitment to one another "will appear again, in fact, in much greater dimension in Steinbeck's next novel, *The Grapes of Wrath*."

The Grapes of Wrath, probably the high point of Steinbeck's career, is discussed here in two essays by John Seelye and Susan Shillinglaw. Seelye takes up the charge Leslie Fiedler issued against the novel in a 1989 address to a major convocation of Steinbeck scholars. On the fiftieth anniversary of the publication of *The Grapes of Wrath*, Fiedler faulted the novel for sentimentality and of course stirred up resentment and a number of heated responses. In his essay, Seelye refutes Fiedler carefully and at length. Comparing *The Grapes of Wrath* with Harriet Beecher Stowe's *Uncle Tom's Cabin*, he reveals an amazing number of parallels between the two novels. Both take on major social issues by addressing great national problems through the lives of a group of particular individuals. In each, an economic system fueled by greed inflicts hardship on many oppressed and disenfranchised people, and each novel contains violence as well as an appeal to the Christian example. The irony in Seelye's comparison is that Fiedler, who castigated *Grapes* as "maudlin, sentimental and overblown," had praised *Uncle Tom's Cabin* as "the greatest of all novels of sentimental protest" in the nineteenth century. Seelye declares *Grapes* to be the twentieth-century *Uncle Tom's Cabin*: like Stowe's novel it does not merely generate idle tears but also spurs its reader to demand social change—the improvement of western migrant laborers' working conditions. Seelye especially defends the ending of the novel, for if sentimentality demands a happy ending there is certainly little of one in *Grapes*. By the close of the story, many members of the Joad family have died or been injured; they have not been able to buy their own place or even find enough work to feed themselves. Rose of Sharon's breast-feeding of the starving stranger is not sentimental but shocking and Christian and spontaneous, and it serves as a warning to Californians that something had better be done, or else, because the grapes of wrath are filling.

As one might suppose, Steinbeck's depiction of California ranchers and farmers and state agencies and affluent citizens in general infuriated many in the Golden State. The responses varied: some spearheaded initiatives to return the Okies to their home state or cut relief benefits, while others, as Shillinglaw discusses at length, issued literary responses. Several writers were commissioned or took it upon themselves to defend California ranchers, farmers, and social programs. The most interesting part of these defenses is that the writers, in the main, were sincere. Californians were frightened by the prospect of unions, which they saw as communist or socialist; frightened by their own precarious affluence in the face of a depression; and solidly and sincerely, if mistakenly, believed that people could rise in the world through their own efforts alone.

Shillinglaw examines several of these apologetic publications, three of them Ruth Comfort Mitchell's *Of Human Kindness*, Frank J. Taylor's journalism, and Marshall V. Hartranft's *Grapes of Gladness*. In many ways *Of Human Kindness* is reminiscent of Old South novels such as *Swallow Barn*. It centers on a hardworking and kind affluent family, the Banners, who care for their help beautifully. In contrast to Steinbeck, Shillinglaw writes, Mitchell bends over backward to be fair and balanced toward the affluent and the impoverished and even suggests that the Okies she is familiar with are not the boorish, unwashed peasants that Steinbeck portrays in his novel. Taylor's journalism as a whole praises the California entrepreneur and California's overly generous governmental responses. In one of his articles, he writes about the Merritt family of the Tagus ranch, the probable site of the strike in *In Dubious Battle*, praising them as hardworking, Jeffersonian yeoman farmers and "benevolent men." Hartranft's *Grapes of Gladness* proposed a scheme by which an Okie family could receive one acre of land, on very generous terms, and earn a living on that one acre, a diminished echo of the forty acres and a mule that freedmen were promised after the Civil War but never received. Collectively, these apologies seem not cynical but well-meaning, if hopelessly naïve. The writers did not and perhaps could not imagine how large and severe the problems were and could offer only "Band-Aid" solutions.

The volume then shifts gears by examining themes prevalent across Steinbeck's work. Warren G. French begins his essay by explaining that Steinbeck's "self-characters" are not autobiographical characters—as is, say, Thomas Wolfe's Eugene Gant—but "underdog" characters with whom Steinbeck in some way identifies, oftentimes through a shared dream. For instance, *Tortilla Flat*'s protagonist, Danny, feels caught between his desire for peaceful prosperity and his yearning for unregulated freedom—a conflict Steinbeck himself felt before he became financially successful. His frustrated desire for community is reflected in three of the 1930s novels—*Tortilla Flat*, *In Dubious Battle*, and *Of Mice and Men*. The protagonists of each dream of community, but each story ends in a literal death and in the death of the dream of community. This is especially vivid in *Of Mice and Men*, for George lives on after Lennie, but now he will be literally alone and lonely. With the success of *The Grapes of Wrath* and the affluence it brought him, Steinbeck was no longer exactly an underdog, but he was not confident that his success would last. He identified with his latest protagonist, Tom Joad, who declares in his final speech that he will go out into the world and be not a revolutionary at the barricades but a voice for change and an inspiration to anyone who would listen.

James C. Kelley takes up Steinbeck's interest in science and his friendship with marine biologist Ed Ricketts in "John Steinbeck and Ed Ricketts: Understanding Life in the Great Tide Pool." He details how both men studied early ecology texts—Ricketts more formally at the University of Chicago—and came to believe that humans are just one of many threads in nature, not above or separate from it, and that creation is a kind of "superorganism" larger than the sum of all its parts. The mythologist Joseph Campbell, a mutual friend of theirs whose later work in mythology would conclude that people everywhere on the planet shared the same myths and the same Jungian collective unconscious, strengthened their belief. Kelley also takes up the question of the proper attitude toward science. Should we fear science? Is it a tool humankind uses to despoil the planet? Will it be our salvation? Finally, he concludes, science and scientific understanding are just one more step in our progress toward being in harmony with the universe.

John H. Timmerman takes yet another approach to Steinbeck's pre-occupation with science and ethics. It is generally agreed that the later years of Steinbeck's career was a "moral phase." In *America and Americans* and *Travels with Charley*, Steinbeck decried the waste, carelessness, abuse of the land and its natural resources, and the many examples of human greed that he saw around him. He was irritated by what he thought of as the country's incessant haste; people seemed to him to rush from place to place and seldom pause to enjoy and be in awe of the natural world and its power. He professes that affluence is often the enemy of morality and leads to callous abuses of the earth.

Some critics see these sentiments as the complaints of an old man, one eaten up with nostalgia for an idyllic past that probably never in fact existed. Yet Timmerman demonstrates that these concerns were in Steinbeck's works from the very outset of his career. Joseph Wayne in *To a God Unknown* tries and fails to control the natural cycles of rain and drought; at least some of the valley residents of *The Pastures of Heaven* live in harmony with nature; and, late in Steinbeck's career, the canneries in *Sweet Thursday* are silent and rusting because, foolishly, the fishermen have caught all the pilchards. Nature is rich but not inexhaustible and Steinbeck, Timmerman shows, had been working on this question of humankind's proper relationship to the natural world all his writing life.

Over the past three decades, opinions of Steinbeck's depictions of women have vacillated. Jackson J. Benson's biography of the author shows that, without doubt, there were many women in Steinbeck's life, many of them strong teachers and with great influence upon him. Why, then, are most of the women in his fiction either at home tending to domestic matters and ignored or tyrannizing those husbands or living and working in brothels?

In her "Steinbeck and the Woman Question: A Never-Ending Puzzle" Mimi Gladstein focuses on *East of Eden* especially, finding the amoral Kate Trask one of literature's most vile villainesses. With the exception of Abra, Gladstein finds the rest of the women "pallid, hysterical, mean and/or stupid." She also examines the evolution of Curley's nameless wife in *Of Mice and Men* as the novel was transformed into stage play and film. Each representation of Curley's wife, she claims, reflects the changing interests of its generation.

Along with what we might call "the woman question," Steinbeck's critics attend to the author's portrayals of various ethnic and minority groups. Susan Shillinglaw acknowledges that Steinbeck has sometimes been accused of portraying minorities stereotypically and as primitives but believes this to be a misunderstanding. First of all, Shillinglaw reminds us, Steinbeck knew many minorities, especially Mexicans, firsthand because as a young man he worked side by side with them in factories and fields. At a time when most minorities were invisible in California, he not only knew of them but also lived and worked beside them.

Steinbeck, who had a streak of mysticism in him, might also be faulted for romanticizing minorities. He felt, as D. H. Lawrence did, that Native Americans and others minorities have freer access to other dimensions of reality. Yet, as Shillinglaw argues, Steinbeck's portraits are never derogatory—in *To a God Unknown*, the Indians, isolated, silent, and in harmony with the earth, try to warn Joseph Wayne about his foolish attempts to dominate the earth. Further, certain white male characters seem to have the same knowledge and powers as Steinbeck's minority characters. Mac in *Tortilla Flat* or Doc in *Cannery Row*, for instance, can also be spontaneous, instinctive, and nonteleological. Shillinglaw also points out that where there is racial stereotyping in the novels, it is presented as one character's opinion of another or, in many cases, such as *Lifeboat*, written into the films made from Steinbeck writings but not into the writings themselves.

Steinbeck may be lodged in the popular imagination as a California writer, not a "war" writer as Hemingway was, but Robert E. Morsberger makes the claim that Steinbeck wrote more about World War II than any other major American novelist: one novel, one play, three movies, and two volumes of nonfiction, not to mention his postwar novels that include veterans still suffering the aftershocks of war. The most important of these writings is *The Moon Is Down*, both novel and play, which were published and produced just three months after the United States declared war on the Axis powers. *Moon* was critically attacked, although, it seems clear now, the attacks were extremely ill-conceived. Although Steinbeck extols the courage and resilience of the citizens of *Moon*'s unnamed occupied country and although the work predicts absolutely the victory of the invaded over the invaders, reviewers could not stand it that Steinbeck's invaders are human—sometimes guilt ridden, often homesick and miserable. After the war it became clear that, although even possessing a copy of the novel was punishable by death in the occupied countries, their citizens had nevertheless read it avidly and taken great inspiration from it. The king of Norway even awarded Steinbeck his country's highest honor.

Less well known these days are Steinbeck's other wartime writings. *Bombs Away* is an account of the assembly and training of an air force bomber crew in which Steinbeck asserts that this task is more possible in America than elsewhere because of the nation's egalitarian, democratic society. This is fanciful but probably true! Morsberger also discusses *Lifeboat,* especially the movie, which Steinbeck strongly disliked and from which he asked that his name be removed. The film version transformed Steinbeck's U-Boat Captain into a kind of superman, even if a supervillain, and the black steward, Joe, into a "stock comedy Negro."

Most interesting, and taken up at length in the biographies, is Steinbeck's actual participation in the war. As a war correspondent, he traveled in Europe from February 1943 to January 1944, in the course of which he spent six weeks in combat in the Mediterranean with a secret commando unit, launching raids on Axis-held islands between Algeria and Sicily and along the Italian coast. After the war, his dispatches concerning activities that were not classified—such as the London Blitz, his visits to the wounded in hospitals, and the talks and poker games he held with GIs—made up the volume *Once There Was a War*.

Toward the end of his career, Steinbeck published one more California epic, *East of Eden*. Many commentators have discussed the novel as a study of polarities—of good versus evil and of Cain versus Abel—but Carol L. Hansen goes further. She sees the novel's arch villainess, Cathy, as an amoral character—"a force beyond good and evil, a force of perverse freedom." The norm seems monstrous to her, Steinbeck has said, and he has Cathy identify with Alice of *Alice in Wonderland*, who is "caught in a nightmare world."

In 1954 Steinbeck published the third volume in his Monterey trilogy, *Sweet Thursday*, a book that was poorly received and called fantastic and sentimental. Yet Robert DeMott believes it was ahead of its time and that critics, more than usual, just didn't get it. This is an early experimental, postmodern novel, he asserts, not a reprise of either the California as Eden theme or the "group man" theory. It is a comic novel, true, but also a novel about creativity, about writing. Several of the characters are writing or trying to write; Doc especially is frustrated by writer's block. Some critics condemned the novel as a "cartoon," to which DeMott replies, "exactly." Steinbeck was a huge fan of Al Capp's comic strip *Li'l Abner*, DeMott remarks, and may have felt he was, like Capp with Dogpatch, creating a new fictional world. This world, Cannery Row, is playful, exaggerated, not mimetically sound, making the novel not social protest or even social satire, but pure comedy.

Finally, this volume closes with an interview, conducted by Donald V. Coers in 1993, with Elaine Steinbeck, John Steinbeck's widow. Elaine—Steinbeck's third wife, whom he married in 1950 and remained with until his death in 1968—is perfectly forthcoming in this conversation that brings Steinbeck to life. He was himself a shy, quiet, sometimes gruff man who did not speak in public easily and did not like reporters very much, yet here Elaine speaks for him. She insists that Steinbeck only wrote what he wanted to—neither publishers nor critics nor his wife controlled his work. Elaine is especially interesting when discussing Steinbeck's deep and abiding interest in Arthurian legend and is engaging about their trips to the Soviet Union and to Stockholm to receive the Nobel Prize in Literature. Readers will be amused to read of Steinbeck's first meeting with William Faulkner, who talked even less willingly than Steinbeck himself, and to learn that Elaine became good friends with Ernest's widow, Mary Hemingway, with whom she obviously had a lot in common. She concludes that John "believed in *man*" and believed that "man will never be perfect, but he has to strive for it."

CAREER, LIFE, AND INFLUENCE

On John Steinbeck_____

Don Noble

In working on a project such as this one, I have found that certain things seem to stand out. Rereading the works of John Steinbeck, I was again delighted at how much pleasure the comic novels such as *Tortilla Flat* or *Cannery Row* still give and how moved one still is by the story of the Joads in *The Grapes of Wrath* or the tragic ending of *Of Mice and Men*. Rereading the criticism written about Steinbeck over the decades, I was struck by something quite different—by how, in large part, it is so defensive. John Steinbeck was both a Pulitzer Prize winner and a Nobel Prize laureate, yet so many of the essays seem apologetic. Many respond to, say, Edmund Wilson's claim that *In Dubious Battle* is "dated," of historical interest only, or refute Leslie Fiedler's assertion that *The Grapes of Wrath* is "sentimental." It seems that the terms of the debate are controlled by a few naysayers. I find this absurd.

Steinbeck himself, in his Nobel Prize acceptance speech, declared his pride in his profession and its many practitioners and announced that he would not "squeak like a grateful and apologetic mouse," but would stand up and "roar like a lion out of pride." This same exhortation might be addressed to Steinbeck fans and critics as well as the compilers of anthologies and producers of syllabi and canons. *Roar like a lion. Stop countering old charges and bringing up the old cavils.* By referring to them over and over, constantly by basing new essays on them, we bring them to the fore again and refresh them in the public consciousness. There is an adage in teaching: never, in some fit of pedagogical jeu d'esprit, write anything on the blackboard that is not correct. The students will read it, write it in their notebooks, and remember that piece of misinformation forever.

Besides which, there is much to be proud of in the works of John Steinbeck, no excuses needed. Humor, for example—literature that gives us pleasure and causes us to smile—is a rare and valuable commodity. There are, surely, too few comic novels in the world, and the

Monterey trilogy is a gift, nothing to be apologetic about. Surely no one wishes Shakespeare had written only tragedies and histories.

Moreover, when he does give us tragedy, Steinbeck is equally gifted. Though critics often pan him for sentimentality, looking closely at how he draws out our tears reveals that he never falls back on the tricks of the sentimental author. In *Of Mice and Men*, as in *King Lear*, the death of the protagonist is inevitable and tragic, not gratuitous. The tears Lennie's death draws from us are real and earned, as are those drawn from us by the grim and uncertain endings of *In Dubious Battle* and *The Grapes of Wrath*.

There is also no reason to apologize for Steinbeck's writing style. True, he is not usually as poetic as Fitzgerald or as ornate as Faulkner or as tellingly terse as Hemingway. But perhaps Steinbeck's style is best compared to that of Billy Collins. Both styles appear to be clear, plain, and simple and are often described as "accessible," and both, besides providing satisfying superficial readings, yield further depths upon rereadings. Steinbeck often wrote that there were layers in his novels. Even in a comedy such as *Cannery Row*, he insisted, there were as many levels of meaning as the reader could bring to it.

But perhaps the best reason to roar about Steinbeck is his continued relevance. Critics have accused some of his most popular novels— especially *Of Mice and Men*, *In Dubious Battle*, and *The Grapes of Wrath*—of being dated, yet this charge seems to me particularly specious. Are the problems of migrant workers solved? Is the question of workers' rights and unionization settled? Have banks and large corporations ceased to be impersonal or amoral? Has corporate greed been checked? These do not, in the year 2010, seem like issues long ago resolved.

And as we learn more about the environment and our relationship to it, Steinbeck's thoughts on ecology seem strikingly prescient. Several of his novels, as well as the nonfiction work *Sea of Cortez*, treat nature, pollution, waste, man's relationship to the earth, and the proper kind of stewardship we must practice if life is to be sustained on this planet.

These subjects are receiving the most positive attention from scholars lately and are of special interest to readers as we all try to answer these questions in our own lives.

Further, Steinbeck's speculations on "group man," or phalanx man, which are notably taken up in *In Dubious Battle* and *The Grapes of Wrath*, are finding new validation from the scientific community. As Jim Casy speculates (perhaps taking a cue from Ralph Waldo Emerson and his idea of the oversoul), maybe we don't each have a separate soul but all share a piece of one great big soul—a notion that Joseph Campbell may have passed on to Steinbeck from his reading of Carl Jung, who believed that all humans, worldwide, share in a "collective unconscious." Though it may sound hokey to some, it is a theory that one of America's foremost naturalists and two-time winner of the Pulitzer Prize, Dr. E. O. Wilson, propounds. Wilson's *Sociobiology: The New Synthesis* (1975) suggests that there may be certain bits of knowledge as well as behaviors and "propensities" that are specieswide and genetically inherited. More recently, a book Wilson coauthored with Bert Hölldobler, *The Superorganism: The Beauty, Elegance, and Strangeness of Insect Societies* (2009), offers the pair's observations of ants, wasps, and bees and convincingly argues that these colony insects should be understood less as individuals and more as parts of a single living entity. Steinbeck studies will doubtless soon be making use of Wilson's work as well as that of ethologists such as Robert Ardrey, Konrad Lorenz, and Desmond Morris, all of whom study the nature of social humankind and how people function in groups.

Sometimes, as is all too often the case with Steinbeck, the critical establishment takes popularity as prima facie evidence of mediocrity. Yet this patently is ridiculous. Lord Byron, Charles Dickens, and William Styron were all popular authors. *The Great Gatsby* and *The Sun Also Rises* sold well, and *For Whom the Bell Tolls* sold very well. That a novel wins a place on the best-seller list is no absolute indicator of its excellence, but neither is it a mark of its inferiority.

The real test, accepted by everyone, I should imagine, is the test of time. *The Bridges of Madison County* sold very well but is thoroughly forgotten now. On the other hand, seventy-one years after its publication, the best-selling *Grapes of Wrath* continues to sell about two hundred thousand copies per year. Likewise, though *Tortilla Flat* was published seventy-five years ago and *Of Mice and Men* seventy-three, both of these books sell briskly today. If the acid test of art is time, Steinbeck's works are certified.

There is much to roar about. We have every reason to be optimistic about the future of Steinbeck studies and confident that Steinbeck will regain his rightful place in the American literary canon.

Biography of John Steinbeck_____

Gordon Bergquist

John Ernst Steinbeck was born in 1902 in Salinas, California, of German and Irish parentage. His father was of German origin and was variously a bookkeeper, accountant, and manager, and he eventually became the treasurer of Monterey County. The elder Steinbeck was an avid gardener (throughout his life, his son would always have to have a garden wherever he lived) and a somewhat introspective man. Steinbeck's mother was of Irish descent, a woman of energy and determination, emotional and sensitive to art, and fond of stories of fantasy and enchantment. The later dichotomies observed in Steinbeck, between the romantic and the hardheaded naturalist, between the dreamer and the masculine tough guy, may be partly accounted for by inheritance from the Irish and German strains of his parents.

The young Steinbeck had a local reputation as a loner and a bit of a dreamer. He read much on his own, his favorite writings being those of Robert Louis Stevenson, Alexandre Dumas, père, Sir Walter Scott, the Bible, and especially *Le Morte d'Arthur* (1485), by Sir Thomas Malory. This last would remain an influence throughout his life, with many of his stories displaying Arthurian parallels and influences; the work which occupied much of his time in the last years of his life was a translation or redaction of the Arthurian stories, unfinished at his death.

Steinbeck grew to be a tall, gangly youth with broad shoulders, a barrel chest, and a large head. He early developed a fondness for words and a passion for language that was never to leave him. He was independent-minded, not to say stubborn, and as a freshman in high school determined to be a writer. He was graduated from high school in 1919, at best an average student and athlete. For the next six years, he attended Stanford University on and off but never took a degree. As in high school, he took what interested him and cared little for other courses, even if required; the courses he took were those he thought would help him in his writing.

During his many vacations from Stanford Steinbeck worked for the local sugar company in the field and in the office; he also worked on ranches, on a dredging crew, and in the beet harvest. He came to know well the Mexican-American workers alongside whom he labored. He rather enjoyed working with his hands and was certainly throughout his life never afraid of hard work; he also became a notable handyman and maker of gadgets. After leaving Stanford for good in 1925, he worked sporadically during the next three years at a lodge in the High Sierra near Lake Tahoe as a caretaker and handyman. The job gave him much time, especially in the winter, for writing. Steinbeck briefly sought his fortune in New York, where he worked on construction and as a cub reporter. He returned to California in the summer of 1926.

Since his early years in high school, Steinbeck had been writing. His first published stories were in a Stanford literary magazine; his first paid story, "The Gifts of Iban," was published pseudonymously in 1927. By 1930, his apprenticeship could be said to be over: In that year, his first novel, *Cup of Gold*, was published, he married Carol Henning, and he met Edward F. Ricketts, who was to have a notable effect upon the ideas and content of his further work.

Cup of Gold was not widely noticed, and Steinbeck and his new wife, while not subjected to grinding poverty, did live a rather hand-to-mouth existence. The publication of *Pastures of Heaven* (1932) and *To a God Unknown* (1933) increased his critical reputation in narrow circles but did little for his finances or fame. Finally, the publication of *Tortilla Flat* (1935) made the breakthrough; the book was a best seller and brought Steinbeck fame and money. Though Steinbeck complained about lack of money for the rest of his career, after this date he was never in any financial distress. This book was the first full-length presentation of those themes and characters that have come to be particularly associated with Steinbeck. He turned away from the mythic and legendary materials of *Cup of Gold* and *To a God Unknown* and dealt with contemporary issues, especially the plight of the socially and economically dispossessed. Like the great majority of Steinbeck's works, *Tortilla Flat* presents familiar, ordinary characters based on his own firsthand acquaintance. His next major works, *In Dubious Battle* (1936), *Of Mice and Men* (1937), and *The Grapes of Wrath* (1939), would continue to exploit these characters and themes.

These works also displayed some of the effects of Steinbeck's friendship with Ed Ricketts (1897-1948), a marine biologist. Steinbeck had earlier been interested, if only haphazardly, in natural science. His naturalistic view of men, especially in groups, was at least reinforced by his friendship with Ricketts. Ricketts was an exponent of non-teleological thinking (seeing what *is* rather than what might be, should be, or could be). This attitude accorded well with Steinbeck's own naturalistic impulses, at least as fictional method; Steinbeck did not always accept the grim conclusions implicit in a naturalistic view of man and maintained his belief in human progress and free will. The most straightforward presentation of such views may be found in *The Log from the Sea of Cortez* (1951), by both Steinbeck and Ricketts. The book provides the philosophical and organizational background for a tidepool collecting and survey trip taken by Ricketts and Steinbeck in 1940 in the Gulf of California.

During World War II, Steinbeck produced only a few minor works until *Cannery Row* (1945). He served for a few months as a war correspondent in Europe, was divorced in 1942, and married Gwyndolyn Conger in 1943. He moved to New York and for the remainder of his life traveled frequently with New York as a base. During these years he also spent much of his time writing film scripts and stage plays based on his works. As much as any other American novelist, Steinbeck was attracted to and involved in the stage and the cinema.

After the war, he began the major work that critics and the public were expecting after *The Grapes of Wrath*. The work was eventually to be *East of Eden* (1952), a long generational novel into which Steinbeck poured much of his own personal experience and which he regarded as his major work and expression of whatever he had learned over the years. The public did not share Steinbeck's regard, and the novel is perhaps best known today in its film version, starring the cult figure James Dean. Before *East of Eden* appeared, however, Steinbeck had published *The Wayward Bus* (1947), which was a Book-of-the-Month Club selection, and *Burning Bright* (1950). After *East of Eden*, Steinbeck published only three more novels: *Sweet Thursday* (1954), *The Short Reign of Pippin IV: A Fabrication* (1957), and *The Winter of Our Discontent* (1961). The latter is considered to be the best of the three and expresses Steinbeck's view of the malaise into which postwar America had fallen.

Steinbeck had divorced his second wife in 1948 and was remarried, in 1950, to Elaine Scott. In the postwar years he traveled often, seeming unable to settle down in a single place. He went several times to Russia, Europe, and especially England, but when abroad he would frequently long for home. After *East of Eden*, Steinbeck became preoccupied with nonfiction work. He wrote regular editorials for the *Saturday Review*, his wartime dispatches were published (1958), he published *Travels with Charley* (1962, a record of a three-month trip by truck around America with his dog), and he completed the essays that compose *America and Americans* (1966), designed to accompany a series of photographs showing the spirit and diversity of America and its people. In 1967, Steinbeck, who had done some speechwriting for President Lyndon B. Johnson, went to Vietnam at the request of the president and recorded his views and impressions in a series of newspaper reports. His long career as a writer was capped in 1962 with the award of the Nobel Prize in Literature. He died of coronary disease in New York in December, 1968, and his ashes were later scattered with the wind on the California coast.

In the course of his career, Steinbeck was held to be a sentimental romantic and a grim naturalist, a Communist and a Fascist, a mere journalist and the spokesman of a generation. It is a tribute to the man that his work has inspired such varying views; clearly, he has made a mark on American consciousness. Steinbeck was the writer (he disliked the word "author") of at least one major masterpiece—*The*

Grapes of Wrath—and several excellent works of lesser scope: *Tortilla Flat, Of Mice and Men, The Red Pony, In Dubious Battle*, and *Cannery Row*. All, except perhaps the last, are standard readings in high school and college English courses, as well as the subject of a large and growing body of critical analysis and opinion.

His particular contribution to the American ethos was to make uniquely his own the portraits of migrant workers, the dispossessed, dirt farmers, and manual laborers. He provided authentic portraits of a class of people seldom seen in fiction before his day. His pictures of stoop laborers, strikes, and the Depression are today the standard images by which those things are known and imagined. *The Grapes of Wrath* has become not only an artistic creation but also an authentic view of many of the plagues of the 1930's. For most people, *The Grapes of Wrath* is what the Depression was, at least in the western United States.

Perhaps the greatest general qualities of Steinbeck's work, qualities which help his works continue to interest, are life and immediacy. Steinbeck was enamored of life and gloried in it. He re-created it vividly in many of his works, with color and accuracy. He took great pains to research most of his works and believed he was thus attaining to some sort of truth, as well as reality. His generally nonteleological view of life led him to concentrate on the moment, on what *is*. At his best, mostly in works before World War II, he re-created authentic American types and characters and placed them in contexts which partook of the great myths and patterns of life and literature: the Bible, the Arthurian myths, the eternal cycles of nature. He had a strong faith in the natural processes of renewal and continuity and thus expanded his tales of the small and the insignificant to give them resonance and universality.

His accuracy and realism can perhaps best be seen in his care for the dialogue of his novels, even to the extent, in his later works, of reading into a tape recorder his own dialogue and playing it back for himself until he felt he had got it right, testing it constantly on the ear. It was probably this attention to authentic speech which made so many of his novels good candidates for stage and screen. None of his novels made bad films and some were outstanding, notably *The Grapes of Wrath* and *Of Mice and Men*. With only a few exceptions, his characters and events were equally genuine, dealing as they did with specifically American and specifically contemporary events.

Finally, Steinbeck was a patriot, but not of the flag-waving, jingoist persuasion. He displayed a deep feeling for the American people and the land both early and late in his career. He saw the values—perhaps felt them would be more correct—of family and social cohesion. He saw man as a part of a whole, often against a background of the disintegration of larger social and economic units and systems. At roughly the same time as Sinclair Lewis was skewering the middle class of America, Steinbeck was giving his public an equally authentic view of a very different class of Americans, though with less satire and more affection.

From *Dictionary of World Biography: The 20th Century.* Pasadena, CA: Salem Press, 1999. Copyright © 1999 by Salem Press, Inc.

Bibliography

Astro, Richard, and Tetsumaro Hayashi, eds. *Steinbeck: The Man and His Work.* Corvallis: Oregon State University Press, 1971. One of the first full-length works published after Steinbeck's death, this superb collection of essays presents opinions which regard Steinbeck as everything from a mere proletarian novelist to an artist with a deep vision of humans' essential dignity.

Benson, Jackson J. *The True Adventures of John Steinbeck, Writer.* New York: Viking Press, 1984. This biography emphasizes Steinbeck's rebellion against critical conventions and his attempts to keep his private life separate from his role as public figure. Benson sees Steinbeck as a critical anomaly, embarrassed and frustrated by his growing critical and popular success.

DeMott, Robert. *Steinbeck's Typewriter: Essays on His Art.* Troy, N.Y.: Whitston, 1996. A good collection of criticism of Steinbeck. Includes bibliographical references and an index.

Fontenrose, Joseph. *John Steinbeck: An Introduction and Interpretation.* New York: Holt, Rinehart and Winston, 1963. A good introduction, this book discusses some of the symbolism inherent in much of Steinbeck's fiction and contains some insightful observations on Steinbeck's concept of the "group-man"—that is, the individual as a unit in the larger sociobiological organism.

French, Warren G. *John Steinbeck's Fiction Revisited.* New York: Twayne, 1994. The chapter on *The Long Valley* in this revision of French's earlier Twayne book on Steinbeck provides brief discussions of the major stories, including "Flight" and "Chrysanthemums."

George, Stephen K., ed. *John Steinbeck: A Centennial Tribute.* New York: Praeger, 2002. A collection of reminiscences from Steinbeck's family and friends as well as wide-ranging critical assessments of his works.

Hayashi, Tetsumaro, ed. *Steinbeck's Short Stories in "The Long Valley": Essays in Criticism.* Muncie, Ind.: Steinbeck Research Institution, 1991. A collection of new critical essays on the stories in *The Long Valley* (excluding *The Red Pony*), from a variety of critical perspectives.

Hughes, R. S. *John Steinbeck: A Study of the Short Fiction.* New York: Twayne, 1989. A general introduction to Steinbeck's short fiction, focusing primarily on critical reception to the stories. Also includes some autobiographical statements on short-story writing, as well as four essays on Steinbeck's stories by other critics.

Johnson, Claudia Durst, ed. *Understanding "Of Mice and Men," "The Red Pony," and "The Pearl": A Student Casebook to Issues, Sources, and Historical Documents.* Westport, Conn.: Greenwood Press, 1997. This casebook contains historical, social, and political materials as a context for Steinbeck's three novellas. Contexts included are California and the West, land ownership, the male worker, homelessness, and oppression of the poor in Mexico.

McCarthy, Paul. *John Steinbeck.* New York: Frederick Ungar, 1980. Though much of this study is a recapitulation of earlier critical views, the book has the virtues of clarity and brevity and contains a fairly thorough bibliography.

McElrath, Joseph R., Jr., Jesse S. Crisler, and Susan Shillinglaw, eds. *John Steinbeck: The Contemporary Reviews.* New York: Cambridge University Press, 1996. A fine selection of reviews of Steinbeck's work.

Noble, Donald R. *The Steinbeck Question: New Essays in Criticism.* Troy, N.Y.: Whitston, 1993. A collection of essays on most of Steinbeck's work; most important for a study of the short story is the essay by Robert S. Hughes, Jr., titled "The Art of Story Writing," Charlotte Hadella's "Steinbeck's Cloistered Women," and Michael J. Meyer's "The Snake."

Parini, Jay. *John Steinbeck: A Biography.* New York: Henry Holt, 1995. This biography suggests psychological interpretations of the effect of Steinbeck's childhood and sociological interpretations of his fiction. Criticizes Steinbeck for his politically incorrect gender and social views; also takes Steinbeck to task for what he calls his blindness to the political reality of the Vietnam War.

Steinbeck, John. *Steinbeck: A Life in Letters.* Edited by Elaine Steinbeck and Robert Wallsten. New York: Viking Press, 1975. An indispensable source for the Steinbeck scholar, this collection of letters written by Steinbeck between 1929 and his death forty years later shows a writer both well read and well disci-

---

plined. Those letters to his friend and publisher, Pascal Covici, shed light on the writer's working methods and are particularly revealing.

Timmerman, John H. *The Dramatic Landscape of Steinbeck's Short Stories*. Norman: University of Oklahoma Press, 1990. A formalist interpretation of Steinbeck's stories, focusing on style, tone, imagery, and character. Provides close readings of such frequently anthologized stories as "The Chrysanthemums" and "Flight," as well as such stories as "Johnny Bear" and "The Short-Short Story of Mankind."

the PARIS
REVIEW

The *Paris Review* Perspective _____

Hua Hsu for *The Paris Review*

As Preston Sturges's 1941 film *Sullivan's Travels* begins, we find its titular barnstormer, a naïve but well-meaning Hollywood filmmaker, adrift in his own idealism. Sullivan has grown weary of the dim-witted box office hits that finance his lifestyle: he wants to adapt a Depression best seller called *O Brother, Where Art Thou?* and remind audiences of the suffering, poverty, and leaden spirits their beloved movies too often ignore. In order to prepare himself—after all, he knows nothing about such travails—Sullivan sets out on a fact-finding adventure to reconnect with the common man, only to discover that his prospective heroes aren't all that different from his native caste. As the film draws to a close, its sundry classes, races, and generations united by a common love of fluffy, escapist fare, the audience finally sees a close-up of this book that inspired Sullivan's silly quest. Its author: Sinclair Beckstein, an amalgamation of virtue-driven, activist-minded authors Upton Sinclair, Sinclair Lewis, and John Steinbeck.

That Steinbeck was worthy of lampooning would not have seemed likely just a few years earlier. Whereas Sinclair and Lewis had established their credentials as muckraking authors decades prior, he was a newcomer to the world of literary celebrity. Throughout the 1930s, Steinbeck had published ten books of varying quality, most of them soulful sketches of life in California's quiet, fertile valleys and remote, seaside communities. Although Steinbeck had tasted success—*Of Mice and Men* (1937) had been a Book-of-the-Month Club selection— few anticipated that he would produce a novel as powerful or ambitious as his 1939 breakthrough, *The Grapes of Wrath*. "If only a couple of million overcomfortable people can be brought to read it," the critic Clifton Fadiman wrote in *The New Yorker*, "John Steinbeck's *Grapes of Wrath* may actually effect something like a revolution in their minds and hearts."

Steinbeck's revolution certainly was not an aesthetic one. During a period of American literary history best remembered for urgent challenges to notions of propriety and style, Steinbeck's voluminous oeuvre offers a folksy, earnest, at times old-fashioned optimism. Even then, his spare, workmanlike prose rarely bettered contemporaries such as Ernest Hemingway or Willa Cather, who shared a similarly direct style. Instead, Steinbeck's legacy was his expansive vision—his willingness to take the world in whole where lesser spirits (such as his fictional disciple Sullivan) had blushed. His best works celebrate the democratic resolve of the masses. They imagine communities forged through radical gestures of empathy rather than the accident of geography. They are celebrations of America's discarded and dispossessed, swampers and fishermen, "bindlestiffs" and *paisanos*, bedraggled wanderers searching for a day's pay, and immigrants misshapen for the American Dream. His visions are haunting, as with the penetrating bond between the clever, cynical George and the gentle, guileless Lennie of the tragic novella *Of Mice and Men* (1937); some, like the remarkable act of communion that closes *The Grapes of Wrath*—still one of the most haunting final pages in American literary history—proved too controversial for genteel readers. Few authors, then or now, rendered these anonymous classes with such care, not as exotic curiosities but as individuals with dreams and dignity. Here, too, he perceived himself a man apart. "It is the fashion now in writing to have every man defeated and destroyed," he reflected in his private journals (reprinted in *The Paris Review*). "And I do not believe all men are destroyed."

Steinbeck's upbringing helps explain this spirit. He was a rarity among his literary peers: a Californian. Born in 1902 to a middle-class family in present-day Monterey County, there was no shortage of settlers, laborers, and immigrants to spur his imagination. California then was largely unsettled, with few literary heroes beyond Jack London or Frank Norris. Steinbeck attended Stanford University intermittently through the late 1910s and 1920s, never graduating. Instead, he worked a range of jobs that would become formative to his literary career. Stints at local hatcheries and ranches introduced Steinbeck to the real-life misfits who would be reborn in his fiction, while a brief spell as a newspaper reporter in New York sharpened his skill for description. All of these experiences would open his sympathies to leftist causes.

Steinbeck's late 1930s successes guaranteed his celebrity—but it's possible they also insured his ultimate undoing. The success of *The Grapes of Wrath* allowed him to reverse the course of the novel's Joad family, heading East to the almost-mythical cultural beacon of New York. He continued to be productive through the 1940s and 1950s, eventually tallying twenty-seven books, at least a dozen of which were adapted as movies, and in 1962 he received the Nobel Prize in Literature. But, as his dear friend Elia Kazan observed to Steinbeck biographer Jay Parini: "Steinbeck was a Californian, never a New Yorker. It was a great mistake for him to leave the West Coast. That was the source of inspiration."

Indeed, Steinbeck was rarely better than when he was writing about the thing he knew best: California—its people and its possibilities, both of which were new for the times. He considered *East of Eden* (1952), an ambitious and wildly uneven fictionalization of his family history, his best work. But his love for home is best captured in the wondrous opening line of his more modest *Cannery Row* (1945): "Cannery Row in Monterey in California is a poem, a stink, a grating noise, a quality of light, a tone, a habit, a nostalgia, a dream." Steinbeck's appeal is for those who hail from unfamiliar parts but feel obliged to shout its praises to any who will listen. He believed in good and bad, at times simplistically, but he also believed these qualities were randomly and unpredictably distributed among the population.

He wrote for those who saw the stirrings of a nation among the scattered many who agreed to tend to the needs of the same valley. His books are for those who seek to answer someone else's plea: *O Brother, Where Art Thou?*

CRITICAL
CONTEXTS

John Steinbeck's Critical Reception_____

Matthew J. Bolton

The critical reception of John Steinbeck's work is a study in contrasts. Forty-some-odd years after the author's death, Steinbeck's novels are still immensely popular: *The Grapes of Wrath*, for example, has never gone out of print and, along with *Of Mice and Men*, is one of the most commonly assigned novels in middle school and high school classes. Yet in critical and academic circles, one could argue that Steinbeck's work has never truly entered the canon. He may be a late contemporary of F. Scott Fitzgerald, Ernest Hemingway, and William Faulkner, but he is rarely deemed their equal. Just as there is a gap between Steinbeck's popularity and his critical acclaim, so is there a gap between how he has been received at home and abroad. During the 1940s and 1950s Steinbeck was lauded overseas for his left-wing politics and for his solidarity with the occupied nations of Europe, and the same strain of didacticism and sentimentality that seemed to alienate American critics electrified European ones. The 1962 awarding of the Nobel Prize in Literature to Steinbeck seemed to write large this difference between how the author was seen in the United States and how he was seen in the rest of the world. Finally, there is a tremendous range within Steinbeck's work and a concomitant range of critical responses. While this is true of most writers, rarely is it true to such an extreme: Steinbeck's books vary greatly in theme, genre, and quality, and one can love one stack of Steinbeck's books while loathing another. Readers who wanted the author to keep producing novels just like *The Grapes of Wrath* (1939) were inevitably disappointed as Steinbeck moved from one form to another in the second half of his career. It is important to keep these various gaps and contrasts in mind in surveying the wide range of reactions to Steinbeck over the past eighty years. His literary fortunes illustrate the divisions between popular and literary fiction, between American and European criticism, and between the kind of novel that inspires a nation and the kind that leaves it cold.

Steinbeck was born in 1902 in Salinas, California, the state that would be his spiritual homeland and the setting for his most enduring novels. He grew up in a comfortable, middle-class home, the only boy among three sisters. His father was emotionally distant, his mother strict and overbearing, and the shy and awkward boy would often retreat from his family to read in his upstairs room or to play in the woods. While the gabled Victorian on Central Avenue was his home, two other locations rivaled it in his affections: his family's seaside cottage in Pacific Grove and his grandfather's farm sixty miles south of Salinas. Both sites would inform the characters and settings of Steinbeck's later novels. After graduating from Salinas's small high school, he attended Stanford University, taking classes intermittently over the course of six years but never receiving a degree. Writing had already become his passion, and, though he often neglected assignments and skipped classes, he put tremendous energy toward reading what interested him and toward producing fiction. At Stanford he benefited from working with professors in the English department, particularly Margaret Bailey and Edith Mirrielees. The latter's fiction course was an early example of what would become the university creative writing program. If Steinbeck was lackluster academically, he thrived socially, making strong friendships and becoming involved with literary groups that would foster his creativity.

During summers and his intermittent breaks from Stanford, Steinbeck worked a series of manual and menial jobs. He dug trenches, did odd jobs on farms, worked at a sugar plant, built a dam, served as a clerk in San Francisco, and was a jack-of-all-trades for a lodge on Lake Tahoe. Altogether, Steinbeck probably spent a year of his time at Stanford working in these various capacities. The experiences furnished Steinbeck with material that he would draw on for the rest of his life. Biographer Jay Parini writes: "Nothing was ever wasted on Steinbeck; he instinctively knew how to milk his experience for what it was worth in imaginative value. One can tie a huge number of characters, incidents, and settings from his later fiction to early working experiences acquired during periods away from Stanford" (27).

Deciding he had spent enough time at Stanford, Steinbeck set out to live a writer's life. Drawn to the bohemia of New York City's Greenwich Village, he signed on to a steamer sailing from San Francisco through the Panama Canal. In New York, Steinbeck spent a hardscrabble year working first in construction and then as a reporter. When he was fired from the latter job, he holed up in his shabby efficiency in Gramercy Park and wrote a collection of short stories. He returned to the West Coast and to a radically different situation: as caretaker of a Lake Tahoe estate, where he spent two winters alone in a cottage, working on a novel.

The product of Steinbeck's solitude at Lake Tahoe was *Cup of Gold* (1929), his first published novel. The story of pirate Henry Morgan, the book struck an uneasy balance between its swashbuckling theme and Steinbeck's realistic treatment. A reviewer for the New York newspaper the *Evening Post* identified this as the novel's principal flaw, writing that *Cup of Gold* "seems to fall between two stools of style," in that its "historical subject" and "modern naturalistic" style "do not harmonize" (in McElrath, Crisler, and Shillinglaw 4).[1] The *New York Herald Tribune* made a similar point: "Strangely enough, the tale lacks the color and spirit traditional to its genre, perhaps because the author has preferred to tinker with a realistic method" (3). This muted critical response was matched by lackluster sales; the book sold just over fifteen hundred copies.

Nevertheless, *Cup of Gold* helped to legitimate Steinbeck's efforts in his own eyes and in those of his friends and family. He was a published novelist now, a fact that seemed to give him a renewed confidence in both his personal and his creative life. Soon after the publication of *Cup of Gold*, Steinbeck married Carol Henning, who would be his wife for the next decade. Steinbeck and Carol moved to Pacific Grove, where they lived in a series of rented houses and surrounded themselves with a loose-knit crowd of Steinbeck's bohemian friends. It was here, by the coast of Monterey, that Steinbeck wrote and published his next several books. Each of these would, in one way or another, draw on the countryside and inhabitants of Salinas, where he had grown up, or Monterey, where he began his married life.

The Pastures of Heaven (1932), Steinbeck's second book to be published, was much stronger and more compelling than *Cup of Gold*. The book consists of twelve linked stories set in a fertile California valley and owes a debt to *Winesburg, Ohio* (1919), Sherwood Anderson's seminal short-story cycle. Steinbeck's stories are linked through their location and through the characters' connections to the Monroe family, a financially successful but spiritually doomed line who seem to stand for an American loss of innocence. The great breakthrough of *The Pastures of Heaven* was Steinbeck's realization that modern-day Northern California would be a rich setting for him to draw on. Though *The Pastures of Heaven* sold only a little better than had *Cup of Gold*, the reviews were far more favorable. Robert M. Coates, writing for *The New Yorker*, said that Steinbeck's "grasp of the whole sweep of the valley, and the people in it and their lives, is comprehensive and sure" (13). Other critics sounded notes that would prove prescient as Steinbeck's career unfolded. A reviewer for *The Nation* compared Steinbeck to Faulkner but suggested that Steinbeck was missing a critical element in his writing: "If he could add social insight to his present equipment he would be a first-class novelist" (18). Steinbeck would do this within the next few years, for *In Dubious Battle*, *Of Mice and Men*, and, of course, *The Grapes of Wrath* would be animated by a social consciousness that is largely absent in *The Pastures of Heaven*. A reviewer for the *Times Literary Supplement* identified a weakness that Steinbeck would less readily compensate for; in the context of a largely favorable review, the critic wrote that Steinbeck's characters "do not live as individuals" (19). A decade later, Edmund Wilson would make this argument in a far more vocal and condemning way, and it was one that would dog Steinbeck throughout his career.

Steinbeck's next book was *To a God Unknown* (1933), a work he had actually finished before *The Pastures of Heaven* but the publication of which was delayed. A spiritual and mythic story of a man's relationship to the land, *To a God Unknown* owes much to two of Steinbeck's friends, Toby Street and Joseph Campbell. Street, with whom Steinbeck studied at Stanford, had written a play called *The Green Lady* that essentially served as the model for Steinbeck's novel. Grafted onto this was the interest in mythology and Jungian archetypes that Steinbeck shared with his Monterey neighbor Campbell, who was on his way to becoming a prominent scholar and popularizer of mythology. *To a God Unknown* is an uneven book that met with generally cool critical responses. A reviewer for the *New York Times* wrote of the novel, "The elements of realism and symbolism fail to cohere and it oversteps all the bounds of convincingness even on the mystic plane" (25). This line of criticism is reminiscent of the reception *Cup of Gold* had received; in both novels, Steinbeck was said to have combined two disparate styles that did not truly cohere. *The Times* review ended with a stinging *bon mot*: "*To a God Unknown* is a novel which attempts too much; and by any standard it achieves too little" (25).

Whereas *To a God Unknown* was something of a failure financially and artistically, Steinbeck would score a ringing success with his next novel. *Tortilla Flat* (1935) was a best seller that met with glowing reviews. The *New York Herald Tribune* declared, "John Steinbeck is a born writing man, and *Tortilla Flat* a book to cherish" (34). The *Saturday Review* sounded a similar note, saying, "The flavor of this book is something new; the setting and the people carry thorough conviction; and the extraordinary humors of these curiously childlike natives are presented with a masterly touch" (35). *Tortilla Flat* would make Steinbeck, who had struggled in relative poverty and obscurity for years, a success. It also further marked Northern California as Steinbeck country, an association that for better or worse remained with Steinbeck throughout his career.

Readers and critics who laughed their way through *Tortilla Flat* were surprised at the topic and tone of Steinbeck's next book, *In Dubious Battle* (1936). In what would become a characteristic pattern, Steinbeck responded to success by writing in a radically different vein.

Rather than write a second picaresque novel, he produced a proletarian protest novel about an agricultural strike. The reviewer for the *San Francisco Chronicle* wrote: "In this new novel, John Steinbeck has done something totally different; something as startling in its way . . . as though say P. G. Wodehouse should have written *Germinal*. This *In Dubious Battle* is just as little like its immediate predecessor as you could very well imagine" (51). The *New York Times*, which had been critical of *To a God Unknown*, lauded *In Dubious Battle*, claiming that it "marks Mr. Steinbeck as the most versatile master of narrative now writing in the United States" (54). The *New York Herald Tribune* presciently wrote, "There is now nothing to prevent him from doing something very big, perhaps even great" (62).

Indeed, Steinbeck had entered what many would consider the most important phase of his career. In February 1937 he published *Of Mice and Men*, a short novel that continues to be widely read and that has become a fixture in American schools. As with so many of Steinbeck's novels, there was a readily apparent gap between its popularity and the critical response to it. The book was a best seller; as a main selection of the Book-of-the-Month Club, it reached a wide audience. Within two years it would be adapted for the Broadway stage and soon after that would be made into a successful Hollywood film. John Steinbeck was becoming a household name. The critical reviews of *Of Mice and Men*, however, were less wholly positive. Some reviewers lauded it; the *Chicago Tribune*, for example, called it "a remarkable literary feat" (75). Yet many of the most influential literary critics of the time took issue with the novel's sentimentality and its contrivances. Mark Van Doren, writing in *The Nation*, made what was becoming a familiar objection to the broadness of Steinbeck's characterization, stating, "All but one of the persons in Mr. Steinbeck's extremely brief novel are subhuman if the range of the word human is understood to coincide with the range thus far established by fiction" (qtd. in Parini 183). Though Steinbeck would often associate this sort of vitriolic review with New York City intellectuals, there were biting comments closer to home as well. A reviewer for the *Peninsula Herald*, a newspaper in Steinbeck's own adopted town of Monterey, wrote: "The plot is not great, nor are its characters great, but they are both real and carried through to completion. It is a plot upon which the characterizations and story are laid as effectively as flesh upon bone" (75). This is a backhanded compliment, to be sure, and one that highlights the tremendous importance that the critical establishment of the 1930s placed on psychological realism. *Of Mice and Men*, like so many of Steinbeck's novels, has an element of fable, allegory, or parable, which literary critics of the time found off-putting. The subsequent Broadway and Hollywood adaptations of the novel were extremely successful, solidifying Steinbeck's reputation and underscoring the gap between his popular reception and his critical reception.

Steinbeck's next two books, the linked stories of *The Red Pony* (1937) and the short-story collection *The Long Valley* (1938), met with much the same reception as had greeted *Of Mice and Men*: they sold well and were roundly criticized. William Soskin, a reviewer for the *New York Herald Tribune*, asserted that the range of stories gathered in the latter volume allowed one to "weigh the various merits and faults" of Steinbeck's style (134). This is the general pattern of the reviews of *The Long Valley*: critics contrast the stories in which Steinbeck's strengths as a storyteller shine with those that are weighed down by stiff characterization and clumsy symbolism. Many of the critics of the time singled out the stories that had previously been collected in *The Red Pony* as the highlight of the collection. It is interesting to note that even some stories that would go on to become classics of the form, such as "The Chrysanthemums," met with mixed reviews. Soskin, for example, called the story "weak" and argued that "Steinbeck's traffic with sophisticated women and female emotion in these stories is his weak point. The only women he does well are mothers, ranch wives, eccentrics, and clods" (135).

For his own part, Steinbeck was deeply stung by the critical response to his work. Under his bluster, he was a deeply sensitive man, prone to depression and self-doubt, and he took bad reviews to heart. He would term literary critics "these curious sucker fish who live with joyous vicariousness on other men's work and discipline with dreary words the thing which feeds them" (Steinbeck 165). Decades later, as he received the Nobel Prize, Steinbeck still mounted a defense against the criticism that had dogged him his whole career. In accepting his award—one that many American newspapers had suggested he did not deserve—Steinbeck said, "Literature was not promulgated by a pale and emasculated critical priesthood singing their litanies in empty churches—nor is it a game for the cloistered elect" (447).

Yet adulation was, in a way, as hard for Steinbeck to accept as criticism. His next book, *The Grapes of Wrath* (1939), would bring him both. By any account, the publication of *The Grapes of Wrath* would be the high-water mark of Steinbeck's career, and the author would founder in its wake. In 1936, he had secured a commission to write a series of articles for the *San Francisco News* on the plight of migrant workers fleeing the Dust Bowl for the promise of prosperity in the California fields and orchards. Steinbeck spent considerable time in a government-sanctioned camp for migrant workers and was shocked by the appalling poverty he saw there, though he recognized that the camp's director, Tom Collins, was doing everything he could to help the workers in the face of the landowners' cruel indifference. Steinbeck published his articles but also saw that he had the materials for what could be a great and important novel. He wrote *The Grapes of Wrath* in 1938 during six months of tremendous concentration, producing what has always been regarded as his masterpiece.

The book was an instant success when it was published in March 1939, and it stayed on the top of the *New York Times* best-seller list throughout 1939 and into 1940. In the more than seventy years since, *The Grapes of Wrath* has never gone out of print and has been translated into dozens of languages. Yet, as with Steinbeck's previous work, the popular success of this novel did not necessarily translate into critical success. A review in *Time* magazine was decidedly mixed, acknowledging the power and popularity of Steinbeck's narrative but also dismissing the parts of the novel in which Steinbeck most directly addresses the plight of the migrant worker, saying that these polemics are "not a successful fiction experiment. In them a 'social awareness' outruns artistic skill" (163). The influential critic Edmund Wilson argued that Steinbeck had written a successful novel but not a great one. According to Wilson, Steinbeck was lacking some essential quality that the great modernists possessed: "Mr. Steinbeck has invention, observation, a certain color of style which for some reason does not possess what is called magic" (187). A decade later, in his survey of 1940s literature, Wilson would expand on this argument in a devastating way, arguing, "The characters in *The Grapes of Wrath* are animated and put through their paces rather than brought to life; they are like excellent character actors giving very conscientious performances in a fairly well written play" (42).

Whereas literary critics objected to *The Grapes of Wrath* on aesthetic terms, some residents of both Oklahoma and California objected to it on moral and political grounds, and Steinbeck was pilloried as a liar in both states. In fact, Steinbeck began to fear that he would be the victim of some kind of reprisal or smear campaign at the hands of the Associated Farmers. In a 1939 letter he wrote that he was now "careful not to go anywhere alone nor to do anything without witnesses" (qtd. in Parini 230). The Federal Bureau of Investigation was investigating him, and, on the whole, Steinbeck seemed to wish that the country would forget about him and his book.

He was also disconcerted by the attention, both positive and negative, that *The Grapes of Wrath* had brought him. In what was becoming a characteristic move for him, he responded to the success of this novel by writing in an entirely different vein. After making his name with the ribald *Tortilla Flat*, he had written a proletarian novel. Now, after writing a novel that had become an instant classic, Steinbeck abandoned fiction altogether. He set out on a voyage down the coast of California and Mexico with his wife and his friend Ed Ricketts, a marine biologist. The book that documented this journey was *Sea of Cortez: A Leisurely Journal of Travel and Research*. As Steinbeck's subtitle implies, this was an uneasy admixture of travel narrative and amateur marine biology. The book was printed in a very limited run of seventy-five hundred copies and was generally reviewed with a sort of indulgent bemusement. The *New York Times* saw the book as further evidence that Steinbeck had much in common with Hemingway, who had written nonfiction books exploring his interest in bullfighting and in Africa (203). *The New Yorker* read it as confirming Edmund Wilson's characterization of Steinbeck as a "biological novelist" (204). It was a book that aimed less to categorize marine life on the Baja coast than "to explain Steinbeck's view of life and mode of thinking" (204).

Steinbeck's interest in Mexico drove another project as well: he wrote the text for a documentary film called *The Forgotten Village*, which was eventually published in 1941 as a collection of film stills accompanied by Steinbeck's text. Book and film alike chronicled traditional life in a Mexican village and the introduction of Western medicine to better the lives of its inhabitants. Many reviewers saw this project as an extension of Steinbeck's interest in the lives of the dispossessed. A reviewer for the *New York Tribune* made the point that Steinbeck is not "hard boiled" but "a Francis in store clothes" (196). For others, this sentimentality was a form of condescension. The *San Francisco Chronicle* claimed that Steinbeck's "mystico-poetical text succeeds only in talking down to the reader" (197). In a particularly damning—but insightful—observation, the reviewer identified in Steinbeck's work an "insistent diminishment of his human characters . . . by which the author-creator unconsciously magnifies himself in relation to them" (197). Less than two years after the stunning success of *The Grapes of Wrath*, the jury was in on Steinbeck. Throughout the 1940s, 1950s, and 1960s, two critical commonplaces would tend to greet each new book he published: first, that Steinbeck's interest in symbolism, biology, and politics kept him from drawing convincingly human characters; and second, that the author had done his best work with *The Grapes of*

Wrath, and each new work represented only a further diminishment of his powers.

With World War II now raging across Europe and the Pacific, Steinbeck wrote two works that sought to give hope to the Allies and to the occupied nations of Europe. *The Moon Is Down*, released as a novel in 1942 and as a play the next year, told the story of an unnamed nation occupied by a totalitarian invader. The work sold well both in print and on stage but met with the vitriolic critical reaction that Steinbeck was becoming used to. Clifton Fadiman, writing in *The New Yorker*, said of the novel, "The form is deceiving and its message is inadequate" (217). In *The Nation*, Margaret Marshal compared the work unfavorably to novels such as *The Grapes of Wrath*, arguing that here, "the form . . . seems contrived, the simplicity becomes pretentious, the understatement and matter-of-fact tone sentimental" (220). Writing of the play, Mark Van Doren objected to Steinbeck's vaguely sentimental portrayal of the invaders and termed the work "a humanely conceived but woodenly written play" (244). Yet when Steinbeck visited Europe after the war, he found himself and his play the object of great admiration in Denmark, France, and other nations that had been occupied by the Nazis. *The Moon Is Down* had played in Europe to great acclaim and was embraced uncritically as a work that offered solidarity to the occupied. *Bombs Away* (1942), Steinbeck's journalistic account of a bomber squad's wartime activities, met with general approval. As a writer for the *Chicago Sun* noted, "We don't judge *Bombs Away* on its literary merits alone" (266): the United States was at war, and this book was one of Steinbeck's contributions to the war effort.

After the war, Steinbeck continued to write and publish prolifically. He had settled in New York City with his second wife and their young sons, but his subject throughout the 1940s remained Northern California and Mexico. *Cannery Row* (1945) was a sequel to *Tortilla Flat*. It sold well, and its critical reception was better than one might expect. Edmund Wilson, with a backhanded compliment, called it "the least pretentious of his books" and "the one I have most enjoyed reading"

(278). Other critics objected to its thinness of plot and incident. This line of criticism would be more vociferous a decade later, when Steinbeck published *Sweet Thursday* (1954), the third of the picaresque Monterey novels.

The Wayward Bus (1947) again sold well but was critically savaged. The story of a disastrous expedition by bus down a deserted stretch of the Baja coast, it was roundly panned. Eleanor Clark's article in *The Nation*, "Infantilism and Steinbeck," argued that Steinbeck has "faulty vision" and "a will to irresponsibility" (305). His depictions of the lower class and of relationships between men and women are inherently false, according to Clark. In *Commonweal*, Frank O'Malley noted, "The publication of this latest work of Steinbeck raises a very grave question: why do so many of our serious American writers deteriorate?" (307). The novella he published that same year, *The Pearl* (1947), has become a classic and is often assigned in middle school classrooms. Despite its brisk sales, however, it was generally taken as one more sign of Steinbeck's deterioration. The *Saturday Review* noted that during the 1930s Steinbeck had moved from allegorical and picaresque stories to social criticism and wondered "why Steinbeck has now returned to this earlier and less satisfactory vein of his work" (316).

Steinbeck had long enjoyed the theater and as a New Yorker now was closer to Broadway than he had been before the war. His third wife, Elaine, had an acting background and introduced Steinbeck to several important Broadway personages. His 1950 play *Burning Bright* delved into the symbolic and allegorical concerns that had driven *To a God Unknown*. Steinbeck's working title had been *Everyman*, and that medieval morality play was present in the stiff, deliberately artificial language of *Burning Bright*. The play flopped, closing after only thirteen performances. The *New York Times* called it "cramped, literal, and elementary," and on its closing noted, "Everything connected with *Burning Bright*, except the script, evoked general commendation" (357). Steinbeck would take one more stab at the theater, writing the libretto for *Pipe Dream*, a Rodgers and Hammerstein adaptation of *Sweet Thursday*. When that, too, failed, Steinbeck gave up on the stage.

Steinbeck made a triumphant return to fiction by writing in the form that had brought him his greatest success: the long, epic novel *East of Eden* (1952) was a tremendous popular success, selling well and leading to a hit film starring James Dean. Many critics noted the looseness of the novel's structure and Steinbeck's tendency toward purple prose, yet the reviews tended to compare *East of Eden* favorably to Steinbeck's work of the past dozen years. The *New York Times* review was representative of the general tenor of the novel's reception:

> John Steinbeck's best and most ambitious work since *The Grapes of Wrath* is published today. . . . Clumsy in structure and defaced by excessive melodramatics and much cheap sensationalism though it is, *East of Eden* is a serious and on the whole successful effort to grapple with a major theme. (383)

The *Saturday Review* saw the novel in similar terms, writing, "Perhaps East of Eden isn't a great novel . . . [but] it is one of the best novels of the past ten years and the best book John Steinbeck has written since *The Grapes of Wrath*" (386).

Steinbeck's next three novels fared less well. The previously mentioned *Sweet Thursday*, the last book in the Monterey trilogy, was widely dismissed as being insubstantial. *The Short Reign of Pippin IV* (1957), Steinbeck's burlesque satire on modern politics, was greeted with puzzlement and exasperation by critics. Nevertheless, the book sold well, particularly as it was listed as a Book-of-the-Month Club choice. Steinbeck's final novel was *The Winter of Our Discontent* (1961). With it, the author had returned to the long novel form that had served him well in *The Grapes of Wrath* and *East of Eden*. But the critical response to *The Winter of Our Discontent* was largely negative. *Time* wrote that Steinbeck had tried but failed to recapture his youthful ardor: "The book contains more pose than passion, and the moral anathema sounds curiously like late-middle-aged petulance" (455).

The *New York Times* argued that Steinbeck's form undercut his content: "The manner of the writing of this satire robs it of much of its force. Mr. Steinbeck's prose is jocular, gay and flippant" (457). In the *Saturday Review*, Granville Hicks objected to "the slick way in which Steinbeck has carpentered this novel" (459).

Yet the 1960s brought Steinbeck great acclaim as well. Steinbeck had always found himself highly regarded on his trips to Europe; in Scandinavia, Russia, France, and Italy he was treated like a celebrity. It should therefore not be surprising that the Nobel Prize committee saw the elderly Steinbeck as a great author who deserved this highest of recognitions and awarded him the Nobel Prize in 1962. In the United States, however, Steinbeck's reputation had fared poorly over the previous two decades. The *New York Times* ran an editorial questioning the validity of awarding such a prestigious prize to "a writer who, though still in full career, produced his major work more than two decades ago" (qtd. in Parini 445). This line of argument was echoed in many other quarters, and Steinbeck was stung by such a vocal rejection by his own countrymen, though he did receive the U.S. Presidential Medal of Freedom in 1964. He had become friends with President Lyndon Johnson, and Steinbeck and Elaine were regular visitors at the White House. It was largely out of a sense of loyalty to Johnson that Steinbeck lent his support to the escalating war in Vietnam. Increasingly frail and beset by health problems, he nevertheless visited Vietnam and spent time with various American military units there. His refusal to oppose the war—and by extension his tacit support of it—alienated him from some of his friends and from much of the literary and artistic community in his adopted home of New York City.

Steinbeck's last major work was a ringing success. *Travels with Charley* (1962), Steinbeck's memoir of traveling across country with his dog, sold well and was reviewed well. The author's encounters with everyday Americans and his readiness to write about the ugliest aspects of American life—such as the fierce opposition to racial integration in the New Orleans schools—represents a return to the themes that animated his great socially engaged books of the 1930s. A final book, *America and Americans* (1966), might be read as a quiet coda to *Travels with Charley*.

Steinbeck died in 1968, and the following decade saw a series of efforts to publish posthumous work and to consolidate the author's reputation. Steinbeck's journal and letters chronicling the writing of *East of Eden* were published in 1969 as *Journal of a Novel*, and his retelling of Mallory's *Morte D'Arthur* appeared in 1976 as *The Acts of King Arthur and His Noble Knights*. The bulk of Steinbeck's letters were published in the 1975 *Steinbeck: A Life in Letters*, while his correspondence with Elizabeth Otis, his agent, would come out in 1978 under the title *Letters to Elizabeth*. The last major posthumous publication was *Working Days: The Journals of "The Grapes of Wrath," 1938-1941* (1989), a fascinating record of Steinbeck's process of composition.

Around the time of Steinbeck's death, several important institutions were founded to promote Steinbeck scholarship. The Steinbeck Society, which had been formed in 1966, began publishing the *Steinbeck Quarterly* in 1968. This journal, along with the conferences that the society organized, became an important forum for scholars of Steinbeck's work. The society would go on to host international conferences and to sponsor a Steinbeck Monograph Series. Founder Tetsumaro Hayashi would also release collections of dissertation abstracts connected to Steinbeck—a valuable resource for students and scholars seeking to do new research on the author. In 1974, Professor Martha Heasly Cox founded the Steinbeck Research Center at San Jose State University. The Center, which would eventually be renamed the Martha Heasly Cox Center for Steinbeck Studies, has made several important contributions to Steinbeck studies. It hosts conferences and, through its fellowship program, funds Steinbeck scholars. The center's Web site offers a range of resources from teacher lesson plans to a searchable bibliography of Steinbeck research and criticism. Many other universities, particularly ones located in California, boast similar centers devoted to Steinbeck studies.

The first major biography of Steinbeck would arrive in the 1980s. Jackson J. Benson's *The True Adventures of John Steinbeck, Writer* (1984) is a seminal book: thoroughly researched, exhaustive, sympathetic, and insightful. Benson had access to many of Steinbeck's friends and contemporaries, and his book performs an invaluable service in recording their memories of the author for posterity. Jay Parini's subsequent biography *John Steinbeck* (1995) draws on Benson's work as well as on interviews with Steinbeck's wife Elaine, his friend Burgess Meredith, and other sources close to Steinbeck. Parini's biography is shorter than Benson's and in many respects may be of more interest to the casual reader. The book contains much new research, detailing some aspects of Steinbeck's life that are not addressed in Benson's book.

Because novels such as *The Red Pony, Of Mice and Men, The Grapes of Wrath*, and *The Pearl* have remained a mainstay of middle school and high school classrooms, there are an abundance of study guides and critical collections devoted to these books. The Twayne Series and Harold Bloom's various imprints are two of the most readily available of this kind of collection. Each gathers a representative sampling of critical work on a given novel or set of novels. There are also many academic monographs on Steinbeck each year.

Several bibliographies and compilations are of tremendous use to anyone doing research on Steinbeck. Robert DeMott's *Steinbeck's Reading: A Catalogue* lists all of the books that Steinbeck owned—a great resource for scholars working on Steinbeck's literary influences. *John Steinbeck: The Contemporary Reviews* (1996), edited by Joseph R. McElrath, Jr., Jesse S. Crisler, and Susan Shillinglaw, gathers representative critical responses to all of Steinbeck's books and plays, offering firsthand source material regarding the author's critical reception. *The Critical Responses to John Steinbeck's "The Grapes of Wrath"* (2000), edited by Barbara A. Heavlin, serves a similar function for Steinbeck's most famous novel, and John Ditsky's *John Steinbeck and the Critics* (2000) offers an overview of Steinbeck criticism.

Yet the gap between Steinbeck's popularity and his critical reputation persists. In academia, he is still, as Jackson J. Benson puts it, "the favorite author we love to hate" (in Heavlin xv). The best testimony to Steinbeck's enduring power is therefore found not in the various publications and institutions devoted to his work but in the tremendous number of new readers who discover this author each year. Steinbeck remains a vital author not because of any critical or academic community but simply because he is still read when so many other authors are not. Something about Steinbeck's greatest novels and stories still speaks to the American experience, and it is this quality that continues to ensure his legacy.

Note

1. Unless otherwise noted, page numbers cited for all quotations from reviews of Steinbeck's work refer to McElrath, Crisler, and Shillinglaw's collection *John Steinbeck: The Contemporary Reviews*.

Works Cited

Ditsky, John. *John Steinbeck and the Critics*. Rochester, NY: Camden House, 2000.

Heavlin, Barbara A., ed. *The Critical Responses to John Steinbeck's "The Grapes of Wrath."* Westport, CT: Greenwood Press, 2000.

McElrath, Joseph R., Jr., Jesse S. Crisler, and Susan Shillinglaw, eds. *John Steinbeck: The Contemporary Reviews*. New York: Cambridge UP, 1996.

Parini, Jay. *John Steinbeck*. New York: Henry Holt, 1995.

Steinbeck, John. *Journal of a Novel: The "East of Eden" Letters*. New York: Viking Press, 1969.

"Roar Like a Lion":
The Historical and Cultural Contexts
of the Works of John Steinbeck_____

Jennifer Banach

When John Steinbeck was awarded the Nobel Prize in 1962, he expressed, quite humbly, that he was uncertain if he deserved the honor ahead of so many of his colleagues. Yet, cast in such a position, he was prepared to speak strongly and passionately about the true purposes of his profession:

> It is customary for the recipient of this award to offer personal or scholarly comment on the nature and the direction of literature. At this particular time, however, I think it would be well to consider the high duties and the responsibilities of the makers of literature.
>
> Such is the prestige of the Nobel award and of this place where I stand that I am impelled, not to squeak like a grateful and apologetic mouse, but to roar like a lion out of pride in my profession and in the great and good men who have practiced it through the ages. (paras. 2-3)

He went on to discuss not only the job of the writer (a purpose that he likened to William Faulkner's hope of promoting understanding and dissolving fear) but also his views on human beings' responsibility to one another, a responsibility that had, he said, grown only greater in modern times as humans had appropriated more power over nature and over one another. The modern world—which had become, in large part, industrialized and driven by technology and which had been drastically altered by two world wars—had imparted a new power to humankind and, subsequently, new responsibilities:

> We have usurped many of the powers we once ascribed to God. . . .
>
> Having taken Godlike power, we must seek in ourselves for the responsibility and the wisdom we once prayed some deity might have.

Man himself has become our greatest hazard and our only hope.

So that today, St. John the apostle may well be paraphrased: In the end is the Word, and the Word is Man—and the Word is with Men. (paras. 20, 23-25)

When Steinbeck presented his speech in Stockholm, he had already endured many years of criticism, the burning and banning of his books, and ongoing interrogation into the nature of his character. Though critics would later describe him as "modest and soft-spoken," as someone who "had trouble defining himself as a subversive, an unpatriotic man" (Wagner-Martin viii), and as "more often than not extremely humble and self-deprecating" (DeMott, "Introduction" viii), Steinbeck had consistently produced novels, short stories, news articles, nonfiction, film scripts, and plays that evinced a deep interest in the great cultural and social issues of his time and challenged social norms. By recalling the words of St. John in his speech, he recognized the potential of the *written* word to influence and shape mankind. And if the word was man itself, writers were bearers of this word, spokespeople with deep responsibilities. Steinbeck accepted that this role was not without controversy and, indeed, he faced criticism from conservatives and liberals alike. His books were banned, burned, and censored for their coarse language, for their depictions of the harsh realities of American society, and for their unconventional themes. Conservative critics accused him of being a Communist or a socialist, and leftist critics complained that he was not sufficiently dedicated to their agendas. Still, his interest in the cultural problems of his time and his concern for basic human rights never waned. The criticisms of his detractors were, to him, simply part of the job, and his instinct as a writer—to roar like a lion, rather than squeak like a mouse—became emblematic of his life's work.

As with many great authors, much of Steinbeck's work is rooted in the events of his own life. As James Gray explains in a 1971 study of Steinbeck, "Some among the distinguished array of American novelists after World War I now seem rather far removed from us. The writers [like Steinbeck] who developed themes that were highly personal to their own experience stand apart" (5). Steinbeck's most successful (and controversial) works, *Of Mice and Men* and *The Grapes of Wrath*, grew out of his personal life. They bore witness to the hardships he had seen in his own life and home state, taking as their setting the places he had come to know and care about, such as the Salinas Valley and the Monterey community in California. His characters—even those deeply complex and tragic characters such as Lennie Small of *Of Mice and Men*—were inspired by people he encountered in his everyday life. And yet Steinbeck's work is more than merely personal. All of the details he took from his life are housed within a framework of major historical events: the Okie migration from the Dust Bowl during the 1930s, the Great Depression, two world wars, the Cold War, McCarthyism, and the political and social upheavals of the 1960s. What Steinbeck saw in the Salinas Valley and translated into literature became both a symbol of the plight of specific Americans facing specific tragedies and an allegory for all people who face hardships.

John Steinbeck spent the majority of his life in the Monterey area of California, especially in Salinas, where he was born on February 27, 1902. The town was named for its proximity to the Salinas River, the state's largest, which made irrigation easy and transformed the valley into an agricultural hotbed. In the 1930s, it would become a magnet for migrant workers when severe dust storms swept through large areas of Oklahoma, Texas, New Mexico, Colorado, and Kansas, devastating the farmlands. The Steinbeck family was prosperous. Steinbeck's father, John Ernst, worked as an accountant and manager for a few local milling companies, and Steinbeck grew up in a large Victorian home with three sisters.

After his first novel, a picaresque story about the pirate Henry Morgan titled *Cup of Gold* (1929) that largely went unnoticed, Steinbeck found in Monterey one of his signature subjects. *The Pastures of Heaven* (1932) was a book of interlocking short stories set in a farming community in a Monterey valley discovered by a Spanish corporal while he was trying to recapture escaped Native American slaves. The story's simple characters and their struggles with delusion and conformity reflect the people and struggles of the Monterey Steinbeck had grown up in. Although it was generally well received upon its publication, the book failed to find lasting success. As James Nagel explains:

> In the early 1930s . . . [Steinbeck] was a struggling writer committed to a literary life but still searching for subject and style. He found the first in the area he knew best, the farm country near his home in Salinas, California, and the simple people who settled there. This was the subject that was to inform the best of his work and to underlie his reputation as a writer of intellectual substance and social significance. (vii)

The Red Pony, which Steinbeck began publishing in magazines one year later (it was finally published as a book in 1937, a year after the last magazine story appeared), is also one of his great California stories. Semiautobiographical (Steinbeck had had a pony himself as a child), it told the story of a boy named Jody and his life on his father's California ranch and also doubled as a portrait of American life. By including Jody's grandfather in the story, Steinbeck was able to portray significant historical events of the American West, such as the crossing of the Oregon Trail. Throughout the 1930s California would be Steinbeck's chief backdrop: four novels—*Tortilla Flat* (1935), *In Dubious Battle* (1936), *Of Mice and Men* (1937), and *The Grapes of Wrath* (1939)—and a collection of short stories, *The Long Valley* (1938), would all be set in California and become some of Steinbeck's most widely read works. Like *The Pastures of Heaven*, they all feature vivid, earthy characters who struggle with hardships imposed by both the California landscape and California society. And though Steinbeck looked to other landscapes after the 1930s, he also circled back to California three times with *Cannery Row* (1945) and its sequel *Sweet Thursday* (1954) as well as *East of Eden* (1952), an epic story of a family of settlers in the Salinas Valley during the early twentieth century and Steinbeck's most personal novel.

It was in California, too, that Steinbeck became friends with the marine biologist Ed Ricketts. The two were constant companions during the 1930s, much to the annoyance of Steinbeck's wife at the time, Carol Henning, and Ricketts appears in several of Steinbeck's works, including *Cannery Row* (as Doc) and the 1935 short story "The Snake" (as Dr. Philips). Though Steinbeck was likely familiar with the naturalist writers who had preceded him a few decades before, it is likely because of Ricketts that an element of naturalism creeps into Steinbeck's work. The biologist was a holistic ecologist who believed that, to understand an animal, one had to also understand how it functions within its habitat and how it relates to other animals. The creatures living in a tidepool, for instance, are not individual creatures with independent lives, but part of an interconnected microcosm on which they are all dependent. Ricketts would go on to elaborate this view in *Between Pacific Tides* (1939), and coauthored with Steinbeck an account of their 1940 specimen-collecting expedition along the Gulf of California. Ricketts's influence can be seen throughout Steinbeck's work: Many of his characters are at the mercy of their environments and prey to forces beyond their control. In *The Grapes of Wrath*, the manmade ecological disaster of the Dust Bowl forces the Joad family to abandon their Oklahoma farm and travel to California in search of work and a better life. Yet once they arrive, they find that the state is overrun with other migrants just like them, making jobs scarce and wages low. That the Joads are caught up in a social and economic system beyond their control Steinbeck makes clear in one of the early interchapters when he writes, "The bank is something more than men, I tell you. It's the monster. Men made it, but they can't control it" (33). And in *In Dubious Battle*, which depicts a fruit pickers' strike, Steinbeck's hero, Doc Burton, explains, "A man in a group isn't himself at all; he's a cell in an organism that isn't like him any more than the cells in your body are like you" (113).

Yet, unlike the naturalist writers who preceded him, Steinbeck was much more than a mere social determinist. An abiding mysticism—which, like his naturalism, likely stems from his belief that all men are interconnected—leavens Steinbeck's work with a sense of hope. Perhaps the most famous example comes from *The Grapes of Wrath*, in which Jim Casy speculates, "Maybe all men got one big soul ever'body's a part of'" (32), but the tendency can be seen in Steinbeck's earlier work, too. While writing his third novel, *To a God Unknown*, Steinbeck noted in a journal:

> The story is a parable . . . the story of a race, growth and death. Each figure is a population, and the stones, the trees, the muscled mountains are the world—but not the world apart from man—the world *and* man—the one indescribable unit man plus his environment. (qtd. in DeMott, *Typewriter* 115)

It is perhaps in this novel that Steinbeck most fully expresses his mysticism and his preoccupation with myth. He adapted its title from the title of a Vedic hymn, "To the Unknown God," and, like many of his later works, his characters have biblical resonances, especially Joseph Wayne, who, like the biblical Joseph, embarks on a journey to "the promised land" (qtd. in DeMott, *Typewriter* 126) of California to fulfill his dying father's dream of establishing there a new, more prosperous farm. Like the biblical Joseph, Steinbeck's Wayne is a "dreamer and visionary" (126) who comes to believe that his father's soul is living in an oak tree on his land. When Joseph's three brothers join him in California, the farm flourishes until one, worried that Joseph is becoming a pagan because of his long talks with the oak tree, kills the tree and leaves. With the tree's death, a severe drought sets in, and Joseph's wife is killed when she falls from a rock. Not long after her death, the stream that springs from the rock dries up. As the story reaches its end, the drought worsens, and Joseph, finding that the local priest will not pray for rain, climbs atop the rock and cuts his wrists in an act of self-sacrifice. As he dies, it begins to rain.

Frederic I. Carpenter, in a study of *The Grapes of Wrath*, perceptively identified Emerson as an influence on Steinbeck, writing:

> Like Emerson, Casy came to the conviction that holiness, or goodness, results from this feeling of unity [with nature]. . . . But the corollary of this mystical philosophy is that any man's self-seeking destroys the unity or "holiness" of nature. . . . Or, as Emerson phrased it, while discussing Nature: "The world lacks unity because man is disunited with himself. . . . Love is its demand." (316)

Yet even in as early a novel as *To a God Unknown*, one can find Emerson's influence as Joseph Wayne, whom Steinbeck holds up as a sort of Christ figure, feels himself a part of the land and sacrifices himself out of love for it and its people.

About the time that Steinbeck was revising *To a God Unknown* for publication, he became friends with Ed Ricketts's neighbor, the mythologist Joseph Campbell. Campbell, then in his mid-twenties, was already developing the ideas that, when published in 1949 as *The Hero with a Thousand Faces*, would establish him as an expert on world mythology. Like Steinbeck, Campbell was fascinated by Carl Jung, a Swiss psychologist, who drew on myths and archetypes to understand human psychology and developed the theory of the collective unconscious, which holds that people unconsciously organize their experience according to preexisting, inherited archetypes that are shared by all people, regardless of culture or individual experience. In essence, Campbell believed that myth "is the secret opening through which the inexhaustible energies of the cosmos pour into human cultural manifestation" (3). Analyzing myths from around the world, Campbell found that they all shared common images and themes; thus, he concluded, all mythologies and all religions are just particular manifestations of one transcendental truth.

Steinbeck, who had been attracted to myths since childhood (the Arthurian legends were among his lifelong favorites), was electrified by

Campbell's ideas and, in addition to discussing the works of other writers with him, also asked for his help while revising *To a God Unknown*. His influence on the novel can be seen in how Steinbeck reworks the stories of the Old Testament throughout the narrative. As noted in Brian Railsback and Michael J. Meyer's *Steinbeck Encyclopedia*:

> The giant oak tree that contains Wayne's father's spirit comes from Joshua 24:26. . . . Wayne . . . is unable to get water from *his* stone as Moses did (Numbers 20:15), at the end of the novel he dies like Aaron at the top of a mountain (Numbers 20: 23-4). Aaron, however, was denied any entrance to the Promised Land by God, so he sent his son on with his brother, Moses. In an inverted echo, Wayne sends his son on with his own irreligious brother. (380)

Though Steinbeck's friendship with the mythologist ended when Campbell confessed that he had begun an affair with Steinbeck's wife, Campbell's influence can be seen throughout Steinbeck's work. Many of the novelist's other works are also revisions of biblical stories—the Joads' journey to California draws on the Israelites' exodus from Egypt, and *East of Eden* is based on Genesis' Cain and Abel—and a few draw on Steinbeck's beloved Arthurian legends; the close-knit friendships of *Tortilla Flat*, *Cannery Row*, and *Sweet Thursday* suggest the friendships of the knights of the Round Table, and many novels, such as *The Grapes of Wrath* and *Of Mice and Men*, reenact the grail myth as their characters set out in search of some unattainable ideal.

Even Steinbeck's nonfiction works demonstrate his interest in myth: *The Forgotten Village*, a 1940 documentary of the lives of native Mexican Indians, pays special attention to the culture's myths and superstitions.

Yet as the Great Depression ground on, Steinbeck began to temper his mythologizing tendencies with a greater concern for politics and social justice. *In Dubious Battle*, his first novel to directly engage in politics, was also his first to generate controversy. Its protagonist is an activist for "the Party" (unnamed, but presumed to be the American Communist Party) who helps to plan a major strike by fruit workers who are being abused and exploited by capitalists. Published at the same time that Upton Sinclair and other proletarian writers were using novels to protest social injustices and advocate socialism, *In Dubious Battle*, though a commercial and critical success for Steinbeck, was widely misunderstood as a proletarian novel and divided readers along political lines.

The misunderstanding was likely a sign of the times. As more and more of the United States descended into poverty and unemployment rates shot up as high as 25 percent, the country was plunged into political turmoil and polarization. Leftists took the Depression as a sign of capitalism's inherent instability and began swelling the ranks of the American Communist Party and the Socialist Party of America; meanwhile, those on the Right, angered by what they saw as the careless spending and excessive government regulation of President Franklin Delano Roosevelt's New Deal, began to agitate for more conservative social and financial policies. Workers, too, became agitated as they struggled with unemployment and low wages. When the 1933 National Industrial Recovery Act and the 1935 National Labor Relations Act gave workers the right to join unions, union ranks swelled as workers came together to demand higher wages and better working conditions. Strikes became more common and, at times, violent.

Living in Salinas Valley at the time, a region whose fertility had brought prosperity to the owners of its large industrial farms, Steinbeck observed firsthand the hardships and desperation the Depression brought to the workers who labored on these farms. In 1933, two years before *Tortilla Flat* was published, he began research for a new novel that would center on a worker's strike. In the course of his research, he interviewed an organizer for the Communist Party's Cannery and Agricultural Workers Industrial Union, which was then attempting to unionize California's agricultural workers, and eventually transformed his experiences into *In Dubious Battle*. It brought Steinbeck acclaim, but it also drew criticism from both conservatives, who viewed it as pro-labor, and those on the far Left, who took exception to Steinbeck's depictions of the Communist Party. What went unnoticed was that Steinbeck, for the first time, had successfully integrated his interests in morality and myth into a novel that also dealt with the concerns of his time and country. Though ostensibly a novel about labor, its title is taken from a description in *Paradise Lost* of conflict between God and Satan, and its protagonist, Jim, functions as a Christ figure as he sacrifices himself for the Party. In a letter to his friend George Albee, Steinbeck explained, "I have used a small strike in an orchard valley as the symbol of man's eternal, bitter warfare with himself" (*Letters* 98).

Though *In Dubious Battle* was Steinbeck's first novel to implicate the agribusiness for workers' plight, it was by no means his last. With the success of the novel, the *San Francisco News* commissioned Steinbeck in 1936 to write a series of articles about the migrant workers who were flooding into California from the Midwest to escape the devastation of the Dust Bowl. The Dust Bowl was a human-made ecological disaster that struck the southern plains states shortly after the onset of the Depression, exacerbating the poverty that the fall in crop prices had already brought as the stock market crashed. Years of deep plowing and overcultivation had killed the native grasses that helped to hold the topsoil in place, and when a severe drought caused the soil to dry up, high winds swept it up into clouds that reached as far across the country as the East Coast. Hundreds of thousands of tenant farmers and agricultural workers were forced to abandon their homes in search of new jobs. Many traveled to Steinbeck's Salinas Valley, as word circulated that the area promised an abundance of well-paying agricultural jobs. Yet, as Steinbeck discovered when he began writing his articles, upon arriving, many migrants found that jobs were scarce, wages low, and the living conditions wretched.

Later collected as *The Harvest Gypsies*, the articles are at once a vivid portrait of despondent and exploited workers who have lost their homes and livelihoods and a call for reform. Tom Collins, the manager of a government migrant camp whom Steinbeck met while researching the articles, was by far the most influential of Steinbeck's sources. Steinbeck stayed with him for several days at the Weedpatch Camp he managed, and Collins drove Steinbeck around to visit other migrant camps in the area. In his articles, Steinbeck would voice many of Collins's ideas for reform, including the need to allow the camps to be partly self-governing so that the migrants could feel some pride of ownership in them. Years later, while writing *The Grapes of Wrath*, Steinbeck would name his Weedpatch Camp for the camp Collins oversaw and model his camp's manager, Jim Rawley, on Collins.

At the same time that he was writing the articles, Steinbeck was also finishing work on *Of Mice and Men*, which, like *In Dubious Battle*, centers on labor problems. It tells the story of George Milton and Lennie Small, migrant ranch workers during the Depression who dream of making enough money to buy their own land and realize the Jeffersonian ideal of having a small ranch of their own. The book, which became emblematic of the American quest for independence and ownership, concludes with the desecration of the American Dream when the mentally challenged Lennie accidentally kills his employer's son's wife, ending any chance of the new life he has planned with George. To spare Lennie the fury of a lynch mob, George shoots him. The book's tragic tone gives voice to the economic powerlessness of workers of the era.

Yet Steinbeck's outrage at the injustices of the era is best remembered from *The Grapes of Wrath*, which contains this indelible passage in one of its interchapters:

> There is a crime here that goes beyond denunciation. There is sorrow here than weeping cannot symbolize. There is a failure here that topples all our success. The fertile earth, the straight tree rows, the sturdy trunks, and the ripe fruit. And children dying of pellagra must die because a profit cannot be taken from an orange. And coroners must fill in the certificates—died of malnutrition—because the food must rot, must be forced to rot. (349)

Also set during the Depression, it depicts the travails of a family of sharecroppers, the Joads, as they migrate from Oklahoma to the Salinas Valley in the hopes of escaping the poverty inflicted on them by the Dust Bowl. Like *In Dubious Battle*, it is a successful integration of myth, mysticism, and politics. The Joads' journey to California parallels the Israelites' exodus from Egypt and their search for the Promised Land; Emerson's oversoul can be seen in Steinbeck's concept of "the manself," which Jim Casy and then Tom Joad discover; and the plight of the Joads and the other migrants is based on the hardships and squalor Steinbeck found in the migrant camps while writing *The Harvest Gypsies* articles. And like *In Dubious Battle*, the book, though a commercial and critical success, polarized the country. Again, as Linda Wagner-Martin explains, Steinbeck left himself open to conservatives' charges that he was a radical leftist:

> In this long narrative about the dispossessed Okies . . . who traveled to California in search of any kind of work on profitable farms, Steinbeck seemed again to sympathize with collective strategies, to hint that communist cooperation was the way to settle economic inequities in the United States. (vii)

Some agricultural groups, such as the Associated Farmers of California, were aggravated by Steinbeck's depictions of the agribusiness's attitudes toward migrant workers, which they considered inaccurate and irresponsible. The book was banned from several school districts and public libraries in California and Oklahoma. At the same time, actual socialists and communists criticized the novel for failing to call for no less than a revolutionary uprising against American capitalism and the government that supported it.

Though the furor over *The Grapes of Wrath* calmed with time—the novel is now one of the most frequently assigned novels in high school and college classrooms—controversy would continue to dog Steinbeck, even as he held true to his vision of the common humanity of all people and updated it to take in contemporary events.

With the outbreak of World War II in September 1939, Steinbeck became a fierce opponent of fascism and deeply involved in the war effort, even meeting with President Roosevelt in June 1940 to discuss how the United States could aid the Allies by creating propaganda to equal the Nazis'. Throughout the war, he served in two government intelligence agencies, the Office of the Coordinator of Information (COI) and the Office of Strategic Services (OSS), was the foreign news editor for the Office of War Information, and was a member of the Writer's War Board. In the space of five years, he created a tremendous amount of propaganda to support the war effort, writing a novel (which he also adapted into a play), a nonfiction account of a bomber crew, radio scripts, a film treatment for Alfred Hitchcock's *Lifeboat*, a short story that became the film *A Medal for Benny,* and a collection of news articles about the war, *Once There Was a War.*

Though most of this work was well received at the time (modern critics have since largely dismissed it as cheap propaganda), the novella *The Moon Is Down* came under heavy fire. Steinbeck began writing it in the fall of 1941 at the request of the OSS, drawing on interviews he had conducted with refugees from Norway, Denmark, Belgium, France, and the Netherlands for material. The novella was published in March 1942, just four months after the attack on Pearl Harbor. Set in a town in an unidentified northern European country, it depicts the invasion of the country by an unidentified (though clearly German) aggressor. Deprived of their freedoms, the townspeople struggle against their occupiers, suggesting that a free, democratic society will defy a totalitarian one. Though contraband translations of the novella were hugely popular in the occupied countries, especially Norway, in the United States, critics attacked Steinbeck, calling his humanistic portrayal of totalitarian occupiers naïve.

As the war entered its final years, Steinbeck began his return to literary fiction with *The Pearl* (1945), a novella set in the 1900s, which tells the story of an impoverished pearl diver, Kino, whose son, Coyotito, is stung by a scorpion. In order to save Coyotito, Kino and his common-law wife, Juana, set out in search of a pearl valuable enough to pay a doctor; yet their success meets with only more tragedy as dealers and Kino's fellow villagers try to trick him into giving up his pearl for a pittance and even attack him and attempt to steal it. At the same time, Kino's growing obsession with the pearl changes him—he draws blood while fending off a would-be thief and abuses Juana when she tries to take the pearl from him and destroy it. In the end, Coyotito accidentally is killed by one of the would-be thieves, and Kino, realizing how he has been seduced by wealth, flings the pearl back into the sea.

As Linda Wagner-Martin explains in her introduction to *The Pearl*, Steinbeck wrote the novella in the midst of a deep personal crisis. After laboring for years in poverty and obscurity, the success of *The Grapes of Wrath* had brought him fortune and fame. Yet, having achieved the American Dream, Steinbeck still felt unsatisfied and began to interrogate the reasons for his dissatisfaction. The resulting work, *The Pearl*, was meant to be a parable of how material wealth can corrupt a person's greatest treasure—his soul. Yet many critics and readers overlooked the novella's biblical resonances (the original parable of the pearl comes from Matthew 13:45-46) and instead found it full of socialism and contempt for American capitalism.

In the years following the war, Steinbeck also became worried about how the sudden influx of postwar wealth was affecting American values. The same year that *The Pearl* was published, Steinbeck also published *The Wayward Bus*, an allegorical novel about a collection of characters representing a sort of cross section of American society—including a businessman, a black manual laborer, a stripper, a salesman, and a waitress—who find themselves traveling cross-country on a bus driven by a half-Irish, half-Mexican man named Juan Chicory. As Stephen K. George writes, it is Steinbeck's attempt to tackle the problems faced by postwar America:

The Wayward Bus is a sustained attack on the morals of postwar America, particularly postwar American business. Steinbeck uses the novel to address some of the most important issues of the time, issues that remain important today: questions of business ethics, the difference between good work and immoral work, and the relationship between business and sexuality. (155)

Following *The Wayward Bus*, Steinbeck turned to the Cold War and, with photographer Robert Capa, in the late summer of 1947 set off on a forty-day tour of the Soviet Union. As the two explained to an official at the USSR Society for Cultural Relations with Foreign Countries, their purpose was to "avoid politics, but to try to talk to and to understand Russian farmers, and working people, and market people, to see how they lived, and to try to tell our people about it, so that some kind of common understanding might be reached" (*Journal* 24).

Written in a documentary style, *A Russian Journal* (1948) again pleased very few reviewers. Some faulted it for superficiality, saying that Steinbeck's objective stance prevented him from digging into the darker side of communism, and others took issue with Steinbeck's criticisms of Soviet bureaucracy. Again, Steinbeck was suspected of communist sympathies, a suspicion that the Federal Bureau of Investigation had shared since 1943, when it opened an investigation of Steinbeck and found him unfit for a commission in the army because of his associations with the Communist Party in the 1930s while gathering material for his novels. Yet, despite the controversy, Steinbeck would continue to try to foster understanding between the United States and the Soviet Union. In 1956, he joined People to People, a private program initiated by the Eisenhower administration with the intention of facilitating contact between prominent U.S. figures and ordinary Soviet citizens and of persuading Soviets to adopt democracy. Despite its best intentions, though, the group's only real success was securing the release of Ezra Pound from a Washington, D.C., mental hospital, where he had been sent after being found unfit to stand trial for treason for his activities in Italy during World War II.

As the 1950s worn on, Steinbeck grew increasingly dispirited about America's morality and politics. Joseph McCarthy's and the House Un-American Activities Committee (HUAC)'s unfounded harassment of hundreds of people suspected of holding communist sympathies was one factor. The trial of playwright Arthur Miller, who was charged with contempt of Congress for refusing to testify before the committee, particularly disturbed Steinbeck, and in 1957 he published an attack on the HUAC and a defense of Miller in *Esquire*. Adlai Stevenson's failed 1952 and 1956 presidential campaigns were another factor. Stevenson, an eloquent liberal Democrat with an intellectual bent, campaigned in both elections on a platform of progressive reforms, and Steinbeck was a strong supporter of Stevenson in both campaigns. In addition to writing speeches for Stevenson, he traveled to report on both national conventions for more than forty newspapers. He also wrote a foreword for a collection of Stevenson's speeches, remarking:

> I think Stevenson is more durable, socially, politically and morally. . . . As a writer I love the clear, clean writing of Stevenson. As a man I like his intelligent, humorous, logical, civilized mind. (*America* 222)

Years later, upon Stevenson's death in 1965, Steinbeck expressed bitter regret that Stevenson had failed to win the presidency: "My first reaction to his death was one of rage that Americans had been too stupid to avail themselves of his complete ability" (*Letters* 825).

Steinbeck wrote his sole political satire, *The Short Reign of Pippin IV: A Fabrication* (1957), during these years. The book, which made light of the turmoil of France's postwar government (the country would have seventeen prime ministers before the government was dissolved in 1958), told the story of an astronomer and supposed descendent of Charlemagne, Pippin Héristal, who is appointed king of France. Pippin, who would much rather enjoy the privacy of being a citizen, at first tries to dodge his royal responsibilities by dressing like a commoner and riding around on a motor scooter. In time, though, he resolves to try to improve his country and make it more just, only to discover that his appointment was made only so that the Communists would have a monarchy to revolt against. In the end, Pippin is dethroned as the people finally rise up against him. Characteristically, Steinbeck voices his outrage at social and economic injustices through Pippin:

> "I did not ask to be king . . . but I am king and I find this dear, rich, productive France torn by selfish factions, fleeced by greedy promoters, deceived by parties. . . . The riches of France, which should have some kind of distribution, are gobbled up. . . . And on this favored land the maggots are feeding." (137-38)

It is a light work whose satire muffles the disillusionment Steinbeck gave full voice to in his last novel, *The Winter of Our Discontent* (1961). *Winter* revisited the themes of many of Steinbeck's previous works but sounded a more despondent note. As it opens, Steinbeck's protagonist, Ethan Allen Hawley, works in a grocery store that he used to own. Under pressure from his wife and children, who are discontent with their low social status and poverty, Hawley resolves that he will get back his store and notifies the Immigration and Naturalization Service that the store's new owner, an Italian named Alfio Marullo, may be in the country illegally. Faced with deportation, Marullo gives the store to Hawley, who soon becomes a successful and powerful local businessman. In time, he's drawn into local business and political corruption. For awhile he is able to rationalize his immorality, but when he catches his son unremorsefully cheating, Hawley realizes how far he has fallen and resolves to commit suicide. As the novel finishes, however, he feels the tug of his family's love for him and changes his mind, though Steinbeck does not reveal whether he is able to escape the secluded cliffside alcove where he has hidden himself and which is quickly being surrounded by the incoming tide. As Susan Shillinglaw explains in her introduction to the novel, it grew out of Steinbeck's unease about the immorality and materialism of postwar America, which he expressed in a 1959 letter to Stevenson:

> [There's] a creeping, all pervading, nerve-gas of immorality which starts in the nursery and does not stop before it reaches the highest offices both corporate and governmental. . . . [And] a nervous restlessness, a hunger, a thirst, a yearning for something unknown—perhaps morality. Then there's the violence, cruelty and hypocrisy symptomatic of a people which has too much, and last, the surly ill temper which only shows up in humans when they are frightened. (*America* 108)

In his last years, Steinbeck continued to observe and try to understand American culture and politics. In 1962, he set off with his dog Charley on a roughly three-month road trip across America to search for answers to one question to which he no longer knew how to reply: What are Americans really like? *Travels with Charley: In Search of America* (1962), though humorous and compassionate, seems to suggest that neither Steinbeck nor the Americans he encountered had found any way to combat the confusion and materialism of postwar America: "Well, you take my grandfather and his father," one New England farmer tells him:

> "My grandfather knew the number of whiskers in the Almighty's beard. I don't even know what happened yesterday, let alone tomorrow. He knew what it was that makes a rock or a table. I don't even understand the formula that says nobody knows. We've got nothing to go on—got no way to think about things." (26)

Approaching Seattle, Steinbeck wonders why "progress looks so much like destruction" (181), and, traveling through the South, he is repulsed by the rampant racism (numerous people, spying the blue poodle Charley in Steinbeck's front seat, think it a fine joke to remark, "I thought you had a nigger in there").

Shortly after *Charley*, Steinbeck published his final work, a collection of essays titled *America and Americans* (1966). Like *Charley*, it takes a dim view of the country's postwar prosperity: "I have named the destroyers of nations: comfort, plenty, and security—out of which grow a bored and slothful cynicism," Steinbeck intones (400). Shortly after its publication Steinbeck again became embroiled in controversy, this time over the Vietnam War. Beginning in December 1966, he embarked on a six-week tour of the war-torn country as a correspondent for *Newsday*, riding along in U.S. military helicopters, shadowing marines in the jungle as they made preparations for a ground attack, and interviewing North Vietnamese refugees. A fervid opponent of totalitarianism in any form, Steinbeck was convinced prior to his trip that the war was a humanistic endeavor to protect the people of South Vietnam from the oppressions of communism. At a time when young men were burning their draft cards, he also found in the soldiers, of whom his son John IV was one, the sort of noble determination that he had admired years before in the Dust Bowl migrants. Yet after observing the war firsthand, he privately came to believe that it would be impossible for the United States to win. Nevertheless, the articles he wrote, titled "Letters to Alicia," were unremittingly patriotic and supportive of the soldiers, outraging liberals, who, opposed to the war, branded him a traitor for failing to criticize it. When Steinbeck died in 1968, the controversy over his support for the war left his critical reputation in limbo.

Nevertheless, decades after his death, Steinbeck is best remembered as a fierce critic of social injustice and one whose works are much more than mere protest literature: they illuminate the human will to endure, the desire to do better, and the desire to strive in the face of defeat, and they bear witness to what Steinbeck called the potential of the "perfectibility" of man. Through them, Steinbeck strove to draw his readers to this purpose:

The ancient commission of the writer has not changed. He is charged with exposing our many grievous faults and failures, with dredging up to the light our dark and dangerous dreams for the purpose of improvement.

Furthermore, the writer is delegated to declare and to celebrate man's proven capacity for greatness of heart and spirit—for gallantry in defeat—for courage, compassion and love. In the endless war against weakness and despair, these are the bright rally flags of hope and of emulation.

I hold that a writer who does not believe in the perfectibility of man has no dedication nor any membership in literature. (Nobel Speech paras. 10-12)

More so than any other writer of his time, Steinbeck strove to both document his time and his world and to offer his readers hope that, by understanding themselves and their society, they could change both for the better. By turns stern and compassionate, he offered a vision of the world that, as Carpenter observes of *The Grapes of Wrath*, was at once pragmatic, democratic, and deeply spiritual.

In a journal he kept while writing *Of Mice and Men*, Steinbeck remarked:

In every bit of honest writing in the world . . . there is a base theme. Try to understand men, if you understand each other you will be kind to each other. . . . There is writing promoting social change, writing punishing injustice, writing in celebration of heroism, but always that base theme. Try to understand each other. (qtd. in Shillinglaw vii)

Despite cries from critics, what unifies Steinbeck's works, despite their varied genres and styles, is his commitment to understanding. While Steinbeck was willing to roar like a lion, his message was simple and peaceful: the best we can do is try to understand one another.

Works Cited

Campbell, Joseph. *The Hero with a Thousand Faces*. New York: Meridian Books, 1956.

Carpenter, Frederic I. "The Philosophical Joads." *College English* 2.4 (Jan. 1941): 315-25.

DeMott, Robert. Introduction. *To a God Unknown*. By John Steinbeck. New York: Penguin, 1995. vii-xxxvii.

_____. *Steinbeck's Typewriter: Essays on His Art*. Troy, NY: Whitston, 1996.

George, Stephen K. *The Moral Philosophy of John Steinbeck*. Lanham, MD: Scarecrow Press, 2005.

Gray, James. *John Steinbeck*. St. Paul: U of Minnesota P, 1971.

Nagel, James. Introduction. *The Pastures of Heaven*. By John Steinbeck. New York: Penguin, 1995. vi-xxix.

Railsback, Brian, and Michael J. Meyer, eds. *A Steinbeck Encyclopedia*. Westport, CT: Greenwood Press, 2006.

Shillinglaw, Susan. Introduction. *Of Mice and Men*. By John Steinbeck. New York: Penguin, 1994. vii-xxvi.

Steinbeck, John. *America and Americans, and Selected Nonfiction*. New York: Penguin, 2003.

_____. *The Grapes of Wrath*. 1939. New York: Penguin, 2006.

_____. *In Dubious Battle*. 1936. New York: Penguin, 2006.

_____. Nobel Prize Acceptance Speech. 1962. 15 Nov. 2009. http://nobelprize.org/nobel_prizes/literature/laureates/1962/Steinbeck-speech.html.

_____. *The Short Reign of Pippin IV: A Fabrication*. 1957. New York: Penguin, 2000.

_____. *Steinbeck: A Life in Letters*. 1975. Ed. Elaine Steinbeck and Robert Wallsten. New York: Penguin, 1989.

_____. *Travels with Charley: In Search of America*. 1962. New York: Penguin, 1997.

Steinbeck, John, with Robert Capa. *A Russian Journal*. 1948. New York: Penguin, 1999.

Wagner-Martin, Linda. Introduction. *The Pearl*. By John Steinbeck. New York: Penguin, 1994. vii-xviv.

Wollenberg, Charles. Introduction. *The Harvest Gypsies: On the Road to "The Grapes of Wrath."* By John Steinbeck. Berkeley, CA: Heyday Books, 1988.

John Steinbeck, Frank Norris, and Literary Naturalism_____

Gurdip Panesar

As the author of multiple searing portraits of society such as *The Grapes of Wrath*, *Of Mice and Men*, and *In Dubious Battle*, Steinbeck is often classed within the school of American naturalism. Such a classification, however, also prompts a debate about just what naturalism is, particularly the American version, and how far Steinbeck subscribed to its tenets. The "naturalist" tag certainly seems set to stay with Steinbeck, however, as it has done from his time to ours, and as such it is worth examining his work in the light of another writer generally credited as being a founder of the American literary naturalist movement at the beginning of the twentieth century, Frank Norris. Despite the fact that the two authors are often lumped together under this label, there have been few attempts at detailed comparison between the two. Such an approach reveals interesting similarities and illuminating differences. In this essay, Norris's novels *The Octopus* and *McTeague* will form the principal focus of discussion, together with some of Steinbeck's most prominent works.

We can begin with a brief consideration of what "naturalism" could mean. Historically, there has not been too much agreement on this, among either European or American observers. What is beyond dispute, however, is that naturalism has its roots in the idea of scientific determinism, which gained currency in the late nineteenth century in the wake of rapid social changes, such as industrialization and urbanization, and the rise of new scientific and philosophical ideas (most notably Darwin's theory of evolution) that threw traditional religious beliefs into question. Put simply, the naturalists believed that individuals' lives and characters are governed and determined by impersonal natural laws and forces, such as social conditions, the environment, and heredity. They took their cue from Darwin and played up the biological and hereditary factors that constrained individuals as well as the idea that life is a struggle and only the fittest survive. To this end, many naturalists focused their work on those who are worst off in society, emphasizing the role of instinct in survival and depicting realities, such as sex, that, at the time, seemed sordid. The French novelist Émile Zola remains perhaps the single best-known exponent of the school.

The naturalists ostensibly tried to treat their material scientifically. They aimed to strip their fiction of all illusion and dispassionately record the objects, actions, and forces of their societies. But few if any of the naturalist authors successfully executed this program; after all, as has often been noted, it works against the very ideas of fiction and of art, which necessarily require a degree of artifice. Furthermore, as Jackson J. Benson, an eminent Steinbeck biographer, notes, the idea that all human beings are doomed at every moment to act or be acted upon according to circumstances external to them, such as birth and class, hardly makes for interesting fiction: "That man can act, that he has a measure of free will, and that the choices he makes are from genuine alternatives . . . this is what we call a story" (106-7). The naturalist writers believed it their duty to have an unflinching fidelity to the harsh realities that rarely intruded into nineteenth-century realist novels, but they realized that their fiction needed to be something more than mere documentation. For many naturalist writers, the movement in fact provided a new scope for a different kind of tragedy, fatalism under a new scientific name, and their art, they argued, became a search for the great fundamental truths about the human condition that they felt that the prevailing mode of realism could not encompass, as it merely scratched "the surface of things" (Norris, "Plea" 1166). In America, naturalism included alike Jack London's tales, which were set in the wilderness, away from the protection of civilization, and included both human and animal characters; Stephen Crane's and Theodore Dreiser's stories, which centered on the elemental passions at the very edges of society that peeped through the thin veneers of duty and convention; and Norris's stories, which depict the struggles of common men and, in some cases, the slow reversion of a man to a brute. No one declared this search for truth in more grandiose terms than Norris, who extolled naturalism as a new kind of romanticism (exemplified, for him, in the writings of Zola), and decreed that such writing exposed "the unplumbed depth of the human heart, and the mystery of sex, and the problems of life—and the black, unsearched penetralia of the soul of man" (1169).

Born in Chicago in 1870, Norris moved with his family to San Francisco when he was fourteen. He studied art in Paris 1887 and 1888, and it was there that he was first fired with enthusiasm for the writings of Zola. While attending the University of California between 1890 and 1894, he was exposed to the evolutionary theory that was to make such an impact on his work as writer. He worked as a journalist with the *San Francisco Wave*, was later a war correspondent in Cuba for *McClure's Magazine*, and eventually joined the Doubleday publishing firm in 1898. His journalistic experience helped to form one of his major literary projects, *The Octopus* (1901), the first book of a planned trilogy, "An Epic of Wheat," that became his best-known work with the exception of *McTeague* (1899). The second novel in this trilogy, *The Pit*, followed in 1902: however, the third installment was never written as Norris died of a ruptured appendix in 1902 at the age of thirty-two.

Born in the year that Norrris died, Steinbeck never publicly acknowledged any literary debt to him, and a direct lineage between the two authors is not often sought out by scholars.[1] However, even a casual comparison of their careers immediately reveals parallels. Norris was fairly widely read in the early twentieth century as a "muckraking" writer, particularly for his portrayal, in *The Octopus*, of a tragically violent confrontation between ranchers and a railroad trust that was inspired by a real-life event. The Mussel Slough Tragedy of 1880 saw a bloody clash between agents protecting the Southern Pacific Railroad and ranchers who had hoped to buy the land they had been renting from the railroad only to find that the company was demanding that they pay exorbitant prices. Norris meticulously researched the event and the lives of ranchers in the area and used this material as the basis for his depiction of the injustice inflicted on ordinary working people by corporate forces intent on making profits. He wanted to use the medium of the novel to expose social injustices, as he made clear in his usual declamatory style: "[the modern novel] . . . may be a great force, that works together with the pulpit and the universities for the good of the people, fearlessly proving that power is abused, that the strong grind the faces of the weak" (Norris, "Novel" 1200).

Steinbeck also, of course, worked as a journalist and agreed with Norris when he wrote that "one job of a writer is to set down his time as nearly as he can understand it" (*Russian Journal* 25) and that the American writer's job in particular is to be "the watch-dog of society . . . . to satirize its silliness, to attack its injustices, to stigmatize its faults" (158). Thus he tended to focus his stories on real-life people who had been exploited by American society, such as the striking fruit pickers of *In Dubious Battle* and the migrant farmworkers of *The Grapes of Wrath*, all the time, like Norris, drawing on his wealth of journalistic experience.

Moreover, both Steinbeck and Norris wrote of California; *The Octopus* is subtitled "A California Story." Unlike Steinbeck, Norris was not born in California, but he did spent his formative years there and imaginatively engaged with it. *McTeague* captures the San Francisco streets in assiduous detail and also portrays the state's great mountains and valleys and its miner communities; *The Octopus* captures California ranch life, and several of Norris's short stories also depict miner communities. Steinbeck, in turn, writes memorably of places such as Salinas and Monterey, and both engage in lengthy descriptions of the distinctive California landscape. At times they take a mythic approach, conceiving of the California earth as a kind of mother goddess. Take, for instance, this passage from *The Octopus*:

> It was the season after the harvest, and the great earth, the mother, after its period of reproduction, its pains of labour, delivered of the fruit of its loins, slept the sleep of exhaustion, the infinite repose of the colossus, benignant, eternal, strong, the nourisher of nations, the feeder of an entire world. (614)

This is comparable with Steinbeck's descriptions of Joseph Wayne's land in *To a God Unknown*, a book in which Steinbeck's mythologizing tendencies are most evident. His farm is located in the valley tellingly known as Our Lady, but the Christian reference veils the sense of a deeper and more ancient earth-religion that Norris makes more explicit in the aforementioned passage. The land's lush fertility (before the coming of the droughts that presage disaster) is overwhelming, and Wayne is intoxicated by it: "His eyes smouldered with lust. . . . He willed that all things about him must grow, grow quickly, conceive and multiply" (27).

At other times, both writers focus more on the grimmer side of the California landscape, emphasizing its inhospitable and arid aspects. For instance, Death Valley appears at the close of *McTeague*:

> Before him and upon either side, to the north and to the east and to the south, stretched primordial desolation. League upon league the infinite reaches of dazzling white alkali laid themselves out like an immeasurable scroll unrolled from horizon to horizon; not a bush, not a twig relieved that horrible monotony. Even the sand of the desert would have been a welcome sight; a single clump of sage-brush would have fascinated the eye; but this was worse than the desert. It was abominable, this hideous sink of alkali, this bed of some primeval lake lying so far below the level of the ocean. The great mountains of Placer County had been merely indifferent to man; but this awful sink of alkali was openly and unreservedly iniquitous and malignant. (560)

Steinbeck strikes a similarly grim note with the wholly ironic first glimpse that the Joads have of California, their Promised Land: "They looked dully at the broken rock glaring under the sun, and across the river the terrible ramparts of Arizona" (101).

Another way in which the two writers can be compared is in their intentions to write about contemporary American life in the epic strain. Steinbeck, as has often been noted, consciously drew on biblical refer-

---

ences in his novels, for example with his use of the Cain and Abel story in *East of Eden* (whose very title, of course, is biblical) and the motif of the journey to the Promised Land that he uses in *The Grapes of Wrath*; the title of *In Dubious Battle* is taken from *Paradise Lost*. Also, Steinbeck often subtly uses biblical phrasing. For example, Jim Casy's final speech in *The Grapes of Wrath*—"You don't know what you're doin' " (344)—alludes to Christ's words on the Cross, "Father, forgive them; for they know not what they do" (Luke 23:34). There are also times when Steinbeck uses a biblical turn of phrase satirically, as with this scathing observation from *Cannery Row*: "What can it profit a man to gain the whole world and to come to his property with a gastric ulcer, a blown prostate, and bifocals?" (18), which reworks one of Jesus' lessons, "For what shall it profit a man, if he shall gain the whole world, and lose his own soul?" (Mark 8:36).

Religion played a part in Norris's upbringing, too—scholars have examined his Calvinist background as a predisposing factor for his fatalism[2]—but his epics of the American West are cast in secular terms. Presley, the middle-class, educated idealist in *The Octopus*, through whose eyes we see most of the action, initially dreams of writing a poem "of the West, that world's frontier of Romance, where a new race, a new people—hardy, brave, and passionate—were building an empire; where the tumultuous life ran like fire from dawn to dark, and from dark to dawn again, primitive, brutal, honest, and without fear" (584). However, he quickly comes to realize that this kind of epic, like a naturalist novel, will have to be tempered by more unsavory realities: "He searched for the True Romance and in the end found grain rates and unjust freight tariffs" (587).

Steinbeck and Norris also share the dubious distinction of attracting a fair amount of criticism for their style. Steinbeck has often been accused of sentimentalism. Warren French remarks that many of his poor and downtrodden characters seem to undergo "an awakening of . . . consciousness that coincides with the awakening of . . . conscience" (92) as they, as embodiments of a universal "life-force," struggle to "endure and triumph over" hardship (102). For some critics this program leads to mawkishness, particularly in a work such as *The Grapes of Wrath*; Howard S. Levant condemns the "hollowed rhetoric" of the novel's final chapters, in which, he writes, the characters become mere allegorical mouthpieces, especially Jim Casy and Tom Joad, who is effectively Casy's disciple and whose closing speech to Ma refers to a mythical Emersonian oversoul of which he is part (128). Levant sees Ma's pronouncements about the endurance of the common people to be in a similar vein and also criticized the famous last scene, in which, in a supreme act of selflessness, Rose of Sharon, having lost her baby, breast-feeds a starving man. One might also point to the equally well-known closing scene in *Of Mice of Men*, in which George performs an act of mercy by shooting his big, simple friend Lennie to prevent him being lynched. Steinbeck's sentimentality can even be seen in later works such as *Cannery Row*, in which the lowest of the low, who live among the canneries, are called "saints and angels and martyrs and holy men" (7), although the prevailing humor in this work has largely deflected such criticisms as those aimed at *The Grapes of Wrath*.

Norris, meanwhile, is often castigated for his unashamedly grandiloquent style and his melodrama. In his defense, he felt that he had to use such a style to match his grand plans for literature and to portray his most fearsome and awe-inspiring scenes, a lead which he took from Zola: "The world of M. Zola is a world of big things, the enormous, the formidable, the terrible" ("Zola" 1107). Still, more than one critic has seen Norris's zeal for Zola as a regrettable misunderstanding on his part. W. M. Frohock has observed, "Norris simply mistakes Zola's idiosyncratic penchant towards melodrama for the characterising trait of naturalism as a whole" (9).

Neither author's work lacks for sensationalism. Norris's *McTeague* includes drunkenness, abuse, and violent murders; in *Vandover and the Brute*, the title character is afflicted with lycanthropy; and there are a violent shootout, bomb attacks, starvation, and prostitution in *The Octopus*. Steinbeck, too, shows ordinary people in extreme situations, some of which culminate in grim deaths. Nolan's lifeless and, it is implied, faceless body amid the crowd of strikers forms the center of *In Dubious Battle*'s final, lurid scene. The migrants of *The Grapes of Wrath* are exposed to violence and a series of degradations. Both Steinbeck and Norris have been taken to task for their sensationalism, but both felt that they were fulfilling the true duty of the novelist by presenting extreme situations that allowed the fundamental truths of the human condition to emerge.

In the best tradition of the naturalists, Norris and Steinbeck focus on common individuals and often allegorize the common people. In *The Octopus*, Norris writes of the ordinary people who live and work on the ranches, claiming that they form "the starting point of civilization, coarse, vital, real and sane" (682). In his short story "The Wife of Chino," the miners of Placer County also embody these exemplary primitive and straightforward ideals:

> Things were done "for all they were worth" in Placer County, California. When a man worked, he worked hard; when he slept, he slept soundly; when he hated, he hated with primeval intensity; and when he loved he grew reckless. (15)

Steinbeck also portrays the people who live close to the earth in poverty or near poverty, but he generally goes further than Norris in portraying them realistically, especially through dialogue, which is generally one of Norris's weak points. One of the most notable examples of Steinbeck's skill is *The Grapes of Wrath*'s Okie farmer Muley Graves (his name is, of course, instantly symbolic), whose bare, repetitive speech describes the gradual decimation of his old life and the people he knew: "An' I got wanderin' round," he tells Tom Joad and Jim Casy, "just wanderin' round . . . there ain't nothin' to look after. The folks ain't ever comin' back. I'm just wanderin' round like a damn ol' graveyard ghos'" (53). Steinbeck shows his mastery of dialect here, effectively capturing the underlying lilt of the old man's apparently rugged and repetitive speech and transfiguring it into art as it unmistakably takes on something of the stark beauty of a folk ballad.

Even in the midst of modern urban life, some of Steinbeck's and Norris's characters retain the same simple outlook as the farmhands, ranchers, and miners who populate the author's other novels. For instance, the all-wise Doc of *Cannery Row* remarks, "All of our so-called successful men are sick men, with bad stomachs, and bad souls, but Mack and the boys are healthy and curiously clean. They can do what they want. They can satisfy their appetites without calling them something else" (114). Such remarks may cast the characters in a somewhat sentimental light, but Steinbeck also counters this tendency by making less flattering comparisons, at one point writing that Mack and the boys have much in common with mean creatures like "the coyote, the common brown rat . . . the housefly and the moth" because they all have the "gift of survival" (17). At times, Steinbeck also writes of the mob, the "group man" or "phalanx," especially in *In Dubious Battle*. Here, the mob mentality and indeed its very appearance and movement becomes brutelike: "It was just one big—animal, going down the road" (79). This kind of description is also much in evidence in *The Octopus*; for instance, the ranch hands' mealtimes are described as "the feeding of the People . . . gorging of the human animal" (682). Later, when they first hear about the rail trust's exorbitant land rates, the ranchers are depicted as "the human animal hounded to its corner . . . the tormented brute" (795).

Just as the ordinary people are depicted collectively as a "brute," both authors figure the forces that oppress as collective monsters. Norris's steam train in *The Octopus* is "a vast power, huge, terrible, flinging the echo of its thunder over all the reaches of the valley, leaving blood and destruction in its path; the leviathan, with tentacles of steel clutching into the soil" (795). In this inflated description, with its incongruous mixing of animal and mechanical imagery, the train becomes a representative of inhuman forces. The railroad cannot be controlled, as Shelgrim, one of its founders, points out to Presley:

You are dealing with forces, young man, when you speak of Wheat and the Railroads, not with men. There is the Wheat, the supply. It must be carried to feed the People. There is the demand. The Wheat is one force, the Railroad, another, and there is the law that governs them—supply and demand. Men have only little to do in the whole business. Complications may aris*e*, conditions that bear hard on the individual—crush him maybe—*but the Wheat will be carried to feed the people* as inevitably as it will grow. . . . Blame conditions, not men. (1037)

Compare this with Steinbeck's portrayal of the bank as a dehumanized, uncontrollable monster in *The Grapes of Wrath*:

The bank is something more than man. It happens that every man in a bank hates what the bank does, and yet the bank does it. The bank is something more than man. . . . It's the monster. Men made it, but they can't control it. (35-36)

Both writers evince an allegorical tendency as they render the oppressors of ordinary people symbolically and the people themselves collectively as a massive, human animal.

More interesting, however, are both author's portrayals of the individual as a brute. For instance, Norris writes of Trina, the wife of the title character in *McTeague*:

A good deal of peasant blood still ran undiluted in her veins, and she had all the instinct of a hardy and penurious mountain race—the instinct which saves without any thought, without idea of consequence—saving for the sake of saving, hoarding without knowing why. (358)

When her prudent hoarding turns to greed, however, it becomes the single dominating passion of her life amidst all of her ill treatment and degradation, even overshadowing how her earlier prudence was a seemingly praiseworthy trait. Elsewhere, Norris's treatment of the primitive theme is more simplistic. In "The Wife of Chino," the beautiful but degenerate Felice becomes a melodramatic figure of unrestrained lust and vengeance:

> All the baseness of her tribe, all the degraded savagery of a degenerate race, all the capabilities for wrong, for sordid treachery, that lay dormant in her, leaped to life at this unguarded moment, and in that new light, that now at last she had herself let in, stood pitilessly revealed, a loathsome thing, hateful as malevolence itself. (21)

The primitive strain in Trina is considerably more intriguing than this—as is the portrayal of McTeague himself, perhaps Norris's single most unforgettable character. His animalism and the limitations it sets on him are apparent at the outset: "McTeague's mind was as his body, heavy, slow to act, sluggish. Yet there was nothing vicious about the man. Altogether he suggested the draught horse, immensely strong, stupid, docile, obedient " (264). McTeague, then, is not particularly savage or even unlikable—he is even described as being like a "good-natured Saint Bernard" (359), and we can laugh a little at his wife's efforts, early in their marriage, to make him more civilized, to make him less boorish. Later, too, we can feel for him when his rivalry with Marcus Schouler causes him to lose his living as a dentist and he and Trina are plunged into a downward spiral from which they never recover. Norris writes that, even as the pretensions of civilization fall from him and he is forced to revert back to the ways of his bachelor days, McTeague misses the "animal comforts," like "good tobacco," that Trina taught him to enjoy (462). It is a measure of Norris's achievement in this novel that, even as McTeague begins to abuse his wife, he remains at least partially sympathetic; in essence, he appears not as a monster but as a kind of pathetic creature (his rage against Trina is exacerbated by the fact that she sells his concertina, his most prized object), and, in the end, he is left literally trapped, chained to his hateful and dead enemy in the pitiless Death Valley. In many ways, *McTeague*

---

is Norris's most understated work: his protagonist is not particularly judged; rather, the reader is left to ponder his character, his story, and his ultimate fate.

This is not dissimilar from Steinbeck's approach in *Of Mice and Men* and his portrayal of Lennie Small. Though Steinbeck conceives of some of his characters in animalistic terms, such as Thomas Wayne in *To a God Unknown* (although Thomas remains a rather flat and undeveloped figure), Lennie is drawn more subtly. His complete simplicity, mental slowness, and unwitting physical strength connote primitivism, but in Lennie, Steinbeck also more fully explores McTeague's pathos. He kills and injures but never means to; throughout the story, his abundant good nature is always in evidence and the reader's sympathies remain entirely with him.

Where Lennie appears most animalistic is probably at the end of the novel when he is shot by George; he is, in effect, put down as Candy's old dog is put down. But here, too, Steinbeck's foremost concern is the all-too-human pity that George feels for his friend. Steinbeck's handling of this scene foregrounds his eminently human and humanistic concerns, and it is in these concerns that he differs from Norris. Compare, for instance, *The Grapes of Wrath* with *The Octopus*. The former, at times, explodes into ringing indictments of the existing social order, one of the most fervent being Steinbeck's condemnation of the agribusiness for letting fruit rot while poor children die of malnourishment: "There is a crime here that goes beyond denunciation. There is a sorrow here that weeping cannot symbolize" (365). His sympathies lie firmly with the impoverished migrants; in a journal entry dating from the time of the novel's composition, Steinbeck wrote: "Every effort I can bring to bear is and has been at the call of the common working people to the end that they may eat what they raise, use what they produce, and in every way and in completeness share in the works of their hands and their heads" (qtd. in DeMott xxiii).

In *The Octopus*, Norris does at times appear to subscribe to a straightforward condemnation of big business (particularly in his simplistic portrayal of the odious and cowardly S. Behrmann) and a glo-rification of the honest, hardworking ranchers. When invited to din-ner at the house of one of the vice presidents of the railroad trust, Presley indulges in an apocalyptic vision in which the rich are made to pay:

> He saw for one instant of time that splendid house sacked to its founda-tions, the tables overturned, the pictures torn, the hangings blazing, and Liberty, the red-handed Man in the Street, grimed with powder smoke, foul with the gutter, rush yelling, torch in hand, through every door. (1063)

We can compare this with Steinbeck's description in *The Grapes of Wrath* of the poor encroaching upon the consciousness of the rich:

> Men who had never been hungry now saw the eyes of the hungry. Men who had never wanted anything very much now saw the flame of want in the eyes of the migrants. And the men of the towns and of the soft suburban country gathered to defend themselves. (295)

At the conclusion of *The Octopus*, there is a somber reflection on how the railroad's actions have crushed and beggared the ranchers, not only taking their lives but also breaking their spirit: "Yes, the Railroad had prevailed. The ranches had been seized in the tentacles of the octopus; the iniquitous burden of extortionate freight rates had been imposed like a yoke of iron" (1096). However, *The Octopus* contains more than a simple dichotomy of good and evil, of rich versus poor. *The Grapes of Wrath* ends with an abiding image of human selflessness, verging on the mythical: a "mysterious smile" passes over Rose of Sharon's face, symbolizing how the human spirit, even in the very worst of times, will prevail and even triumph. Norris, however, offers an ultimately imper-sonal vision of the ravaged ranches:

But the WHEAT *remained.* Untouched, unassailable, undefiled, that mighty world-force, that nourisher of nations, wrapped in Nirvanic calm, indifferent to the human swarm, gigantic, resistless, moved onward in its appointed grooves. Through the welter of blood at the irrigation ditch, through the sham charity and shallow philanthropy of famine relief committees, the great harvest of Los Muertos rolled like a flood from the Sierras to the Himalayas to feed thousands of starving scarecrows on the barren plains of India.

Falseness dies; injustice and oppression in the end of everything fade and vanish away. Greed, cruelty, selfishness, and inhumanity are short-lived; the individual suffers, but the race goes on. The larger view always and through all shams, all wickednesses, discovers the Truth that will, in the end, prevail, and all things, surely, inevitably, resistlessly work together for good. (1097-98)

The exalted pitch of this passage, coming, as it does, immediately after the mournful litany for the suffering of the ranchers, may seem like a mishmash ending, as several critics have noted.[3] Yet, through it, Norris moves beyond the personal dimension and individual human concerns to talk, if rather vaguely, of a greater good, of an inscrutable scheme or universal plan that forces people in one part of the world to suffer so that people elsewhere may eat. Ultimately, in *The Octopus*, there is no good or evil, only the mysterious workings of natural laws.

Thus there are important differences between the works of Norris and Steinbeck that are more than mere differences of style. Steinbeck's foremost concern is the human level. His fiction is grounded in earthly dialogue and actions and memorable, individualized characters. Only glimpses are offered of the overarching human spirit, at first in terms of the "group man," or the mob, but later taking in the more elevated concept of "Manself." Norris, on the other hand, is more preoccupied with overriding abstractions, even as he creates individual characters—a legacy of nineteenth-century thought as well as his temperament. He is more willing than Steinbeck to overlook human individuality and instead figure his characters against a background of impersonal forces, symbolized by the wheat of his unfinished trilogy.

Notes

1. There is no doubt that Steinbeck was familiar with a lot of Norris's work; indeed, he was even accused by F. Scott Fitzgerald of basing his account of George relating his dream to Lennie in *Of Mice and Men* closely on a scene in *McTeague* in which Maria tells old Zerkow her dreams of wealth. See Jesse Crisler for further comparison of the two novels.

2. See Torsten Pettersson for a discussion of the influence of Norris's Calvinist up-bringing on his work.

3. See George Wilbur Meyer for a defense of the novel's ending.

Works Cited

Benson, Jackson J. "John Steinbeck: Novelist as Scientist." *John Steinbeck*. Ed. Harold Bloom. New York: Chelsea House, 1987. 103-23.

Crisler, Jesse. "Frank Norris and John Steinbeck: The Critical Reception of Naturalistic Art." *Steinbeck Newsletter* 8.1-2 (Winter/Spring 1995): 9-12.

Davison, Richard Allen. "*Of Mice and Men* and *McTeague*: Steinbeck, Fitzgerald, and Frank Norris." *Frank Norris Studies* 17.2 (Autumn 1989): 219-26.

DeMott, Robert. Introduction. *The Grapes of Wrath*. By John Steinbeck. Harmondsworth: Penguin, 2000. ix-xlvi.

French, Warren. *John Steinbeck*. Boston: Twayne, 1975.

Frohock, W. M. *Frank Norris*. St. Paul: U of Minnesota P, 1968.

Holman, Hugh C., and William Harmon. *A Handbook to Literature*. New York: Macmillan, 1992.

Levant, Howard. *The Novels of John Steinbeck: A Critical Study*. Columbia: U of Missouri P, 1974.

Meyer, George Wilbur. "The Original Social Purpose of the Naturalistic Novel." *Sewanee Review* 50.4 (1942): 563-70.

Norris, Frank. *McTeague*. 1899. *Frank Norris: Novels and Essays*. Ed. Donald Pizer. New York: Viking Press, 1986. 261-572.

_____. "The Novel with a 'Purpose.'" *Frank Norris: Novels and Essays*. Ed. Donald Pizer. New York: Viking Press, 1986. 1196-1200.

_____. *The Octopus: A Spy of California*. 1901. *Frank Norris: Novels and Essays*. Ed. Donald Pizer. New York: Viking Press, 1986. 573-1098.

_____. "A Plea for Romantic Fiction." *Frank Norris: Novels and Essays*. Ed. Donald Pizer. New York: Viking Press, 1986. 1165-79.

_____. *Vandover and the Brute*. 1914. *Frank Norris: Novels and Essays*. Ed. Donald Pizer. New York: Viking Press, 1986. 1-260.

_____. "The Wife of Chino." *A Deal in Wheat and Other Stories*. 1903. Middlesex: Echo, 2006. 12-22.

_____. "Zola as a Romantic Writer." *Frank Norris: Novels and Essays*. Ed. Donald Pizer. New York: Viking Press, 1986. 1106-08.

Pettersson, Torsten. "Deterministic Acceptance Versus Moral Outrage: A Problem of Literary Naturalism in Frank Norris' *The Octopus*." *Orbis Litterarum* 42.1 (1987): 77-95.

Steinbeck, John. *Cannery Row*. 1945. London: Pan, 1974.

_____. *The Grapes of Wrath*. 1939. Harmondsworth: Penguin, 2000.

_____. *In Dubious Battle*. 1936. Harmondsworth: Penguin, 1992.

_____. *A Russian Journal*. 1948. With Robert Capa. New York: Penguin, 1999.

_____. *To a God Unknown*. 1933. London: Heinemann, 1970.

"You're Kind of Untouchable":
Women, Men, and the Environment in *The Long Valley*_____

Cynthia A. Bily

Readers of Steinbeck's short-story collection *The Long Valley* (1938) have long been touched by its richly drawn characters: Jody, the young man who undergoes painful rites of passage as he earns the right to his own red pony; Harry Teller, the lonely husband who deliberately shoots the white quail that gives his wife pleasure; Dick and Root, two union organizers who bravely accept a beating; and Elisa Allen, who grows the biggest chrysanthemums in the valley. Elisa's story, "The Chrysanthemums," opens the collection and features one of the most memorable of Steinbeck's female characters. But hers is the only female consciousness presented in the volume; all of the other women characters—and there are few of them—are presented primarily through the perceptions of the men around them, men who take center stage in the other stories. This is true not only in *The Long Valley* but also in much of Steinbeck's other work.

The question of why women appear so infrequently in Steinbeck's fiction, and in such minor and subservient roles, is one that has been turned over and over again, especially by readers of the novels. Mimi Gladstein surveys this "chorus of voices raised in question of Steinbeck's portrayal of women" (85) in the aptly titled essay "Missing Women: The Inexplicable Disparity Between Women in Steinbeck's Life and Those in His Fiction" and traces Steinbeck's biography to show that he, unlike many of his characters, was mentored and inspired by intelligent women with active careers. Gladstein observes that it seems peculiar, in light of Steinbeck's own experiences, that "the women in his novels are from the lower classes, uneducated and domestic. Their spheres of influence are the home and the brothel" (97). Clearly, this description also fits the female characters who appear in the short stories in *The Long Valley,* where the only women who work outside the home are those who work in the "fancy houses" (117) Peter visits during his yearly business trips to San Francisco in "The Harness," and where the women who stay home occupy themselves with cooking, gardening, and avoiding sex with their husbands.

The scarcity of female characters, however, and their lack of action in the stories' plots, does not mean that they are unimportant. Instead, we can acknowledge that most of the stories are told from a male point of view and still see the female characters as representative of something mysterious and essential. Critic Lorelei Cederstrom, in an essay titled "Beyond the Boundaries of Sexism: The Archetypal Feminine Versus Anima Women in Steinbeck's Novels," identifies "Steinbeck's holistic conception of life and deep appreciation for the value of the feminine" (190). Rather than look at Steinbeck's female characters as underdeveloped and unrealistic, she writes, one can read them as representations of the archetypal feminine, as symbols of the natural world, as reminders of "the balance between masculine and feminine upon which not only every man/woman relationship but also the health of the earth itself depends" (204). In highlighting the relationship between the female and the natural, and in identifying the "health of the earth itself" as a theme in Steinbeck's novels and in her own work, Cederstrom engages a body of thought known as "ecofeminism." The lens of ecofeminism, this essay will show, can also raise interesting questions about the short stories in *The Long Valley*.

Ecofeminism has its origins in the growing ecological awareness of the late 1960s and early 1970s and in the feminist movement that was growing at the same time. (For a brief introduction to the origins of ecofeminism, see Barbara T. Gates, "A Root of Ecofeminism: *Ecoféminisme*.") Many feminists came to see that the oppression women suffered under the patriarchy—the hierarchical society organized, operated, and controlled by men—mirrored the oppression of the earth under capitalism. In other words, just as men have sought to conquer and dominate nature, they have sought to do the same with women. Even the language is similar; we remember from tales of the explorers their determination to "conquer untamed wilderness" or their placing special value on "virgin territory," and we are familiar with the labeling of degradation of land as a "rape." Ecofeminism evolved over the next four decades as a tree with distinct branches; for example, some ecofeminists believe that women are essentially different from men and that women have a closer connection to the earth than men do, while others emphasize the ways in which men and women are essentially the same and encourage all people to act on a renewed awareness of their place as part of the natural world. In examining the relationships among men and women and nature, and in exploring the connections between the dominance over women and what Karla Armbruster calls "the destruction and misuse of nonhuman nature" (97), ecofeminist literary criticism offers a cluster of questions that shed light on *The Long Valley.*

Ecofeminism is ultimately a political and social movement, seeking to restore harmony to the damaged earth before it is too late. It asserts that Western patriarchal culture is out of balance, cut off from the feminine Earth Mother/Mother Earth, and that the job of the critic is to expose and counteract this sickness in order to transform the culture. One way literary critics can do this is by examining what Glynis Carr and others call "dualisms." Patriarchal thought, she explains, "constructed around dualisms, imagines production, culture, the mind, and rationality in terms gendered 'male,' while reproduction, nature, the body and feeling are gendered 'female'" (16). Carr is not saying that men are more essentially rational while women are more essentially emotional; she is saying that patriarchal culture has *labeled* these qualities masculine and feminine. This does not mean that the roles of men and women are irrelevant. As Riane Eisler puts it in "The Gaia Tradition and the Partnership Future," "The way a society structures the most fundamental human relations—the relations between the female and male halves of humanity without which the species could not survive—has major implications for the *totality* of a social system" (26). By examining the connections between men and women in a culture, then, one can infer important things about the connections between humans and the rest of the natural world.

So what can ecofeminism tell us about Steinbeck's short stories? What is Steinbeck trying to tell his readers about the male/female, about culture/nature, about production/reproduction? What roles do the women in *The Long Valley* serve?

Few women have prominent roles in *The Long Valley,* but when they do appear it is often in the role of nurturer. Steinbeck's most well-known treatment of woman as nurturer, as provider of nourishment, occurs in his novel *The Grapes of Wrath* (1939), when Rose of Sharon famously offers her breast milk to a starving man after her own child is stillborn. This scene, which falls at the end of the novel, offers a bit of hope after a long story of suffering brought about by environmental degradation; it seems to say that, in the end, Mother Earth will forgive, and will nurture. Cederstrom examines Rose of Sharon's gesture in an essay titled "The 'Great Mother' in *The Grapes of Wrath*," in which she describes the scene as "an affirmation of the power to give life and to take it, to nourish even while surrounded by the death and destruction [the Great Mother] has wrought" (77). For Cederstrom, Rose of Sharon evokes "not Christian iconography but the culmination of the pagan, earth-derived values of the Great Mother" (76). Here, Steinbeck associates nature with the feminine, offering life to the waiting male.

The Long Valley presents another breast-feeding woman in the simple story "The Breakfast," whose narrator encounters a family living in a tent and surviving as day laborers picking cotton. Walking alone in the valley in a dreamlike state as the sun rises, he sees the tent, an outdoor cook stove, and then "a young woman beside the stove," who "carried a baby in a crooked arm, and the baby was nursing, its head under her waist out of the cold. The mother moved about, poking the fire, shifting the rusty lids of the stove to make a greater draft, opening the oven door" (86). Throughout the brief story, the woman continues her work, preparing and serving bacon, biscuits, gravy, coffee, and all the while the baby continues nursing. She does not go with the men to pick cotton; when they are fed, her role in the story is done.

Carroll Britch observes that "Breakfast" is only about eight hundred words long and that nearly one-third of those words describe the young woman's movements as she cooks food for the rest of the family. Unlike Cederstrom, Britch finds in the nursing mother a bridge between orthodox Christianity and the pagan: "She is drawn in a likeness of the Madonna," Britch writes, and "this Madonna is conceived as a mother of the earth" (17). Indeed, the young woman is seemingly as untouchable as the Madonna; there is no hint of sexuality about her. The narrator describes her grace and efficiency, but makes no comment about her appearance. Although the presence of the baby clearly indicates that there has been a sexual union between the woman and the younger man, there is no suggestion during the meal that the younger man responds any differently to her than the older man or their guest does or she to him. When the narrator revisits this small event, "recalling it again and again" (85), his highest praise is reserved for "frying bacon and baking bread, the warmest, pleasantest odors I know" (86). The narrator does not seek out the woman or her family; he does not want their companionship or the work they offer to help him obtain. They are simply there, and when he has eaten he moves on.

Other women in the collection are also seen offering food—and usually to men. Jody's mother in "The Red Pony" is generally seen in the kitchen, preparing or cleaning up after a meal. When Emma suffers her annual spell of sickness in "The Harness," the neighbors want to help, but "there was nothing you could do for her when she was ill, except to take pies and cakes to Peter" (112). In "Johnny Bear," the Hawkins sisters' home is known around town as "the place where a kid can get gingerbread. The place where a girl can get reassurance" (161). Jelka, the wife of Jim in "The Murder," takes pleasure in feeding him: "No matter what time Jim came in . . . his dinner was exactly, steamingly ready for him. She watched while he ate, and pushed the dishes close when he needed them" (172). Even after he beats her bloody for having an affair, she asks him, "Did you have any breakfast at all?" (183). In "Flight," Mama gives her son Pepé jerky and bullets when he flees for his life and reminds him how to alternate eating jerky and grass so as not to upset his stomach. Even the mildly sinister woman who wants to buy a snake from Dr. Phillips in "The Snake" brings sustenance to a male in her own strange way: "I want to come here and look at him and feed him and to know he's mine" (76). When Phillips tells her that the snake does not need to eat, she insists, "I want to feed him" (76); "I want to feed my snake" (77); "I want him to eat" (78); "I want to see him eat it" (80). Watching the snake eat a rat satisfies something mysterious in the woman; when he is done eating, she leaves and never returns.

There is no suggestion that cooking is satisfying to these women, that it serves them as a form of self-expression or a point of pride. They are providing fuel for working men. But this does not mean that these are dull women, who aspire to nothing more than providing for men. Cederstrom makes the point that what the women in Steinbeck's fiction think and do is less interesting to Steinbeck than how the men around them respond to them. In other words, these are not stories about women who have nothing interesting to offer but rather stories about men who are not much interested in women. Most of these stories are narrated by male characters, of course, and each narrator reveals the details that are important to him. It may be that these nurturing women have lives of their own—friends, hobbies, wishes—but these details are less interesting to the men than their own hunger. Are men and women essentially different in their connections to nourishment? In *The Long Valley* it appears that they are—that women are here to feed men.

What about the ways in which women and men use the land? In another publication, I have explored the differences between Elisa Allen and her husband Henry in this regard. In that essay, I concluded that "The Chrysanthemums" does show women and men to be fundamentally different. Elisa's connection to the land, demonstrated and strengthened by the flowers she grows, is much richer than Henry's or the tinker's; the men see the land as something to struggle against, to conquer, and to earn a living from. Charlotte Hadella, in her essay "Steinbeck's Cloistered Women," also examines "Elisa Allen in her fenced-in chrysanthemum garden" (52), and sees her as one of Steinbeck's "guarded, fenced, repressed" women who must be "chastised, purified, and controlled" (51). I agree with Hadella that the story reflects "Steinbeck's sensitivity to the female's struggle for autonomy in the early part of the twentieth century" (57). Yet rather than seeing the fence around Elisa's garden as a male attempt to keep her *in*, I prefer to think of it as her attempt to keep men *out*, to protect her little patch of earth from the moneymaking parts of the farm, "from cattle and dogs and chickens" (5).

Flowers are important symbols for Steinbeck—remember, the name of the young woman who offers her breast in *The Grapes of Wrath* is Rose of Sharon. Like Elisa Allen, Mary Teller in "The White Quail" also grows flowers, "cinerarias, big ones with loads of flowers . . . ranging in color from scarlet to ultramarine" (21). In Mary's case, it is clear that her garden is more important to her than her husband, Harry. Indeed, as the narrator notes, "the garden was herself" (22). With this line, Steinbeck highlights the ways in which the story of Mary and Harry Teller is an exaggeration, a cruel parody, of the story of Elisa and Henry Allen. Elisa is proud of her flowers, yes, and of her "planter's hands" (5), but she is not consumed by her garden the way Mary is. Elisa's flowers are big and colorful, but they are strong and sturdy, and the "stems seemed too small and easy for her energy" (4). By contrast, Mary's flowers, also big and colorful, are perversions, "so heavy they bent the stems over" (21). Elisa's garden and yard are surrounded by land of utility and beauty, with "black earth shining like metal" and "thick willow scrub along the river [that] flamed with sharp and positive yellow leaves" (3). Mary's garden is an artificial, geometrical oasis right beside a more threatening landscape, where "the hill started up, wild with cascara bushes and poison oak, with dry grass and live oak, very wild" (21). Most important, Elisa does all the work in her garden, from starting new seedlings to destroying invading insects with her fingers, while Mary's garden, though designed by her, was built by workmen, and Mary's favorite view of it is from "the window seats behind the dormer windows . . . piled with bright, fadeless fabrics" (24). When it is time to "kill slugs and snails" in Mary's garden, Mary holds the flashlight "while Harry [does] the actual killing" (25).

If Elisa Allen feels a connection with the natural world more powerful and enriching than the men in "The Chrysanthemums" do, the same cannot be said of Mary Teller. Mary sees the world outside her garden as "the enemy," as "the world that wants to get in, all rough and tangled and unkempt" (26). She wants to attract birds with her cement-lined heart-shaped pool, but when Harry comments that the poison she wants him to put out for the cats could make "animals suffer terribly," she responds, "I don't care" (34). Hadella emphasizes Mary's isolation in a world that she has created, finding that she is "at one with her perfect, sterile garden" (66). The word "sterile" here is important: Mary's garden is not genuinely alive.

From the examples of the first two stories in the collection, then, it appears that Steinbeck does not intend to offer a monolithic vision of women as earth mothers, as stand-ins for the natural world. He rejects, it seems, the dualism that says women love nature while men seek to dominate it. What of the other gardeners in the collection? At the Randall farm in "The Harness," most of the land is turned over to hay, beets, and apples, but "the immediate yard was fenced, and in the garden, under Emma's direction, Peter raised button dahlias and immortelles, carnations and pinks" (110). Emma is tiny and frequently sick, so perhaps she is not strong enough to do her own gardening, but more likely her flower garden is just one more way she shows her dominance over her husband. In this marriage, Peter manages the money crops as Henry Allen does, and he also grows the flowers—under Emma's direction. Once Emma dies, and Peter is free to do as he wishes, he decides to plant a large field in sweet peas: "Think of how it'd be to sit on the front porch and see all those acres of blue and pink, just solid. And when the wind came up over them, think of the big smell" (119). He does not care that growing sweet peas is risky from a business stand-point, and he does not care that Emma never approved of this plan. Like Mary Teller, he turns toward his flowers and away from other people, suddenly refusing to engage in valley farmers' typical preplanting chatter. "Peter . . . made it plain that his crop was a secret" (121).

But Peter does not represent an overturning of the production/ reproduction dualism. He does seem to enjoy the sweet peas in flower, sitting on his porch in a rocker every afternoon: "When the afternoon breeze came up, he inhaled deeply" (123). But the other men are suspicious in a way that they never are about the flowers women grow. Perhaps it is because the amusements of women are simply less important than the serious business of men. Only when it is clear that Peter's sweet pea crop will make money do the other men realize that they feel "a new admiration and respect for him" (124). And at the end of the story Peter admits that he has taken no pleasure from the sweet peas be-cause Emma has been worrying him from the grave. He has attempted to find a balance, to grow something both utilitarian and beautiful, but in the end he is unable to do it. Are the women of *The Long Valley* more connected to the land than the men? Do they grow flowers in harmony with nature while the men grow crops in subjugation of it? Elisa Allen tempts us to think so, but as Mary and Peter show, this dualism does not always operate in Steinbeck's world.

As mentioned earlier, Cederstrom writes that "the superficial and seemingly sexist characteristics of the women in Steinbeck's novels are much less at issue than the attitudes of the male characters toward them" ("Beyond" 204). So while it is true, as Gladstein notes, that the women of *The Long Valley* are those who inhabit "the home and the brothel" (97)—in addition to "the noisy girls at the Three Star" (173)—Steinbeck is more concerned with how the men respond to these women. Throughout the collection, the men experience women as sep-arate, untouchable, and mysterious, and this echoes the detachment and alienation they feel from the natural world. But it is also true that women feel separate from men, echoing their own alienation.

Poor Harry Teller realizes early on that he will never connect with Mary in the way he imagined. He admits that he is afraid of her and says, "You're kind of untouchable. There's an inscrutability about you" (25). Mary knows that she is a puzzle to him, that "he wanted to understand, and he never quite succeeded" (28). Dr. Phillips, owner of the laboratory in "The Snake," is attracted to and repelled by the woman who visits him, but all of his knowledge "about psychological sex symbols . . . doesn't seem to explain" her (82). And Jim Moore, not long after marrying his beautiful Slavic wife Jelka, realizes "before long that he could not get in touch with her in any way" (172). Even Henry Allen, the best of the bunch, has no idea what to say to Elisa. His joke about taking her to the fights falls flat, and his well-meaning attempt to tell her she looks "nice" only makes her angry and leaves Henry "bewildered." "Henry!" she exclaims, "Don't talk like that! You don't know what you said!" (16). The more men reach out to women, the more women push them away. It is as though they speak different languages, have different needs.

Although the women are lonely, too, this is a book about men, and what men need. The women characters in these stories provide food and nourishment, but it is not enough to satisfy their men. Though they seldom put it into clear language, the men seek to connect with other people, with women, with nature, with their own natures, in the most intimate way—through sex. Having no better way to say it (and because Steinbeck was restricted by different rules about what was acceptable to write about in the 1930s), they speak of hunger, or they respond to hunger. Kissing Mary for the first time, Harry Teller tells her, "You're so pretty. You make me kind of—hungry" (23). After Peter Randall's wife, Emma, dies, and he is free for the first time to indulge his own desires, he shouts, "I want fat women, with breasts as big as pillows. I'm hungry, I tell you" (119). Britch uses the same language when he describes what the narrator of "The Breakfast" really wants:

"Beyond the want of breakfast, he hungered in every way for the light of human warmth" (27).

Of course, Harry's hunger both startles and annoys Mary, but it does not please her. Perhaps it is because he is not sure enough about what he wants to ask for it. At night, after Mary retires to her own room, she sometimes hears Harry quietly trying to open her door, but "the door was locked. It was a signal; there were things Mary didn't like to talk about" (30). Although in the beginning she "let him" kiss her (22), she seems to have no physical desire for her husband. In fact, it is only when she sees the white quail for the first time that "a shiver of pleasure, a bursting of pleasure swelled in Mary's breast" (33). Emma Randall apparently knew all along that her husband was visiting "fancy houses in San Francisco" on his annual business trips, but although she punished him when he came back, "she never said anything" (117). And Hadella observes that Elisa is unable to tell Henry what she needs and that we cannot tell "whether Henry could ever be capable of satisfying Elisa were she to supply the romantic context and direct her passions toward him" (61) because we do not know enough about what Henry thinks and feels.

Whatever their level of sexual interest in their husbands, neither Elisa Allen, Mary Teller, Emma Randall, nor Jelka Moore is a mother, another rejection by Steinbeck of the production/reproduction dualism that says men raise crops while women raise children. The most obvious exception to these asexual women is Miss Amy Hawkins, whose "edges were soft. Her eyes were warm, her mouth full. There was a swell to her breast" (155). In the most direct mention of sexual union between any two people in the collection of stories, Miss Amy has had an affair with a Chinese sharecropper and becomes pregnant. But Steinbeck does not allow her to enjoy her sexuality. Amy has been acting on feelings she felt in the night, but her voice is "low and hoarse with misery" when she tells her sister, "I can't help it. I can't help it" (151). When she learns that she is pregnant, she kills herself. Hadella compares the long valley with an Eden in need of restoration, and argues, "Since an attempt to regain Eden motivates Steinbeck's characters, Woman, as the initiator of the original Fall, must be chastised, purified, and controlled" (51). Miss Amy's fate demonstrates the confused and contradictory ways that the feminine has often been received: woman is worshipped as a bringer of life but punished for participating willingly in sex.

The young woman in "The Breakfast" does have a nursing baby, but curiously there is no hint of sexuality about her. And when Dr. Phillips, annoyed with the woman who intrudes into his laboratory, feels "a desire to arouse her" (73), he means only that he wants to frighten her with his casual way of killing animals. Because "The Red Pony" focuses on the consciousness of Jody, it is appropriate that the sexual lives of his parents are not explored, but one more mother deserves mention here. Nellie the horse submits to the stallion who impregnates her, becoming "coquettishly feminine" (263) in a way that none of the women in these stories ever does. The moment when the two horses meet is vivid and powerful, the sex scene that Steinbeck could not depict with any of his human couples. In pregnancy, Nellie is "complacent" and carries herself "with the calm importance of an empress" (265). But in the end, she dies horribly, killed with blows to the head from a hammer so Billy Buck can rip her open to deliver her (male) colt. It would be unfair to say that the story treats Nellie with respect only as long as she is a useful vessel for her male child or to claim the longing of a twelve-year-old boy for a pony of his own as representative of a male pattern of thought, but it is fair to wonder about the extent to which Steinbeck uses Nellie's role to explore attitudes that would make us recoil if Nellie were a woman.

Although ecofeminism analyzes the ways in which the patriarchy has dominated both women and the natural world, in *The Long Valley* men are often dominated by women. Are the women more powerful, or have men conveniently surrendered their power—and their responsibility—to the women? The most obvious example of this dominance is Emma Randall, who literally makes her husband Peter wear a harness to keep his shoulders back and his stomach in, who directs him to grow flowers in the garden, and who refuses to allow him to grow sweet peas in the field. "I don't know how she made me do things," he says. "She had a way of doing it" (119). Hadella describes Mary Teller's "ability to dominate Harry so thoroughly that he is only capable of symbolic violence" (68). Dr. Phillips in "The Snake" is powerless to resist the woman's unreasonable request to purchase and feed the snake. When he says, "It's the most beautiful thing in the world. . . . It's the most terrible thing in the world" (79), he could be speaking for many of the male characters in this book, attracted and repelled, hungry and afraid, desiring and fearing the feminine and the natural. Michael J. Meyer, in "Fallen Adam: Another Look at Steinbeck's 'The Snake,'" presents the conflict as between emotions and knowledge, and returns to the myth of Eden. He equates the woman with Eve, and Dr. Phillips with Adam, and awards her the power over Phillips's decision: "Despite his revulsion, the hypnotic eyes of the woman persuade Phillips to let her have her wish. Adam, seduced by Eve, gives in to her request" (104). Phillips has internalized the dualism of rationality/feeling; he has no trouble killing cats or interfering with starfish reproduction in the name of science, but a woman feeding a rat to a snake and *enjoying* it is more than he can handle.

The exception to this female power is Jim Moore, who is outsmarted by his wife Jelka for a time, but who regains his dominance by following her father's advice and beating her "bad as I could without killing you" and then "tenderly" (183) cleaning her wounds as her eyes smile at him for the first time. Although he was reluctant at first, Jim seems to have embraced the patriarchal dualisms. Jelka is his property as surely as the other animals he strokes and pats are, as the deputy sheriff understands; if the only way to regain control over Jelka is to conquer her physically, then that is what he will do. Although he plans to build a new house and start a new life with Jelka, this will be a new life in which each man and woman knows his or her place.

Carr sums up her task as an ecofeminist literary critic this way: "In broadest terms, ecocritics are concerned with the many ways that literature and criticism might teach us to better love this world and its inhabitants" (18). In *The Long Valley,* there is precious little love to be found. Instead, men and women are continually frustrated with each other, farmers and ranchers are continually struggling against the earth, people are fed yet still hungry, and everyone is lonely. Still in his thirties when he wrote *The Long Valley* and *The Grapes of Wrath*, Steinbeck may not have found a solution to alienation, but he demonstrates clearly in these books that the status quo was not working for anyone.

Since the 1990s scholars have debated Steinbeck's relationship to the environment as well as his relationship with the feminine, looking for a cohesive philosophy or ethic in his large body of work. Perhaps the most useful synthesis is offered by John H. Timmerman in an essay titled "Steinbeck's Environmental Ethic: Humanity in Harmony with the Land": "From his earliest years he was exploring an ethical attitude—a pattern of right living—based upon a belief in the possibility of a harmonious relationship between humanity and the environment" (322). Cederstrom declares that in Steinbeck's greatest novel, *The Grapes of Wrath,* the members of the central family, the Joads, "confront the Great Mother within: the women learn to understand themselves as a part of the natural cycles of life and death; the men are forced to atone for their sins against life and are either transformed or die in the process" ("Great Mother" 90). No such resolution awaits the characters in *The Long Valley,* who instead face bleak futures of loneliness and doubt. Perhaps the most that can be said is that the stories in this early collection raise questions that would haunt Steinbeck throughout his career—questions about the connections between men and women, between culture and nature, between rationality and feeling—and that as a young man he was not yet ready to answer.

Works Cited

Armbruster, Karla. "'Buffalo Gals Won't You Come Out Tonight': A Call for Boundary-Crossing in Ecofeminist Literary Criticism." *Ecofeminist Literary Criticism: Theory, Interpretation, Pedagogy.* Ed. Greta Gaard and Patrick D. Murphy. Urbana: U of Illinois P, 1998. 97-122.

Bily, Cynthia A. "The Chrysanthemums." *Short Stories for Students.* Vol. 6. Ed. David Galens. Detroit: Gale, 1999. 67-71.

Britch, Carroll. "Steinbeck's 'Breakfast': Godhead and Reflection." *Rediscovering Steinbeck: Revisionist Views of His Art, Politics, and Intellect.* Ed. Cliff Lewis and Carroll Britch. Lewiston, NY: Edwin Mellen, 1989. 7-32.

Carr, Glynis. Introduction. *New Essays in Ecofeminist Literary Criticism.* Ed. Glynis Carr. Lewisburg, PA: Bucknell UP, 2000. 15-25.

Cederstrom, Lorelei. "Beyond the Boundaries of Sexism: The Archetypal Feminine Versus Anima Women in Steinbeck's Novels." *Beyond Boundaries: Rereading John Steinbeck.* Ed. Susan Shillinglaw and Kevin Hearle. Tuscaloosa: U of Alabama P, 2002. 189-204.

_____. "The 'Great Mother' in *The Grapes of Wrath.*" *Steinbeck and the Environment: Interdisciplinary Approaches.* Ed. Susan F. Beegel, Susan Shillinglaw, and Wesley N. Tiffney, Jr. Tuscaloosa: U of Alabama P, 1997. 76-91.

Eisler, Riane. "The Gaia Tradition and the Partnership Future." *Reweaving the World: The Emergence of Ecofeminism.* Ed. Irene Diamond and Gloria Feman Orenstein. San Francisco: Sierra Club, 1990. 23-34.

Gates, Barbara T. "A Root of Ecofeminism: *Ecoféminisme.*" *Ecofeminist Literary Criticism: Theory, Interpretation, Pedagogy.* Ed. Greta Gaard and Patrick D. Murphy. Urbana: U of Illinois P, 1998. 15-22.

Gladstein, Mimi Reisel. "Missing Women: The Inexplicable Disparity Between Women in Steinbeck's Life and Those in His Fiction." *The Steinbeck Question: New Essays in Criticism.* Ed. Donald R. Noble. Troy, NY: Whitston, 1993. 84-98.

Hadella, Charlotte. "Steinbeck's Cloistered Women." *The Steinbeck Question: New Essays in Criticism.* Ed. Donald R. Noble. Troy, NY: Whitston, 1993. 51-70.

Meyer, Michael J. "Fallen Adam: Another Look at Steinbeck's 'The Snake.'" *The Steinbeck Question: New Essays in Criticism.* Ed. Donald R. Noble. Troy, NY: Whitston, 1993. 99-107.

Steinbeck, John. *The Grapes of Wrath.* New York: Penguin Classics, 2006.

_____. *The Long Valley.* New York: Penguin, 1986.

Timmerman, John H. "Steinbeck's Environmental Ethic: Humanity in Harmony with the Land." *Steinbeck and the Environment: Interdisciplinary Approaches.* Ed. Susan F. Beegel, Susan Shillinglaw, and Wesley N. Tiffney, Jr. Tuscaloosa: U of Alabama P, 1997. 310-22.

CRITICAL
READINGS

John Steinbeck:
The Favorite Author We Love to Hate_____

Jackson J. Benson

Pauline Pearson, who has worked with the John Steinbeck Library in Salinas, taping interviews with old-timers and locating historical sites, tells of the time when she took a group of Steinbeck enthusiasts on a tour of local points of interest. The bus stopped at the cemetery, and Pauline led a dozen people to the family plot and John's marker, where she began to give a talk about the author's death and burial. After a few minutes, right in the middle of her presentation, the sprinklers suddenly came on all around the group, getting everyone wet. Some groundskeeper was apparently registering his protest that John Steinbeck should be revered in this way by outsiders.

This small incident represents very well the mixed reaction that one of our most popular authors still evokes from people. John Steinbeck has made for himself a very special place in the hearts of many around the world—people seem to relate to him in a way, very personally and very emotionally, that they don't relate to other writers. He was a writer who not only created memorable stories, but he really cared about people, particularly the dispossessed and the persecuted.

This was a quality that the writer apparently had from childhood. Herbert Hinrichs, one of the very few people left in Salinas who remembers Steinbeck as a boy, recalls,

> If John could talk you into doing something, he delighted in that, especially if it got you into trouble. You wouldn't think John could show compassion at all. He was surly. He never laughed but he was always there to help somebody. He was always standing up for this one boy that the other kids picked on. One day, I asked him why. He said, "When you're down, someone's got to help you." That was John. I've never forgotten that.[1]

It is the genuineness of this caring, that he demonstrated throughout his life and in all of his work, that I think is the secret of his enduring appeal.

Some measure of this appeal can be seen in the thousands who come to the Steinbeck Library every year. Unfortunately, there is not much to see. The library has not had the money to expand, and so the first editions, manuscripts, letters and possessions of the writer must be displayed in a small room off of the main lobby, the bulk of the material stored in a basement vault. But people come from every state in the union and nearly every country in the world to stand and look in that small room, some with tears in their eyes.[2]

Visitors have included Ministers and members of parliament from several nations. Once, the librarians tell me, they observed a limousine which cruised around and around the block passing each time the front of the library. At last the automobile stopped, and a chauffeur got out and came into the library. The Ambassador from Japan, he said, would like to know if they could tell him anything about Steinbeck. Could they visit the house where he was born?[3]

The writer's appeal has been nearly world-wide and it has been strong. A book dealer in Denmark wrote to him to report that "a woman rowed in an open boat over eight miles to bring two chickens to my store to exchange for one of your paperback books" ("Our Man" 43). Once when he was in Paris, he had a visit at his hotel from an old French farmer who had travelled all night on the train in order to have the writer sample his wine (Benson 601). But the foreigners most attracted to Steinbeck have been the Japanese. One always wonders, however, how well an author's work can be translated into the language of a culture so very different from ours. Once when Elaine, Steinbeck's widow, was in Nagasaki, she asked an English-speaking bookstore clerk if he had any of her husband's books. "Oh yes," he said, "I have *Angry Raisins*."

Several hundreds of thousands of Steinbeck's books are sold every year (neither Viking nor the Steinbeck family will give out precise figures, but it has been estimated that *The Grapes of Wrath* sells two hundred thousand alone), and various books by him are required reading in high school and college classrooms across the country. But even more to the point, during the years I was working on the biography, I had so many people—from plumbers to librarians to electrical engineers—come up to me and tell me how much they enjoyed Steinbeck's work, that while I have no statistics to support it, my impression is that Steinbeck is nearly everyone's favorite author. And when he is loved, he is loved passionately.

Several years ago the National Endowment for the Humanities put out a list of the most important books a high school graduate should read. Citizens, including groups of well-known intellectuals and high school teachers attending NEH summer seminars, made out lists of the ten books they would recommend. These were compiled, the works ranked, and a list of thirty books then published by the National Endowment. The only twentieth-century writer to make the top ten was Steinbeck, whose *Grapes of Wrath* was ranked eighth (after Shakespeare, American historical documents, Mark Twain, the Bible, Homer, Dickens, and Plato) (Bencivenga n.p.).

I think it is significant that the other American writer singled out in the top ten is Mark Twain, since Twain and Steinbeck were both writers of the people, rather than writers that wrote to please the academy, and both have survived despite a great deal of snobbish disparagement over the years. Among literary scholars and critics generally, there is no doubt that Steinbeck's reputation is low, although not as low as it was in the 1960s. After I wrote my biography, it received a huge number of reviews, testimony to Steinbeck's continuing appeal, although many of the reviewers used the excuse of my book to express their disdain for the novelist. In *Newsweek*, for example, Walter Clemons wrote, "Fifteen years after his death, nearly all Steinbeck's books are in print [inaccurate—all of them are]; but until someone can make a stronger case for him, he will probably survive best as a classic young-adult author" (80). I suppose that Clemons felt he was assigning Steinbeck to the Siberia of teenage fiction, but I can't help but recall that was precisely what happened to the fiction of one [Samuel Langhorne Clemens]—whose major works were for decades consigned to children's literature (although they were also often banned as presenting a corrupting influence).

Snobbishness is, of course, the curse of the literary and academic worlds, and Steinbeck has become, just as Thomas Wolfe was for years, the goat of those who find satisfaction in playing the role of the cool, detached intellectual. I remember several years ago writing to a professor in the Midwest for some information about someone who knew Steinbeck. He replied that he would be glad to give me the information, but he was surprised to hear that anyone other than an undergraduate would be interested in Steinbeck's work.

A couple of years ago, a young high school teacher, Irvin Peckham, wrote a little essay for the *English Journal* called "Thank You, John" in which he mourned the fact that although he had an M.A. in English literature, he had never read a word of Steinbeck. Worse, he was taught by his professors to despise him:

"Steinbeck? Are you kidding?" I said when someone asked whether I was including his novels in one of the cast-off courses I had inherited at Live Oak High School. Never mind that the course was called California Literature and that Live Oak was thirty miles north of Salinas, Steinbeck Country. "Who reads Steinbeck?" I said.

Although I had been cloned in academia, I at least had the intelligence to discard the avocado green anthology of California Literature. Nosing around a dusty corner of the bookroom, I discovered a few copies of *Cannery Row*. I took one home, and I have been a Steinbeck addict since. He has added an immeasurable richness to my life and to the lives of my students, and that richness will spread.

Back when we had money for new texts, I sneaked other Steinbeck novels into the curriculum over the protests of a well-meaning assistant principal who worried about the dirty language in *Of Mice and Men*. In a department littered with singletons, my one section of California Literature swelled into six, all of them packed. . . . Steinbeck is [largely responsible] because he has a way of reaching out of his books, grabbing my students by their shirts and shaking them until they cut the bullshit and think and talk and write about things that really matter—their pride, their fear of censure, their repressed violence, their sexual confusion and desire, their loneliness and desperate need for love. (31)

Irvin Peckham is not alone in his experience. Your chances of reading Steinbeck in an English class in a major university are very low and in the Ivy League, practically zero. For example, I just got a letter from a friend who recently received her Ph.D. from Yale in American literature after graduating from Wellesley as an English major who wrote to me that she would never have read Steinbeck except that her husband is a marine biologist. Astounded that she, a teacher of courses in American literature, had never read Steinbeck, her husband and his scientist friends shamed her into reading *Cannery Row*, and that in turn led her to read the rest of the novels. Steinbeck is still included in American literature anthologies, but he is represented so meagerly that one has the feeling that it is a kind of tokenism. And now that it is the fashion to include more women and ethnic writers—which is, I think, generally a good trend—Steinbeck, unfortunately, will probably be one of the first white males to be left out.

The problem for the anthologists is that in addition to his continuing popularity, he remains historically so important—he is *the* spokesman for the thirties, as well as having written perceptively about other periods in our recent history. One measure of the mixed feelings held by anthologists toward Steinbeck can be seen in the explanatory material provided by Blair, Hornberger, Miller, and Stewart, who edited the Scott, Foresman *The Literary History of the United States* (I quote here from the abstraction of interchapter material published as *American Literature: A Brief History*). Their comments are largely condescending, particularly toward the later work:

Steinbeck . . . maintained his popularity, although most critics found his work after *The Grapes of Wrath* inferior and uneven. Some surprise was expressed when he was awarded the Nobel Prize in 1962. The public, however, followed him faithfully through *East of Eden* (1952), *Sweet Thursday* (1954), *The Winter of Our Discontent* (1961), and a number of lesser pieces, widely circulated in paperback. (259)

(Note that some of the author's best work is not included on this list: *Cannery Row* [1945], *The Pearl* [1947], and *The Log from the Sea of Cortez* [1951].)

At the same time as they heap scorn on his later work and consign him to cheap paperback popularity, the anthology editors turn to Steinbeck in order to describe the spirit of the post-WWII period:

The development of technology in the last few decades, however, has unquestionably added to world-wide anxiety about the future. Can the instruments of death be destroyed or banned? Can the vast new sources of power be used to improve the human condition rather than to set the stage for a world-wide holocaust? These are questions which all Americans, and all thoughtful and informed men everywhere, continue to ask. Their effect upon the American psyche is well summed up by the central character in Steinbeck's *The Winter of Our Discontent*. (246)

The editors go on to quote a paragraph from the novel. Am I the only one who sees a certain contradiction in all of this?

The main factor that seems to cause such mixed signals is that scorn of Steinbeck is not so much a matter of discriminating taste or the result of reasoned rejection, as it is a matter of fashion. Just as some people have to wear certain name brand T-shirts or jeans with a label or logo prominently displayed on breast or hip in order to assure their status, so, too, academics have to assure their status by showing they know what's in and what's out, what's hot and what's not. How did Steinbeck get on the "out" list? I think it has been a combination of factors. First, he is a Westerner, and Western writers have always had a hard time impressing the Eastern establishment critics. Second, he was a popular writer, and academics have always been suspicious (and perhaps jealous) of popularity. Third, he has written comedies, and few writers of comedy are ever considered important. Fourth, he has been accused of being sentimental, which is the worst of literary sins. And fifth, although he personally was nearly apolitical in his approach to his work, it has frequently been judged not on literary, but political grounds.

Steinbeck was a Western writer in a country that still, after two hundred years, looks to the East coast for cultural guidance, and with an Eastern literary establishment that looks to Europe to set its fashions. One wonders what Mark Twain would say about Jacques Derrida. Let me give you an example of this prejudice in regard to Eastern treatment of a Westerner. I am currently working on a critical biography of another author—Wallace Stegner. He is an extremely accomplished author who lives in California, who usually writes about the West, and who has received just about every award and honor a writer can be given except the Nobel Prize. Of the two novels which were given major prizes, *Angle of Repose* for the Pulitzer and *The Spectator Bird* for the National Book Award, neither was reviewed at the time of publication in the *New York Times Book Review*. Just a year ago at the age of 78, he published his eleventh novel, a marvelous one, called *Crossing to Safety*. It was reviewed by Doris Grumbach, who praised it inordinately, but the review was safely tucked away in the back pages—on page 14, as a matter of fact. Can you imagine a book by Updike, or Roth, or Mailer receiving that kind of treatment?

In writing about Steinbeck, two of our most prestigious critics, Edmund Wilson and Alfred Kazin, have both declared that it is impossible for any novelist writing out of and about California to produce great literature. The tradition is too short-lived and diverse and the culture too thin. You may not care for California, but such a statement would be stupid if applied to *any* state or region of the country. Regardless of its stupidity, the judgment has stuck and influences still the Eastern media and, in turn, academics all across the country.

In our book culture, one finds several obvious paradoxes. One is that unless a writer is discovered and trumpeted by the media, his career may, like Stegner's, languish. Appearing on the cover of *Time* and *Newsweek* did more for John Cheever's career than any number of literary awards. On the other hand, if you become a media darling, as Ernest Hemingway or Truman Capote were for many years, the literary establishment becomes irritated with you. The same thing is true of sales and popularity. If an author does not have at least one great popular success, he or she may well be ignored by reviewers and academics, but if he or she is constantly popular, the critics become suspicious of the writer's serious intentions. Steinbeck had the good luck, from a financial point of view, of having nearly every book he wrote, starting with his fourth, *Tortilla Flat* (1935), sell well, even though he never wrote fiction with an eye on potential sales and never used his serious work to try to make money. But as the quality of his work generally declined in his later years, he had the bad luck, in terms of his reputation, of continuing to hit the best-seller lists.

Even a book like *The Short Reign of Pippin IV*, which he wrote as a tongue-in-cheek experiment and which he thought would have almost no sales at all, was, much to his amazement—and amusement—chosen as a Book-of-the-Month Club selection. The popularity of such works led the critics to accuse him of writing junk to please a mass audience, and the author, feeling put-upon by a barrage of criticism, began to wish for more modest sales, particularly for works that in retrospect he realized had not achieved the artistic success he had aimed for. What argues against the idea of Steinbeck as a writer of potboilers is his seriousness of purpose, even in a light and funky—too funky, as it turned out—comedy such as *Sweet Thursday*, as well as his dedication throughout his life to the art of fiction. What is both amusing and a bit sad is that Steinbeck—who had comparatively little ego and almost no snobbishness—himself looked down on the sort of best-selling author that he was often taken to be.

In addition to the popularity which undermined his reputation, there was the extensive use of his books in junior high and high schools which suggested to elitist critics and academics that his work was simple-minded and fit only for younger, less sophisticated readers. As *The Grapes of Wrath* became more and more often a part of the high school curriculum, colleges and universities tended to shy away from it, partly for fear of repeating material already studied, but also because they came to believe that such adoptions demonstrated that the novel was not college-level material.

Another strike against the author's reputation is that we have a tendency to discount the work of anyone who writes comedy. Neil Simon, no matter how well he writes, will never be taken seriously—or *as* seriously as Tennessee Williams or Arthur Miller—by the literary establishment. Frequently discarded or overlooked, Steinbeck's comic trilogy—*Tortilla Flat*, *Cannery Row*, and *Sweet Thursday*—is not even considered as part of the canon by some critics. The scorn heaped upon *Cannery Row* at the time of its publication came largely, in my view, for political reasons and suggests why all the comedies have been viewed so negatively: in brief, the author was thought to be trivializing serious social problems.

While the fantasy-comedy of *Tortilla Flat*, an early work, was largely forgiven, the fantasy-comedy of *Cannery Row* aroused outrage—not too strong a word—among those who felt the author had abandoned his social responsibility. The book was called inconsequential; it "smells," one reviewer declared, "of fish and reeks with kindness" and was "as sentimental as a book can be" (*Commonweal*). "Sentimental" is the ultimate pejorative in modern literary criticism, tending automatically to disqualify anything tinged with it from further serious consideration. The term has stuck to Steinbeck, partly because his themes, even when they were recognized, seemed irrelevant to Eastern, urban critics, and partly because he was, in fact, sentimental at times.

As I said at the beginning, we value Steinbeck precisely because he was a kind and compassionate man who cared deeply for people in trouble. But this sense of caring can occasionally degrade his fiction when it lapses into mere tearful sadness. If there is one episode in *Cannery Row* that qualifies as sentimental, it is Chapter 10, concerning the mentally retarded boy, Frankie, who wants so desperately to please, but who cannot deal with society's rules. Designed to break the reader's heart with the injustice of Frankie's fate, the segment reflects two themes that are almost Steinbeck obsessions: society's failure to accept the handicapped on their own terms, and the intolerance and hypocrisy of respectability. Here, as occasionally elsewhere, the author's emotions have led him into artistic excess.

What saves this artist from constant excess is that his compassion is, in much of his writing, balanced and disciplined by a very objective view of the world and of man. Although not an expert, he wrote out of a more-than-casual knowledge of biology, anthropology, and astronomy, and a biological-ecological view of man's nature and place dominated his thinking. He saw mankind not at the center of creation, but as just another species, one, which, after the advent of nuclear weapons, he had little faith would survive its own "self-hatred," as he called man's propensity toward war, terrorism, and brutality. When, for example, he writes of the plight of Lennie and George in *Of Mice and Men*, he does so with a strange mixture of compassion and distance. There is no motivation for social reform behind the novelette at all— simply the presentation of a story, of a "Something That Happened," as he first called his manuscript. It was the social reformers who made this, a very deterministic picture of man's fate, a novel which calls for social action.

On this basis, one might be inclined to believe that for the most part, those who have felt that Steinbeck has "sentimentalized the folk," to use Richard Hofstadter's phrase, have brought their own sentimentality with them. As early as *In Dubious Battle*, Steinbeck showed that he had no illusions about the dispossessed whom he presents in that novel as sometimes careless, greedy, and easily manipulated. Although the tourists that flocked to Monterey after the publication of *Tortilla Flat* may have considered the *paisanos* as quaint or cute, that did not reflect the author's attitude, which was one of distanced respect for their dignity and for their best attributes in a grasping, materialistic society.

The paisanos, like the down-and-outers of *Cannery Row* and *Sweet Thursday*, are material not for the sociological study or political tract that the Marxists would have desired, but for fables which alter our perspective so that we might re-examine our values. What bothered the political-minded was that these works, dealing with the dispossessed in our society, were essentially apolitical. Accusing the author of sentimentality, leftists would have substituted their own brand: the melodrama of the proletarian novel with its noble workers and wicked bosses.

"Perspective" is a key word here, for Steinbeck's fiction invariably asks us to step out of our traditional way of looking at things to take another point of view. We might note that in *Cannery Row* Doc is given a microscope and in *Sweet Thursday*, a telescope, so that the whole range of seeing is thereby covered. The range is crucial, for what leads Steinbeck to object to politics, in the immediate, short-sighted sense, is its narrow view of the world. We should stop and look and consider as the scientist would, and we should approach life with the scientist's objectivity and distance. For Steinbeck, one can be detached in his observations on the one hand, while at the same time express compassion on the other. This combination, which has been often mistaken by negative critics of Steinbeck for sentimentality, is really quite the opposite when examined closely. Detachment and compassion together are major components of an overall attitude toward the universe—nature, including that speck of dust called "man"—which Steinbeck calls "acceptance."

To "accept," in the sense that Steinbeck employs it, is to stand aside from all those factors that limit our vision and confine our sympathies and to see people and events within the indefinite continuums of time and space. It is to be broadminded in the largest possible sense. Contrary to the behavior of the weepy-eyed, sentimental liberal, the person who practices acceptance is open-eyed and realistic—he or she not only casts aside preconceptions and prejudice, but also looks to see people and events clearly for what they actually are. Sentimentality, within Steinbeck's scheme, is simply another avoidance, another self-deception, another mode of categorizing so that we can feel righteous or superior. We would do well not to approach Mac and the boys from the motives of the do-gooder or naive bleeding heart, for we are likely, first, to be taken to the cleaners and then, second, shocked by their independence and ingratitude.

One of the great ironies of Steinbeck's career was that although he was only mildly political in life and almost apolitical in his approach to writing, his work was very often judged from a political point of view. From nearly the beginning of his career, with the publication of *In Dubious Battle* in 1936, reactions to his work, condemning him in the most abusive terms, have come from both the right and the left. For Steinbeck's home region, an ultra-conservative rural area, the writer had "betrayed his class" by deserting the upper-middle class Republicanism of his parents to embrace the plight of the despised and dispossessed. One can only think that it has been greed that has led a dozen very wealthy lettuce growers in the Salinas Valley to resist tooth and nail, for over sixty years, anything that might improve the lot of their workers, and greed that has led to their abiding hatred of the author who told their workers' story. Much of the public, throughout the author's career, automatically associated him with Communism, although he was never a Marxist and never endorsed its doctrines. It is a sad commentary on our society that anyone who takes the part of the underdog, the powerless, and the persecuted should so often be tarred with the blackest brush in our political vocabulary.

While throughout his career he was attacked by the conservative press—Randolph Hearst's newspaper chain, Colonel McCormick's *Chicago Tribune*, Norman Chandler's *Los Angeles Times*, and Henry

Luce's *Time* magazine—he was also squeezed on the other side by expressions of snobbish disdain by liberal intellectual journals, particularly the *New Republic* and the *New York Times Book Review*. He was too liberal for the right and not liberal enough for the left, and I think this had a profound effect on his reputation, since throughout most of his career the print media was essentially conservative, and disapproving, and many of the most influential critics in the Eastern literary establishment were Marxists or sympathetic to Marxism, and disapproving.

The novels that caused the most political furor, *In Dubious Battle* and *The Grapes of Wrath*, were not written out of political motives and came out relatively early in the author's career, yet the political labels attached to him then followed him for the rest of his life. For over thirty years *Time* expressed its antagonism for him as a "proletarian" writer (a code word for communist) and never gave him or his work a kind word until it wrote his obituary. It is hard to imagine the depth of hatred for Steinbeck held by someone on that magazine, presumably Henry Luce, which would feed on itself and fester for so long, so consistently. On the other hand, leftists, who tended to applaud his early writing and who tried to use Steinbeck for their own purposes in whatever way they could, scolded him when he turned away from the subject of farm labor.

For example, Stanley Edgar Hyman wrote that he began to lose interest in Steinbeck after the shift in "social commitment" as marked by *Of Mice and Men* versus *The Moon Is Down*. That shift away from social commitment seemed to him confirmed by *Cannery Row*, which he found "merely an insipid watering down of Steinbeck's engaging earlier book *Tortilla Flat*." "I stopped reading him," he adds. Later, however, he was sent *The Winter of Our Discontent* for review but decided that it was "far too trivial and dishonest a book to waste space on." Then when he learned of the Nobel Prize, given in response to Steinbeck's recent publication of *Winter*, he found the choice and its occasion incredible. He reread the book and found it confirmed his earlier impression of it. "It is the purest soap opera, a work of almost inconceivable badness." When he discovered on the dust jacket that the book had been praised by Lewis Gannett and Saul Bellow, Hyman declared that "to assume their honesty I must disparage their intelligence" (113).

As if this were not nasty enough, liberal-radical attacks on Steinbeck in his late years were particularly acrimonious. During the early years of the Vietnam War he was only one of many writers and correspondents who tended to have hawkish views. Yet, the bitterest commentary was reserved for Steinbeck—the Marxists were particularly upset with him for acting what was, in their minds, a traitor. They had the gall first to make him a Marxist, which he never was, and then to accuse him of betraying that which they had made him out to be. Peter Collier, for example, compares him to Ezra Pound during WWII and thus presumably to Pound's fascism and giving of aid and comfort to the enemy. This is a very peculiar comparison when one considers that Steinbeck's "crime" was *support for* American troops fighting under difficult circumstances in a foreign war. Most of the time, Collier insists, Steinbeck sounds "like a naive political hireling mouthing platitudes." Steinbeck's betrayal comes down to this: "It is unaccountable that Steinbeck should not be able to see how similar these Vietnamese peasants are to the Joads" (61). Regardless of how one feels about the Vietnam War, its rights and wrongs, which were plentiful on both sides, it is difficult not to ask how many times the Joads set off a Claymore at a crowded bus stop or threw grenades into a restaurant filled with women and children. The aftermaths of two such incidents were witnessed by Steinbeck as a war correspondent—hospital wards filled with screaming children, many of whom were missing at least one limb.

Now that the author is dead, the political attacks on his books continue, coming now particularly from the New Right, the Moral Majority, and allied groups that have worked to ban or censor books that do not fit their political agenda. In addition to objections to realistic uses of language, to any depictions of sexuality, and to any questioning of the traditional role of women, they have also objected to any material that points out injustice and turmoil in American history.[4] Needless to say, John Steinbeck has been one of their favorite targets. While a number of challenges have been made on the basis of language, there is reason to believe that this is a smoke screen for attacking books that in the view of the New Right undermine faith in the free enterprise system.

Irvin Peckham, the high school teacher I quoted earlier, speaks of the fear of dirty language in *Of Mice and Men*, and both it and *The Grapes of Wrath* have been banned every year by school districts, from the classroom or the library, and by public libraries all across the country. But these are not the only Steinbeck books banned, and they are not banned just in the provinces by backwoods school boards. In 1980 *The Red Pony* was banned by a school district in New York because it was "a filthy, trashy sex novel."[5] Steinbeck has had the dubious distinction, usually having two books on the most-banned lists published annually by library and publisher associations, of probably being the most banned author in the nation.[6] In 1988 *Of Mice and Men* led the lists.[7] Of course, such wholesale negative reactions to his work would not be possible if his books were not so admired and frequently taught. Once again we are brought back to our thesis—that while John Steinbeck may be our most beloved author, he is also, by all evidence, the most hated.

In defending Steinbeck from what I believe to be prejudice and misunderstanding, I don't mean to imply blanket approval for all his work or all of his ideas. Some of the things he wrote, particularly at the beginning and the end of his career, were failures or only partial successes. He took a lot of risks in his work, and as a result the quality of his fiction is very uneven. But whatever else one might say, one must note that he has written one book, *The Grapes of Wrath*, which seems destined to join *Moby Dick*, *The Scarlet Letter*, *The Adventures of Huckleberry Finn*, and *The Red Badge of Courage* as an American classic.

Frank Kermode, in his study *The Classic: Literary Images of Per-*

manence and Change, distinguishes two types of classic works of literature: the work that encapsulates an era and thus allows us to reenter it mentally and the work that states our basic humanity so well as to triumph over time and space (43-44, 130). It seems to me that *The Grapes of Wrath* performs both functions admirably. There is no doubt in my mind that Faulkner and Hemingway are two great American writers of prose fiction in our century. Yet, I cannot think of a work by either, taken alone, which has a chance to achieve the status that *The Grapes of Wrath* seems to be achieving. Almost exactly fifty years after its publication, Steinbeck's novel has demonstrated a remarkable staying power, transcending its original categorization as a propaganda novel or social document. No other novel of this century seems quite so typically American. No other American novel of our time seems so firmly planted on land while it reaches out, not for the American dream in a small sense, but the dream of our founders, a vision of liberty and justice for all.

Notes

1. Ellen Uzelac. "Salinas Tries to Remember Its Once Least-Favorite Son." *The Sacramento Bee* 17 August 1988, final ed.: D6.

2. John Gross, Director, Salinas Library, personal interview, 3 February 1989.

3. Mary Gamble, Steinbeck Archivist, John Steinbeck Library, personal interview, 6 February 1989.

4. Heather Dewar. "Decade of the Censors?" *The Commercial Appeal* (Memphis, Tennessee) 29 May 1983: G1.

5. Maury Chauvet. "Bookstore Celebrates the Freedom to Read." *The Daily Aztec* (San Diego State University), (clipping) n/d: 1.

6. See monthly *Newsletter on Intellectual Freedom*; and the yearbook *Banned Books Week 1981 [yearly to 1988]: Celebrating the Freedom to Read* (Chicago: American Library Association, 1981-1988).

7. "Censorship Continues Unabated; Extremists Adopt Mainstream Tactics." *Newsletter on Intellectual Freedom*, November 1989: 193.

Works Cited

Bencivenga, Jim. "Must-Read List for High School." *The Christian Science Monitor* (clipping) n/d: n/p.

Benson, Jackson J. *The True Adventures of John Steinbeck, Writer.* New York: Viking Press, 1984.

Blair, Walter, Theodore Hornberger, James E. Miller, Jr., and Randall Stewart, eds. *American Literature: A Brief History.* Glenview, IL: Scott, Foresman and Company, 1974.

Clemons, Walter. "Cursed by Success." *Newsweek* 6 February 1984: 80.

Collier, Peter. "The Winter of John Steinbeck." *Ramparts July* 1967: 61.

Grumbach, Doris. "Crossing to Safety." *The New York Times Book Review* 20 September 1987: 14.

Hyman, Stanley Edgar. "John Steinbeck and the Nobel Prize." *Standards: A Chronicle of Books for Our Time.* New York: Horizon Press, 1966.

Kermode, Frank. *The Classic: Literary Images of Permanence and Change.* New York: Viking, 1975. I am in debt to Louis J. Budd's "Introduction" to *New Essays on "Adventures of Huckleberry Finn"* (New York: Cambridge University Press, 1985): 6, for this definition.

"Our Man in Helsinki." *The New Yorker* 9 November 1963: 43, 45.

Peckham, Irvin. "Thank You, John." *English Journal* 75.7 (1986): 31-32.

Review of *Cannery Row. Commonweal* 26 January 1945: 379-80.

Tortilla Flat and the Creation of a Legend_____

Joseph Fontenrose

Steinbeck has loved no town so much as Monterey. It has been his town in a way that Salinas, Pacific Grove, and New York have not. It has an Old World flavor that has lingered from the days when it was the seat of Spanish and Mexican governments. The Steinbeck Monterey, which is not necessarily the same thing as the real Monterey, fights a losing battle against twentieth-century civilization, but has not yet gone under. "Monterey sits on the slope of a hill, with a blue bay below it and with a forest of tall dark pine trees at its back. The lower parts of the town are inhabited by Americans, Italians, catchers and canners of fish. But on the hill where the forest and the town intermingle, where the streets are innocent of asphalt and the corners free of street lights, the old inhabitants of Monterey are embattled as the Ancient Britons are embattled in Wales. These are the paisanos." This purlieu is Tortilla Flat, a purely fictitious subcommunity of Steinbeck's Monterey which represents the town's paisano population. "What is a paisano? He is a mixture of Spanish, Indian, Mexican and assorted Caucasian bloods. His ancestors have lived in California for a hundred or two years."

The paisanos are a people to whom Steinbeck is sympathetic. Paisano characters had appeared in *To a God Unknown* and in short stories later to be collected in *The Long Valley*. Steinbeck himself knew paisanos, talked and drank with them, listened to their tales, and some paisano lore, Moore [Harry Thornton Moore, ed.] says, he learned from Susan Gregory, a resident of Monterey, to whom *Tortilla Flat* is dedicated. He put these people into a novel which has delighted many readers, but the book's unexpected popularity had its disconcerting features: readers liked the paisanos for wrong reasons, for being quaint curiosities, contrary to Steinbeck's intention.

Tortilla Flat at first sight appears to have a loose construction like *The Pastures of Heaven*, several stories set within a frame and written about the same people. It is, in fact, much more tightly constructed. Every story has the same central characters, Danny and his friends; we do not move from one family to another as in *The Pastures*. And it has a perceptible plot with a gradual rise and a swifter fall.

Danny, returning from the war, found that he had inherited two houses in Tortilla Flat. He rented one to Pilon, who never had money to pay rent. Pablo Sanchez and Jesus Maria Corcoran moved in with Pilon, but they never had money either. Relations between Danny and Pilon were becoming strained when Pilon's house burned down. Then the three friends moved in with Danny. The four admitted the Pirate, a half-witted man, and his five dogs to the house, hoping to get the Pirate's hoard of money; and he did bring a big bag of quarters to them for safekeeping, explaining that he had vowed a golden candlestick, worth a thousand quarters, to Saint Francis for the recovery of a dog. The friends were loyal to their trust, and the bag of quarters became "the symbolic center of the friendship." Soon afterward Joe Portagee joined the group and stole the Pirate's bag. His housemates gave him a beating and, recovering most of the money, found that the Pirate had enough to buy his candle. Several adventures occurred before and after the fulfillment of the vow; but finally the good days of the fellowship came to an end. Danny deserted his friends and ran wild; when he came back, he was listless and melancholy. To rekindle his spirits his friends gave a big party, which all Tortilla Flat attended. Danny had a last uproarious fling, surpassing all his past exploits of drinking, wenching, and fighting, until he ran outside to fight "The Enemy who is worthy of Danny," fell into a gulch, and was killed. The evening after the funeral his house burned down and the friends scattered.

It is a picaresque novel: Danny and his friends are pleasant rogues who never work unless extremity drives them to it. They pick up food, drink, and fun as chance offers, thinking nothing of petty theft, prevarication, and trickery, and they get along quite well without running water, electric lights, and a change of clothes. They live for the pleasures of the passing day: all they want is enough to eat, plenty of red wine, a cozy place to sit and talk, an occasional amour or brawl. "Love and fighting, and a little wine," said Pilon, "then you are always young, always happy." They use money and barterable goods mainly for buying wine or presents for women. Although they literally break the law often enough, they are not criminals. Nor do they lack conscience and moral feelings (except perhaps Joe Portagee). Still, they are hardly paragons of virtue and reliability, and he who puts his trust in them is likely to regret it. We may give them credit for keeping faith with the Pirate and keeping his bag of quarters inviolate; yet we should remember that the Pirate's quarters were devoted to Saint Francis, and also that Danny's second house burned down because Pablo, having bought a candle for Saint Francis, had used it profanely instead. "Have you forgotten that this candle was blessed? . . . Here is the principle which takes the waxen rod outside the jurisdiction of physics." Danny and his friends could not risk offending the saint again: they had but one house left.

The paisanos are great moralizers, but their moralizing too often consists in finding noble reasons for satisfying desires at a friend's expense, as when Pilon took Joe's serge trousers. Wanting wine as he sat beside the sleeping Joe on the beach, Pilon pretended to himself that he wanted it for Joe. Searching his own and Joe's pockets for money or some exchangeable object and finding none, he noticed Joe's serge pants. Now Joe's friends wore jeans; the trousers were much too small for Joe anyway, and besides Joe had stolen a blanket from Danny's house and needed punishment. So off came the trousers, which Pilon exchanged for a quart of wine (having asked for a gallon). Drinking the quart at once, he then "thought sadly of his friend out there on the beach," liable to arrest for indecent exposure, because a harpy (Mrs. Torrelli) "had tried to buy Pilon's friend's pants for a miserable quart of miserable wine." As he left Torrelli's he recovered the trousers and, posing as Joe's benefactor, returned them to the awakened and embarrassed Joe.

This is the sort of picaresque episode which has caused many readers to enjoy *Tortilla Flat* as an entertaining account of amiable rascals.

The book, however, is a good deal more than a picaresque novel, and we have not said all that there is to say about its characters when we have called them rogues. As "good people of laughter and kindness" Steinbeck sets them in contrast to the commercial civilization that surrounds them; they "are clean of commercialism, free of the complicated systems of American business." This is a recurring theme of Steinbeck's fiction: the values of a simple people are opposed, as more healthy and viable, to the values of a competitive society.

That income property may damage human relations is an important thesis of *Tortilla Flat*. When Danny told Pilon that he had inherited two houses, Pilon said, "Now the great times are done. . . . Thou art lifted above thy friends. Thou art a man of property." The final phrase, one feels, is deliberately reminiscent of Galsworthy's Soames Forsyte, the man of property who got income from rented houses. The ownership of a rented house did adversely affect Danny's friendship with Pilon, and so when that house burned, Danny gladly gave up the status of rentier, saying, "Now we can be free and happy again." But Danny still owned one house; it was still true that as a house owner he could no longer smash windows at will or joyously destroy property with a clear conscience. "Always the weight of the house was upon him; always the responsibility to his friends." So he fled, and that was the beginning of the end.

The house was the body of an organism. In *Tortilla Flat* Steinbeck's biological point of view becomes explicit, and for the first time he makes deliberate, if humorous, use of the conception of the group as organism. The first words are, "This is the story of Danny and of Danny's friends and of Danny's house. It is a story of how these three became one thing, so that in Tortilla Flat if you speak of Danny's house you do not mean a structure of wood flaked with old whitewash. . . . No, when you speak of Danny's house you are understood to mean a unit of which the parts are men, from which came sweetness and joy, philanthropy and, in the end, a mystic sorrow." The group organism is more than just the sum of its parts, and the emotions of its unit parts coalesce into a single group emotion. When the friends discovered Joe Portagee's theft of the Pirate's money, they waited in the house for his return: "No words were spoken, but a wave of cold fury washed and crouched in the room. The feeling in the house was the feeling of a rock when the fuse is burning in toward the dynamite." So *Tortilla Flat* is on one level the life history of an organism, which was conceived when Danny, just out of jail, met Pilon and told him about the two houses. When Pilon, Pablo, and Jesus Maria moved in with Danny, the organism was born. It grew (when the Pirate and Joe Portagee came in), thrived for a time, had good and bad experiences, became sick, and died; and the burning of the house was the cremation of the organism's body.

Just as individual organisms are units of a group organism, so smaller group organisms may be units of larger group organisms. Danny's household was part of Tortilla Flat, and Tortilla Flat was part of Monterey. Tortilla Flat as a whole had qualities like those of Danny's fellowship, but other qualities too, since each paisano household had its peculiarities. In Monterey as a whole paisano characteristics mingle with other kinds; yet Monterey is in certain respects like Danny's house: "There is a changeless quality about Monterey. . . . On Tortilla Flat, above Monterey, the routine is changeless, too. . . . In Danny's house there was even less change." Monterey too can behave like a single organism: "All Monterey began to make gradual instinctive preparations against the night"; then Steinbeck reports the unvarying acts of several persons and creatures at this time of day, not as acts of autonomous individuals but as coordinated movements of a single organism's parts. The group organism has a nervous system—the pathways of rumor—which carries information and emotions through the whole collective body. In several books Steinbeck expresses his wonder at the uncanny speed and operation of rumor, as in *Tortilla Flat*: "One evening, by that quick and accurate telegraph no one understands, news came in that a coast guard cutter had gone on the rocks near Carmel." Again, when Danny's friends began to plan the final party, the rumor of it flew about Tortilla Flat and beyond into Monterey: "The morning was electric with the news."

This organismic complex—Danny, Danny's fellowship, Tortilla Flat, Monterey—is doomed to defeat before the forces of twentieth-century civilization. Monterey becomes just another American city, and Tortilla Flat fades away into it. The old organism was changeless—that was its *hamartia*—and lacked the resilience and vigor needed for resistance. It was too easily infected by the insidious pride of property ownership.

The organismic complex may also be seen as an ecological community, for Steinbeck's interest in ecology first makes itself plainly felt in *Tortilla Flat*. The paisanos illustrate the ecological principle that every niche in the environment is likely to be filled and that some kind of creature will adapt itself to every possible source of subsistence. In his later foreword, Steinbeck says that the paisanos are "people who merge successfully with their habitat. In men this is called philosophy, and it is a fine thing." The Pirate brought his friends scraps and leftovers collected at the back doors of restaurants, very good fare sometimes, "fresh fish, half pies, untouched loaves of stale bread, meat that required only a little soda to take the green out"; once he had "a steak out of which only a little was missing." After the Pirate had bought his votive candlestick, he spent his daily quarter, earned by selling kindling wood, for food, which he brought to the house. Sometimes the friends threw rocks at fishing boats from the wharf and picked up the fish thrown back at them. They also pilfered food from restaurants and stores and got wine in devious ways. Some paisanos gleaned the bean fields. We perceive, therefore, that the paisanos, particularly of Danny's kind, are symbiotics or commensals (some would say parasites) of the Monterey community, depending upon others for their food, living on the pickings. So in one aspect *Tortilla Flat* is the story of this symbiosis. The paisanos, trying to preserve their own values, pushed into a corner of the habitat, are forced to become scavengers and jackal-like snatchers of others' food.

But more important than the organismic and ecological themes, though merging with them, is the Arthurian theme; for the Arthur story, as Steinbeck has said plainly, provided *Tortilla Flat* its central structure. On the first page Steinbeck says, "For Danny's house was not unlike the Round Table, and Danny's friends were not unlike the knights of it. And this is the story of how that group came into being, of how it flourished and grew to be an organization beautiful and wise. This story deals with the adventuring of Danny's friends, with the good they did, with their thoughts and their endeavors. In the end, this story tells how the talisman was lost and how the group disintegrated." This broad hint was ignored by readers of the manuscript and by reviewers of the published book. The failure of publishers' readers to recognize the Arthurian theme puzzled Steinbeck. In a letter to his agents, early in 1934, he said,

> I had expected that the plan of the Arthurian cycle would be recognized, that my Gawaine and Launcelot that my Arthur and Galahad would be recognized. Even the incident of the Sangreal in the search of the forest is not clear enough I guess. The form is that of the Malory version, the coming of Arthur and the mystic quality of owning a house, the forming of the round table, the adventures of the knights and finally, the mystic adventures of Danny. However, I seem not to have made any of this clear.

When the book appeared in 1935 Steinbeck had provided it with chapter headings in the style of Caxton's Malory: e.g., chapter 1, "How Danny, home from the wars, found himself an heir, and how he swore to protect the helpless."

As recently as 1957 Steinbeck said that *Tortilla Flat* was deliberately based on Malory's book. An author's own statement of his structural plan should be of prime importance for the study and interpretation of a book. Yet in dealing with *Tortilla Flat* critics usually brush aside the Arthurian theme with the remark that there is nothing more to say about it than what Steinbeck himself has said, that the structural similarities which Steinbeck mentioned are so general as to lack signif-icance, and that it is vain to look for detailed parallels. Of course, one must not look for one-to-one correspondences throughout; and if we say, truly enough, that Danny corresponds to Arthur and Pilon to Launcelot (Pablo seems to be Gawaine and Jesus Maria to be Gal-ahad), we need not suppose that Danny is always Arthur, Pilon always Launcelot. This is to misconceive a creative writer's use of a mythical theme. Faulkner's *A Fable* illustrates nicely what a writer does with a myth: the old French Marshal is now God the Father, now Satan, and again Pontius Pilate; the Messiah is married to Mary Magdalene. In taking the Arthurian ingredient of *Tortilla Flat* seriously one is not reading the work as a modern version of the Arthur legend, since obvi-ously the novel is not an Arthurian legend, any more than Faulkner's novel is the gospel story. The structural plan of Malory's *Arthur* had to be condensed for use as model for *Tortilla Flat*, and one rescue of a maid in distress will do for twenty. But Malory's Arthur story did in fact determine the narrative sequence and pervade the whole content.

First notice the narrative sequence. Arthur [Danny] after an obscure boyhood unexpectedly inherited a kingdom [house] and was trans-formed from ordinary manhood to heaven's viceroy as lord of the land [a landlord who experienced "the mystic quality of owning a house"]. The new king had trouble with subject kings and barons [Pilon, Pablo], who refused to pay homage [rent], but were finally defeated [the rented house burned down] and reconciled. Arthur [Danny], chastened by ex-perience of rule, gathered knights [friends] to his Round Table [house] and gave them lands [shelter and a place to sleep]. The knights swore an oath of devotion and fealty [Danny's friends promised to see that Danny should never go hungry]. Arthur and his knights gave their at-tention to Pelles, the Maimed King, and the Grail which he kept [Pirate and his treasure]. Percival, undervalued by the knights (a simpleton in the pre-Malory legend), was placed among humble knights [the Pirate was given a corner of Danny's house, where he slept among his dogs]. The knights (but not Arthur) set out in search of the Grail for the welfare of Arthur's kingdom [the friends, without Danny, searched on Saint Andrew's Eve for mystic treasure for Danny's welfare]. Launcelot [Pilon, who said, "It is because my heart is clean of selfishness that I can find this treasure"] achieved a vision of the Grail [a phosphorescent light above the spot], but failed in the quest [found a Geodetic Survey marker]. Demon women [Sweets Ramirez] tempted Percival and Bors [Danny], who were finally saved from their machinations (the partly successful efforts of Launcelot's friends to draw him away from Guinevere, a later episode in Malory, are merged with the demon women's temptations in the successful effort of Danny's friends to separate him from Sweets). An old man came to Arthur's court with the boy Galahad [a Mexican corporal came to Danny's house with his infant son], who would be greater than his father [as the corporal intended his son to be]. Then the Grail appeared to the knights at supper and supplied them with meat and drink [Danny and his friends "were sitting in the living room, waiting for the daily miracle of food"; soon the Pirate (keeper of the true Grail) came in with a bag of mackerels]. Arthur and his knights, finishing their supper, went to look at the Siege Perilous, where Galahad sat [after their meal Danny and his friends went to look at the corporal's son lying in an apple box]. Galahad did not live long [the child died]. Percival [Joe Portagee] came upon a damsel [Tia Ignacia] who gave him wine to drink; he fell asleep in her pavilion [chair] and afterward made love to her (here Joe with his ill-fitting trousers is also La Cote Male Taile, whom a lady first scorned and then loved). Percival, Galahad, and Bors achieved the quest of the Grail [the friends' true treasure was the Pirate's bag of quarters, "the symbolic center of the friendship, the point of trust about which the fraternity revolved" (and the Pirate kept the house supplied with food, as the Grail provided often for the Round Table)].

After the quest the Round Table knights reassembled [the friends became reconciled with Joe Portagee], Launcelot saved Guinevere from death and again from capture [the friends rescued Teresina Cortez in the bean shortage] and had amorous trysts with her [Teresina found herself pregnant again]. The knights, as formerly, enjoyed tournaments and the fellowship of the Round Table ["Of the good life at Danny's House" (chapter 14)], until Arthur became Launcelot's enemy. Arthur left England to fight elsewhere [Danny left the house and took to fighting elsewhere]. In Arthur's absence Mordred claimed the throne, relying upon the regency which Arthur had granted him and upon forged letters [Torrelli, carrying a deed signed by Danny, claimed ownership of the house]. Arthur's loyal subjects opposed Mordred's claim [Danny's friends foiled Torrelli's attempt to occupy the house]. Arthur returned to England [Danny came back to the house] and in a great last battle defeated his enemies [at the final big party "roaring battles . . . raged through whole clots of men," and "Danny defied and attacked the whole party," prevailing over everybody], but mortally wounded, went off over a lake to Avalon with supernatural companions [Danny, going outside to fight The Enemy, met him and fell into a gulch to his death]. None of Arthur's knights [Danny's friends] was present at his funeral and burial.

The parallels, of course, should not be more obvious than they are. Steinbeck started with tales, true and legendary, about paisanos. He perceived something in paisano behavior that reminded him of Arthur's knights, farfetched as any similarity may seem offhand, and he believed the likeness worth developing. The manner in which he could assimilate paisano deeds and habits to knightly ways is perhaps even better revealed in narrative details than in the more general structural parallels.

Like the knights of old, Danny, Pilon, and Joe Portagee were warriors, having enlisted in the American army in the First World War. And Danny, like every knight, was a horseman: "At twenty-five his legs were bent to the exact curves of a horse's sides," and few men could handle mules as well. Danny's company liked fights with one another or with anybody: Arthur's knights loved jousts and hostile encounters on the road. Both paisanos and knights fought over women, who were likely to favor the victor. Danny and Pilon had "a really fine fight" in the presence of two girls, who "kicked whichever man happened to be down." The knights' ladies were sometimes like that too. It hardly mattered to a certain damsel whether Palomides or Corsabrin won their fight, for she was ready to go with either (Malory 10:47). Another cheerfully spent the night with Epinogris after he had killed her father and a companion knight; the next morning she went off with Helior when he wounded Epinogris; later, Palomides restored her to Epinogris (Malory 10:83). Sometimes several knights attacked one man and took his lady from him; likewise several soldiers twice took the hardly reluctant Arabella Gross from Jesus Maria, and the second time Arabella helped them beat him up. Nor for all their chivalrous talk were Arthur's knights less lecherous than the paisanos. Arthur himself had amorous relations with Lyonors and Lot's wife Margawse, Launcelot with Guinevere and Elaine, Tristram with Isould, Gawaine with Ettard. Moreover, the knights enjoyed good food and wine quite as much as did Danny and his friends.

Tortilla Flat has the same Catholic background as Malory's *Arthur.* In both books references to masses, rituals, and sacred objects are frequent; the characters in both speak as men to whom the Faith is second nature. Miracles occur, visions are seen, in Tortilla Flat as in the kingdom of Logres. The Pirate's dogs saw a vision of Saint Francis—so the Pirate believed—and he almost saw it too. As Jesus Maria lay on the beach near Seaside, the waves washed an empty rowboat ashore. He rowed it to Monterey, sold it for seven dollars, and bought both wine and a gift for Arabella. "God floated the little rowboat to you," said Pilon; and God sent a self-moving boat to Jesus Maria's Arthurian counterpart, Galahad, who on boarding it found a silk crown and a marvelous sword. Another time an empty boat came to Arthur as he stood on a riverbank, and carried him to a castle where he was served with wines and meats.

Danny's bed was the Siege Perilous. When Big Joe tried to lie in it, a stick came down hard on the soles of his feet "so that even he learned the inviolable quality of Danny's bed." Pilon taking the sleeping Joe's trousers and going off in search of wine is Launcelot taking the sleeping Kay's armor and going off in search of adventure (Malory 6:11). Even the paisanos' habit of sleeping in the open likens them to the knights, who often lay down in a forest or by a well; and as harts and deer crossed the knights' paths, so chickens crossed the paths of Danny and his friends. Danny in Monterey jail is Arthur imprisoned in Sir Damas's castle. Petey Ravanno at last won Gracie Montez's love when he tried suicide: Ettard finally loved Pelleas when she thought him dead. Old Man Ravanno, lovesick over a girl, is like Merlin besotted over Nineve; and as Merlin, entering a rock at Nineve's request, was shut therein and died, so when old Ravanno entered a tool house to win Tonia's love by feigning suicide, the door slammed shut, nobody saw him, and he really hanged himself. In many details like these, the paisanos show their kinship with Arthur's knights. They even use the same kind of speech: in courteous expression, statements of moral sentiment, accepted codes of conduct, even in their hypocrisy and insincerity, the paisanos resemble the knights. The use of the familiar second person and the literal translation of Spanish expressions into English have the effect of giving the paisanos a speech like that of Malory's knights.

Having observed the pervasive Arthurian tone of *Tortilla Flat*, we can no longer deny significance to Steinbeck's own statements about his debt to Malory. But how does the Arthurian reading of *Tortilla Flat* harmonize with the organismic and ecological reading? The Round Table, of course, was a group, a community, and therefore a social organism. There may appear to be a great gap between the nobility of the Arthurian cycle and the squalor of the meaner sort of commensal organism. However, it is just this contrast that gives *Tortilla Flat* much of its picaresque quality. And it has a deeper meaning too, a meaning like that of Mark Twain's *A Connecticut Yankee in King Arthur's Court*. After all, the knights were no more industrious and productive than Danny's band: the fact is that they too lived on the products of others' labor. In reading Malory we are now and then reminded that lands which other men tilled gave the knights their living. If these amiable and idle paisanos are parasites, so were the knights. If the knights were courteous men, so are the paisanos.

But the term "mock-heroic" seems misleading if applied to *Tortilla Flat*. Steinbeck is too fond of both paisanos and Arthurian legend to be guilty of belittling either. *Tortilla Flat* both illuminates the Dark Ages and dignifies the paisanos. We are again confronted with an antithesis: the actual lives of men who enjoy fighting, live on others' labor, and shun work are opposed to the legendary lives of men whose mode of life was much the same. If anything, the paisanos are more amusing and less dangerous than the knights. The sort of thing that they do is the stuff that legends are made of, as Steinbeck tells us in his preface: "It is well that this cycle be put down on paper so that in a future time scholars, hearing the legends, may not say as they say of Arthur and of Roland and of Robin Hood—'There was no Danny nor any group of Danny's friends, nor any house. Danny is a nature god and his friends primitive symbols of the wind, the sky, the sun.'"

This quotation may be called the primary oracle of *Tortilla Flat*; for again Steinbeck hints at the pagan myth behind Arthurian legend: Danny is the sun that rises, rules the sky and the wind, has his high noon and brilliant afternoon, and then sets into darkness. The burning of the house is the glory of the sunset—we should notice that in Steinbeck's first five novels (including *In Dubious Battle*) a fire or parching drought (which was a fire in an early draft of *To a God Unknown*) occurs either at the climax or at the conclusion. Notice the portents which posterity will attribute to the great climactic party: "It must be remembered . . . that Danny is now a god. . . . In twenty years it may be plainly remembered that the clouds flamed and spelled DANNY in tremendous letters; that the moon dripped blood; that the wolf of the world bayed prophetically from the mountains of the Milky Way." Thus Steinbeck resumes his opening jest. We are not expected to take Danny's divinity seriously, and yet Steinbeck tells us how gods and heroes are made.

Tortilla Flat thus mingles seriousness with jest, enjoyment with deeper meanings. Its tone blends humor, bittersweet pathos, and the objectivity of a sympathetic and amused narrator of legendary events in a language just different enough from ordinary speech to be distinctive and to place the narrative at one remove from the commonplace. Again and again the reader encounters expressions both surprising and delightful, as Pilon's "One feels a golden warmth glowing like a hot enchilada in one's stomach," Danny's "I have here two great steaks from God's own pig," and the narrator's "Big Joe abhorred the whole principle of shoveling. The line of the moving shovel was unattractive. The end to be gained, that of taking dirt from one place and putting it in another, was, to one who held the larger vision, silly and gainless." Surely not only Mordred, but also Launcelot, had no more love for a shovel.

From *The Short Novels of John Steinbeck*, edited by Jackson J. Benson (1990): 19-30. Copyright © 1990 by Duke University Press. All rights reserved. Used by permission of the publisher.

Sharing Creation:
Steinbeck, *In Dubious Battle,* and the Working-Class Novel in American Literature_____

Thomas M. Tammaro

Peasant Song

When the sun rises, I go to work.
When the sun goes down, I take my rest.
I dig my well from which I drink.
I farm the soil which yields my food.
I share creation, Kings can do no more.

—Ancient Chinese song, 2500 B.C.

Virtually no modern working-class novels are included among those works traditionally found in undergraduate curricula in American literature. Furthermore, working-class novels are rarely, if ever, represented in the major anthologies that give each new generation of college students a sense of our national literature. Yet working-class literature surely deserves a place in our curricula.

"Proletarian literature," a generic name given to certain works produced mostly in the 1920s and 1930s, grew out of two suppositions: that human experience is influenced by the social, economic, and political environments, and that the best way to understand the phenomenon of the individual manipulated by forces beyond his or her control is through Marxist theory, which sees the dialectic between class and culture. Proletarian literature burst on the American scene during the 1920s and 1930s, a time when the social and political climates provided proletarian writers with ample grist for their literary mills. However, the mainstream critical literary consensus is that proletarian literature as a genre "dwindled away as a subject and a theory in the 1940s."[1]

Walter Rideout, in *The Radical Novel in the United States, 1900-1950*, which Frederick J. Hoffman calls the "best book on the subject" of proletarian literature,[2] defines the radical novel as "one which demonstrates, either explicitly or implicitly, that its author objects to human suffering imposed by some socioeconomic system and advocates that the system be fundamentally changed."[3] Hoffman believes that "almost invariably, radical is equivalent to proletarian, and especially in the American thirties."[4] Of Rideout's four types of radical novels, the "strike novel" is best represented by Steinbeck's *In Dubious Battle*, which Hoffman calls "the superior novel of this class."[5] As a type of literature, however, the label "proletarian" is too limited, being closely aligned to Marxist theory; the term "working-class" provides a broader perspective because the term is not so tightly tied to a specific political ideology or dogma.

In his excellent essay "Democratizing Literature: Issues in Teaching Working-Class Literature," Nicholas Coles offers a useful definition of working-class literature: "writing by working-class people—whether they are workers who write ('worker-writers') or professional writers from working-class backgrounds—that deals substantially with working-class life."[6] Coles continues:

> Writers who are also workers, while they write about much else besides work . . . have often sought in writing to explore the effects of the inescapable centrality of work in their lives: describing what they get out of work and what it takes out of them; perhaps asking how the conditions of work got this way and how they might be different. And in doing so, how they may encourage students who are or will be workers to do the same. In focusing on work itself, then, this literature illuminates a customary and perhaps necessary blindspot of much middle-class literature: it makes visible the human labor that invests everything we have and use.[7]

This definition is inclusive, free of ideological or doctrinaire ties. Perhaps one reason why working-class literature has not found its way into the canon is that the romance of modern American literature has not been with blue-collar workers and their lives and issues, but rather with the lives and issues of white-collar workers. And if the business of America is business, we understand, then, why so few working-class novels are represented in the American canon.

An understanding of the working-class experience in America is crucial to our understanding of the American experience. And it is especially crucial to our understanding of the reshaping of the American character in the last decades of the nineteenth century and the early decades of the twentieth as the country moved from an agrarian to an industrial culture and economy. With the rise of corporate America came the shifting concentration of wealth to fewer people (it is estimated that in 1892, 200,000 people owned 70 percent of the country's wealth). With the trend of concentrated wealth came the lowering of income for the masses. According to some estimates by the Brookings Institute, by the time of the crash of 1929 nearly 60 percent of American families lived below the poverty level. Coupled with new waves of immigrants entering the United States to take their places in the rank and files of industry, these explosive changes—changes that eminently revolve around the working-class—forever altered the fabric of American culture.

But why a vacuum in the literature of that experience? Why are those novels and that literature missing from the standard reading lists in our courses and not represented in our anthologies? Are there no writers, no novels, that speak to those issues? There are those who will be quick to say that Upton Sinclair's *The Jungle* is just such a book. Yet when *The Jungle* is read, taught, or represented in anthologies, it is often slighted, taught apologetically, or discussed or dismissed as an aberration, as second-rate, suggesting that working-class issues do not lend themselves to great art, for surely if they did, our *great* writers would have written about them. The implications of classism and elitism become embarrassingly apparent when such criticisms are put forth. When working-class literature is viewed, it is often viewed as merely communist, socialist, left-wing liberal propaganda written by individuals who were short on artistry but long on passion for reform and social conscience, for it is all too easy to remember Sinclair's pro-nouncement that he had come to Chicago's South Side "to write the *Uncle Tom's Cabin* of the labor movement."[8] Because the working-class experience is grossly underrepresented in American literature, verging, in fact, on near invisibility, the arguments used to justify the rightful placement of ethnic and women's literature in the American canon seem relevant in justifying the addition of working-class litera-ture as well.

One reason for the absence of working-class literature in our curric-ula and canon is the failure to see the centrality of the working-class experience in American culture. More than anything else in our collec-tive experience, it is our work that defines us. In fact, no other Ameri-can institution embodies so many of the myths that feed the American psyche. How much of the American character has been nurtured by the myths of upward mobility, equal opportunity, a classless society, the land of opportunity, hard work and reward, pulling oneself up by one's own bootstraps, self-reliance, and rugged individualism? If these are the archetypal American democratic myths, then it is essential for our individual and collective psychological health to examine them care-fully. Good working-class novels—and good working-class literature in general—can help us scrutinize these myths, for these are the myths that nurture young men and women in our culture as they train to take their places among the working ranks in America.

Steinbeck's *In Dubious Battle*—among the best of American work-ing-class novels—can fill this vacuum and address this reluctance to read and study a literature that has too long been ignored and is central to our common experience. If Louis Owens is correct—and I think he is—that *In Dubious Battle* "is the most tightly knit of Steinbeck's work, illustrating a highly complex harmony between structure and materials," and that "it is perhaps his most artistically successful novel and a key work in the whole of his fiction,"[9] and if Warren French is correct—and I think he is also—that *In Dubious Battle* is the "best novel about a strike ever written because Steinbeck refused to become a blind partisan and rather showed how struggles between laborers and employers—however provoked and justified—can inevitably prove only destructive and demoralizing to both parties and also to society as a whole,"[10] then I believe we need to ask why this novel has not taken its place among the important and necessary works of American literature. With *In Dubious Battle* we have a novel about the nature of working-class issues that is rich in both artistry and depth.

Lack of artistry, excessive propaganda, and datedness—that too much time must be spent teaching social history instead of literary criticism—are charges frequently hurled against the teaching of working-class literature. In his essay "Aesthetics of the Proletarian Novel," Frederick J. Hoffman asserts that "the proletarian novels . . . of the Thirties now mainly exist as period pieces, to which one refers from time to time, but almost unbelievingly."[11] Critics have used these very charges to diminish and underscore the second-ratedness of *In Dubious Battle*. Hoffman thought *In Dubious Battle* "the superior novel of its class."[12] Yet even Hoffman—who obviously sees the artistry in Steinbeck's novel and the lack of it in other "strike novels" of proletarian literature—cannot bring himself to call Steinbeck a first-rate writer. He writes that "the fiction of Farrell, Steinbeck, and Dos Passos [survives] and this is largely because it was superior work, less given to formulas and more in the literary tradition of twentieth-century naturalism. None of these is a first-rate writer, but all of them offer a literature that resists the confinement of an ideological source and explanation."[13] Hoffman's curse-by-faint-praise criticism does underscore, however, the fact that *In Dubious Battle* transcends propaganda. More recently, Harold Bloom, in his cursory assessment of *In Dubious Battle* as "quite certainly a period piece . . . of more interest to social historians than to literary critics,"[14] failed to see beyond the dated charge.

Yet *In Dubious Battle* stands next to *The Grapes of Wrath* as one of Steinbeck's greatest artistic achievements. Its polemics and propaganda are negated by its objectivity—which has been discussed in detail by others—and by Steinbeck's failure to choose sides and create flat, unambiguous characters who woo our sympathies. Far from being polemical, *In Dubious Battle* succeeds because it *avoids* polemics and propaganda. Had Steinbeck wanted the novel to embrace polemics, to be a Communist book, all he would have needed to do was bring Doc Burton back into the struggle to take his place among the rank and file. Instead, he makes him disappear, and Doc becomes a kind of working man's "lone ranger" who appears when needed and then conveniently moves on—most likely to the next struggle—leaving behind a trail of good deeds and high philosophical concerns that transcend party line and ideology. Steinbeck's deliberate distancing of himself from Communist ideology in the novel was a stroke of aesthetic genius, placing him squarely on the side of writing informed by both personal vision and social conscience instead of writing informed *only* by social conscience.

Furthermore, the novel is not a period piece. It is not forever wedded to the plight of the agrarian working class of the 1930s, though that is certainly where the story emerges. On the contrary, one of the novel's strengths is that it is teachable and readable without a crash course in the social history of the 1930s. In many ways, one of the triumphs of *In Dubious Battle* is that its meaning and vision are not contingent upon time or place. Removed from its historical context, *In Dubious Battle* loses none of its richness and power. It still stands as the same hard-edged, face-to-face encounter with the human dilemma regarding the nature of work, power, personal freedom, and degree of responsibility and commitment individuals have toward their fellow human beings— all of this played out in a universe of benign indifference.

Other reasons account for the absence of working-class novels and literature in our course syllabi. For example, historically the relationship between organized labor and corporate America has been tenuous, to say the least. Relatedly, unionism has been equated with communism, more out of an anti-communist/anti-Soviet spirit than because of any real threat of communist subversion of the working classes. (Steinbeck cleverly deals with this issue in *In Dubious Battle* by showing how the workers' hunger has more to do with who they follow than their belief in any given ideology.) And the American xenophobic response to the flood of eastern European immigrants—especially during the early years of this century—and the strong ethnic presence in unions (and in working-class literature) certainly must be raised, especially as it is related to working-class issues.

Coles argues that "a preference [in literature] for the obscure and highly wrought, and a bias against the work of those who were not traditionally members of the trained literary elite: the literature of women, of black, of ethnic, and working-class writers . . . was excluded or admitted only by exception, in a form of discrimination that, at bottom, has less to do with valuations of literary quality than with the social distribution of power."[15]

Steinbeck knew he was going against the grain when he chose to write about Mexican-American field workers, *paisanos*, bindle stiffs, migrant workers, strikers, party organizers, and a host of other characters who move outside middle-class and mainstream life. And as Benson and Timmerman have documented, Steinbeck's knowledge of these people and their lives was not second- or third-hand knowledge, as critics have often accused, but rather first-hand knowledge, for as Benson states, "he knew them well from childhood on."[16,17]

In Dubious Battle brings many of the issues of working-class literature to the foreground, and it does so with finely tuned aesthetic and dramatic sensibilities. Coles writes that "engaging in a marginalized tradition such as working-class literature can put us in a position to learn again that there are other ways of reading, and texts that demand to be read in other ways. This discovery is especially important at a time when mostpeople [Coles is borrowing e. e. cummings's word] in all their diversity, go to college and take our literature courses."[18]

"For some students," Coles continues, "texts like these offer revelations of social worlds they had never imagined as existing; they respond like readers of documentary realism, with shock, concern, sometimes political questioning."[19] Thus, we allow our students to "share in creation" when we bring books such as *In Dubious Battle* into our classrooms and make them part of our tradition, because they are part of our tradition—and we can do this without sacrificing artistry and aesthetic excellence.

In Dubious Battle seems as relevant and useful a book in the 1990s as it was when it was published in 1936. We need only to look to the March 26, 1990, issue of *Time* magazine to see how near *In Dubious Battle* is to our times.

In the wake of the March 1990 strike by nine thousand Greyhound bus drivers against Greyhound Company, *Time* reported the results of its poll of American attitudes toward labor unions. While 73 percent of the people polled believed that the American worker still needed labor unions, 40 percent believed labor unions had too much power, while 33 percent believed they had just the right amount of power. Only a little more than one-fifth of those polled believed that unions did not have enough power.

While many believe the death knell of the modern labor movement was rung by Ronald Reagan's decision to fire Professional Air Traffic Controllers Organization strikers in 1981 and replace them with non-union workers, others point to the general decline of unionism since the end of World War II. According to *Time*, union membership in 1945, for example, "made up more than 35% of the non-agricultural work force; by 1980, they had dropped to 22%, and have fallen considerably since."[20] To many, the Reagan years are seen as a time of "open season on unions," and they point to a number of government, private, and public actions that have generally weakened unionism. Many union loyalists believe that too often labor disputes are more about getting rid of unions than they are about wages and fair labor practices.

Working-class literature may be invisible because Americans do not think of work and working as "an art." Instead, work is seen in terms of product and production, a commodity to be consumed and devoured, something to nourish the material body (i.e., we work for our "bread and butter"; we go to the "salt mines"; we "bring home the bacon"; we measure our collective work as a "gross national product"). It is an attitude based upon a materialistic paradigm, not an imaginative or creative one. We work to have "something to put our hands on," to echo Ben's gauge of success in *Death of a Salesman*, Arthur Miller's play about work. That which is made material and concrete in our language is made invisible in our literary canon because it is so much a part of our devalued daily experience. And so we "take vacations from," make temporarily invisible, that which reminds us of our daily struggle to survive.

As a working-class novel, *In Dubious Battle* remains as strong and central a work of literature as ever. Read against today's headlines, it is difficult to dismiss it as a period piece. The issues of labor, work, management—all of which are addressed and explored in *In Dubious Battle*—still remain with us, unresolved, uncertain, and underrepresented in our national literature.

Notes

1. James D. Hart, "Proletarian Literature," in *The Oxford Companion to American Literature* (New York: Oxford University Press, 1983), pp. 610-11.

2. Frederick J. Hoffman, "Aesthetics of the Proletarian Novel," in *Proletarian Writers of the Thirties*, ed. David Madden (Carbondale: Southern Illinois University Press, 1968), p. 184.

3. Ibid.

4. Ibid.

5. Ibid., p. 189.

6. Nicholas Coles, "Democratizing Literature: Issues in Teaching Working-Class Literature," *College English* 48 (November 1986): 667.

7. Ibid., p. 669.

8. Upton Sinclair, *The Jungle* (Urbana: University of Illinois Press, 1988), p. ix.

9. Louis Owens, *Steinbeck's Re-Vision of America* (Athens: University of Georgia Press, 1985), p. 90.

10. Warren French, *John Steinbeck*, 2d ed. (Indianapolis: Bobbs-Merrill, 1975), p. 76.

11. Hoffman, "Proletarian Novel," p. 193.

12. Ibid., p. 189.

13. Ibid., p. 193.

14. Harold Bloom, ed., *John Steinbeck: Modern Critical Views* (New York: Chelsea House, 1987), p. 1.

15. Coles, "Democratizing Literature," p. 665.

16. Jackson J. Benson, *The True Adventures of John Steinbeck, Writer* (New York: Viking Press, 1984), p. 41.

17. Louis Owens raises a related and interesting point in his essay "Writing 'in Costume': The Missing Voices of *In Dubious Battle*." He writes that Steinbeck's aesthetic architecture for *In Dubious Battle*, while creating a highly successful and popular novel, simultaneously and inadvertently silences those minority voices—namely Mexican and Filipino workers—who figure so prominently in the historical, social, political, and economic reality of the novel but are obviously absent from the novel itself. The appropriation of their story without novelistic representation further marginalizes their voices and experiences. The degree to which *In Dubious Battle* is omitted from curricula because of this oversight and inaccuracy is difficult to gauge. If the novel is discussed in the hermetically sealed world of New Criticism, the issue is a moot point. However, discussed in a larger, sociopolitical context, the novel does open itself to this charge. Owens would not deny Steinbeck's right to manipulate the raw materials for his fiction, for *In Dubious Battle* is, ultimately, a fiction, he believes. But what Owens convincingly suggests is an irony: in his desire to write an objective, nonjudgmental book, Steinbeck—confusing a "dramatic method" with "impossible authorial objectivity"—wrote a highly personal and subjective novel.

18. Coles, "Democratizing Literature," p. 666.

19. Ibid., p. 677.

20. Janice Castro, "Labor Draws an Empty Gun," *Time*, March 26, 1990, p. 57.

A Historical Introduction to *Of Mice and Men*_____

Anne Loftis

Steinbeck wrote *Of Mice and Men* midway through the 1930s, the most creative decade of his career. During this time he was becoming increasingly concerned about current social and economic problems in California, and he published three successive novels about farm workers, each distinctive in tone and conception.

Of Mice and Men was a deliberate change from his previous book, *In Dubious Battle* (1936), an imaginative interpretation of a contemporary farm strike and a study of the movement and action of crowds. In the new project he set out to work within a narrow framework, concentrating on a small number of characters in carefully detailed settings, telling his story as economically and dramatically as possible. He explained that he was teaching himself to write for the theater, and in fact he soon did translate the novel into a play.

The subject was less controversial than that of his previous book. He was writing about people who were isolated in the society of their time, who belonged to a group that was fast disappearing from the American scene. Only a short time before, thousands of itinerant single men had roamed the Western states following the harvests. Their labor was essential to the success of the bonanza grain-growing enterprises that had been started in the second half of the nineteenth century and had proliferated so rapidly that by the year 1900 some 125,000 threshers were migrating along a "belt" that extended from the Brazos Bottoms in Texas north to Saskatchewan and Manitoba, and from Minnesota west to the state of Washington. Many of them traveled by rail, arriving in the fields in empty boxcars that were later used to transport the grain.

In the early years they were paid an average wage of $2.50 to $3 a day plus board and room. The "room" was frequently a tent: living conditions were spartan. But wages rose at the time of the First World War when the price of wheat was high, partly through the action of the

Industrial Workers of the World, which established an eight-hundred-mile picket line across the Great Plains states.

In California, where grain was the chief farm commodity in the 1870s and 1880s before the advent of irrigated agriculture, some of the early harvesters were disappointed miners returning from the gold-fields. In the social and occupational hierarchy they were on a level considerably below the mule drivers, who, like Steinbeck's character Slim, were valued for their skill in handling as many as twenty animals "with a single line" and who were generally employed permanently on the ranches.

Steinbeck's recognition of the status of the mule driver epitomizes his re-creation of a working culture that was undergoing a historic change even as he wrote about it. In 1938, the year after *Of Mice and Men* was published, about half the nation's grain was harvested by mechanical combines that enabled 5 men to do the work that had been done formerly by 350. The single farm workers who traveled from job to job by train, or like George and Lennie by bus, were disappearing. They were being replaced by whole families migrating in cars, like the people in Steinbeck's next novel, *The Grapes of Wrath*.

The physical background for *Of Mice and Men* came from Steinbeck's own early years in a California agricultural valley. His native city of Salinas, eighty miles south of San Francisco, is the seat of Monterey County. (His father was the county treasurer for a number of years.) In his childhood he spent a good deal of time on a ranch near King City, south of Salinas, that was owned by relatives of his mother, and during his high school years he worked summers in the fields and orchards near home.

More important in planting the germ of the novel was an experience he had during a period when he dropped out of college. He entered Stanford in 1919, already ambitious to become a writer and determined to follow his own particular interests in the curriculum. Experiencing some difficulty with courses and grades the following year, he decided to break away, shed his identity as a university student, and make his way for a while as a workingman. "I was a bindle-stiff myself for quite a spell," he told reporters some years later. "I worked in the same country that the story is laid in."[1]

Tall and husky, he was hired as a laborer on a ranch near Chualar, a short distance—in miles—from the prosperous neighborhood in Salinas where he was born, and for a time he became a part of this very different world. The fact that he was promoted to straw boss[2] suggests that he got on well with his fellow workers. He had a talent for being inconspicuous: they probably learned very little about him while he was gathering impressions of them.

After he returned to the campus, he published a story in the *Stanford Spectator* about a runaway girl who takes shelter during a storm in the bunkhouse of some Filipino farm workers. She marries the crew leader, who alternately showers her with presents and beats her. Eventually she leaves him.[3] Although the prose is vigorous, this sketch, full of bizarre details that strain the reader's credulity, is an amateur's experiment.

It is instructive to compare this apprentice effort with Steinbeck's achievement as a mature artist a dozen years later. *Of Mice and Men* is a work of symmetry and balance in which the action moves with a compelling momentum toward an inevitable conclusion. The social history which he had learned firsthand is woven seamlessly into the fabric of the story.

In the first scene by the river he introduces the mute evidence of the past: the ash pile left by previous campers and the tree limb overhanging the water, worn smooth by tramps who have come there over the years to jungle up. Linking the past with the present, George and Lennie make their entrance in the tradition of bindle-stiffs, carrying blankets on their backs. The story then moves into the opening dialogue, justly famous in American literature, through which we come to know and believe in the touching partnership of the moronic giant and his gruff protector.

The next scene at the ranch opens with a description of the empty bunkhouse with its tiers of beds, each with an apple box nailed to the wall to hold the meager possessions of men who travel light. The place is not particularly clean. Flies dart through the motes of dust stirred up by the push broom of Candy, the old swamper; a can of bug powder suggests lice or bedbugs in the mattress ticking.

The characters who come in one by one create the social dimension of the place. This rough lodging in which nothing has been provided beyond the bare necessities is governed by the harsh code of the men who live there for a week, a month, or a year. It is a society intolerant of weakness or difference. Old Candy, helpless to stop the shooting of his dog, knows that he too will be banished when he is no longer useful. Crooks, the black stable hand, is excluded except on Christmas when the boss brings in a gallon of whiskey for the entire crew. The rest of the year Crooks plays horseshoes outside with the others, but when they come indoors to sleep, he goes off alone to his bed in the harness room of the barn.

Women are not welcome in this male enclave. Curley's wife wandering around the ranch in a wistful quest for some kind of human contact, is stereotyped by the men, whose experience of women comes from "old Suzy" and her girls in town. Curley's wife (in the novel she has no other name) goes along with the typecasting by playing the vamp, inflaming her jealous husband, who, as the son of the boss, is as powerful as he is vicious. It is on this explosive situation that the plot turns. Lennie, sensing trouble too complicated for a simple mind to unravel, begs to leave after George tells him that Curley's wife is "poison" and "jail bait."

Steinbeck had a different view of her, as he explained in a letter to the actress who played the role in the Broadway production of the play. Curley's wife acts seductively because she "knows instinctively that if she is to be noticed at all, it will be because someone finds her sexually attractive." But her pose is deceptive. "Her moral training was most rigid." She was a virgin until her marriage and had had no sexual experience outside her unfulfilling union with Curley. She had grown up "in an atmosphere of fighting and suspicion" and had "learned to be hard to cover her fright." But she is fundamentally "a nice, kind girl" who has "a natural trustfulness. . . . If anyone—a man or a woman—ever gave her a break—treated her like a person—she would be a slave to that person."[4]

Steinbeck captured this aspect of her character in her final scene with Lennie. In the presence of this childlike man she drops her defenses and expresses her real feelings. Her rambling monologue of blighted hopes and tawdry fantasies is, in effect, a last confession.

Steinbeck has prepared his readers for the shocking climax of the novel through his portrait of Lennie. He might have created a caricature in the mental defective who crushes soft creatures in his powerful hands. He had worked with a real-life Lennie, he told reporters when he was writing the stage version of *Of Mice and Men*. "He didn't kill a girl. He killed a ranch foreman. Got sore because the boss had fired his pal and stuck a pitchfork right through his stomach."[5] The fictional Lennie is passive and nonviolent. Would he be capable of a murderous rage if George was threatened? Perhaps. It is through his connection with his intelligent partner that he becomes believable. In the opening scene Steinbeck establishes the dynamics of their relationship, in which George's exasperated bossing of Lennie appears as a form of protectiveness that masks their mutual dependence.

Loneliness is a recurrent theme in the novel, articulated in George's speech that begins: "Guys like us, that work on the ranches, are the loneliest guys in the world. They got no family. They don't belong noplace."

"*But not us*," Lennie replies. "*And why. Because . . . because I got you to look after me, and you got me to look after you, and that's why.*"

Their plan to find a place of their own, which Candy and Crooks, outcasts on the ranch, are hungry to share, is straight out of the American Dream. They have set down the details in a kind of litany which George recites while Lennie chimes in with the chorus. They repeat the comforting words from time to time like an incantation to ward off trouble and rekindle hope. In the last scene—a final irony in a work compounded of ironies—George, in order to calm Lennie, utters the familiar refrain, which becomes an epitaph for his friend.

* * *

Before he found the apt title from Robert Burns's poem, Steinbeck called his work in progress "Something That Happened." While he was at work on the book he sent revealing bulletins to his literary agent and his friends. Describing a state of mind familiar to writers, he commented in February 1936, "I have to start and am scared to death as usual—miserable, sick feeling of inadequacy. I'll love it once I get down to work."[6]

It was as he predicted. In a postcard to the same friend he reported that "after two months of fooling around my new work is really going and that makes me very happy—kind of an excitement like that you get near a dynamo from breathing pure oxygen." He explained, "I'm not interested in the method as such but I am interested in having a vehicle exactly adequate to the theme."[7]

On April 4: ". . . my new work is moving swiftly now."[8]

Eleven days later: "Pages are flying."[9]

Toward the end of May he reported a setback. His setter pup had "made confetti" of half of the manuscript. "Two months work to do over again. . . . There was no other draft." He tried to be philosophical. The pup may have been "acting critically. I didn't want to ruin a good dog for a ms. I'm not sure is good at all."[10] He finished the work during the summer.

Almost immediately after sending the manuscript to his publishers he set out on a research trip around California in preparation for writing a series of newspaper articles on newly arriving Dust Bowl migrants and the employers who were making life difficult for them. While starting in a direction that led eventually to *The Grapes of Wrath*, he could not ignore the book he had just completed. He reported that there was a mixed reaction to the manuscript. (He didn't say *whose* reaction.) His publisher, Pascal Covici, liked it.[11]

Steinbeck said that he was not expecting a large sale, and he was surprised that *Of Mice and Men* was chosen as a Book-of-the-Month Club selection and that 117,000 copies were sold in advance of the official publication date, February 25, 1937. The reviews were enthusiastic. "The boys have whooped it up for John Steinbeck's new book," Ralph Thompson wrote in the *New York Times*.[12] The novel was praised by, among others, Christopher Morley, Carl Van Vechten, Lewis Gannett, Harry Hansen, Heywood Broun, and Eleanor Roosevelt. Henry Seidel Canby wrote in the *Saturday Review of Literature* that "there has been nothing quite so good of the kind in American writing since Sherwood Anderson's early stories."[13]

In early April it was on the best-seller list in six cities across the country, and it continued to be among the top ten best-sellers in fiction into the fall. Steinbeck, who said that he would never learn to conceive of money in larger quantities than two dollars, was surprised by the large checks he received from his agents. He was not by any means an unknown writer. *Tortilla Flat* (1935) had been a popular success, and *In Dubious Battle* and some of his short stories had been praised by critics. But he was now treated as a celebrity, something he had always feared. As he and his wife Carol passed through New York en route to Europe, his appearance in his publisher's office was considered news-worthy in literary circles.

On his return he worked with playwright George F. Kaufman, who was going to direct the stage version of *Of Mice and Men*. Kaufman wrote Steinbeck that the novel "drops almost naturally into play form," but he had a couple of suggestions for changes. He thought that Curley's wife "should be drawn more fully: she is the motivating force of the whole thing and should loom larger." He told Steinbeck: "Preserve the marvelous tenderness of the book. *And*—if you could feel it in your heart to include a *little* more humor, it would be extremely valuable, both for its lightening effect and the heightening of the subsequent tragedy by comparison."[14]

Steinbeck seems to have ignored the latter idea, but he considerably enlarged the role of Curley's wife, who is presented in the play as a person with strongly articulated feelings about her past history and family relationships. Another change was his decision to end the play with George's speech to Lennie just before he pulls the trigger, an improvement over the anticlimactic group scene in the novel.

Of Mice and Men opened at the Music Box Theater in New York on November 23, 1937, with Wallace Ford as George and Broderick Crawford as Lennie. Claire Luce appeared as Curley's wife. Will Geer, who was prominent in many plays in the 1930s, took the part of Slim. The reviews were ecstatic, and the play drew enthusiastic audiences during a season in which *Tobacco Road, Golden Boy, Stage Door,* and *You Can't Take It with You* were among the offerings on Broadway. It ran for 207 performances and won the New York Drama Critics' Circle Award in competition with Thornton Wilder's *Our Town.*

The film version of *Of Mice and Men,* written by Eugene Solow from the novel and the play, is considered by Joseph R. Millichap to be the most faithful screen adaptation of any of Steinbeck's works.[15] It was a labor of love on the part of the director, Lewis Milestone, who consulted with Steinbeck and visited ranches in the Salinas Valley in his company. Although he shot most of the outdoor sequences in southern California, the landscape has an authentic look. He commissioned Aaron Copland to compose the background music, and he took pains with the casting. He hired Burgess Meredith to play George, Lon Chaney, Jr., was Lennie, and Betty Field played Curley's wife, called Mae. Charles Bickford appeared as Slim. Milestone brought Leigh Whipper from the Broadway cast to repeat his performance as Crooks.

The movie, released in 1939, was not a box-office success. Never as famous as John Ford's *The Grapes of Wrath,* it deserves more recognition than it has received. An excellent television version of *Of Mice and Men* based on Milestone's film was brought out in 1981, featuring Robert Blake, Randy Quaid, Pat Hingle, and Lew Ayres. In 1970 an opera by Carlisle Floyd, who wrote both the music and libretto, had its premiere in Seattle. The composer changed the story slightly (he eliminated Crooks, the black stable buck, and created a chorus of ranch hands), but he was faithful to Steinbeck's theme. One critic, obviously no lover of the original work, thought that the new form was an improvement: "The operatic conventions impose a frame that makes Steinbeck's basic sentimentality infinitely more acceptable."[16]

Warren French has suggested that readers who spoke of *Of Mice and Men* as sentimental should "think of it as an expression of Steinbeck's outraged compassion for the victims of chaotic forces."[17] Criticism of the novel became noticeable at the end of the 1930s when there was an evaluation of Steinbeck's total literary achievement up to that point. On the one hand, he was praised for his versatility, and on the other, denounced for trying to do too much, for mixing romance and realism,[18] for "weakness in characterization" and "puerile symbolism."[19] The most damaging assessment, one that would be echoed by later critics, was Edmund Wilson's statement that Steinbeck's preoccupation with biology led him "to present life in animal terms," to deal "almost always in his fiction . . . either with lower animals or with human beings so rudimentary that they are almost on the animal level." Wilson found a prime example of his point in the character Lennie.[20] (More recently Jackson Benson has given a different interpretation of Steinbeck's concern with biology. According to this view, science and nature provided a philosophical framework for Steinbeck's writing, his conviction that meaning and stability came from a sense of connection with the natural universe.[21] This thesis supports Peter Lisca's emphasis on the importance in *Of Mice and Men* of the camp by the river, "a retreat from the world to a private innocence," and of George and Lennie's dream of the farm, "a safe place," as a symbol of happiness.)[22]

Wilson summarized the novel as "a compact little drama, contrived with almost too much cleverness, and a parable which criticized humanity from a nonpolitical point of view."[23] During the 1940s and 1950s Steinbeck's fiction, in particular the three farm-worker novels on which his reputation was largely based, were criticized on ideological grounds. His work had been popular when it appeared because it expressed the values of the Depression decade: a passion for social justice and concern for the common man. Yet, fittingly for a man of independent judgment, he was attacked by both radicals and conservatives. Left-wing critics complained of his nonconformity to the doctrines with which he was identified by the growers' groups whose actions he had exposed in *In Dubious Battle* and *The Grapes of Wrath*.

It is interesting that *Of Mice and Men*, which represents a break in the sequence of Steinbeck's "problem" novels, took on some political coloration from his other writings and from his ongoing connection with the controversies of the 1930s. In the summer of 1937 the Theatre Union of San Francisco, which supported maritime workers in their fight for unionization, gave what was probably the first stage performance of the work, creating their own script from the novel. Two years later Steinbeck gave permission to some Stanford students to give a benefit reading from the book to raise money to help the migrants. In the 1970s scenes from the play were presented to the supporters of César Chávez's United Farm Workers Union.

Yet the continuing popularity of *Of Mice and Men*, both as a drama and in its original novel form, indicates the degree to which it has transcended its historical context. As a work of literature, it has attained the status of a modern classic. A staple of the middle-school curriculum in England and the United States, it has been translated into a dozen foreign languages. The arguments of the critics will go on, no doubt, but we have come to acknowledge that Steinbeck's "little book"[24] has a quality that defies analysis. It touches our deepest feelings and enlarges our understanding of the human condition. As a tragedy, with the power to arouse pity and terror implicit in that art form, it has drawn readers for half a century and, it seems safe to predict, will reach new generations in the century to come.

From *The Short Novels of John Steinbeck*, edited by Jackson J. Benson (1990): 39-47. Copyright © 1990 by Duke University Press. All rights reserved. Used by permission of the publisher.

Notes

1. "Mice, Men, and Mr. Steinbeck," *New York Times*, December 5, 1937, quoted in Jackson J. Benson, *The True Adventures of John Steinbeck, Writer* (New York: Viking Press, 1984), p. 364.

2. Steinbeck's college roommate, Carlton Sheffield, gives an account of Steinbeck's experience on the ranch in his introduction to *Letters to Elizabeth: A Selection of Letters from John Steinbeck to Elizabeth Otis*, ed. Florian Shasky and Susan F. Riggs (San Francisco: Book Club of California, 1978).

3. John E. Steinback [*sic*], "Fingers of Cloud: A Satire on College Protervity," *Stanford Spectator* (February 1924).

4. John Steinbeck to Claire Luce, 1938, from *Steinbeck: A Life in Letters*, ed. Elaine Steinbeck and Robert Wallsten (New York: Viking Press, 1975), pp. 154-55.

5. "Mice, Men, and Mr. Steinbeck." Jackson Benson suggests Steinbeck may have been putting on a "wild west" act for reporters.

6. Letter to Louis Paul, February 1936, in *Life in Letters*, p. 120.

7. Postcard to Louis Paul, undated, in *Life in Letters*, pp. 123-24.

8. Letter to Elizabeth Otis, Stanford University Library, Department of Special Collections.

9. Letter to Elizabeth Otis, April 15, 1936, Stanford Department of Special Collections.

10. Letter to Elizabeth Otis, May 27, 1936, Stanford Department of Special Collections.

11. Letter to George Albee, 1936, in *Life in Letters*, p. 132.

12. February 27, 1937, review.

13. February 27, 1937, review.

14. Quoted in *Life in Letters*, p. 136.

15. Joseph R. Millichap, *Steinbeck and Film* (New York: Ungar, 1983), p. 13.

16. Frank S. Warnke in *Opera News Review*, March 14, 1970.

17. Warren French, *John Steinbeck* (New York: Twayne Publishers, Inc., 1961), p. 74.

18. James D. Hart, *The Oxford Companion to American Literature* (New York: Oxford University Press, 1941), pp. 722-23.

19. Margaret Marshall, quoted in Peter Lisca, *The Wide World of John Steinbeck* (New Brunswick: Rutgers University Press, 1958), p. 5.

20. Edmund Wilson, *The Boys in the Back Room: Notes on California Novelists* (San Francisco: Colt Press, 1941), pp. 41-43.

21. Jackson J. Benson, "Hemingway the Hunter and Steinbeck the Farmer," *Michigan Quarterly Review* 24, no. 3 (Summer 1985): 452-53.

22. Lisca, *Wide World*, pp. 134-36.

23. Wilson, *The Boys in the Back Room*.

24. So described by Steinbeck in a letter to George and Anne, January 11, 1937, in *Life in Letters*, pp. 133-34.

Of Mice and Men:
The Dream of Commitment_____

Louis Owens

The Eden myth looms large in *Of Mice and Men* (1937), the play-novella set along the Salinas River "a few miles south of Soledad" (*Of Mice and Men*, p. 1). And, as in all of Steinbeck's California fiction, setting plays a central role in determining the major themes of this work. The fact that the setting for *Of Mice and Men* is a California valley dictates, according to the symbolism of Steinbeck's landscapes, that this story will take place in a fallen world and that the quest for the illusive and illusory American Eden will be of central thematic significance. In no other work does Steinbeck demonstrate greater skill in merging the real setting of his native country with the thematic structure of his novel.

Critics have consistently recognized in Lennie's dream of living "off the fatta the lan'" on a little farm the American dream of a new Eden. Joseph Fontenrose states concisely, "The central image is the earthly paradise. . . . It is a vision of Eden." Peter Lisca takes this perception further, noting that "the world of *Of Mice and Men* is a fallen one, inhabited by sons of Cain, forever exiled from Eden, the little farm of which they dream." There are no Edens in Steinbeck's writing, only illusions of Eden, and in the fallen world of the Salinas Valley—which Steinbeck would later place "east of Eden"—the Promised Land is an illusory and painful dream. In this land populated by "sons of Cain," men condemned to wander in solitude, the predominant theme is that of loneliness, or what Donald Pizer has called "fear of apartness." Pizer has, in fact, discovered *the* major theme of this novel when he says, "One of the themes of *Of Mice and Men* is that men fear loneliness, that they need someone to be with and to talk to who will offer understanding and companionship."

The setting Steinbeck chose for this story brilliantly underscores the theme of man's isolation and need for commitment. Soledad is a very real, dusty little town on the western edge of the Salinas River midway down the Salinas Valley. Like most of the settings in Steinbeck's fiction, this place exists, it *is*. However, with his acute sensitivity to place names and his knowledge of Spanish, Steinbeck was undoubtedly aware that "Soledad" translates into English as "solitude" or "loneliness." In this country of solitude and loneliness, George and Lennie stand out sharply because they have each other or, as George says, "We got somebody to talk to that gives a damn about us." Cain's question is the question again at the heart of this novel: "Am I my brother's keeper?" And the answer found in the relationship between George and Lennie is an unmistakable confirmation.

Of Mice and Men is most often read as one of Steinbeck's most pessimistic works, smacking of pessimistic determinism. Fontenrose suggests that the novel is about "the vanity of human wishes" and asserts that, more pessimistically than Burns, "Steinbeck reads, '*All* schemes o' mice and men gan *ever* agley'" [my italics]. Howard Levant, in a very critical reading of the novel, concurs, declaring that "the central theme is stated and restated—the good life is impossible because humanity is flawed." In spite of the general critical reaction, and without disputing the contention that Steinbeck allows no serious hope that George and Lennie will ever achieve their dream farm, it is nonetheless possible to read *Of Mice and Men* in a more optimistic light than has been customary. In previous works we have seen a pattern established in which the Steinbeck hero achieves greatness in the midst of, even because of, apparent defeat. In *Of Mice and Men*, Steinbeck accepts, very non-teleologically, the fact that man is flawed and the Eden myth mere illusion. However, critics have consistently undervalued Steinbeck's emphasis on the theme of commitment, which runs through the novel and which is the chief ingredient in the creation of the Steinbeck hero.

The dream of George and Lennie represents a desire to defy the curse of Cain and fallen man—to break the pattern of wandering and loneliness imposed on the outcasts and to return to the perfect garden.

George and Lennie achieve all of this dream that is possible in the real world: they are their brother's keeper. Unlike the solitary Cain and the solitary men who inhabit the novel, they have someone who cares. The dream of the farm merely symbolizes their deep mutual commitment, a commitment that is immediately sensed by the other characters in the novel. The ranch owner is suspicious of the relationship, protesting, "I never seen one guy take so much trouble for another guy." Slim, the godlike jerkline skinner, admires the relationship and says, "Ain't many guys travel around together. . . . I don't know why. Maybe everybody in the whole damn world is scared of each other." Candy, the one-handed swamper, and Crooks, the deformed black stablehand, also sense the unique commitment between the two laborers, and in their moment of unity Candy and Crooks turn as one to defend Lennie from the threat posed by Curley's wife. The influence of George and Lennie's mutual commitment, and of their dream, has for an instant made these crippled sons of Cain their brother's keepers and broken the grip of loneliness and solitude in which they exist. Lennie's yearning for the rabbits and for all soft, living things symbolizes the yearning all men have for warm, living contact. It is this yearning, described by Steinbeck as "the inarticulate and powerful yearning of all men," which makes George need Lennie just as much as Lennie needs George and which sends Curley's wife wandering despairingly about the ranch in search of companionship. Whereas Fontenrose has suggested that "the individualistic desire for carefree enjoyment of pleasures is the serpent in the garden" in this book, the real serpent is loneliness and the barriers between men and between men and women that create and reinforce this loneliness.

Lennie has been seen as representing "the frail nature of primeval innocence" and as the id to George's ego or the body to George's brain. In the novel, Lennie is repeatedly associated with animals or described as childlike. He appears in the opening scene dragging his feet "the way a bear drags his paws," and in the final scene he enters the clearing in the brush "as silently as a creeping bear." Slim says of Lennie, "He's jes' like a kid, ain't he," and George repeats, "Sure, he's jes' like a kid." The unavoidable truth is, however, that Lennie, be he innocent "natural," uncontrollable id, or simply a huge child, is above all dangerous. Unlike Benjy in *The Sound and the Fury* (whom Steinbeck may have had in mind when describing the incident in Weed in which Lennie clings bewildered to the girl's dress), Lennie is monstrously powerful and has a propensity for killing things. Even if Lennie had not killed Curley's wife, he would sooner or later have done something fatal to bring violence upon himself, as the lynch mob that hunted him in Weed suggests.

Steinbeck's original title for *Of Mice and Men* was "Something That Happened," a title suggesting that Steinbeck was taking a purely non-teleological or nonblaming point of view in this novel. If we look at the novel in this way, it becomes clear that Lennie dies because he has been created incapable of dealing with society and is, in fact, a menace to society. Like Pepé in "Flight," Tularecito in *The Pastures of Heaven*, and Frankie in *Cannery Row*, Lennie is a "natural" who loses when he is forced to confront society. This is simply the way it is—something that happened—and when George kills Lennie he is not only saving him from the savagery of the pursuers, he is, as John Ditsky says, acknowledging that "Lennie's situation is quite hopeless." Ditsky further suggests that Lennie's death represents "a matter of cold hard necessity imposing itself upon the frail hopes of man." Along these same lines, Joan Steele declares that "Lennie has to be destroyed because he is a "loner" whose weakness precludes his cooperating with George and hence working constructively toward their mutual goal." Lennie, however, is not a "loner"; it is, in fact, the opposite, overwhelming and uncontrollable urge for contact that brings about Lennie's destruction and the destruction of living creatures he comes into contact with. Nonetheless, Steele makes an important point when she suggests that because of Lennie the dream of the Edenic farm was never a possibility. Lennie's flaw represents the inherent imperfection in humanity that renders Eden forever an impossibility. Lennie would have brought his imperfection with him to the little farm, and he would have killed the rabbits.

When Lennie dies, the teleological dream of the Edenic farm dies with him, for while Lennie's weakness doomed the dream it was only his innocence that kept it alive. The death of the dream, however, does not force *Of Mice and Men* to end on the strong note of pessimism critics have consistently claimed. For while the dream of the farm perishes, the theme of commitment achieves its strongest statement in the book's conclusion. Unlike Candy, who abandons responsibility for his old dog and allows Carlson to shoot him, George remains his brother's keeper without faltering even to the point of killing Lennie while Lennie sees visions of Eden. In accepting complete responsibility for Lennie, George demonstrates the degree of commitment necessary to the Steinbeck hero, and in fact enters the ranks of those heroes. It is ironic that, in this fallen world, George must reenact the crime of Cain to demonstrate the depth of his commitment. It is a frank acceptance of the way things are.

Slim recognizes the meaning of George's act. When the pursuers discover George just after he has shot Lennie, Steinbeck writes: "Slim came directly to George and sat down beside him, sat very close to him." Steinbeck's forceful prose here, with the key word "directly," and the emphatic repetition in the last phrase place heavy emphasis on Slim's gesture. Steinbeck is stressing the significance of the new relationship between George and Slim. As the novel ends, George is going off with Slim to have a drink, an action Fontenrose mistakenly interprets as evidence "that George had turned to his counter-dream of independence: freedom from Lennie." French suggests that "Slim's final attempt to console George ends the novel on the same compassionate note as that of *The Red Pony*, but Slim can only alleviate, not cure, the situation." Steinbeck, however, seems to be deliberately placing much greater emphasis on the developing friendship between the two men than such interpretations would allow for. Lisca has pointed out the circular structure of the novel—the neat balancing of the opening and closing scenes. Bearing this circularity in mind, it should be noted that this novel about man's loneliness and "apartness" began with two men—George and Lennie—climbing down to the pool from the highway and that the novel ends with two men—George and Slim—climbing back up from the pool to the highway. Had George been left alone and apart from the rest of humanity at the end of the novel, had he suffered the fate of Cain, this would indeed have been the most pessimistic of Steinbeck's works. That George is not alone has tremendous significance. In the fallen world of the valley, where human commitment is the only realizable dream, the fact that in the end as in the beginning two men walk together causes *Of Mice and Men* to end on a strong note of hope—the crucial dream, the dream of man's commitment to man, has not perished with Lennie. The dream will appear again, in fact, in much greater dimension in Steinbeck's next novel, *The Grapes of Wrath*.

Works Cited

Alexander, Stanley. "The Conflict of Form in *Tortilla Flat*." *American Literature* 40 (1968): 58-60.

Astro, Richard. *John Steinbeck and Edward F. Ricketts: The Shaping of a Novelist*. Minneapolis: U of Minnesota P, 1973.

Carpenter, Frederick. "John Steinbeck: The Philosophical Joads." *College English* 2 (January 1941): 324-25.

Ditsky, John. "Ritual Murder in Steinbeck's Dramas." *Steinbeck Quarterly* 11 (Summer-Fall 1978): 72-76.

Fontenrose, Joseph. *John Steinbeck: An Introduction and Interpretation*. New York: Barnes and Noble, 1963.

French, Warren. *John Steinbeck*. New York: Twayne, 1961.

Levant, Howard. *The Novels of John Steinbeck: A Critical Study*. Columbia: U of Missouri P, 1974.

_____. "*Tortilla Flat*: The Shape of John Steinbeck's Career." *PMLA* 85 (1970): 1087-95.

Lisca, Peter. *John Steinbeck: Nature and Myth*. New York: Crowell, 1978.

Pizer, Donald. "John Steinbeck and American Naturalism." *Steinbeck Quarterly* 9 (Winter 1976): 12-15.

Steele, Joan. "A Century of Idiots: *Barnaby Rudge* and *Of Mice and Men*." *Steinbeck Quarterly* 5 (Winter 1972): 8-17.

Wilson, Edmund. "The Boys in the Back Room." In *Classics and Commercials: A Literary Chronicle of the Forties*. New York: Farrar & Straus, 1950.

Come Back to the Boxcar, Leslie Honey:
Or, Don't Cry for Me, Madonna, Just Pass the Milk:
Steinbeck and Sentimentality_____

John Seelye

I want to start by rendering a précis of a famous work of fiction: it is about the breakup of families, chiefly caused by the vagaries of staple-crop agriculture; it is about a man of humble origins and Christly virtues, a lay minister for a time, who emerges during the course of the novel as a scapegoat for the people he represents and who is killed by the forces of exploitative, capitalistic agribusiness, figured as intolerant, bigoted, and ignorant wielders of absolute authority; it focuses on family and on the values promoted by domestic virtues by means of scenes with women who are central to the plot, who prove far stronger than the men with whom they are associated; it stresses the importance of motherhood, figured as a positive force working to maintain the coherence of family even as the domestic unit is torn asunder by centrifugal social forces which have disempowered male authority. This work of fiction is founded on carefully gathered facts; it transcends the particular, however, and is epical in scope, for the action ranges widely along the length of a longitudinal geopolitical axis of the United States; it is a movement through space permitting a documentary series of vignettes demonstrating the social ills caused by an economic system indifferent to the integrity of the family, to the suffering of the dispossessed, to the basic needs of humanity. The action from time to time builds to violence, in which a courageous few do battle with the many who draw their strength from a code of laws that are based on the sacredness of private property essential to the Constitution.

It is a work of sentimental fiction, which attempts to enlist our sympathies, to draw from us tears of grief for the tragic lot of families torn asunder by economic forces, to move us to better the lot of our fellow human beings. It ends with the conversion of a son of one of the farming families to radicalism, virtually swearing on the grave of his Christ-like friend that he will join the growing ranks of those aroused to anger and action by the tragic inequities permitted in American society. We as readers are reached out to by his conversion, which is intended to move us to do likewise, to enlist us in the same struggle. We weep tears of anger but they are not idle tears. Thousands of our fellow readers weep also, a torrent of water that will sweep away the iniquities to which we have been vicarious witnesses, that will turn the wheels of the millstones of God, grinding a wrathful vintage from the perpetrators of injustice. A great war is coming, just beyond the closing pages of this book, a war that will lift the intolerable burden of suffering and poverty from the families and open the doors of opportunity wide to them.

The novel is, of course, *Uncle Tom's Cabin*, by Harriet Beecher Stowe. James Baldwin has called *Uncle Tom's Cabin* "Everybody's Protest Novel," in an essay that I for many years, not having read it, thought was about *The Grapes of Wrath*, by John Steinbeck, a novel which bears a certain resemblance to *Uncle Tom's Cabin* (149). These points of similarity are worth consideration, if only because Leslie Fiedler, who in *Love and Death in the American Novel* pronounced Stowe's book "the greatest of all novels of sentimental protest" (264) of the nineteenth century, has denounced *The Grapes of Wrath* as "maudlin, sentimental, and overblown" ("Looking Back" 55).

Now Fiedler is an icon, whose courage to make outrageous statements provides a model inspiring us not to walk the line but dance along the edge. It was courageous in 1960 to praise *Uncle Tom's Cabin*, and positively foolhardy in 1989 to stomp on *The Grapes of Wrath* in the presence of a host of Steinbeckians: From this pressing came no sweet communion wine, but, as I have been informed, tears shed in maudlin and overblown grief at having to witness the public dismantling of a beloved object. But that has been Fiedler's mode ever since he shocked the literary establishment by proposing that the love between Huck and Jim was the kind that passeth the laws of Mississippi. Fiedler is a kind of lumberjack, whose critical dynamite loosens up academic log jams and gets the wood moving again, rafting it downstream toward the pulp mills that roll out the paper on which, according to Fiedler, our greatest masterpieces are written. And regarding his attack on Steinbeck's sentimentality, I am as always grateful to Fiedler because he has provided the fulcrum for the lever I am about to set in motion. To my mind, Steinbeck's book is assuredly the greatest sentimental novel of protest of the twentieth century.

Moreover, like *Uncle Tom's Cabin* in the 1960s, which owed its advent in the curriculum to the increased attention being paid to African Americans during the struggle for Civil Rights, *The Grapes of Wrath* is greatly relevant to the present, a time when the problems of migrant workers are once again being brought forward. And as for the homeless, well they are always with us, but never in such numbers I think as now. To borrow President Clinton's imaginative and highly evocative metaphor, if there is a bridge to the twenty-first century, a broken-down automobile with a family living in it is stuck half-way across, from which vantage point you may see a group of foreign nationals wading over to the farther side.

Before we join them, pending the universal loss of tenure, let us for a time consider the meaning of the word "sentimental," that being the problematic half of the whole, for surely all of us can agree what a protest novel is. And it is at the start important to point out some differences between Stowe's novel and Steinbeck's, which like the similarities are helpful in defining what the sentimental was to writers of far different cultural origins and historical generations.

First off, let me say that Steinbeck probably never read Stowe's novel, which during the 1920s and 1930s was thought of, when it was thought of at all, as a literary curiosity of the nineteenth century, which survived largely through the Tom shows that were a regular part of traveling carnivals. Steinbeck surely knew about Uncle Tom. Everybody knew about Uncle Tom, especially James Baldwin, for whose generation Stowe's hero was generally confused with Booker T. Washington as black men who danced Jim Crow to the white man's tune. We now know differently, having over the past thirty years developed a much more intimate and informed acquaintance with Stowe's novel, and realize that Uncle Tom is a latter-day Christ, who in refusing to take up the whip and flog his fellow slaves at the behest of Simon Legree guarantees his own crucifixion. It is an act not of cowardice but great courage, an act moreover that strikes at the very heart of the system of which Tom and his fellow slaves are victims, which corrupts whites as well as blacks because of the effects of absolute power. It is an extreme version of the civil disobedience about which Thoreau was writing at the time, and for which he logged a famous night in the Concord jail. It is, that is to say, an intensely political act, that reaches for its impetus beyond the laws of men to that higher law to which Thoreau himself had reference.

But where Thoreau thought of the higher law in general, perhaps even deistic terms, as that body of self-evident truths to which Jefferson made reference in the Declaration of Independence, Uncle Tom (and Harriet Beecher Stowe) were thinking about gospel truths. Tom draws his strength from the Bible, from the example of Christ. As Nietzsche observed, Christianity was the religion of women and slaves; it was (and is) the religion of the oppressed, that holds out the consolation of heaven to those who suffer without hope of relief here on earth. Women and slaves were equals in Rome in the time of the Caesars as persons without power; it was a situation that had not much changed by 1850 in America. Harriet Beecher Stowe responded in a characteristic evangelical manner, by holding out to women and slaves the promise of power implicit in the Gospels; indeed, she gave that power to the women and the slaves in her novel, as an example to her readers of what could be done through the liberating agency of faith—in opposition to the oppressiveness of man-made and unjust laws. That power is essential to the force of sentimentality in fiction.

Suffering in sentimental fiction, according to Jane Tompkins, may cause tears, but they are tears of identification and sympathy. Women, in effect, by prayerfully suffering abuse from drunken husbands and dying pious deaths from tuberculosis and other lingering diseases, gain terrific power by imitating Christ in his passion, who died from the effects of entrenched Orthodoxy and the Roman empire. But we need to add a third factor here; in Stowe's novel suffering in imitation of Christ is not empowerment per se, but is used to give impetus to the abolition movement. Along with her emphasis on the family, a strategy to gain the interest of her middle-class readers, Stowe's use of Tom as a black Christ, however heart-felt, was an effective device that appealed to that class of Americans who had political power. Hers once again is a protest novel, the strategy of which is to move her readers to take action; a call from the author herself comes at the very end of the book, when she instructs her readers to do that which makes them feel good. Obviously doing nothing was not what Stowe had in mind.

It perhaps helps here to remember that for Jane Tompkins the pluperfect sentimental novel is *The Wide, Wide World* by Susan Warner, the end of which brings the heroine to an absolute sense of her own unworth, a humility born of Christian doctrine that promises the ultimate reward: a heaven on earth identified with marriage to a minister. There is no reference in Warner's book to the social and economic inequities of her day, even though she and her sister were victims of the very unstable commercial situation that was typical of speculative capitalism in mid-nineteenth century America. For Christians like Warner, then and now, the evils of this world are simply irrelevant to the larger design, which is preparing oneself for the next and far, far better world to which they will be going, having done those far, far better things for others to which Charles Dickens, the ultimate sentimentalist of the day, made frequent reference. Dickens for his part was well aware of the inequities of this world, which are displayed in full in his fiction, but though he showed Stowe and Warner how sentimentality could be used to good effect in arousing sympathy for the underprivileged and dispossessed, Dickens did not write novels of protest. Thus, in *Oliver Twist*, having exposed the horrors of workhouse life, he proposed no alternative solution to poverty. Instead, he put considerable emphasis on personal benevolence, that is, the happy hearthside condition which his long-suffering orphan boy finally attains, not because of any government program, but through the agency of his regained birthright, an action that is providentially determined.

On the other side of the Civil War we have the instance of Bret Harte, who was, to borrow the title of his popular poem, "Dickens in Camp." Mark Twain sneered at Bret Harte's "saintly whores and sanctimonious sons-of-bitches," but Harte, like Stowe, owed a great debt to Dickens, from whom he abstracted the idea of his golden-hearted gamblers and open-handed gold miners. Harte went Dickens one better, for he had no social agenda at all; indeed, the world he wrote about had already disappeared by the time he began writing about it. He was merely playing with an idea that was given warrant by a situation, namely the essentially male makeup of California mining-camp life. But in eliciting his readers' often tearful sympathy for these rough-surfaced but tender-hearted and sensitive West-Coast guys, Harte was providing an almost linear demonstration of what is much more complex in both Dickens and Stowe, namely the exponential diagram implicit in "The Luck of Roaring Camp," in which the presence of a child brings out the mother in all of the men resident in the place, rendering "Roaring Camp" ambiguous in implication, at least to modern ears. For what are we talking about here but cross-dressing? But the effect of this transformation is to bring out as it were the mothers in all of us as well, so that we brim over with human sympathy and then weep at the ending when a sudden flood wipes out the camp and leaves the little Luck dead in the arms of one of the rough miners, who died in trying to save him. There is a certain element of mischief in Harte's fiction, and the flood that destroys the camp and child is the kind of water that turns the works in sentimental fiction. For the kid misnamed Luck is a male version of Little Nell and Little Eva, not used by Harte to move us to promote social reforms but assuredly to move us to tears.

What, you may be wondering, has all this got to do with John Steinbeck? Well, what Bret Harte demonstrates to a fault is the function of sentimental literature that is essential to protest fiction, which is to redeem what have been considered marginal persons by bringing them into the domestic center. It is a movement invariably associated, in Dickens, Stowe, Warner, and Harte, among many others, with women and children, whose mere presence can act to reveal the essential feminine in us all. By contrast, yet in complete synchronization with Harte, let me cut to the scene in which the remnants of the Joad family, along with other dispossessed emigrants, take refuge from rising flood waters in a boxcar on a railroad embankment. The men have struggled to preserve their vehicles from the flood by erecting a flimsy levee, a mud wall that is subsequently torn apart by a fallen tree in an episode that is diagrammatically illustrative of Steinbeck's naturalistic view of causality. During this same episode Rose of Sharon gives birth to a stillborn baby, a tiny corpse that her uncle sets adrift on the flood that rises above the cars and trucks so essential to their survival. We may doubt that Steinbeck was making a conscious allusion to the ending of Harte's most famous story, but the connections, as with parallel elements in *Uncle Tom's Cabin*, are useful here.

Because what the rising flood and the dead baby arouse in us are not tears of sympathetic grief, but a concomitant despair; we abandon hope not only for the Joads and their companions in adversity but for the humankind of which they are the lowest common denominator. The baby, ordered by Uncle John to "go down" like Moses and instruct America, can hardly set his people free. But then there occurs that final and famous moment in which Rose of Sharon gives her breast to a starving man, a gesture encouraged by her mother and which elevates these two women to a salvational and central position in the terminal tableau. It is a situation that would seem to recommend itself to us as a prototypical instance of the sentimental, yet though it draws upon our feelings, it does not I think move us to tears. It may end the novel on a note of affirmation, but not that rising organ chord associated with the operatics of soap. Fiedler admits to admiring this final moment, which attains the "mythopoeic" power, the "archetypal resonance," he finds in texts like

Gone With the Wind, *Tarzan of the Apes*, and *The Adventures of Sherlock Holmes* ("Looking Back" 60). He even allows that it redeems all the rest of the book, with its cosmeticized sharecroppers, noble truck-drivers, and golden-hearted waitresses (Harte's miners, gamblers, and whores updated). He tells us that "Steinbeck himself has confessed . . . that [this] strange conclusion to a revolutionary and intendedly hopeful fable forced itself on him unbidden, which is to say, emerged out of his deep unconscious" ("Looking Back" 63). In contrast to the rest of the book, with its simplistic account of a complex economic and political situation, the ending is highly ambiguous, and ends with the word "mysterious." For Fiedler the transforming, even redeeming moment *has* to emerge from an archetypal resonance. Notably, the terminal passion of Uncle Tom famously came to Harriet Beecher Stowe in a dream vision, also.

Fiedler reminds us that the Hollywood version of the novel ends with the Joads attaining the felicity of a government camp, a clean, well-lighted place with the added bliss of flush-toilets, a heaven on earth conceived by a middle-class sensibility and an equivalent to that Dickensian center of domesticity which the characters in all sentimental fiction, including Bret Harte's, struggle to attain. But Steinbeck relegates the camp episode to an interlude, a periodicity that puts the government program into perspective, as a palliative perhaps but not a solution. Instead, he carried the remnants of the Joad family to that desperate hour on the railroad embankment and the final scene in the barn. This conclusion may, as Fiedler insists, have been generated in Steinbeck's unconscious, but it was also a carefully contrived artifact, which the author defended to Pascal Covici in a famous letter. There were those editorial readers who felt that the nameless vagrant to whom Rose of Sharon offered her breast should have been more tightly woven into the story, that the moment of hope should not have been a casual encounter but should have had some kind of foreplay by way of extenuating circumstances. But Steinbeck would have none of that. "The giving of the breast has no more sentiment than the giving of a piece of bread," he wrote. "If there is a symbol, it is a survival symbol, not a love symbol, it must be an accident, it must be a stranger, and it must be quick. To build this stranger into the structure of the book would be to warp the whole meaning of the book" (*SLL* 178).

Steinbeck seems to have wanted the moment to have the same accidental force as the toppling of the cottonwood tree by the flood and its subsequent destruction of the feeble levee erected by the desperate men, who are forced to stand by as helpless witnesses to the event. Moreover, it is this emphasis on chance as a definitive force that provides a link between *The Grapes of Wrath* and Steinbeck's other novels about migrant workers: Like the disappearance of Jim Nolan's sister, in *In Dubious Battle*, the falling tree "was one of those things that happen." Like the murder by Lennie of Curley's wife in his second novel about migrant workers, originally entitled "Something That Happened," the encounter between Rose of Sharon and the starving man was a moment without causality, as casual as casual sex, "an accident, with a stranger, and quick." Most important, it was explicitly not, as Steinbeck emphasized, a sentimental gesture, which it might well have been had the man been tightly woven into the preceding events of the novel. Despite the familial grouping, centered by women, it was a classical moment, that, as Fiedler demonstrates, drew on a long iconographic tradition, Christian surely in implication, but not sentimental.

That is why Fiedler is drawn to it, as he tells us, such allusiveness being an archetypal resonance. But Fiedler is drawn to the conclusion of *The Grapes of Wrath* for other reasons, also: our leading connoisseur of kink, for whom all American fiction worth discussing has a sexual subtext, usually pathological, Fiedler was chiefly interested in *Uncle Tom's Cabin* because of the "rape" of Uncle Tom and the subliminal seductiveness of Little Eva. His *Love and Death in the American Novel* traces those aspects of our fiction that contain the gothic continuity, and there are no gothic bones showing in *The Grapes of Wrath*. Moreover, when Steinbeck deals with sexuality, it is seldom in a subliminal package but out in the open air, under a bush perhaps with Jim Casy but in plain view.

Fiedler, however, does manage to find an Oedipal message in *The Grapes of Wrath*, identified with the disempowerment of Pa Joad and the "loving" bond between Tom and his mother. These Freudian elements are agents of archetype that provide Fiedler welcome relief from the depressing soup kitchen of sentiment that is for him the novel as a whole, and they lead up to that final scene, in which Rose of Sharon as a perverse Madonna nurses an impotent father figure, "a total reversal of conventional generational roles" ("Looking Back" 62). But Fiedler's sexual "archetypes," can also be read as essential to the sentimental idea: if Pa is disempowered by his loss of patriarchal authority, which derives from an honest day's work, so Ma gains terrific strength, validating the maternal center of the sentimental mode; Tom's deep regard for his mother works to a similar end, for the action of the novel is clearly intended to move Ma Joad toward the center of power. It is a movement that, as in *Uncle Tom's Cabin*, identifies that center with the domestic idea, which likewise warrants the final scene in the book, even while that scene turns against its sentimental potential. Once again, the sentimental impulse is essential to novels of social protest.

But then Fiedler has never been much interested in either sentimentality or social protest, for having grown up in the age of hard-boiled realism and agitprop, he is immune to both. It was Fiedler, we should remember, who defended the execution of the Rosenbergs, the Mom and Pop of the Communist Party who, third in line to Major André and Sacco and Vanzetti, were the dubious beneficiaries of liberally shed tears. Fiedler's was a position which in the 1950s took real guts. He is tough, the Mike Hammer of literary critics, and having punched out Steinbeck's generous truckers and butt-kicked "the improbably soft hearted waitress," he blows away what he calls the "pastoralism" of Steinbeck's novel, the Joads' fanciful dream of finding a little farm somewhere in California that will sustain their agrarian ideal ("Looking Back" 57).

But the Joads do not find that farm, a failure consistent with Stein-beck's intention, and in keeping with his decision to override the senti-mental potential of his novel with his carefully chosen conclusion. *The Grapes of Wrath* may posit a pastoral ideal, but in terms of plot it is an epic, an action that moves not toward the domestic resolution of the *Odyssey*, nor the Promised Land of *Exodus* and the *Aenied*, but toward what in naturalistic terms must be called a tragedy. In sum, Steinbeck's greatest novel most certainly has sentimental elements, which work in the traditional, nineteenth-century way, engaging our sympathies with the characters. But in denying the Joads their dream, turning the plot away from a positive, hopeful resolution, Steinbeck turns the senti-mental mode back on itself, a movement of which the dead baby, the flood, and the final scene with the starving, anonymous man are signi-fiers.

In an earlier moment in the novel, not discussed by Fiedler, the Joad family prepares to leave their Oklahoma farm. Departure from the home place has epical overtones but is an essentially sentimental event, as Uncle Tom's forced exile demonstrates, because it raises the domestic ante to an intolerable level of deprivation. Ma Joad is shown going through and discarding the memorabilia of her youth, as the mel-ody from "Red River Valley" fills the air—in the movie, not the novel, not always easy to keep apart. Now we may harden our hearts like Fiedler, and ask how many Okie farm wives kept boxes of nostalgic keepsakes hidden away like a secret memory, but the function of this scene is not to provide us a realistic inventory of Okie farm-wife mem-orabilia. It is to arouse the sympathy of the reader/viewer for Ma Joad, and through her for all of the women who were displaced by the god-awful Dust Bowl depression and forced to join the westward-moving army of the kinds of people we now call the Homeless.

Much as Harriet Beecher Stowe reached out to touch the hearts of her middle-class, white women readers by asking them if they had ever lost a child—not to slavery, of course, but to death—so Steinbeck is playing the same tune, albeit in a minor key, which in a protest novel in the United States must be gauged to harmonize with the values of the great American middle class, always the instrument of change then and now in this country. And most women of the great American middle class have a box in a closet somewhere filled with precious trinkets saved from their youth and understand what it means to have to discard a faded and shriveled rose of long ago, a memento not of death but of a past life hidden away, a sustaining secret memory of love.

It is moments like this, perhaps unconsciously conflated with the movie, that warrant Leslie Fiedler's charge of sentimentality, and there are other episodes, like the deaths of the Joad grandparents, that also correspond to tropes of the nineteenth-century model. For like Harriet Beecher Stowe, Steinbeck wanted to move his readers, and he could only do so by engaging them with the predicament of the Joads, which meant moving that family not only to California but into the familial center occupied by the great American middle class. At the same time, as his letter to Covici indicates, Steinbeck introduced elements that consciously worked against sentimental possibilities: significantly, having removed a few valuable trinkets, presumably to sell them, Ma Joad consigns her ephemeral treasures to the fire. It is a burning away of the past that like the deaths of that Anchisean pair, Granma and Granpa Joad, is an allusion to one of the several classical epics whose framework undergirds the family's heroic passage westward.

Although always drawn toward romantic models, like the Arthurian matter, Steinbeck is one of our great neoclassical writers, for whom form is a highly traditional even mandatory inheritance. The same may be said for his use of biblical patterns, whether the Exodus migration or the passion of Christ, which play such sustaining roles in *The Grapes of Wrath*, as they do in *Uncle Tom's Cabin* as well, albeit to much different ends. To put it briefly, Stowe's epic is Judaic-Christian in its implications, but for Steinbeck it is the classical version that holds, a Homeric, Virgilian, Mosaic errand underwritten by no providential guarantees but entirely dictated by the vagaries of chance, witnessed by the drought and the flood with which the action is framed. And of all the classical models, it is perhaps the *Iliad* that *The Grapes of Wrath* most closely resembles, being essentially a battle epic with no happy, empire-founding, promised-land-regaining conclusion.

Not only does the notion that life is dictated by casual happenstance connect Steinbeck's three labor-intensive novels, but chance is the factor that rules in all of his fictions, the accidentalness of events that disrupt the plans of men. And chance as the determining force of the universe is a notion foreign to the impulse that moves sentimental fiction. It is an ideology bordering on nihilism that operates, as in *Moby-Dick*, against the very basis of the sentimental tradition, which is so fruitfully rooted in the Christian idea of universal redemption. Once again, from Dickens's romances to Stowe's, causality in sentimental fiction derives from the gospel promise; it gives meaning to suffering and takes its form from the idea of salvation; God rules this world through the gracious intervention of Jesus Christ. Even the little Luck in Bret Harte's tearful parable suggests the redemptive role of Christ-child, for in the Christian plan the fall of a sparrow is part of a great and benign plan, providentially determined. The tears of sadness we are called upon to weep will yield to tears of gladness.

Thus, an emphasis on mere causality, on accident as the determinant factor of life, would seem to be downright hostile to the sentimental impulse. After all, we can identify this idea with realistic and naturalistic fiction, with the great continuity that connects Stephen Crane, Edith Wharton, and Theodore Dreiser with Hemingway, Glasgow, and Faulkner, among many others. It is a tradition which likewise operates outside the frame of social literature, the tradition of Dos Passos, Richard Wright, and Jack Conroy, which is shaped to illustrate a generally Marxist argument. For Marxism is keyed to a faith in immutable laws akin to those sustaining Judaic Christianity, not to the idea of the universe as an accident. It is perhaps not necessary to point out with Fiedler that *The Grapes of Wrath*, despite its points of similarity with texts like *Manhattan Transfer* and *U.S.A.*, is no more Marxist in its ideology than conventionally Christian. True, Tom Joad is not only given a messianic profile but is last seen shouldering a radical errand, which last, like Steinbeck's attack on what he defined as the "Fascist" elements of American agrarian capitalism, inspired ferocious reactions on the part of his contemporaries who assumed he was himself a Socialist when in fact his novel was in sync with Roosevelt's attempts to rescue the United States from Revolution.

In short, Steinbeck is a gravely misunderstood writer, as Leslie Fiedler's dismissal surely demonstrates. But that in some ways is his own fault, for much as Steinbeck, though a realist, often uses symbolic frameworks derived from archetypal sources, structures essentially romantic in implication, so as a realist he is anomalous in his use of sentimentality. But let us remember that Harriet Beecher Stowe was herself an early proto-realist, who turned from writing melodramatic protest novels to stories that are thought of as the foundation of the local color movement. Moreover, later, bona fide realists like Mark Twain, despite his contempt for Bret Harte and female purveyors of flapdoodle, could evoke the sentimental spirit as well. The reverse imprint of *Uncle Tom's Cabin* is *The Adventures of Huckleberry Finn*: The raft is an intensely domestic place. And Louisa May Alcott, who began her career writing penny dreadfuls, in *Little Women* provided a necessary corrective to *The Wide, Wide World*, not for its sentimentality but for its unbearable Christian burden. For American writers like Stowe, Alcott, Twain, and Steinbeck, the sentimental mode has its uses but was not an invariable necessity. Use it, as the saying goes, don't abuse it. Consider, then, some of the uses to which Steinbeck put sentimentality—and how he did not abuse it and why.

Let's start with *The Red Pony*, which veers toward the sentimental in its final, added chapter, when the grandfather recalls the pioneer past in which he took part only to be dismissed by the boy's father, thereby setting up a bond of sympathy between the boy and the old man and between the readers and both old man and boy. But in the original version of the book—which includes only the first three stories—there is no such opportunity, although there are plenty of situations that could have been worked for tears, like the death of the pony in the title. Deaths of horses are sentimental occasions, surely, or *Black Beauty*, published by the Humane Societies of Great Britain and America, was written in vain. *Black Beauty* is another sentimental novel written to forward reform, and when first published was subtitled *The Uncle Tom's Cabin of the Horse*, which makes the connection complete. Cut to *Bambi*, and the death of the deer mother, which makes the union of the fawn and his father, the great stag, possible; cut to *Love Story*, in which the death of Jenny makes the reunion of Oliver and his father possible. These are all sentimental fictions, and you may pick those which use tears to work reforms and those for which tears, as in Tennyson's poem that provides the title of the sentimental novel that serves as a target for aesthetic darts in *The Rise of Silas Lapham*, are merely idle, being for the sake of a good cry only. These are lachrymose lubricosities as it were, a kind of pornography of tears, intended to move us—but only to move us.

It serves a useful purpose here, I think, to mention also *The Yearling*, Marjorie Kinnan Rawlings's clone of *The Red Pony*, which plucks at your heartstrings to no purpose that I have been able to detect, or *My Friend Flicka*, a hybrid horsey out of *The Red Pony* and *The Yearling*, but with no perceivable connection to the ultimate horse's tale, *Black Beauty*. We are in these fictions set in Bret Harte country, which is to say we are back in California, the artistic capital of which is Hollywood, the place where Lassie always comes home. And it was of course Hollywood that added "Red River Valley" to Ma Joad's moment with her treasured past, whereas the song Steinbeck had chiefly in mind as he wrote his novel was "The Battle Hymn of the Republic," which keys both the epical and the gospel elements of the novel and provides another useful link to *Uncle Tom's Cabin*.

Let us now turn to Steinbeck's other novels about dispossessed field workers, specifically to *Of Mice and Men*, which took its title from a beloved poem by Robert Burns, the Robert Frost of his own day and as often misconstrued. It is about a plowman who has turned up by accident a mouse's nest, and who, holding the quivering victim in his hand, philosophizes about the vicissitudes to which all living creatures are heir, and over which they have no control. Now there is a sadness that permeates much of Burns's poetry, he who wrote what might have served as the epithet for much sentimental literature, that "Man's inhumanity to man/ Makes countless thousands mourn!" ("Man Was Made to Mourn" 56-57). And the image of the "wee, sleekit, cow'rin', tim'rous beastie" in "To a Mouse" with the "panic" in its "beastie" like Bambi is certainly susceptible to a sentimental reading (2). The plowman, holding the mouse, begs its pardon for having destroyed its home, for in asserting "Man's dominion," he has broken "Nature's social union" (7-8). But a companion poem is Burn's "To a Mountain Daisy," which contains the following stanza, starkly unsentimental and yet in keeping with the concluding line from "To a Mouse" that Steinbeck took as his title:

> Ev'n thou who mourn'st the Daisy's fate,
> That fate is thine—no distant date;
> Stern Ruin's ploughshare drives elate
> Full on thy bloom,
> Till crush'd beneath the furrow's weight,
> Shall be thy doom.
>
> (49-54)

Of Mice and Men, like the poem from which it takes its title, does seem susceptible to a sentimental reading. Fiedler's dismissive essay ignores Steinbeck's still highly popular novel, which enjoys sales of over 300,000 paperback copies a year, preferring for obvious reasons to attack *The Grapes of Wrath*, which sells only 150,000 copies a year. His preference gives heft to his notion that Steinbeck, like Dos Passos and James Farrell, is no longer read, as mythopoetic an idea as any conjured up by Edgar Rice Burroughs. But for our purposes, *Of Mice and Men* is particularly useful, not only because it is still widely read, but because, although it deals with the lives of migrant workers, it does not have a social agenda of any detectable kind. Indeed, from a modern, feminist perspective, it is probably Steinbeck's most politically incorrect work of fiction, errors of attitude that turn on the role played by the woman known only as Curley's wife, whose actions disrupt and finally destroy the vision of a male-centered paradise, the Edenic parable beneath the pastoral weave.

In Lennie and George we have a pair recalling the two men in Bret Harte's "Tennessee's Partner," in which male bonding is taken to a sentimental extreme. As in "The Luck of Roaring Camp," moreover, domesticity in this novel is identified with the male hegemony, for the Joad family's dream of owning a little farm is shared not only by Lennie and George but by the other migrant workers they are cast among, a green, pastoral hope we are called upon to share likewise, but which finally proves futile.

Likewise, Lennie's proclivity for taking up little furry creatures in his hand seems to be a sardonic reference to the sentimental plowman in Burns's poem, given what happens to them as a result. And when he holds and then crushes Curley's wife, we must I think regard him as a heedless and callous natural force, arbitrary and casual in its effects. Lennie's attraction to little furry things is sentimentality itself but what he does to them destroys the sentimental impulse along with the little furry thing. And when George administers an anaesthetic of sorts to Lennie, by pointing to the distant green prospect of their long deferred domestic paradise before shooting him, we have a perfect diagram of Steinbeck's use of the sentimental mode, which is to hold it out to us in a promising form and then, like Lennie with a wee mousie, crush it.

Steinbeck's is not, however, a cynical gesture. It is in keeping with his non-teleological view of the world, which is essentially unfriendly to linear and progressive literary forms, the kinds of discourse that sustain an argument or a thesis or a solution, whether it be Christian or Marxist doctrine. The sentimental mode, like the pastoral and epic with which it is often conjoined in protest novels, is one of the most linear of forms, pointing always to some happy and regenerative—even trans-figuring—conclusion, and when used for the purpose of protest literature it holds out a socially determined solution to a social problem.

Once again, there is no solution posited for the problems overwhelming the Joads and their fellow migrant workers, only expedient palliatives. That momentary relief experienced by the family in the government camp was derived from actual experience, as we know, but Steinbeck in his letters and articles also made it clear that the fascistic vigilante bands organized by local authorities in California were furiously antagonistic to those camps, fearing that they would provide the workers the opportunity to organize themselves into an effective force for change. In the novel, the migrants are able to forestall the attempts to invade their camp, but in truth the real strength, as in *In Dubious Battle*, was in the hands of local authorities who kept the vigilantes on a purposefully loose leash. And as for the vow that Tom Joad takes on the grave of Jim Casy, with its vague promise of a syndicalist agitation, we know from *In Dubious Battle* also how skeptical Steinbeck was about the activities of labor organizers, for whom the actual welfare of workers is secondary to furthering the Socialist cause in which the organizers serve.

In Dubious Battle, the critical first in Steinbeck's labor-intensive trilogy, would seem to be the one of the three that is without any bid for sentimental sympathy. It is also intensely male-centered, with only marginal roles for women, although the young mother, Lisa, with her ambitious husband, is clearly a prefatory sketch for that American Madonna, Rose of Sharon. Indeed, throughout the book we find points of contingency with *The Grapes of Wrath*, starting with Jim Nolan, the protagonist, who shares certain qualities with Tom Joad, but who, as his family name suggests—borrowed from that of the protagonist in Edward Everett Hale's "Man Without a Country"—is a permanent exile in the world, without family connections. As the central figure, a young man who is undergoing an education in radicalism, Jim should attract reader sympathy, and his sudden death in a vigilante ambush is certainly shocking. But in the end he serves merely as the occasion for yet another appeal by his mentor, the labor agitator, Mac, for the workers' attention and solidarity, forwarding a strike already defined as doomed.

With Mac slipping into his familiar rhetoric as he stands over Jim's bleeding corpse, Steinbeck obviously is blocking any bid for empathy with his cause, for where Mac is obviously appealing to the sentimentality of the fruit pickers, Steinbeck, by calling our attention to that ploy, puts massive distance between the reader and the message. The ending is not only unsentimental but also grimly realistic, holding out little hope for casual laborers in those factories in the field, the orchards of California. It is in this novel, once again, that the idea that things just happen is first made explicit. And though Steinbeck expresses the phalanx idea through the reflections of young Dr. Burton, we see no sign that the men Mac attempts to organize can muster anything but sporadic efforts to join in a common effort to better their lives. Mac's career seems a little better than an extended exercise in futility, from which he protects himself with a thick callus of rationalization, the repeated mantra that even a failed strike will serve a useful purpose. Likewise, the cost to the men he purports to help is written off as a kind of expense account, necessary to effect a greater good, resulting in another kind of protective callus, on the heart not the head. His is a higher realism, which Steinbeck's carefully flattened prose intensifies.

Yet at a critical point Burton observes that "Sometimes I think you realists are the most sentimental people in the world" (209), and a few pages later he tells Mac that he is "the craziest mess of cruelty and hausfrau sentimentality, of clear vision and rose-colored glasses I ever saw" (212). Increasingly it is Jim Nolan who sees "the big picture," the Marxist vision, and who by the time he dies has become a thorough socialist zealot, while Mac again and again gives way to a human impulse, a warmth perhaps attributable to his Irish blood but which I think is essential to the meaning of the book, and hence to Steinbeck's use of sentimentality in *The Grapes of Wrath* as well. As Warren French suggests, it is in Mac's mouth that Steinbeck places the words that will in terms of sentiments be repeated by Tom Joad, when he promises his mother that he will become an omnipresent force among the migrant families, being "there" wherever a few are gathered together, in effect becoming a secular Christ (14).

There is a depth of humanity in this connection that is I think essential to Steinbeck's often perverse use of sentimentality, his *lacrimosus interruptus*. If Tom Joad does play that role so central to sentimental fiction, the human semblance of Jesus Christ, it is not, however, the suffering Christ, the passive victim of established authority who in rendering unto Caesar what was Caesar's included his corporal identity, with the expectation that his spirit would rule in heaven, to which destination and triumph he recommended the meek and lowly of the world. That was the role, once again, of Uncle Tom, not Tom Joad. Let us return in that connection to the theme song of *The Grapes of Wrath*, "The Battle Hymn of the Republic," which is about quite a different Christ from the one found in sentimental literature, whose robes fit so easily on the suffering protagonists engendered by writers like Stowe and Susan Warner.

The Christ of Julia Ward Howe is the militant Savior, not warranted by the Gospels but produced by the uneasy union of Christianity and the old Pagan religion it displaced, with its furious berserker gods for whom violence and vengeance were a way of life. Howe's is the Puritan Christ, as well, that compound of the Old and New Testaments, the Gideon-like wielder of the sword of divine judgement. We should always keep in mind that deep within "The Battle Hymn of the Republic" there dwells not the moldering body but the undying spirit of Captain John Brown, whose solution to the problems dramatized in *Uncle Tom's Cabin* was quite different from Harriet Beecher Stowe's—not colonization but insurrection.

The Grapes of Wrath is, like *Uncle Tom's Cabin*, a very emotional book, but the emotion is one of anger. Steinbeck's letters from California during the period of the novel's gestation seethe with fury over the plight of the migrants, starving and drowned out by social and natural forces, victims of laws both man-made and natural over which they have no control. His anger was chiefly aimed at the vigilante groups who persecuted the Okies, and we know that the novel was first drafted as an attack on those groups, a version that lingers in detectable fragments in the book that finally emerged from Steinbeck's fury. And it is anger I think that he hoped to inspire in his readers, moving them to tears not of sad resignation but outrage over the fate suffered by the Joads as they strive to attain what was and is still a middle-class ideal, a decent job that could permit a degree of self-respect. Leslie Fiedler snorts the epithet "middle-brow" ("Looking Back" 61) but that was precisely the point, nor were Steinbeck's efforts to ennoble the Joads any different from the end sought by photographers like Dorothea Lange, whose sympathetic portraits of noble Okies and Arkies are patent exercises in primitivism that somehow escape Fiedler's censorious eye.

Moreover, Steinbeck saw in the anger of farm workers in California the seeds of a war, a populist uprising, much as John Brown saw in Nat Turner's and other slave rebellions hopeful signs that a general insurrection was possible in the South. Surely we take Tom Joad's promise to his mother as a threat to established order, as an errand that will carry Jim Casy's populist gospel to the circling watchfires of the migrant workers' camps. This is not to say that Steinbeck hoped by means of his novel to stir up revolution in California. Though he may have borrowed technique from *U.S.A.*, he hardly shared Dos Passos's Marxist ideology. It is to say that *The Grapes of Wrath* is a text that, like Luther's, is pinned as a warning to the gates of Heaven that something had better be done or else. Why otherwise the insistence on reprinting "The Battle Hymn of the Republic" on the endpapers entire, the hints to Pascal Covici that the song contained the essential message of his book?

That is, if he hoped to arouse outrage and anger in his readers, he also seemed to have sought to strike terror into the hearts of the authorities in California, and he appears to have been successful in this last regard, given the reaction of many Californians to his book. But like John Brown's raid, Steinbeck's literary terrorism was counterproductive in the long run, for if his only solution to the problem of the migrant workers was essentially the palliative already in place, those government camps that the fruit growers feared and hated as staging grounds for the revolution Steinbeck hoped to evade, then the record shows that his novel did not serve as an effective vehicle for change, and may even have worked against his purposes. On another plane, Steinbeck may have hoped that his rhetoric would override the essential circumstances of life, but things do just happen, and the greatest irony framing *The Grapes of Wrath*, as Fiedler points out, is the fact that a war did indeed end the plight of the Okies, not a revolution but the anti-Fascist conflict that America finally entered in 1941.

That is, the Okies and Arkies who seemed in 1939 at the point of taking up arms against their troubles escaped them by finding employment in armament factories. But Fiedler does not acknowledge that those jobs enabled many of the former migrants to realize their pastoral dream, buying the farms seized from resident Japanese, who were interned by those same paranoid fascist authorities who were aroused to panicked action by an invasion of swarms of alien migrants seeking a small piece of California landscape for themselves. And as the Okies and Arkies moved toward the middle-class center where Steinbeck had sought to place them, so the dispossessed Nisei were removed to camps far from the American gaze, most of them deported finally to the land of their ancestors as the Okies and Arkies became solid, even reactionary citizens of California.

In denying Steinbeck's novel the power of archetype, Fiedler overlooks the transforming role of the popular cinema, to which Margaret Mitchell's novel also owes its mythic force. By means of that mystic liminal grove known as Hollywood, Tom Joad as Henry Fonda became Mr. Roberts, and died a hero's death in the War, fighting fascism but not suffering martyrdom in the cause of the IWW. By such means he became "there" in a way hardly foreseen by John Steinbeck, suffering a death which, like those of Uncle Tom and Jim Casy, inspired the conversion of yet another, younger man to the cause of rebellion against arbitrary power (I speak of Ensign Pulver, soon enough grown old and grumpy). And in a former identity Tom Joad as Henry Fonda had been Jesse James's younger brother Frank, in the Hollywood version a populist hero whose career of robbing trains was revenge against the railroad company for the murder of his mother, who in the movie was played by Jane Darwell, who is Ma Joad in the movie version of *The Grapes of Wrath*. Tom/Henry's daughter, also Jane, in her time espoused radical causes also, but then went on to marry a man who owned stuff like cattle ranches and baseball teams, including a television network that occasionally shows the Hollywood version of *The Grapes of Wrath*. None of this, once again, was the work of John Steinbeck, who, as we know, hated Hollywood as an alien presence that corrupted literature, but it is, I think, a marvelous irony that the movie is populated by actors who appear like members of some radical repertoire company in any number of films of the Thirties. For many of these movies celebrate, often by sentimental means, the common people who sustain the American economy or who, when betrayed by it, begin to think revolutionary thoughts and engage in revolutionary activities, which is ever the lesson of Captain John Brown, never mind Baby Face Floyd.

In conclusion, John Steinbeck's use of sentimentality is intrinsically and idiosyncratically his own, at once revealing the warm and passionate heart of a man who was moved to anger and outrage by the suffering of his fellow human beings but who in creating the kind of fiction that would call attention to that suffering stopped well short of calling for revolution or even holding out hope for positive social change. His belief in the accidentalness of life, a fatality without a supernatural agency behind it, was an ideological frame that blocked the championship of purposeful action. Steinbeck was, if you will, a Prometheus in chains of his own fashioning, whose rage was a signal of his powerful identification with the suffering of humanity, an anger exacerbated not, as Fiedler would have it, by guilt, but by a frustrating realization that bad things happen to good people, and cannot be set right by a specific political action.

Yet through all his fiction we find a terrific energy at work, the sort of force that across the highway drives the old tortoise, seeds borne between his drought-hard skin and carapace; that drives the Joads to California, that keeps them going against all adversity; that drives zealots like Mac to pick themselves up and hurl their bodies again and again against an apparently indifferent wall of inert mankind, that doubtful battle to which the epithet from Milton has reference. It is a characteristic that bonds Steinbeck's works to those of William Faulkner, in which endurance leads to prevalence, and no one has ever accused Faulkner of sentimentality in the negative sense, or "A Rose for Emily" was written in vain. So if you must ask to whom and for what purpose Rose of Sharon offers her breast, then I say she offers it to thee.

Works Cited

Baldwin, James. "Everybody's Protest Novel." *Within the Circle: An Anthology of African American Literary Criticism from the Harlem Renaissance to the Present*. Ed. Angelyn Mitchell. Durham, NC: Duke UP, 1994. 149-55.

Bentman, Raymond, ed. *The Poetical Works of Burns*. Boston: Houghton Mifflin, 1974.

Dos Passos, John. *U.S.A.* London: Constable, 1938.

Fiedler, Leslie. "Looking Back After 50 Years," *San Jose Studies* 16.1 (1990) 54-64.

_____. *Love and Death in the American Novel*. New York: Dell, 1996.

French, Warren. Introduction. *In Dubious Battle*. John Steinbeck. New York: Penguin, 1992.

_____. *John Steinbeck*. New York: Twayne, 1961.

_____. *John Steinbeck's Fiction Revisited*. New York: Twayne, 1994.

Melville, Herman. *Moby-Dick*. 1851. New York: Vintage, 2000.

Steinbeck, John. *The Grapes of Wrath*. 1939. New York: Penguin, 1992.

_____. *In Dubious Battle*. 1936. New York: Penguin, 1992.

_____. *Of Mice and Men*. 1937. New York: Penguin, 1994.

_____. *Of Mice and Men: A Play in Three Acts*. New York: Covici-Friede, 1937; rpt. Kyoto: Rinsen, 1985.

_____. *Steinbeck: A Life in Letters*. 1975. Eds. Elaine Steinbeck and Robert Wallsten. New York: Viking, 1989.

Tompkins, Jane. *Sensational Designs: The Cultural Work of American Fiction, 1790-1860*. New York: Oxford UP, 1985.

California Answers *The Grapes of Wrath*_____

Susan Shillinglaw

Four months after publication of *The Grapes of Wrath*, John Steinbeck responded sharply to mounting criticism of his book: "I know
what I was talking about," he told a *Los Angeles Times* reporter. "I
lived, off and on, with those Okies for the last three years. Anyone who
tries to refute me will just become ridiculous."[1] His angry retort is
largely on target—but the opposition was in earnest and had been even
before his novel was published.

In 1938 corporate farmers in California responded forcefully to the
consequences of continued migration: the twin threats of unions and a
liberal migrant vote.[2] Beginning early that year a statewide publicity
campaign to discredit the "migrant menace" had been mounted by the
Associated Farmers and the newly formed CCA, or California Citizens
Association, a group with the broad support of banks, oil companies,
agricultural land companies, businesses, and public utilities.[3] Well-
funded and well-placed, the CCA and the Associated Farmers produced scores of articles meant to discourage further migration, to encourage Dust Bowlers already in California to return to their home
states, and to convince the federal government that California's migrant problem was a federal, not a state, responsibility. These articles
vigorously defended farmers' wage scales and housing standards.
They complained about the state's generous relief, which, at almost
twice that of Oklahoma and Arkansas, had "encouraged" migration.
And they often maligned the state's newest residents. "The whole design of modern life," noted an article in the *San Francisco Examiner*
entitled "The Truth About California," "has stimulated their hunger for
change and adventure, fun and frippery. Give them a relief check and
they'll head straight for a beauty shop and a movie."[4] The publication
of Steinbeck novel in March 1939—followed shortly thereafter by
Carey McWilliams's carefully documented *Factories in the Field*—
simply gave the outraged elite a new focus for their attack.

The campaign took on a new intensity. Editorials and pamphlets, many underwritten by the Associated Farmers, claimed to expose Steinbeck's "prejudice, exaggeration, and oversimplification," the thesis of one tract, or to discredit the "Termites Steinbeck and McWilliams," the title of another.[5] Of greater impact, however, were the more sustained efforts to counter what were perceived as Steinbeck's factual inaccuracies. I shall examine four of the most important respondents. Two who defended California agriculture were highly respected professional writers: Ruth Comfort Mitchell, the author of *Of Human Kindness*, and Frank J. Taylor, a free-lance journalist who covered California business, farming, and recreation for the state and national press. And two were highly successful retired farmers, to use the word loosely: Marshall V. Hartranft, the Los Angeles fruit grower and real estate developer who wrote *Grapes of Gladness: California's Refreshing and Inspiring Answer to John Steinbeck's "Grapes of Wrath,"* and Sue Sanders, touted as the "friend of the migrant," who wrote and published a tract called "The Real Causes of Our Migrant Problem." Since each contributed to what can only be called a hysterical campaign against the migrant presence and Steinbeck himself, it is difficult not to cast them as villains. What must be recognized, however, is that each with great sincerity and, to a large extent, accuracy, described another California—a brawny, confident state that bustled with entrepreneurial zeal. Each defended California against Steinbeck's charges largely by ignoring much of the agony and cruelty he chronicled. Each sought an answer to the "migrant question" without fully comprehending—or perhaps, more significantly, empathizing with—the "problem," the migrants' plight. To understand each writer's perspective is to appreciate better the intensity of the political clashes of the 1930s, a period when, as liberal activist Richard Criley observed, "Social issues were so sharp and so clear . . . we were pulled to take a position because things were so acute, so terrifying in the need to change."[6] These interpreters of the California scene resisted change.

In the late 1930s, Los Gatos novelists Ruth Comfort Mitchell (1882-

1954) and John Steinbeck shared a magnificent view of the Santa Clara Valley from their mountain homes six miles apart.[7] Similarities in perspective end there. The author of sixteen novels and several collections of poems, as well as short stories and articles published in *Woman's Home Companion, Century, Good Housekeeping, and McCall's*, Mitchell claimed as her fictional terrain the uncertain ground of young love. When she wrote a vaudeville sketch on the "great question of labor" in 1907, it was lauded as an "uplifting" piece that helped give the stage a more wholesome image. Mitchell's play, noted the reviewer, "holds the human emotions paramount and introduces the labor and capital strike feature as secondary."[8]

That comment holds true for much of her work. Mitchell always "liked to take the bright view," noted her obituary in the *New York Times*. Neither by temperament nor by class was she fitted to fully comprehend Steinbeck's Joads. She was one of California's elite, raised in comfort and married to wealth. "I know nothing about that stimulating lash of adversity that all of you people who have had to fight for your foothold talk about," she admitted to one reporter.[9] Her only contact with migrant labor was on her husband Sanborn Young's dairy farm south of Fresno, where the two lived for several years until Young became a state senator—and notorious strike buster—in 1925.[10] As early as 1918, when they built their *Los Gatos* summer home, she took to wearing only green, writing on only green stationery using green ink and stamps, and driving only green cars (a pose that Steinbeck almost certainly satirizes in the effete Joe Elegant of *Sweet Thursday*, whose manuscript is on "green paper typed with a green ribbon"). Mitchell's eccentricity was seen as part of her charm, and this prolific and witty author was much in demand as a public speaker for women's groups both locally and nationally. Often she discussed writing, read her poetry, or commented on her recent work. But just as often in the late 1930s Mitchell—state president of the National Association of Pro America, a Republican women's association—lectured on international politics.

The publication of *The Grapes of Wrath* gave her a fresh platform much closer to home. As novelist, popular lecturer, wife of Farmer/Senator Young, and efficient political organizer, she was the ideal candidate to help launch a campaign against Steinbeck's novel. In league with the Associated Farmers—in fact, she gave the keynote speech at their annual convention in December 1939—she threw her considerable resources into the superbly organized attack against the novel. On August 23, 1939, the day after *Grapes* was banned in Kern County, William B. Camp, president of the Associated Farmers, announced a statewide plan to recall the book.[11] In that same week, Mitchell was chair and key speaker at a meeting of Pro America in San Francisco, where "five hundred persons . . . heard speakers denounce recent books dealing with California's migrant problem, call for cessation of relief for transients, and praise efforts of individual farmers to better conditions for migratory workers."[12] This meeting may serve as a touchstone for all such gatherings and may demonstrate why Steinbeck could with truth call the "Ass Farmers"—his term—ridiculous. It was here that Mitchell contended that California farms were becoming smaller, and another speaker maintained that "farmworkers of California are better paid and better housed than agricultural workers anywhere else in the world."[13]

Even if such exaggerated claims characterized many attacks on the novel, it cannot be said that defenses of California agriculture rested on overstatement alone. The central thrust was not to ban Steinbeck's text statewide, although some in Kern County attempted to do so, or to discredit the man, although many tried. Rather, it was to replace one picture of California farm and migrant life with another. Mitchell set out to prove that California was a rural paradise, farmed by energetic, committed Americans. In June 1939 she began writing what became the longest and most highly publicized response to *Grapes*, her novel *Of Human Kindness*, published by D. Appleton-Century Company in 1940. As she was writing her book, she repeatedly declared to audiences and reporters that she told "the other side of the story," insisting that in doing so she did not intend to attack Steinbeck, merely to defend the ranchers' position. Indeed, both she and her publisher took pains to dissociate her book from Steinbeck's. Her novel, she asserted, was fully outlined before Steinbeck's book was published. But this seems unlikely, since Mitchell's novel is crafted to dovetail with the Associated Farmers' own campaign.[14]

In their many tracts the farmer is invariably a heroic figure, a hardworking man protecting his home and minimal profits, enduring the uncertainties of weather and insects that affected his crops. Prolific pamphleteer Philip Bancroft, farmer and Republican candidate for the state senate in 1938, described himself as enjoying the "out-of-doors life, simply and economically."[15] Cut from the same cloth, Ed Banner, Mitchell's dairyman farmer, is as patriotic as his last name suggests—a point hammered home by his daughter's fiancé, who calls her "Star Spangled." The Banners are "San Joaquin Valley pioneers, third generation in California; plain people, poor people, proud people; salt of the earth."[16] Their success, as Mitchell never tires of making clear, was achieved not through wealth, but by working "sixteen hours out of the twenty four." Indeed, the Banner matriarch "out-earth mothers" Ma Joad, thus proving the family's superior Americanism; she is supremely fair-minded, a "Dowager Empress in her authority, her calm, her composure, her wisdom. Old Buddha in a faded gingham dress" (*OHK*, p. 72). And she is altruistic to a fault: her own home is "less good than the cabins she had built for her men." Their farm community is similarly archetypal: poor but energetic, closely knit and supportive—the neighbors banding together to help the Banners clean their new house and to break up, rather gently, a strike.

In presenting the "other side," Mitchell takes pains to show that farm life, like migrant life, could be "hard and harsh and uncompromising" (*OHK*, p. 75). Only one farmer enjoys wealth and leisure, and he is compared to Simon Legree. This benighted farmer is "always undercutting the prevailing wage, charging them fifteen cents to ride out to the field, [and building] shacks a self-respecting pig wouldn't live in" (p. 221). But this "blood-sucker," "gorilla," and wife tormenter, Mitchell shows, is far from the norm.

This rural tycoon is as exaggerated a type as are the interlopers who threaten Arcadia. One Okie, Lute Willow, the "okie-dokie Boy," intrudes and elopes with the Banner daughter. But the guitar-slinging Lute is hardly representative. His family owns a dairy farm in Oklahoma, and he came to California by choice, not because he was driven out of his home. Most significantly, under Ed Banner's tutelage he learns to work hard. And so Ed, initially rejecting the "dumb and shiftless" Okies, learns to accept this superior specimen. Mitchell's point is clear: a few migrants can be integrated into the valley communities if they are willing to work as diligently as have the farmers—precisely the Associated Farmers' announced position. In "The Truth about John Steinbeck and the Migrants," the laborers are said not to be the "beasts" Steinbeck portrays, but "honest, intelligent, and assimilable people."[17]

Neither Mitchell nor her supporters, however, were prepared to accept leftists who, they charged, entered the state only to inflame the workers. Most "replies" condemned the Communists. In Mitchell's text, the chief spokeswoman for what is clearly perceived as Steinbeck's position is a new history teacher who looks like a rabbit. Rude, flat-chested, sallow, and lesbian, Pinky Emory corrupts the valley children—the Banner son included—by arguing that migrants were "lured out to California by the farmers so oodles and oodles would come and they could get cheap labor and pay starvation wages!" (OHK, p. 81). This is, of course, Steinbeck's novel in a nutshell. There is also a union organizer, a "Carmen—and Delilah—Borgia" (p. 206), a "Black Widow" (perhaps modeled on labor organizer Caroline Decker),[18] who seduces the son, betrays the history teacher who adores her, and, after sending Pinky to her death, seizes her body and uses it to inspire the workers to action in a scene that echoes Mac's reaction to Joy's death in In Dubious Battle. The organizers are clearly a bad lot whose sexual deviance redundantly condemns their already perverse politics. As

Philip Bancroft had earlier noted in an article characterizing the Communists: "Some of the most rabid and dangerous are attractive and educated women."[19] For Mitchell, the women's position is synonymous with Steinbeck's, and their siren songs are as fatal as his text. Indeed, what may have been most inflammatory about *Grapes* was its sympathy with collective action. In championing the "family of man" Steinbeck seemed perilously close to embracing a socialist ideal, and Mitchell, like all these interpreters, would not betray her faith in American individualism, its excesses notwithstanding.

What may be most remarkable about Mitchell's novel, however, is not her sublimely ridiculous characters—the noble farmers, sapphic leftist organizers, and uniquely respectable Okie—all of whom she judges against the Banner ethos and the rhetoric of the Associated Farmers. Rather, it is that, while waving the virtuous Banners—Ed and Mary—so vigorously before the reader, Mitchell nonetheless proclaims her objectivity. Clearly she wants the reader to believe that her novel is grounded, not in the self-interest of the landed class, but in fair-mindedness. Not merely a narrative stance, fair-mindedness is realized by her strong female characters: the Banner matriarch, Helga the public nurse, and the semiautobiographical heroine, Mary Banner, whose perspective is the broadest in the book. Armed with an urban education and a rural practicality, Mary—like Mitchell herself—"bend[s] over backwards trying to be fair" (*OHK*, p. 221). (It was an acrobatic attitude many pamphleteers also assumed.) Thus, Mary articulates the book's (and, to a large extent, the Associated Farmers') central tenet: "I know just as well as you do that there's injustice and graft and greed here and everywhere, and ignorance and filth and suffering, but it's utterly false to say the world isn't better and going to be still better!" (pp. 178-79). And it is the farmers, not the staid city dwellers, who are most open to the meliorism she envisions, even though such change is gradual and often slow. When the students picket in support of their teacher, the politically chromatic Pinky, it is a farmer who tells the others that "most of us are too far to the right. We've got to do some fact-facing ourselves" (p. 190). Later, the feisty Ed Banner, initially denouncing the Okies, learns to accept both his Okie son-in-law and his own political obligation to run for the state senate. For Mitchell, it is axiomatic that good farmers adapt. Hard and demanding rural life molds fair-mindedness. This seems to be Mitchell's central position, the objective "other side" she championed against the "prejudice, exaggeration, and oversimplification" seen in *Grapes*.

If Mitchell best articulated the Associated Farmers' position in fiction, Frank J. Taylor, free-lance journalist, was the farmers' most formidable advocate in nonfiction. Taylor (1894-1972) also attended the Pro America evening at the Palace Hotel in San Francisco late in the summer of 1939. For the previous ten years, he had covered the West Coast for national magazines, first writing articles on Yellowstone and the National Park Service, and then, as a self-styled "roving reporter" for the conservative *Country Gentleman*, covering California agriculture. Being a "scout for farming stories," he notes in an autobiographical piece, "quite naturally turned up some characters who were good material for the *Sat Eve Post*, *Colliers*, *Nation's Business*, and the *Reader's Digest*. These stories had to be slanted at people who lived in cities, rather than at farmers, who were the Gent's readers."[20] Writing for these conservative national magazines and an urban audience, Taylor excelled in human interest stories about California entrepreneurs: beekeepers, vintners, and firework makers; the Burpees of seed company fame; UC Berkeley's Dr. Gericke, originator of "soil-less crops"; Walt Disney; and "Mr. Gump—of Gump's."[21] Taylor was a dyed-in-the-wool California booster. He admired the "shrewd individualists" who shaped the "Many Californias," men who wrested sizable fortunes from flowers, gold mines, and Oriental art, men who forged the state's cooperative farming and shipping interests. His perspective was, in fact, nearly identical to Mitchell's: positive, forward-looking, and pragmatic. Living and working in "the biggest and best" state, he looked around for what made it run smoothly.

Farmers did. As his 1938 article "The Merritt System" makes clear,

Taylor champions the farmer's work ethic as vigorously as does Mitchell. The Merritts, father and son, owned the huge Tagus Ranch, probable site of Steinbeck's *In Dubious Battle*. But Taylor's ranch is most definitely not Steinbeck's. The benevolent Merritts "brought to farming the restless search for efficiency the elder Merritt had learned in the industrial world, and they have made Tagus Ranch a year-round producer." Furthermore, Taylor notes that they have created a utopian community for their workers, who live in "glistening white" houses they rent for two to four dollars a month, buy food from a company store at "chain store prices" (where the "Merritts manage to lose a cent or two on every dollar of sales—purposely"), and send their children to the Tagus school, where they are given cod-liver oil if they appear malnourished despite the hot chocolate and graham crackers they are fed at recess.

The only flies in the ointment, reports Taylor, are the "radical labor organizers" who, seemingly without cause, "descended in force on Tagus Ranch" a few years earlier and "dragged fruit pickers from their ladders [and] threatened women and children." And, in a note at the end, he reports that the Merritts also have problems with Okies who are so accustomed to living in one-room shacks that they "chopped out partitions" in the cottages and "burned them when firewood was free for the cutting."[22] Clearly, Taylor admires the Merritts' industry and perceived goodwill toward workers. His detailed account of housing conditions is meant to counter frequent charges that farmers provided only substandard housing for workers. If Steinbeck looked for and found squalor, Taylor, like Mitchell, looked for and found the benevolent master.

He featured other farmer-entrepreneurs. In 1935, he published an equally glowing piece on "Teague of California," a wealthy man and "a farmer from the soil up . . . [who] wrested a sizable fortune from the California soil, starting with nothing in the way of assets but energy and ability and a willingness to work."[23] For Taylor, the Merritts and Teague were not capitalists but Jeffersonian gentlemen farmers, benevolent men, Horatio Algers of the soil. Yearly, they courageously faced uncertainties of weather or labor unrest; they were "beset even in times of industrial tranquility by unusual hazards such as long-haul freight rates, danger of spoiling, cost of packing, and whimsies of the market."[24] But farmers endured, a point Taylor reiterates in several articles. As American icons, these energetic, courageous, and generous owners ("Mr. Teague has never received a red cent for the vast amount of time he has devoted to the citrus and walnut cooperatives") shaped California's destiny, and their produce helped make California farming vital to the nation's economy. To threaten their crops was to steal food from tables across America.

Communist organizers are thus, for Taylor as for Mitchell, serpents in the garden. Prior to 1939 Taylor wrote several articles on the labor situation in California. No reactionary, he does not denounce unions; indeed, he features businessmen who have learned to "play ball" with unions. Nor is he unsympathetic to workers, to the Okies' "natural urge" to "dig their toes into a patch of ground . . . and settle down."[25] What he, like so many Californians, could not tolerate was the organized threat to commerce—particularly agriculture. "Communists," he declared in a 1937 article on the Associated Farmers, "had singled out California agriculture for special attention because of the vulnerable nature of its perishable crops."[26] Thus, for Taylor, the farmers, who quite naturally rose to defend the land and their rights to market their produce, were the "minute men of California agriculture." In the Salinas lettuce strike of 1936, they "transformed themselves into bands of embattled farmers, armed and imbued with a Bunker Hill determination to fight it out."[27] Taylor's metaphors define his sympathies. For him, as for Mitchell, the Associated Farmers defended the homeland against aliens—and often the issue of unfair wages was simply ignored or dismissed.

After publication of *Grapes*, DeWitt Wallace, the editor of *Reader's Digest*, asked Taylor to "trace the travels of the Joad family" in order to "tell the rest of the world about California."[28] The resulting piece, published in both *Forum* and *Reader's Digest* in November 1939, is an impressively detailed defense, supported by statistics and by Taylor's own observations. He begins, "I made one inquiry during the winter of 1937-38, following the flood which Steinbeck describes; I made another at the height of the harvest this year."[29] What he sees on both trips—and in his fifteen-year residence in the Santa Clara Valley—are the migrants as field workers, "stoops," the lower class. During both trips, he is most impressed, not by the migrants' plight but by the state's relief efforts. And he is most interested in the health officials' responses to the migrants; at least one of them, Dr. Lee Stone of Madera County, was a virulent Okie hater. His reputation for scrupulous reporting notwithstanding, Taylor could not fully acknowledge the human misery that Steinbeck had seen in his two years of trips, nor could he bear witness to the tragic flooding in the spring of 1938. Undoubtedly well intentioned, Taylor, quite simply, shared Mitchell's elitist perspective. For these two, as for the majority of Californians, field workers were—and in fact still are—an invisible population. When the state was finally forced in 1938 to acknowledge the numbers of the Dust Bowl migrants and, unlike the Mexican workers they replaced, their determination to settle in California, most Californians could hardly be expected to see the state's newest residents objectively.

To bolster his own observations, Taylor marshalled impressive statistics to show that the migrants' lot was not "the bitter fate described in *The Grapes of Wrath*." California wages, he notes, were higher than those in the southwestern states. Often true, but the cost of living was also higher. Relief payments in California, he continues, were almost twice as high as those in southwestern states, and thus migrants swarmed to California to claim this "comparative bonanza" ("CGOW," p. 233), which they were allowed after a year's residency. True, payments were higher, but, as Walter Stein observes, what many "neglected to admit was the critical role the Okie influx played in keeping wages so low that local residents actually lost money if they went off relief in order to pick the crops."[30] In addition, recent studies have shown that relief payments were not the key consideration in the migrant movement westward.[31]

To further demonstrate that migrants were well cared for, Taylor notes that during the first year, when ineligible for state relief funds, migrants could obtain emergency food and funds from the Farm Security Administration, "which maintains warehouses in eleven strategically located towns" ("CGOW." p. 233). That program, he fails to explain, had been approved only in 1938 and, more importantly, destitute migrants often could not travel, could not overcome their pride to ask for relief, could not help but fear unknown authorities. Finally, as he discusses at some length, hospitals and health facilities cared for the migrants. Like the above statistics, this was true, particularly in Kern and Madera counties. But concerned health officials could not eliminate all squalor and sickness, however impressive their efforts. Tom Collins's reports, Carey McWilliams's prose, and Dorothea Lange's portraits bear witness to the fact that outlying squatters' camps were as filthy as those in Steinbeck's novel. Both Taylor's observations and his facts demonstrate that the migrants were, for him, a group to be studied, classified. Striving for objectivity, he nonetheless accepted the Associated Farmers' absurd claims that "neither the Association nor the Bank [of America] concerns itself with wages. Rates of pay are worked out through the farmer cooperatives in each crop or through local groups" (p. 238). He recorded, as a subsequent letter to *Forum*'s editor states, "only what is profitable to his state."[32] While the solidly middle-class Steinbeck, Collins, Lange, and McWilliams saw the poor as individuals, Taylor, like so many others, viewed them primarily as a social problem.

The central point of Mitchell's argument is the farmers' integrity, while Taylor's "defense" rests chiefly on the state and federal governments' benevolence to the migrants. Yet another emphasis is to be found in *Grapes of Gladness*, a book by the retired realtor and grower Marshall V. Hartranft, whose text underscores the migrants' potential for a self-sufficient existence. "Two men looked out from their prison bars," states the epigraph to the text. "One saw the mud, the other the stars."[33] Hartranft opts for stargazing and, cursing the mud-gazer "Steinbitch," invokes the spirit of Thoreau to prove that migrants can claim their own bit of land and become self-supporting.

Only Hartranft's enthusiasm for bountiful California qualified him as respondent to *Grapes*. As a fruit grower near Los Angeles he had been, in 1893, the first to sell at auction West Coast oranges to the East Coast market; subsequently, he settled in Los Angeles and founded horticultural trade dailies, the Los Angeles and the New York *Daily Fruit World*, which helped in "advertising the distinctive products of California and advancing the interests of the producers."[34] More significantly, as a Los Angeles real estate agent, he was "instrumental in the development of many of the state's large farming lands," primarily through the California Home Extension Association, which encouraged "group colonization" of desert lands. In his book, he sets out to prove Steinbeck wrong by enthusiastically summarizing his life's two projects—colonizing and cultivating California.

If the migrants' plight were taken out of the politicians' hands, he declares in the Foreword, and put into the hands of social engineers like himself, the Joads would settle as happily in California as do his own "authentic" family, the Hoags of Beaver, Oklahoma. Traveling west, the Hoags by some good fortune continue toward Los Angeles rather than swinging to the north. Highway 66 is their road to glory, papered with signs announcing the availability of "garden acres." "Population creates land values," these posters declare, as did Hartranft whenever founding one of his several land colonies. "We will loan an acre farm to any enterprising family of worthy American people," he writes. "Near Los Angeles industries, agricultural activities, and only one or two miles from the beach. You must dig a cess-pool for your first payment; carry the 6% interest of $4.00 a month—and taxes. We require no other money payment for five whole years. You must build at least a two room cottage within a year" (*GOG*, p. 17). The next one hundred pages tell how the Hoags' skepticism—most particularly Pa's—turns to partisanship as they do, indeed, find their fruitful acre.

What is most impressive about Hartranft's reply is its optimism, its wholehearted endorsement of the Edenic myth, which Ma reads about as they drive into Los Angeles. "Taking a living in California," preaches the literature they have picked up along the way," is almost as easy as the natives have it in the South Sea Islands where they gather their living from the wild trees" (*GOG*, p. 58). Midway through the book, a Thoreauvean sage wanders into the Hoag camp, munching carob bean and "radiating" Thoreau's doctrines of simplicity and economy. Thus inspired, the optimistic Ma takes to reading Thoreau—"through its first chapter at least" (p. 61)—and to believing that they too can survive off the land. With another family, the Hoags find their garden plot on the outskirts of Los Angeles. And they learn "acre-culture," to live off what their gardens produce; to own pigs, not pups; to plant food-bearing trees that also have "foliage that would make a peacock stutter" (p. 105). Self-sufficiency is thus given highest priority—and government assistance is scorned.

Indeed, Hartranft's reply is as American a document as is Mitchell's—and Steinbeck's. What is particularly striking about these rebuttals is that the values endorsed are shared by Steinbeck's own migrants. The Joads, the Hoags, and the Banners all believe in hard work, in community loyalty, in family honor, in land ownership. What differs is not the values, but a belief in their ability to succeed. From the beginning of his career, Steinbeck rejected the axiom that any human, through individual efforts, is guaranteed happiness. Perhaps at some visceral level, what Mitchell and Hartranft found most subversive about Steinbeck's novel is that it radically questions the American faith in the efficacy of work. The wealthy Mitchell, the successful Taylor, and the enterprising Hartranft simply could not comprehend that worthy, energetic people could fail. Hartranft's book ends with a rather touching tribute to his faith; his Hoags, having recently read about their friends in a book (obviously *Grapes*), are heading toward Shafter to rescue them. The recent converts to the gospel of work have become its evangelists.

Sue Sanders was undoubtedly a Kern County phenomenon, the author of a small pamphlet of limited circulation, "The Real Causes of Our Migrant Problem."[35] Hers is a personal testimonial to her equally strong faith in the initiative of migrants. Neither her tract nor Hartranft's received the national attention given the others, but she deserves brief mention in order to clarify one other central tenet in the anti-Steinbeck campaign. What is intriguing about these defenses is their ambivalence toward the migrant. On the one hand, Okies were said to be far more "filthy and unenterprising" than Steinbeck had suggested. Prejudice against the southwesterners ran deep, particularly in the Central Valley. But defenses of the migrants were as common as denunciations, perhaps because, as Mitchell, Hartranft, and Sanders show, these white farm workers, unlike the Mexicans, were perceived as pioneers. They were farmers, only one generation removed from many Oklahomans who had migrated to California in the 1920s. And they exhibited early on that most admirable of American traits, the determination to make a go of it on the last frontier.

In short, Sue Sanders's tract is, like Hartranft's, a hymn to the pioneer spirit of the staunch American farmer. In mid-1939 she launched a one-woman campaign to solve California's migrant problem by proposing that the newcomers go back to Oklahoma to farm their home turf, or what was left of it. First, as she reports in her pamphlet, she toured the camps at Arvin and Shafter and confirmed the fact that these migrants were not, as she feared, shiftless. She writes: "I could be just as proud of these people as I had ever been" (*RCMP*, p. 12). So she traveled to more camps and lifted spirits by promising destitute migrants that she would, like the Wizard of Oz, help them return to the Midwest. She organized "Okie Farm Hours" at the camps and sponsored competitions with "cash prizes for the best talks on the Farm Hour on such subjects as 'How I Would Plant a Forty-Acre Farm in My Home State,' or 'My Methods of Canning Fruits and Vegetables,' or 'How I Would Make a Salad.'" With admirable naïveté, she then went to Oklahoma and asked farmers to give the migrants land. They refused. So she sadly returned to the camps and told her migrant friends that they couldn't go home again—but they could resist relief. "A country can go bankrupt in more ways than one," she concludes. "I'm not sure but that the most fatal way is by wasting the character resources of its citizens. That is exactly what is going on under the system of giving relief. We need a system of helping. Yes, by all means. But not a system that doles out charity and takes away initiative and self respect" (p. 70). Although her solution fizzled, her faith did not.

On the one hand, Sanders's and Hartranft's enthusiastic projects are ridiculous "defenses," just as Steinbeck declared. Hartranft's garden acres helped a tiny proportion of migrants who came to Los Angeles, while Sanders's visions of deportation improved spirits but temporarily. These "solutions" were Band-Aids, and the wound continued to fester. But in company with Mitchell's and Taylor's more searching analyses, these documents share an idealism that is far from ridiculous. It is staunchly American. Theirs is the faith in individual initiative. Theirs is the belief in land ownership, in the virtues of the yeoman farmer. All four demonstrated that any conscientious migrant could make it without clamoring for state aid or collective action. What Sanders discovered as she traveled among the migrants was that "They do so well with what they have. . . . They are clean and neat" and have "ingenuity in getting along with very little."[36] What was inimical to this way of thinking was the idealism of Tom Joad, a call for action as fully American as theirs, but one rooted in group, not individual, initiative. "The Battle Hymn of the Republic," which Steinbeck insisted be printed in full on the end papers of his text, calls for a collective march onward. And Steinbeck's novel marches to the same drummer. Californians attacked *The Grapes of Wrath* so viciously not only because of its language, but also because of its vision of poverty, and its attack on a system that, in fact, many agreed was flawed. These Westerners, proud and independent themselves, lambasted a book that flouted what seemed to them irrefutable American ideals.[37] The idealism of Mitchell, Taylor, Hartranft, and Sanders was, quite simply, irreconcilable with the idealism of Tom Joad.[38]

Notes

1. Tom Cameron, "*The Grapes of Wrath* Author Guards Self from Threats at Moody Gulch," *Los Angeles Times*, July 9, 1939, pp. 1-2.

2. James N. Gregory, *American Exodus: The Dust Bowl Migration and Okie Culture in California* (New York: Oxford University Press, 1989), p. 88.

3. Walter J. Stein, *California and the Dust Bowl Migration* (Westport, Conn.: Greenwood Press, 1973), p. 97. Gregory calls this stage of reaction "the second anti-migrant campaign" (*American Exodus*, p. 88). Since the mid-1930s, valley residents had viewed the Southwestern migrants with increasing disdain, complaining of their poverty and strange ways and, more pointedly, of their need for schooling and health care, which had sent taxes soaring. The crisis in the migrant problem came in 1938, when the second Agricultural Adjustment Act set new controls for California cotton, resulting in fewer acres planted and fewer jobs for migrants.

4. Elsie Robinson, "The Truth About California: Red Ousters Urged as State's Only Solution to End Migrant Evil," *San Francisco Examiner* ["March of Events" section], January 14, 1940, p. 1.

5. See George Thomas Miron, "The Truth About John Steinbeck and the Migrants" (Los Angeles, 1939), p. 4, Bancroft Library, University of California, Berkeley; and John E. Pickett, "Termites Steinbeck and McWilliams," Pacific Rural Press, July 29, 1939.

6. Interview with Richard Criley, June 21, 1990.

7. Similarities between the two are intriguing. Like Steinbeck, Ruth Comfort Mitchell loved dogs, the outdoors, and music, believing that of all the arts, "music is the only art that restores us to ourselves." While still a teenager, she, too, devoted her time to writing; her first poem, "To Los Gatos," was published in the local paper when she was thirteen, and at nineteen she had launched a successful career as a writer for vaudeville. Also like Steinbeck, she refused to see her most popular productions during their New York runs. When Mitchell and her husband built a house in Los Gatos in 1916, she, like Steinbeck, built a study "with the floor space of a postcard" where she wrote for four to twelve hours daily. See Stella Haverland, "Ruth Comfort Mitchell," pp. 122-26, Ruth Comfort Mitchell Papers, San Jose Public Library.

8. *Pittsburgh Dispatch*, August 29, 1909.

9. *Los Angeles Times Sun*, Ruth Comfort Mitchell Papers, San Jose Public Library.

10. Sanborn Young owned the two thousand-acre Riverdale Ranch, a dairy ranch near Fresno in the San Joaquin Valley; he was also part owner of the New Idria quicksilver mine in San Benito County. He took his new wife to his dairy farm after their marriage in 1914; it was during her few years on that farm and in subsequent visits that she gained her perspective on California's labor problems.

A senator from 1924 to 1928 and 1930 to 1932, Young became a prominent voice in state politics, largely through his support of narcotics control. In 1931 he and Mitchell attended an international conference on narcotics in Geneva (May 27-July 13), and nine years later he remained a chief spokesman for this issue, claiming that "California has between 3000 and 6000 narcotics addicts, and addiction to marijuana—Indian hemp—is rapidly increasing" (*Los Gatos Times*, March 10, 1939, p. 3). Less highly publicized was his support for the Associated Farmers and, in all likelihood, for the CCA.

11. Tim Kappel, "Trampling Out the Vineyards—Kern County's Ban on *The Grapes of Wrath*," *California History* 61 (Fall 1982): 212.

12. "Pro America Gives 'Other Side' of Story to Migrant Problems," *Los Gatos Times*, August 25, 1939, p. 1.

13. *Fresno Bee*, a report of a meeting on the status of California farm workers, August 23, 1939.

14. Mitchell repeatedly denied that her novel was written in response to Steinbeck's. In a letter to a friend, JHJ, she says: "Will you please PLEASE emphasize the fact—as you so kindly did once before—that it wasn't an 'answer' or 'challenge to GRAPES OF WRATH,' that it was planned, plotted, named before I read G-O-W, that I yield to no one in my admiration for the genius of John Steinbeck? . . . I sent JS a copy from a 'Los Gatos wild cat to a literary lion,' and he sent me IN DUBIOUS BATTLE, which is my favorite, altho' MICE AND MEN is a gorgeous pattern." (This was probably written May 8, 1940.) Mitchell Papers, Bancroft Library, University of California, Berkeley.

Mitchell's protests notwithstanding, her book played a part in the Associated Farmers' campaign. Mitchell was "preparing to give California's answer as principal speaker at the banquet on December 7 which opens the two-day convention of the Associated Farmers of California at Stockton" ("Ruth Comfort Mitchell to Address Meeting of Associated Farmers," *Los Gatos Times*, November 24, 1939, p. 5). She spoke on "her version of 'The Grapes of Wrath'" ("Noted Authoress Answers Charges of Novel, Defends Migrants," *Stockton Record*, December 8, 1939, pp. 1, 21). (See also "Writer to Discuss Steinbeck Book Before Farmers Meet," *Stockton Record*, December 5, 1939, p. 13.)

Furthermore, records indicate that she did indeed write in response to Steinbeck's text. The first notice of Mitchell's book in the Los Gatos paper is June 30, 1939—nearly three months after publication of *Grapes*. The contract for *Of Human Kindness* was not signed until October 19, 1939, and the book was not published until May 1940. (See also *New Republic 103* [September 2, 1940], p. 305, where Carey McWilliams shows that Mitchell publicly responded to Steinbeck on many occasions.)

15. Philip Bancroft, "The Farmer and the Communists," [San Francisco] *Daily Commercial News*, April 29, 30, 1935.

16. Ruth Comfort Mitchell, *Of Human Kindness* (New York: D. Appleton-Century Co., 1940), p. 5. Hereinafter identified as *OHK*.

17. Miron, "Truth about Steinbeck," p. 21.

18. Labor historian Anne Loftis pointed out this possible parallel to me. Stein, however, sees the "Black Widow" as Steinbeck himself.

19. Bancroft, "Farmer and Communists," p. 7.

20. Frank J. Taylor, "One Story Leads to Another," Frank Taylor Papers, Department of Special Collections, Stanford University Libraries.

21. See "The Flowers and the Bees," *Collier's* (September 9, 1939); "Color from California: More than Half the World's Supply of Flower Seeds Come from This State," *California—Magazine of Pacific Business* (November 1939); "Mr. Gump—of Gump's: A Romance of Treasure Trove in San Francisco," *California—Magazine of Pacific Business* (April 1937); "Soil-less Crops," *Country Home* (September 1936), pp. 18-19; "Mickey Mouse—Merchant: A Personality Sketch of a Native Son and California's No. 1 Merchandiser," *California—Magazine of Pacific Business* (March 1937); "What Has Disney Got that We Haven't," *Commentator* (October 1937). I wish to thank Frank J. Taylor's son, Robert Taylor, for generously showing me scrapbooks of articles written by his father.

22. Frank J. Taylor, "The Merritt System," *Commentator* (November 1938), pp. 84-87. (The article was reprinted in *Reader's Digest* 35 [February 1939], pp. 104-6. Frank Taylor Papers, Department of Special Collections, Stanford University Libraries.)

23. Frank J. Taylor, "Teague of California," *Country Home* (November 1935), p. 36.

24. Taylor, "The Right to Harvest," *Country Gentleman* (October 1937), p. 8.

25. Taylor, "Labor on Wheels," *Country Gentleman* (July 1938), p. 12.

26. Taylor, "The Right to Harvest," p. 8.

27. Taylor, "Green Gold and Tear Gas: What Really Happened in the Salinas Lettuce Strike," *California—Magazine of Pacific Business* (November 1936), p. 18.

28. Taylor, "The Story Behind 'The Many Californias—An Armchair Travelogue'—*R.D.*, January 1952." Frank Taylor Papers, Department of Special Collections, Stanford University Libraries.

29. Taylor, "California's *Grapes of Wrath*," *Forum* 102 (November 1939): p. 232. Hereinafter identified as "CGOW."

30. Stein, *California and Migration*, p. 41.

31. Gregory, *American Exodus*, pp. 19-35.

32. Maud O. Bartlett, "Wrath on Both Sides," *Forum* 103 (January 1940): p. 24.

33. Marshall V. Hartranft, *Grapes of Gladness: California's Refreshing and Inspiring Answer to John Steinbeck's "Grapes of Wrath"* (Los Angeles: DeVorss and Co., 1939), p. 1. Hereinafter identified as *GOG.*

34. John Steven McGroarty, *History of Los Angeles County* (Chicago: American Historical Society, 1923), p. 767.

35. Sue Sanders, "The Real Causes of Our Migrant Problem" (1940). Herein identified as *RCMP.* I wish to thank John Walden of the Kern County Library for his help with material relating to Sue Sanders and the film "The Plums of Plenty" (see below).

36. Mae Saunders, "Migrants Regard Sue Sanders as True Friend," *Bakersfield Californian*, October 21, 1939, pp. 12, 19.

37. One other response to *Grapes* should be mentioned, a short film, now lost, entitled "The Plums of Plenty." Perhaps because of its catchy title, this work is often referred to but seldom identified. In "Steinbeck and the Migrants: *A Study of The Grapes of Wrath*," an M.A. thesis written by John Schamberger at the University of Colorado in 1960, the film's history is summarized: "Emory Gay Hoffman, the manager of the Kern County Chamber of Commerce at the time of publication of *The Grapes of Wrath*, wrote a short story entitled 'Plums of Plenty' in answer to Steinbeck's novel. According to Hoffman, the six-thousand-word draft of 'Plums of Plenty' was lost which precluded its publication. However, a 'movie short' was published from the notes and . . . much of the colored motion picture was used by the old Kern County Chamber of Commerce and 'News of the Day,' a Movie Tone release. Hoffman stated that William B. Camp had sponsored the authorship of his book and the motion picture" (pp. 64-65).

38. On February 11, 1952, Steinbeck gave an interview for the Voice of America, and he was asked if he saw "any changes in the conditions since the time that you were there [in the Dust Bowl] during the research for your novel?" Steinbeck's reply provides a fitting footnote to *Grapes* and to this article: "Oh yes. I found a great many changes. . . . When I wrote *The Grapes of Wrath* I was filled naturally with certain anger and certain anger at people who were doing injustices to other people, or so I thought. I realize now that everyone was caught in the same trap." In California, the migrants "met a people who were terrified, for number one, of the depression and were horrified at the idea that great numbers of indigent people were being poured on them, to be taken care of. They could only be taken care of by taxation, taxes were already high and there wasn't much money about. They reacted perfectly normally, they became angry. When you become angry you fight what you are angry at. They were angry at these newcomers. Gradually through government agency, through the work of private citizens, agencies were set up to take care of these situations and only then did the anger begin to decrease. So when the anger decreased these two sides, these two groups, were able to get to know each other and they found they didn't dislike each other at all."

Steinbeck's "Self-Characters" as 1930s Underdogs

Warren G. French

John Steinbeck's agent, Elizabeth Otis, greeted a letter from the author, dated 26 April 1957, as "one of the most impressive letters that you or anyone else has ever written" (qtd. in Benson 811). Steinbeck considered this letter important enough to send a duplicate copy to his friend and advisor, Chase Horton, who was assisting him with his research on Sir Thomas Malory in connection with Steinbeck's long-planned modernization of Malory's *Morte d'Arthur*. In this letter, he explains his concept of a "spokesman" in a work of fiction, who can be called a "self-character," a central figure with whom the novelist, perhaps unconsciously, identifies and into whom "he puts not only what he thinks he is, but what he hopes to be. You will find one in every one of my books and in the novels of everyone I can remember" (*TAKA* 303-5). Since Steinbeck's main purpose in this letter was to identify Malory's Sir Lancelot as the author's "self-character," he mentions no specific examples from his own writings, but adds: "I suppose my own symbol character has my dream wish of wisdom and acceptance." He thus expresses the importance of recognizing that his "self-characters" do not necessarily share his experiences as thinly disguised self-portraits like Thomas Wolfe's Eugene Gant and Jack Kerouac's Jean Duluoz. In the same letter he mentions Ernest Hemingway as a novelist whose "self-characters" were "most simple and near the surface."

Despite the importance of these "self-characters" to understanding the "dream wish" underlying Steinbeck's fiction, little effort has been made to identify them. The importance, however, of understanding Steinbeck's sense of personal involvement in his fiction has been dramatically disclosed in another pair of self-searching letters to his editor/publisher, Pascal Covici, and his agent, Elizabeth Otis, written in 1938 and published, apparently with his consent, in 1946 in a revised edition of Covici's anthology *The Portable Steinbeck*. Explaining his reasons for destroying the manuscript of an eagerly awaited novel tentatively titled "L'Affaire Lettuceberg," Steinbeck lamented the consequences that his impulsive action might have for Covici's nearly bankrupt firm; he justified his action by explaining, "My whole work drive has been aimed at making people understand each other and then I deliberately write this book, the aim of which is to cause hatred through partial understanding" (qtd. in Benson 376). He found the manuscript unsuitable for publication because he saw himself as a writer with a mission—if not always a pleasant one for readers—to try to open closed eyes and closed minds to a better understanding of the conflicting forces at war in human nature. As he put this conception in a letter to his friend George Albee in 1935, when he was writing *In Dubious Battle*, "man hates something in himself. He has been able to defeat every natural obstacle but himself" (*SLL* 98). Steinbeck's aim, in short, was to connect with his readers through broader understanding of self.

That wish to connect is, perhaps, most clearly evident in three novels that solidified Steinbeck's reputation: *Tortilla Flat* (1935), *In Dubious Battle* (1936), and *Of Mice and Men* (1937). Each is an identifiable stage in the development of Steinbeck's "self-characters" that has been largely overlooked by critics because attention has focused on the dramatic events of the individual novels rather than inter-relationships between and among these three powerful stories produced in such rapid succession. *Tortilla Flat* is usually admired for its quaint local color but often dismissed as an escapist idyll of the devil-may-care paisanos' irresponsible lives and deaths. *In Dubious Battle* has been praised as America's greatest fictional depiction of a workers' strike and its potentially disastrous consequences, while *Of Mice and Men* is lauded as a timeless evocation of the poignant tragedy of nature's misfits. But all have also been criticized for not proposing solutions for the tragic problems that they dramatize, despite Steinbeck's frequent protests that he is writing *novels* not tracts. When I was asked to write the introduction to *In Dubious Battle* for the much-needed Penguin Twentieth

Century Classics collected edition of Steinbeck's work, I began to reconsider it in conjunction with its predecessor and successor.

Looking at *Tortilla Flat* as something more than a tragicomic chronicle of a mock Arthurian roundtable on the edge of a sleepy California city, I perceived the novel as rather the downbeat story of Danny trapped between the contending forces of freedom in the wild woods behind his house and subservience to authority in the town. From the time that he is released from jail, where he has been incarcerated for antisocial behavior, inherits two houses, and assumes a respectable position in the community until the night he makes an unsuccessful attempt to return to life in the woods and struggles with an unidentified "Enemy" (who is the only one worthy of him), Danny is caught between the twin urges for peaceful prosperity and unregulated freedom. The mysterious foe on the night of that wild party is the pressure from the "civilized" community that was beginning to weigh heavily on Steinbeck himself. Danny is a creature of the wild whom society does not need to destroy because he destroys himself by seeking to change his nature. The novel is his eulogy.

Looked at from the perspective that *Tortilla Flat* provides, *In Dubious Battle* can be perceived as Jim Nolan's eulogy. Often, however, the novel has been read as dated social history, a book that both chronicles an apple-pickers' strike against heavy odds and highlights an unresolved debate between a labor organizer (Mac) and the humanitarian Doc Burton, who provides essential medical aid to the strikers, about the difference between men acting on their own and melding together in an organized and directed group. The prominence of this debate over Steinbeck's "phalanx" or group man theories led the prolific Yale critic Harold Bloom to claim, in 1987, that at its half-century mark, the novel is "now quite certainly a period piece, . . . of more interest to social historians than to literary critics" (1).

The difficulty about this judgment is that it turns the novel into not just a tract, but a pointless one, since the dispute between the theorists is never resolved and their contribution to the immediate action is never examined as part of the closure—the narrative ends abruptly with Jim Nolan's grotesque death after assuming a leadership role for which he was not ready. The movement of the narrative is relentlessly focused upon Jim from the moment when, like Danny in *Tortilla Flat*, he is released from jail, where he had been confined on trumped-up charges; to when he decides to join Mac's Party, which is organizing the local strike; to his death a few days later in that Party's service. His eulogy is a timeless account of impetuous youthful ambition and noble intentions gone amok in an exploitative world.

Of Mice and Men ends also with the death of a principal character and may also be viewed as a eulogy for another victim whose fate is inevitable. The final emphasis in this novel, however, is not on the inescapable demise of the physically powerful Lennie, who does not have the mental ability to control his great strength, but on George, a physically less powerful but more thoughtful and visionary individual in control of his actions, but unable to protect Lennie, around whom he has built a dream world from an unpleasantly real world that Lennie cannot understand or control. When George must finally kill Lennie himself quickly to protect him from a torturously cruel death at the hands of an enraged lynch mob, he must also destroy his own dream. His is a kind of living death, since he has been forced to destroy what had made his life worthwhile.

All three of these relatively short novels move toward inexorable conclusions that are parallel variations on the tragic failure of schemes that "gang aft agley," in the words of Scottish poet Robert Burns (from whom Steinbeck takes the title *Of Mice and Men*). Social outcasts all, they are on their way to inevitable dooms, though none of the "plans" around which the novels are built could be considered among the "best laid." All three portray the outcome of aspirations that exceed one's potential. The trio can be most cogently categorized as *Bildungsroman* ("education novels") that end disastrously with the deaths of dreams as a result of impulsive behavior that robbed key characters of constraints that organized society demanded.

In *John Steinbeck's Fiction Revisited*, I summed up the argument for treating these three interrelated narratives as a trilogy of "underdogs," those at the bottom of society and disappearing even below there: "although there is no evidence that Steinbeck had any conscious intention of shaping these three . . . into a kind of ironic trilogy about men's fate, viewed jointly as a phase in his development, they provide a vision of three principal forces responsible for the 'going under' of one who is not able in the words of Sir Henry Morgan in Steinbeck's first published novel, *Cup of Gold*, to 'split' before 'civilization'" (72). The term "underdogs" here both borrows from and connects the novels with the English translation of the Mexican novelist Manuel Azuela's harrowing novel about his country's dispossessed, *Los de Abajo* (literally "Those from Below")—although I have found no evidence that Steinbeck was familiar with the novel.

But what does the steadily downbeat viewpoint of this trilogy have to do with Danny, Jim and George as Steinbeck's "self-characters" or alter egos? The author was neither an untamable creature of the vanishing woods, nor an aspiring labor leader, nor an itinerant field hand with an unworkable dream. Yet despite his cultured, middle-class difference from his creations, he shared with the trio dreams of what they hoped to become, as he supposed his "symbol characters" would. All three dream of a moderate, comfortable lifestyle that they could share with others who need help. At the time each story unfolds—during the post World War I boom in *Tortilla Flat* and during the Depression—Danny, Jim and George dream of establishing communities that will provide them opportunities for leadership benefiting others; but they have no sound, practical ideas of how to improve their situations in communities that threaten their dreams. By implication Steinbeck reflects a general discontentment with the communities he knew well; but he also projects a vision of a better society in the familiar communities of Monterey and San Jose.

He was very reticent during the 1930s to discuss details of his own life in interviews, which he usually shunned. He was more concerned that outsiders would snoop into his personal problems or criticize his dreams than that they would recognize his characters' problems and share in his search to improve the community. If they could identify with the frustrations of Danny, Jim and George as Steinbeck dramatized them, others might be moved to share his self-searching dissatisfactions with society that could lead to a desire to do something. Even so, one wonders how Steinbeck could continue to identify his dreams with those of his socially marginal characters once his work began to attract profitable attention. Steinbeck's sympathetic relationship to Danny, Jim and George must be viewed in relation to his own insecure situation at the time he was writing the novels and not the time of their subsequent publication, as his situation changed rapidly and materially with the publicity surrounding each.

The three books appeared in rapid succession from 1935 to 1937. By the time he began "Something That Happened," as *Of Mice and Men* was originally titled, he was still plagued by the same doubts and fears with which he was endowing his characters. Although he was not particularly pleased to receive four thousand dollars for the film rights to *Tortilla Flat*, he took the money for government bonds "for the lean years that he was sure were ahead" (Benson 323). Even after he moved into his new home in Los Gatos in July 1936, he mused in his ledger that "for the moment now the financial burdens have been removed. But it is not permanent. I was not meant for success" (qtd. in Benson 330). Only after the success of *Of Mice and Men* as both a novel and a play did Steinbeck feel that his fortunes had turned around, and even then, as Benson observes, he continued to be haunted by the conviction that his success was only a temporary fluke (331)—as the journals kept while he wrote *The Grapes of Wrath* testify. Steinbeck could not easily overcome the underdog syndrome that made him a success.

In short, to recognize the significance of Danny, Jim and George as Steinbeck's "self-characters" is to see why these novels are not "dated" social protest tracts. As Steinbeck explained in the letter to aspiring fellow novelist George Albee in January 1935, "I'm not interested in ranting about justice and oppression, mere outcroppings which indicate the condition. But man hates something in himself. He has been able to defeat every natural obstacle but himself he cannot win over unless he kills every individual" (*SLL* 98). The importance of these three novels lies in Steinbeck's deep psychic relationship with his characters.

His writing about underdogs did not end with this trilogy and its doomed characters any more then did the conditions which inspired them. His next novel focuses even more powerfully and memorably on the lonely figure of a besieged social outcast.

When we first meet Tom Joad in the second chapter of *The Grapes of Wrath*, he has been recently released from jail—like Danny and Jim Nolan. But Tom has not served time for drunken rowdiness like Danny or for ill-timed curiosity like Jim; he was convicted for murder, albeit in self-defense, and he has been released early for good behavior. Yet still he is a killer, and as the novel nears its end, he will kill again in momentarily maddened retaliation for the killing of his mentor and friend Jim Casy, a former preacher turned labor organizer.

The Grapes of Wrath, however, does not end as another tragedy of the bold fighter against overwhelming odds, although both Tom and Jim Casy are certainly underdogs. There is a striking difference between this epic and its three predecessors, all narrowly focused narratives. This novel does not rush readers through a downward movement toward defeat, but interrupts the account of the tribulations of the Joad family with panoramic reflections on past and present situations affecting their lives. And this novel ends with the central character momentarily triumphant and optimistic about his own future role and improvement of his people's situation. Here Steinbeck employs a technique that Charles Dickens used a century earlier in *Hard Times* (which would certainly also be an apt, though less stirring title for Steinbeck's own novel) by leaving the future disposition of his characters in the hands of his readers. The readers' response was a chorus of international praise, though some social activists found the ending too romantic while many fellow Californians condemned it and made threats even against the author's life.

How did this change come about, from the pessimistic conclusions of the "underdogs" trilogy to the inspiring feeling that troubled situations can be improved? Such questions are not easily answered, unless the writer explains his intentions publicly, as Steinbeck was not inclined to do, and the answer on this occasion is even more complicated because of missing evidence.

Between *Of Mice and Men*, in which the last words are those of the sadistic fascist Carlson, who looks at the psychopathic Curley and asks, "Now what the hell ya suppose is eat'in them two guys"—referring to Slim leading away the inconsolable George—and the controversial tableau at the end of the *The Grapes of Wrath*, in which Rose of Sharon Joad offers her breast milk to an old man, there is a missing link in the development of Steinbeck's attitudes as projected through his "self-characters." Perhaps "L'Affaire Lettuceberg," a searing attack on his home town of Salinas, included an important "self-character" who would have been very different from his earlier oppressed "underdogs." A possible clue to the nature of this character might be found in "The Time the Wolves Ate the Vice Principal," a short story which appeared after World War II in the first issue of *'47, The Magazine of the Year.* In this gruesome tale, an overworked public servant from the Salinas High School is coming home exhausted late one night when a pack of hungry wolves falls upon him, as the town sleeps serenely on—another blameless individual like Jim Nolan and George Milton doomed by an unfeeling community and another offshoot of the defeatist vision that shaped the underdog novels.

It can be argued, however, that whatever Steinbeck's reasons for providing this unflattering picture of his home town to a new magazine attempting (unsuccessfully) to establish itself, after completing "L'Affaire Lettuceberg," he had undergone, if only temporarily, the same kind of spiritual change that he portrays through Casy and especially Tom Joad. Both the author and the self-character experience a painful ordeal that ultimately ends not destroying them, but enabling them to achieve a vision that transcends self-indulgent action. I use the term "self-indulgent" here because in devising "L'Affaire Lettuceberg," Steinbeck had, from his own account to his agent and editor, succumbed to a personal pique of the kind that made the Joads put the "fambly fust" without pondering whether hope for survival might depend upon collective action.

While Steinbeck had many times experienced defeat and despair trying to establish himself as a writer, he had not had to face the devastating despair experienced by the Joads and other homeless migrants. Since in *The Grapes of Wrath* he also speaks—even lectures—threateningly in his own voice for the first time in his fiction, he seems distanced from the main action, a troubled observer who feels intense sympathy for his agonized characters but in no way identified with them. He's not writing from his own experience except as a sympathetic observer.

In creating the central spokesman, however, he needed to create a character capable of experiencing the same kind of inspirational change that he had when he realized that he must destroy "L'Affaire Lettuceberg." As a result of Casy's vision, although Casy has insisted he is no longer a preacher, Tom realizes that he must fight for all his people, the underdogs, not just his family; but he realizes also that he must avoid Casy's untimely fate if he is to succeed in his mission. In Tom's climactic conversation with Ma Joad, he explains Steinbeck's enlightened realization that violence is no longer the most effective method of working for his people. Just as Steinbeck refused to join many others seeking a better society by battling at the barricades and chose rather to share his message with a wider audience through his writing, so Tom realizes that he must become an inspiring voice speaking out of the darkness, serving his people unperceived, unrecognized: "I'll be all aroun' in the dark," he tells Ma. "I'll be ever'where—wherever you look" (572). In this much admired passage, Steinbeck has Tom Joad explain what Steinbeck hoped to achieve through writing *The Grapes of Wrath*. He had done an about-face, writing here with a new inspiration and hopefulness replacing the angry despair of the earlier underdog novels. He was taking a great risk and staking his own and his backers' futures on a new vision.

Remarkably, the relationship between the author and the "self-character" in this novel is most unusual. When Tom Joad describes himself as "a voice in the dark," he depicts precisely the author's own long-sought role that he achieved through his novel. He has created a "self-character," who indeed shares his "dream wish of wisdom and acceptance." *The Grapes of Wrath* provides one of those rare, illuminating occasions when a dream comes true. Steinbeck did not extend his trilogy of the underdogs into a tetralogy. The underdog here has become a top dog.

It was risky indeed to contemplate such an outcome for an untested work upon which so much depended for author and publisher; but Steinbeck's faith in his vision during the demanding months of intense writing conveyed the message that he wished: "I hope to God it's good," were the last words he wrote in the journal he kept while writing the novel. Unlike many such high hopes, this one was fulfilled. He had become what he had hoped to be.

Afterglow

Although Steinbeck's cycle of underdog fiction was predominantly tragic in concept and cautionary in tone—even *The Grapes of Wrath* ends equivocally with a voice crying out in the wilderness and a hopeful gesture rather than any promising solution for the migrants' problems—it has generally been overlooked that the cycle did not end until Steinbeck ventured into the new medium of film with one of the most undeservedly obscure of his creative works, *The Forgotten Village.* This short film ends not with a voice coming out of the dark but rather with the proud cry of a young Mexican, shouting as he marches straight toward Mexico City determined to become a doctor who will bring new hope and health to his often oppressed people. "I am Juan Diego," the boy cries.

A young Mexican boy may seem a strange "self-character" for Steinbeck, but I feel that if Steinbeck had been a young Mexican boy, he would have been capable of such a defiant gesture. Juan Diego is as much the author's "self-character" as is Jody Tiflin in his memorable *The Red Pony* stories. By telling Juan Diego's story, he ended a decade of uncertainties as he sought to realize his artistic and humanitarian ambitions on the highest possible, positive note.

Works Cited

Benson, Jackson. *The True Adventures of John Steinbeck, Writer.* New York: Viking, 1984.

Covici, Pascal, ed. *The Portable Steinbeck.* Enlarged Edition. New York: Viking, 1946.

French, Warren. Introduction. *In Dubious Battle.* John Steinbeck. New York: Penguin, 1992.

_____. *John Steinbeck's Fiction Revisited.* New York: Twayne, 1994.

Steinbeck, John. *The Acts of King Arthur and His Noble Knights.* Ed. Chase Horton. New York: Farrar, Straus, and Giroux, 1976.

_____. *Cup of Gold.* 1929. New York: Penguin, 1995.

_____. *In Dubious Battle.* 1936. New York: Penguin, 1992.

_____. *The Forgotten Village.* New York: Viking, 1941.

_____. *The Grapes of Wrath.* 1939. New York: Penguin, 1992.

_____. *Of Mice and Men.* 1937. New York: Penguin, 1994.

_____. *Steinbeck: A Life in Letters.* 1975. Eds. Elaine Steinbeck and Robert Wallsten. New York: Viking, 1989.

_____. "The Time the Wolves Ate the Vice-Principal." *'47, The Magazine of the Year,* Mar. 1947: 26-27. Rpt. in *The Steinbeck Newsletter* 9.1 (1995): 10.

_____. *Tortilla Flat.* 1935. New York: Penguin, 1997.

_____. *Working Days: The Journals of* The Grapes of Wrath, *1938-1941.* Ed. Robert DeMott. New York: Viking, 1989.

John Steinbeck and Ed Ricketts:
Understanding Life in the Great Tide Pool_____
James C. Kelley

One of the most important social changes in these last decades of the twentieth century is, surely, the "greening" of the world population. The widespread concern for the environment and the effect of this concern on the political process and on the amount of money we are devoting to understanding human environmental impacts and reversing their effects are unprecedented in human history. This concern may be a natural response by an organism to environmental change. The Gaia Hypothesis (Lovelock 1972, 215) predicts this sort of response as organisms work to regulate their environment to make it more habitable (such a regulatory effort presumably occurs even if the uninhabitable features are of their own making). To some degree, our environmental awareness must be due to the Apollo space program, which allowed us, for the first time, to see our little water planet from the outside. To some less obvious but no less profound degree, the awareness may have been conditioned by John Steinbeck, who gave expression to Ed Ricketts's philosophical thoughts. These thoughts contain all of the primary elements of what "New Age" writers, thinking they have found something new and revolutionary, call "deep ecology." In fact, the thinking by Steinbeck and Ricketts on the subject is considerably more sophisticated than much of the recent work. This chapter will explore some of these ideas and how they may condition environmental concern.

Ecological Thinking, Rational Understanding
Ricketts's mentor, W. C. Allee, traces the origins of ecology to Empedocles, Aristotle, and Theophrastus but recognizes the development of the field in its modern form as beginning with the use of the name (*Oekologie*, or oecology) by Haeckel in 1869 (Allee et al. 34).

The field experienced a rapid expansion and sophistication in the first three decades of this century, during which both Allee himself and William Emerson Ritter were major contributors. The Gaia concept is, of course, more recent. The term was introduced by Lovelock in 1972 (579), but in 1989 (215) he traced its origins to the work of the remarkable Scottish geologist James Hutton in 1788 (Hutton 209-304).

John Steinbeck was certainly interested in the subject we now call ecology at least from his Stanford years; in 1923, he and his sister Mary took summer session courses in marine biology at the Hopkins Marine Station in Pacific Grove. It was a short walk down from the Eleventh Street house to the tide pools between Lover's Point and Cabrillo Point (China Point), which they visited often as children. The instructor in his summer biology course, Charles Vincent Taylor, was a doctoral candidate at Berkeley, a student of Charles Kofoid, and heavily influenced by the work of William Emerson Ritter, former chairman of the Zoology Department and, in 1911, founding director of Scripps Institution of Oceanography (Benson 1984, 240). As chair, Ritter had taught the University of California's summer marine biology course on the Hopkins property in 1892 (Ritter 1912, 148). Ritter used the "superorganism" model for what we would today call an ecosystem. This model worked well for Steinbeck in the form of the "phalanx" concept for "group man," prominent in *In Dubious Battle*, "The Leader of the People," and *The Grapes of Wrath* (Astro 1973, 61).

When John met Ed Ricketts in 1930, Ed was fresh from the powerful influence of Warder Clyde Allee at the University of Chicago. Allee wrote extensively on group behavior among animals and was interested in the ways in which the group modifies, for example, the feeding or reproductive behaviors of its individual members. Allee developed some of the fundamental principles of the discipline of ecology and certainly was one of the most important contributors to the rapid development of the field in the early decades of this century. He was a powerful personal figure, and the University of Chicago, at the time, was a major force in both ecology and marine biology through his efforts and those of the pioneering and prolific invertebrate zoologist Libbie Hyman.

A third perspective, although not strictly ecological and still in its formative stage, was provided by the young Joseph Campbell, Ed's neighbor on Fourth Street in Pacific Grove and a regular visitor to Ed's lab in 1932. Joe Campbell was, at the time, exploring both the common denominators of the mythologies of the world's peoples and also, after his time in Germany with Carl Jung, the needs of our "collective unconscious" and how and why we develop our mythologies. Joe was infatuated with Carol Henning Steinbeck, and it was Carol who introduced Joe, John, and Ed to the often allegorical poetry of Robinson Jeffers. Jeffers, by then living in Carmel, greatly influenced all three (Larsen and Larsen 179).

The mix of ecological and mythological concepts provides a philosophical basis that pervades much of Steinbeck's work from at least *Tortilla Flat* (1935) to *The Log from the Sea of Cortez* (1951). The ecological treatment of intertidal communities was the significant innovation of *Between Pacific Tides*, by Ricketts and Jack Calvin, and the principle of the interconnectedness of everything is an essential part of Joseph Campbell's later work. He was fascinated by the notion that all humans share a set of primitive ideas, the *Elementargedanken* of German anthropologist Adolf Bastian. In Campbell's analysis these primitive ideas may be born of Jung's collective unconscious (*Masks of God* 45). In this formulation the mythological work yields a basically ecological explanation (i.e., one of the ways in which our species adapts to its environment is by explaining the wonders of the world through our mythology—or through our science).

Transcendent Understanding, "Breaking Through"

John was fascinated with Ed's scientific temperament. In a radio script interview on his advocacy on behalf of the Okies in *The Grapes of Wrath*, the novelist said that "the only heroes left are the scientists and the poor" (Benson 1984, 402). He admired Ed's objectivity and his ability to think nonteleologically, to observe natural phenomena for excruciatingly long periods without drawing conclusions as to the causes of the observed behaviors. The story of Hazel and the stinkbugs in *Cannery Row* provides the ultimate display of nonteleological irony to illustrate this point:

> [When Hazel, observing typical stinkbug behavior, asks] "Well, what they got their asses up in the air for?" . . .
> "I think they're praying," said Doc.
> "What!" Hazel was shocked.
> "The remarkable thing," said Doc, "isn't that they put their tails up in the air—the really remarkable thing is that we find it remarkable. We can only use ourselves as yardsticks. If we did something as inexplicable and strange we'd probably be praying—so maybe they're praying."
> "Let's get the hell out of here," said Hazel. (*CR* 147-48)

Ed Ricketts's ability to study the phenomenon under investigation as it is, without leaping to causal conclusions, is certainly an element of good science, but it led Ed to seek another kind of transcendence. Ed was fond of advocating what he called getting the "*toto* picture," the kind of holistic, synthetic thinking that is essential in ecology (Hedgpeth 1978, pt. 2, 26). It was the pursuit of this kind of systemic understanding that led Ed to develop the philosophy of "breaking through." The idea of breaking through implies the existence of a kind of understanding that goes beyond anything possible by scientific observation and deductive reasoning alone. I will refer to this kind of understanding as *transcendent understanding*.

Ed attributes the terminology to Robinson Jeffers in "Roan Stallion":

Humanity is the mould to break away from, the crust to
   break through, the coal to break into fire,
The atom to be split.
      Tragedy that breaks man's face and a white fire flies
   out of it; vision that fools him
Out of his limits, desire that fools him out of his limits,
   unnatural crime, inhuman science,
Slit eyes in the mask; wild loves that leap over the walls of
   nature, *the wild fence-vaulter science,*
Useless intelligence of far stars, dim knowledge of the
   spinning demons that make an atom,
These break, these pierce, these deify, praising their God
   shrilly with fierce voices: not in a man's shape
He approves the praise, he that walks lightning-naked on
   the Pacific, that laces the suns with planets
The heart of the atom with electrons: what is humanity in
   this cosmos? For him, the last
Least taint of a trace in the dregs of the solution; for itself,
   the mould to break away from, the coal
To break into fire, the atom to be split.
                    (Jeffers 140 [emphasis added])

It should be clear from the emphasized phrase, in this part of the poem, that Jeffers expects science itself to break through. In his 1938 poem, "The Purse-Seine," in a mode very much like Ricketts's own, Jeffers breaks through from the description of sardine fishing to see the sardines in a seine net as symbolic of humans pressed together in cities, dependent on one another and the artificial life support systems that keep them trapped in the urban environment (Jeffers 588).

In another use of the phrase, Ed's professor W. C. Allee, in chapter 11 of *Cooperation Among Animals* entitled "The Peck Order and International Relations," says that the biologist must "break through" the confines of his discipline and try to understand how his knowledge may be applied to international relations. He writes:

> It may have come as a surprise to some that there is evidence from modern experimental studies in group biology that bears on international problems. The biological information at hand is incomplete and must be used with caution, but the urgency of the situation [the world political disarray after World War I] has seemed to me to necessitate breaking through the reticence of the research biologist to set forth, and even to summarize briefly, some of the human implications growing out of recent work with animal aggregations. (202)

If Ed did not take the phrase from Allee, certainly he and John followed the advice with some enthusiasm. Interestingly, Joseph Campbell uses the same phrase in *The Masks of God* (4).

The notion of breaking through, especially when it follows a long period of rational contemplation, is a remarkably Zen idea. The achievement of "satori" was discussed in Zen texts owned by Steinbeck and Ricketts (DeMott 1984, 69 and 108), particularly D. T. Suzuki's *Essays in Zen Buddhism*, which we know was in Ed's library at the lab, as were Lao Tze's *Tao teh Ching* and the Taoist poetry of Li Po in S. Obata's *The Works of Li-Po* (Hedgpeth 1978, pt. 2, 23). These works reverberate with various versions of the phrase "the Tao which can be Tao-ed is not the real Tao." In Lionel Giles's 1905 translation, Lao Tze says, "The Tao which can be expressed in words is not the eternal Tao" (5). In Ed's essay "The Philosophy of Breaking Through," he uses the first translation, which is that of Dwight Goddard. Hedgpeth says that Ed had the 1919 edition in his library and further that "John Steinbeck often looked through Ed's books; and if John read Lao Tse, it was probably Ed's copy. My first sight of John Steinbeck was as he was standing beside a bookshelf in Ed's place with a book in his hand" (Hedgpeth 1978, pt. 2, 23). In the essay Ed focuses on the enlightenment achieved after a long struggle, a theme that spans the cultural range from the *Tao teh Ching* to the Grail Romance (*Masks of God* 197) and that is central to the Judaeo-Christian tradition from the Exodus to the Passion and Resurrection of Jesus Christ.

In "About Ed Ricketts," Steinbeck says of Ed, "He was walled off a little, so that he worked at his philosophy of 'breaking through,' of coming out through the back of the mirror into some kind of reality which would make the world seem dreamlike. This thought obsessed him" (*LSC* lxii).

Visceral Understanding

We have seen an awareness of at least two levels of understanding that were of interest to Steinbeck and Ricketts: the empirical scientific understanding that comes from studying the natural world and a transcendent understanding achieved by breaking through. The second is clearly more than an inductive synthesis from observational results. The full realization of the idea requires transcendence in the mystical sense used in Zen Buddhism. In addition to these two forms, there is a third that I will call visceral understanding. This is an intuitive and innate understanding of the world. Steinbeck used the term "racial memory," and it is clear from the pantheistic exploration of the oneness of man and nature in *To a God Unknown* that John came to this notion independently of Ed, although by the time the novel was published in 1933 it showed Ed's influence (Astro 1973, 61-88). Beginning with Webster Street's unfinished play *The Green Lady*, which already took this pantheistic view, John built on the idea with such passages as "There was a curious femaleness about the interlacing boughs and twigs, about the long green cavern cut by the river through the trees." To take another example, in Joseph Wayne's orgasmic experience on the land: "He stamped his feet into the soft earth. Then the exultance grew to be a sharp pain of desire that ran through his body in a hot river. He flung himself face downward on the grass and pressed his cheek against the wet stems. His fingers gripped the wet grass and tore it out, and gripped again. His thighs beat heavily on the earth" (*TGU* 11). The catharsis appears in Joseph's dying words "I am the land, and I am the rain. The grass will grow out of me in a little while" (*TGU* 261).

Ed Ricketts came to a different but sympathetic idea from his marine work. In his essay "The Tide," he says: "We have to envision the concept of the collective pattern associationally involved in instinct, to get an inkling of the force behind the lunar rhythm so deeply rooted, and so obviously and often present in marine animals and even in higher animals and man" (Hedgpeth 1978, pt. 2, 64). Consider Ed's statement, in the same essay, discussing the notion proposed by George Darwin (son of Charles Darwin) that earlier in earth history the tides were much stronger:

It is nevertheless far-fetched to attribute the lunar rhythm status actually observable in breeding animals of the tide controlled breeding habits of the California grunion, of the Polynesian palolo worm, of Nereis, of Amphineura, etc., wherein whole collections of animals act as one individual responding to a natural phenomenon, to the present fairly weak tidal forces only, or to coincidence. There is tied up to the most primitive and powerful social (collective) instinct, a rhythm "memory" which effects everything and which in the past was probably far more potent than it is now. (Hedgpeth 1978, pt. 2, 64)

John's rewritten version in *Sea of Cortez* reads:

It would seem far-fetched to attribute the strong lunar effects actually observable in breeding animals to the present fairly weak tidal forces only, or to coincidence. There is tied up to the most primitive and powerful racial or collective instinct a rhythm sense or "memory" which affects everything and which in the past was probably more potent than it is now. It would at least be more plausible to attribute these profound effects to devastating and instinct-searing tidal influences active during the formative times of the early race history of organisms; and whether or not any mechanism has been discovered or is discoverable to carry on this imprint through the germ plasms, the fact remains that the imprint is there. The imprint is in us and in Sparky and in the ship's master, in the palolo worm, in mussel worms, in chitons, and in the menstrual cycle of women. (*SOC* 34)

The notion that humans and all living things share some sort of common animus, that we are all interconnected spiritually, is a central theme of the "new" deep ecology. The notions of visceral understanding pervade modern environmentalist, animal welfare, and feminist writing. An interesting example was provided in 1990 when Adrienne Zihlman of the University of California at Santa Cruz and Mary Ellen Morbeck of the University of Arizona organized a meeting on female primatology. They closed the meeting to men on the grounds that "women scientists think differently about those topics than men do— possibly even understanding them better because they are women" (Dusheck 1494). The argument is commonly heard that one cannot really understand what it is like to be black, or gay, or female, for example, unless one is black, or gay, or female. This sort of alleged special knowledge could be gained through experiential learning, but clearly in the female primatology case it is said to be an example of visceral understanding.

One of the tenets of the "New Age" sense of visceral understanding is that it is a shared understanding of the interconnectedness of everything, especially humans, with everything else in the universe. Fritjof Capra, in 1991, writes:

a very useful distinction has emerged during the past two decades, the distinction between deep ecology and shallow ecology. In shallow ecology, human beings are put above nature or outside nature, and, of course, this perspective goes with the domination of nature. Value is seen as residing in human beings; nature is given merely use value, or instrumental value. Deep ecologists see human beings as an intrinsic part of nature, as merely a special strand in the fabric of life. (Capra and Steindl-Rast 85)

But half a century earlier John and Ed wrote:

> "Let's go wide open. Let's see what we see, record what we find, and not fool ourselves with conventional scientific strictures. We could not observe a completely objective *Sea of Cortez* anyway, for in that lonely and uninhabited Gulf our boat and ourselves would change it the moment we entered. . . . Let us go," we said, "into the Sea of Cortez, realizing that we become forever a part of it, that our rubber boots slogging through a flat of eelgrass, that the rocks we turn over in a tide pool, make us truly and permanently a factor in the ecology of the region. We shall take something away from it, but we shall leave something too." (*SOC* 3)

Steinbeck and Ricketts explore other manifestations of this sort of visceral understanding. In the second chapter of *Sea of Cortez*, there is a long discussion about boats and how people, especially men, rapped three times on the hulls of boats on display at Macy's in New York. This is almost certainly John's observation, but of this almost instinctive behavior they write:

> Can this have been an unconscious testing of hulls? . . . How deep this thing must be, the giver and the receiver again; the boat designed through millenniums of trial and error by human consciousness, the boat which has no counterpart in nature unless it be a dry leaf fallen by accident in a stream. And Man receiving back from Boat a warping of his psyche so that the sight of a boat riding in the water clenches a fist of emotion in his chest. . . . This is not mysticism, but identification; man, building his greatest and most personal of all tools, has in turn received a boat-shaped mind, and a boat, a man-shaped soul. His spirit and the tendrils of his feeling are so deep in a boat that the identification is complete. (*SOC* 15)

In another form, visceral understanding may be manifested in group behavior of animals and humans, when, as Ed says in the above lines from "The Tide," "whole collections of animals act as one individual responding to a natural phenomenon." This idea of course pervades Steinbeck's novels and has been explored at length by Richard Astro (1973, 61), where John's formulation is the phalanx concept.

A theme central to the phalanx concept is the notion that the collection of individuals in an ecosystem, a group, or as a superorganism, exhibits a purpose, a personality, and an energy transcending that of the individuals who make up the superorganism. The superorganism, like a person drinking alcohol, may even exhibit behaviors that are inimical to the survival of individual components (e.g., brain cells) of the system. In *In Dubious Battle* Doc Burton says, "The pleasure we get in scratching an itch causes death to a great number of cells. Maybe group-man gets pleasure when individual men are wiped out in a war" (132). When Joy and Jim die, Mac turns the events into energy for the superorganism. "I want to see if it'd be a good idea for the guys to look at him tomorrow. We got to shoot some juice into 'er some way. . . . If Joy can do some work after he's dead, then he's got to do it. There's no such things as personal feelings in this crowd" (185).

The phalanx concept was one that had interested John for some time, but it certainly took shape and developed substance from his conversations with Ed Ricketts. As John wrote to George Albee in 1933,

I can't give you the whole thing [the phalanx concept] completely in a letter, George. I am going to write a whole novel with it as a theme, so how can I get it in a letter? Ed Ricketts has dug up all the scientific material and more than I need to establish the physical integrity of the thing. I have written the theme over and over and did not know what I was writing, I found at least four statements of it in the God. . . . When your phalanx needs you it will use you, if you are the material to be used. You will know when the time comes, and when it does come, nothing you can do will let you escape. (*SLL* 81)

Are Visceral and Transcendent Understanding the Same Thing?

In the Tibetan Buddhist and Hindu sense, transcendence is pretty clearly a monotonic increase in spirituality from one plane of being to a more enlightened one. The sense in which Ed Ricketts uses the concept of breaking through, however, is closer to the Zen Buddhist concept (Suzuki 229-66). In describing the human progression in his "Philosophy of Breaking Through" essay, Ed says:

> Children and probably peasants, maybe old-fashioned farmers and laborers also, are unawakened, unconscious, live unknowingly in the flow of life, naive. The much larger conscious group includes a huge sophisticated majority either seeking, puzzled, bitter, or resigned, and a small mellow minority who, usually later in life, are luminously adjusted to their lot, whatever it may be. . . . In occasional naturally wise people (these are rare), the mellow may proceed directly from the naive. . . . [Usually] There is the original naive, child-like or savage belief in a personal deity. This is ordinarily followed, soon after the function of intellectual cognition develops and is honestly put to work on the problem, by a period of loss, bitterness, and atheistic insistence: the sophisticated stage. Then by breaking through as a result of acceptance of struggle with its challenge of work in attempting a deeper understanding, some feeling for the symbolism of religion, knowledge of the "deep thing beyond the name," of "magic" and if the "dog within," ultimately may illuminate the whole scene. The attempt toward conscious understanding of what formerly was accepted naively as a matter of traditional course, apparently imposes a struggle from which only the breakers-through emerge into the mellow group. (Hedgpeth 1978, pt. 2, 78)

Of particular interest is the sense that Ed portrays of the "deep thing" in, for example, the Indians of Baja California, who are extremely generous—

But some of the things offered, the spiritual and friendship things, I have a feeling are offered out of the "deep thing" which underlies both spiritual and physical; in other words they are given for what they are themselves, without either physical or spiritual expediency. You can't easily tell, because the words and actions are identical for the superficial or expedient thing, and for the deep thing. The only discriminating quality I've heard of is what the Upanishads call "the high and fine intuition of the wise." (Hedgpeth 1978, pt. 2, 134)

Ed raises the same point in his "antiscript" to John's *The Forgotten Village*, in which he talks of the "deep smile" of Mexican peasants as "evidence of internal adjustment and happiness" before they are influenced by modern living (Hedgpeth 1978, pt. 2, 172-82). The perception of native peoples living in ecological balance with the natural world has led to speculation that there is a deep harmony between these people and the environment that is lost when people start driving cars, living in air conditioned buildings, and surviving twice as long through the advances of modern medicine. This is certainly part of Ed's idea of the "deep smile," but whether this sort of instinctive harmony is the same state as is achieved by breaking through is a bit unclear. Ed and John talk of the Baja California Indians as living in a sort of dream state. "They actually seem to be dreaming. . . . They seemed to live on remembered things, to be so related to the seashore and the rocky hills and the loneliness that they are these things" (*SOC* 75). As we have seen earlier, John uses the same term in describing Ed's idea of transcendence: "he worked at his philosophy of 'breaking through,' of coming out through the back of the mirror into some kind of reality which would make the world seem dreamlike. This thought obsessed him." If the two states are the same, then consciousness "wraps around," and transcendent understanding merges into visceral understanding. If the states are different, and are instead end points on a continuum with rational or scientific understanding separating them, the model is obviously a very different one.

Implications for Environmental Understanding

Two common themes in contemporary environmental thinking are (1) that we, as members of the world population, must develop an appreciation of the large-scale, synthetic interconnectedness of everything that happens on the planet ("Think globally") and (2) that we, as individuals, must reestablish local ecological balance by environmentally responsible behavior ("Act locally"). It would seem that the first of these themes is best accomplished by a kind of breaking through, a kind of at least synthetic, if not transcendent, thinking. Certainly Allee would have been comfortable with this extension of his scientific ecological understanding, and neither Ed nor John was particularly shy about these sorts of conceptual leaps. The second of these themes may require rediscovering the "deep smile" of native peoples, reestablishing our connections to the natural world. No one doubts that Ed, through his mystical approach to science, nor John, in his literary celebrations of the natural world, had, to a significant degree in their own lives, accomplished just that.

As we have seen, we can view our understanding of our world as progressing from a sort of instinctive understanding, to an understanding refined by our scientific study of the world, and finally breaking through to an understanding of the global ecosystem as whole. Alternatively, we can view ourselves as coming, shortly after birth, out of a state of harmony with our world, passing through a period of searching in which we struggle to develop a rational understanding of our world, to, finally—if we allow ourselves to do so—achieving an enlightenment that reestablishes our sense of harmony with the universe.

A highly romanticized version of the second view is popular today, in which we hear that primitive peoples are in possession of both the instinctive harmony and the transcendent harmony but that victims of Western civilization, especially those perceived to be responsible for advancing that culture, are trapped in a sort of purgatory of rational disharmony (e.g., the popular films *The Emerald Forest* and *Dances with Wolves*). Some feminist literature suggests that it is not the rational step

---

itself that is at fault but rather the current form of science that is the problem. Harding, for example, suggests changing the rational part of the process:

> Women need sciences and technologies that are for women and that are for women in every class, race, and culture. Feminists (male and female) want to close the gender gap in scientific and technological literacy, to invent modes of thought and learn the existing techniques and skills that will enable women to get more control over the conditions of their lives. Such sciences can and must benefit men, too—especially those marginalized by racism, imperialism, and class exploitation; the new sciences are not to be only for women. But it is time to ask what sciences would look like that were for "female men," all of them, and not primarily for the white, Western and economically advantaged "male men" toward whom benefit from the science has disproportionately tended to flow. (Harding 5)

Capra argues that the current form of the rational step, of science, is simply offtrack and calls for a course correction:

> Many of us in the new-paradigm movement believe that this association of man dominating nature, which is a patriarchal attitude, has to be divorced from science. We would like to see emerge again a science in which scientists cooperate with nature and pursue knowledge in order to learn about natural phenomena and be able to "follow the natural order and current of the Tao," as the Chinese sages put it. That is how I understand the traditional medieval notion of pursuing science "for the glory of God." (Capra and Steindl-Rast 12)

Capra blames Francis Bacon for getting science off course in the first place. "Ever since Francis Bacon, the aim of most scientists has been the domination of nature and the exploitation of nature" (Capra and Steindl-Rast 30). The accusation is interesting because Bacon, rather than arguing for a utilitarian science, clearly advocated full appreciation of nature by a combination of empiricism and rational thought. In "De Augmentis Scientiarum," he writes: "Now the first kind [of natural history] which aims either to please by the agreeableness of the narrative or to help by the use of experiments, and is pursued for the sake of such pleasure or profit, I account as far inferior in importance to that which is the stuff and material of a solid and lawful induction, and may be called the nursing mother of philosophy" (Bacon 430). In "Novum Organum," in a delightfully biological admonition, one that Ed and John would surely have appreciated, Bacon wrote: "Those who have handled sciences have been either men of experiment or men of dogmas. The men of experiment are like the ant; they only collect and use; the reasoners resemble spiders, who make cobwebs out of their own substance. But the bee takes the middle course; it gathers its matter from the flowers of the garden and of the field, but transforms it and digests it by a power of its own" (Bacon 288).

The contemporary environmentalist movement seems somewhat schizophrenic about science as an enterprise. For example, while celebrating the sophisticated biochemistry that provides the understanding of, say, heavy metals in the biosphere, the movement condemns the geochemistry that freed these same metals from the lithosphere. The simple resolution is that science is a tool and can be used for good or ill, but this view clearly begs the deeper philosophical question as to whether science, as one aspect of rational understanding, is an inevitable and necessary step in the human progress from instinct to enlightenment or whether it is a Western European juggernaut, blind to instinct and antithetical to enlightenment, which must be stopped before it destroys what is left of the global ecosystem.

It is clear not only that John and Ed were comfortable with science in those days just prior to World War II but that they viewed science as both a noble human undertaking and an essential step in progress of human understanding, as the requisite antecedent to breaking through to transcendent understanding. While decrying with equal vehemence the war half a world away and the ecological damage to the Sea of

Cortez by Japanese bottom trawlers, they did not conclude that if only we stopped doing science, or if we limited our science to its beneficial utilitarian applications, the world would be a better place. They were comfortable accepting science as one of the ways we find our place in the universe, and they clearly saw that ecology itself is neither deep nor shallow and that the scientist determines the level of synthesis and transcendence of the science: "Perhaps it is the same narrowing we observe in relation to ourselves and the tide pool—a man looking at reality brings his own limitations to the world. If he has strength and energy of mind the tide pool stretches both ways, digs back to electrons and leaps space into the universe and fights out of the moment into non-conceptual time. Then ecology has a synonym which is ALL" (*SOC* 85).

The view that we as humans come into the world with a visceral understanding that is both mystical and instinctive, that we respond to our environment by trying to understand it, perhaps through our science, and that if we succeed in this rational understanding we can break through and see that our "racial memory" and our science are steps in a very human progression toward a global understanding is an optimistic and positive one. It contrasts with the "science as aberration" philosophies advanced by some New Age writers and may well resolve the schizophrenia of some in the environmentalist movement.

John Steinbeck and Ed Ricketts offered a philosophy more than fifty years ago that is increasingly relevant. Their work may have helped to condition us for the "green revolution." Revisiting their writing and their lives may help us understand what is going on in our own environmentally conscious lives of today.

From *Steinbeck and the Environment: Interdisciplinary Approaches,* edited by Susan F. Beegel, Susan Shillinglaw, and Wesley N. Tiffney, Jr. (1997), pp. 27-42. Copyright © 1997 by University of Alabama Press. Reprinted with permission of University of Alabama Press.

Note

I wish to recognize and thank Graham Wilson, with whom I began teaching the course "Steinbeck and Ricketts: Literature and the Sea" nineteen years ago and who has taught me much of what I know about the literature; Joel Hedgpeth and Dora Henry (the barnacle lady in "About Ed Ricketts") who have taught me much of what I know about Ed; Mike Gregory whose stewardship of the NEXA program allowed us to teach the course; and our students who have kept us all going. NEXA is an interdisciplinary program that investigates the areas of "convergence" between the sciences and the humanities in courses in which members of the two faculties teach together on a topic of common interest. Initial funding for NEXA was provided by the National Endowment for the Humanities.

Works Cited

Allee, W. C. *Cooperation Among Animals*. New York: Henry Shuman, 1938.

Allee, W. C., et al. *Principles of Animal Ecology*. Philadelphia: W. B. Saunders, 1949.

Astro, Richard. *John Steinbeck and Edward F. Ricketts: The Shaping of a Novelist*. Minneapolis: University of Minnesota Press, 1973.

Bacon, Francis. *The Philosophical Works of Francis Bacon*. Edited by John M. Robertson. London: George Routledge and Sons, 1905.

Benson, Jackson J. *The True Adventures of John Steinbeck, Writer*. New York: Viking, 1984; Penguin, 1990.

Campbell, Joseph. *The Hero's Journey: The World of Joseph Campbell*. Edited by Phil Cousineau. San Francisco: Harper and Row, 1990.

_____. *The Masks of God: Primitive Mythology*. 1959. New York: Penguin, 1991.

Capra, Fritjof, and David Steindl-Rast. *Belonging to the Universe*. San Francisco: Harper and Row, 1991.

DeMott, Robert. *Steinbeck's Reading: Catalogue of Books Owned and Borrowed*. New York: Garland, 1984.

Dusheck, Jennie. "Female Primatologists Confer—Without Men." *Science* 249 (1990): 1494-95.

Giles, Lionel, trans. *The Sayings of Lao Tzu*. London: J. Murray, 1905.

Harding, Sandra. *Whose Science? Whose Knowledge? Thinking from Women's Lives*. Ithaca: Cornell University Press, 1991.

Hedgpeth, Joel W. *The Outer Shores, Part 1: Ed Ricketts and John Steinbeck Explore the Pacific Coast*. Eureka, CA: Mad River, 1978.

_____. *The Outer Shores, Part 2: Breaking Through*. Eureka, CA: Mad River, 1978.

Hutton, James. "Theory of the Earth; or, An investigation of the laws observable in the composition, dissolution, and restoration of land upon the globe." *Transactions of the Royal Society of Edinburgh* (1788): 209-304.

Jeffers, Robinson. *The Selected Poetry of Robinson Jeffers*. New York: Random House, 1938.

Larsen, Stephen, and Robin Larsen. *A Fire in the Mind: The Life of Joseph Campbell*. New York: Doubleday, 1991.

Lovelock, J. E. *Gaia: A New Look at Life on Earth*. Oxford and New York: Oxford University Press, 1979.

_____. "Gaia as Seen Through the Atmosphere." *Atmospheric Environments* 6 (1972): 579-80.

_____. "Geophysiology, the Science of Gaia." *Reviews of Geophysics* 27 (1989): 215-22.

Ricketts, Edward F. *Pacific Biological Laboratory Biological Specimens*. Pacific Grove, CA: Pacific Biological Laboratory, 1925.

_____, and John Calvin. *Between Pacific Tides*. 1939. Revised by Joel W. Hedgpeth and D. W. Phillips. Stanford: Stanford University Press, 1985.

Ritter, William Emerson. "The Marine Biological Station of San Diego: Its History, Present Conditions, Achievements, and Aims." *University of California Publications in Zoology* 9.4 (1912): 137-248.

_____. *The Unity of the Organism; or, The Organismal Conception of Life*. Vol. 1. Boston: Gorham, 1919.

Steinbeck, John. *Cannery Row* [1945]/*Of Mice and Men* [1937]. New York: Penguin Books, 1987.

_____. *The Grapes of Wrath*. 1939. New York: Penguin Books, 1981.

_____. *In Dubious Battle*. 1936. New York: Penguin Books, 1979.

_____ [With Edward F. Ricketts, Jr.]. *The Log from the Sea of Cortez*. 1951. New York: Penguin Books, 1986.

_____. *Of Mice and Men* [1937]/*Cannery Row* [1945]. New York: Penguin Books, 1987.

_____ [With Edward P. Ricketts, Jr.]. *Sea of Cortez: A Leisurely Journal of Travel and Research*. 1941. Mt. Vernon, NY: Paul P. Appel, 1989.

_____. *Steinbeck: A Life in Letters*. Edited by Elaine Steinbeck and Robert Wallsten. New York: Viking Press, 1975.

_____. *To a God Unknown*. 1933. New York: Penguin Books, 1986.

_____. *Tortilla Flat*. 1935. New York: Penguin Books, 1986.

Suzuki, D. T. *Essays in Zen Buddhism: First Series*. New York: Grove, 1949.

Steinbeck's Environmental Ethic:
Humanity in Harmony with the Land_____
John H. Timmerman

During his later years John Steinbeck entered a period of intense ethical reflection that inevitably influenced his literature. It occurred to such an extent, in fact, that one might be tempted to categorize the work of the last decade as the "literature of moral concern" or the period itself as a "moral phase." If one were to categorize Steinbeck's fiction in such a way, and this essay intends to demonstrate the futility of so doing, one might date the period from the publication of *East of Eden* (1952) with its gnarled philosophical speculations, its exploration of moral obligations and the effects of moral transgression, and its proliferation of biblical allusions as a sounding board for supporting echoes. The works of the next decade might seem an extension of similar speculation, one author musing upon the moral decay and ethical paralysis of a people whom he has long loved but now finds dangerously distanced from a holding center of personal and national virtues.

Such categorization and such terms, however, are decidedly insufficient, suggesting the discovery of something altogether new and unfamiliar. It is as if Steinbeck suddenly caught a moral vision the way one catches a cold—quite by accident of circumstance and condition. At the worst, such terms suggest that the literature of earlier years was somehow bereft of moral concern.

Such terminology, moreover, renders whatever moral concerns Steinbeck held during this period indefinable, simply an amorphous cloud of political opinion, petty grievances, some old-age raillery, and a dyspeptic affliction of conservatism, mixed together on the final horizon of his life. What, precisely, was this so-called moral concern about? The task, when it comes to a consideration of his ethical views as a structured pattern of both moral oughtness and also an enactment of that oughtness in human actions, is to isolate a particular instance as a case study—in this case his sense of an environmental ethic. In so doing, however, one discerns three things: first, his environmental ethic did in fact receive deliberate articulation during the final decade of his life; second, that ethic, nonetheless, had been intuitively held throughout his life; and, third, that ethic infuses his literature by providing thematic pattern and direction.

Perhaps the most overt expression of Steinbeck's moral concern appears in *America and Americans* (1966), wherein Steinbeck is invited, like an elder statesman, to reflect upon things past, the woeful present, and the uncertain future. He doesn't miss a punch. He names the enemies of the moral order as comfort, plenty, security—the very ideals that the nation sought but that, in its marvelous excess, it perverted to a poverty of spirit: cynicism, boredom, and smugness. It is Hadleyburg on a national scale. As Steinbeck lamented in a 1959 letter to Adlai Stevenson, "We can stand anything God and nature can throw at us save only plenty" (*SLL* 652).

In *America and Americans* Steinbeck traces our failure in regard to the environment to a perfidious irresponsibility with roots in the spirit of humanity. While in modern environmental ethics we are inclined to see irresponsibility in terms of criminal actions—that is, littering is a criminal act punishable by a fine, as is toxic waste dumping—Steinbeck sees this irresponsibility as a failure in understanding and sympathy. While littering may not have been, in his time, a criminal action, it was an evil action nonetheless. The distinction is important to the case here, for evil, in Steinbeck's ethics, is a positioning of the heart in regard to other living things. We either devour those things like tigers, as *Cannery Row* had it, or live with them in a respectful equilibrium.

Yet the history of Americans in regard to the land, in Steinbeck's view, is marked by a rapacious attitude that sees the land merely as something to be used or abused. Obsessed with the notion that the land was limitless, early settlers "abandoned their knowledge of kindness to the land in order to maintain its usefulness" (*AAA* 146). Implicitly whatever was not useful could be cast aside to get at what was useful.

But as Grandfather testified in "Leader of the People" in *The Red*

Pony, we have learned that the land is not limitless. We have learned that the land is fragile, that the gouges of our rapacious greed forever mar its face, that taking its hidden treasures always leaves an irreparable scar. We have learned that it is susceptible to decimation and deterioration. We have learned our evil toward the land. When one acquires such knowledge, Steinbeck asserts, a pressure of outrage grows.

It must be admitted that in *America and Americans* Steinbeck does a better job of delineating problems than of offering practical solutions. So too in regard to this environmental ethic. Outrage is an important part of an ethical consideration; it constitutes, in fact, the basic premise of an ethic, for an ethic is always and ultimately incarnated in action.

An ethical person acts against a perceived evil; one who ignores it may be said to be ethically culpable for the evil itself. To do nothing is to permit; to permit is to condone. Steinbeck's ethical action is the work of revelation: to make readers mindful of our despoliation of the land. In regard to a specific program to rectify that course, however, this ethic, at least as delineated in *America and Americans*, is found wanting.

Steinbeck arrays several examples of when a people's outrage led to action, as when a California highway route was changed to avoid a stand of redwoods. But most frequently his response in *America and Americans* is formulated as a fond reminiscence for the way things once were, a profound regret for the way they are, and a tempered hope for better times ahead.

What Steinbeck specified through discursive argument in *America and Americans* was discovered more spontaneously and intuitively, however, in the earlier *Travels with Charley*. It may well be said that this work is Steinbeck's consummate ethical treatise. He undertook the journey, leaving on 23 September 1960, immediately after finishing *The Winter of Our Discontent*, not simply to investigate his country's topography but to discover his own manhood. The heart of *Travels with Charley* arises from these questions: What really matters? What endures? What beliefs do I hold about these matters? In environmental matters also these questions receive studied consideration, not first of all as a rational construct, as is the case in *America and Americans*, but out of the expediency of personal experience. In that way, *Charley* moves much closer to Steinbeck's novelistic technique—a probing of matters of the heart arising from reflection upon experience. It may also be considered the practical, historically positioned premise for the argument in *America and Americans*.

As is the case in the best travel literature, *Charley* moves deeper into the traveler with the journey itself. Here the reflections solidify, through event to a perception of the meaning of the event. In fact, the first two parts of the work seem preoccupied by person and place; the third part initiates the harder probing into uncomfortable regions of the mind and heart. Not coincidentally, that passage occurs as Rocinante heads westward across the Mississippi, noses through the flatland prairies, and nears the environment of Steinbeck's youth. Thus he begins the journey inward, for the recollection of the past and the mindfulness of the present clash with the force of runaway freight trains.

In fact, it seems to occur precisely as Steinbeck crosses the Great Divide and becomes mindful of the fact that "it is impossible to be in this high spinal country without giving thought to the first men who crossed it" (*TWC* 166). He then contrasts our rage for hurry, the fact that "we get sick if the milk delivery is late and nearly die of heart failure if there is an elevator strike" (167), to the sense of awe the first explorers held in their slow trek across a land of grandeur. While the ethical flaw noted in *America and Americans* is always the rapacious greed of a people, the flaw noted in *Travels with Charley* is similarly disturbing. It is our unmitigated hurry that leads to the thoughtless use of the land. It took the relentless throb of tires, the flickering of a speedometer, to make Steinbeck mindful of a division in our hearts, a rupture in harmony, by virtue of our hurry. It seems, at this point, that the entire travel plan of the book itself begins to slow as the traveler himself seeks a new harmony with the land.

In this matter, as in so many, the memorable Charley also tutors him.

Afflicted with polyuria, Charley makes necessary stops that become more frequent and prolonged. While Steinbeck makes light of Charley's micturition, he also admits that "while waiting for him . . . I tried to reconstruct my trip as a single piece and not as a series of incidents" (168). That moment represents a transition, more important than any individual highway interchange, in *Travels with Charley*, for it redirects the way Steinbeck looks at the land. It is as if Charley cautions him to slow down, to observe, to meditate, and to draw conclusions.

He sees the hurry of the people, rushing headlong into time, as both at odds with the land and also destructive of the land. Steinbeck understands well—as his visit to Salinas would inarguably convince him—that one cannot relive the past. The point of his land ethic is not to turn the clock backward. He argues that "this sounds as though I bemoan an older time, which is the preoccupation of the old, or cultivate an opposition to change, which is the currency of the rich and stupid. It is not so" (181). Self-preoccupation, after all, serves poorly as an ethical guide. Instead, his effort is to startle recognition of what we once were, what we now are and are now doing, in order to capture a realistic ethic of living in harmony with the land. Here are the things we have forgotten; here now those we must remember. Upon such lies our future hope.

Repeatedly, then, and in a nondidactic manner, he returns in *Travels with Charley* to the theme of living in harmony with the land, capturing the theme in personal events and vignettes that lace the story to its conclusion. In effect, he takes his time—makes time—for the land's tutoring and his appropriation of its lessons. He stands in a magnificent stand of redwoods and ponders the sense of awe and respect he derives from them. These are spiritual qualities, not utilitarian ones. They are lessons of the land. And they have the capacity to change our measure of time itself, for as the great trees work their power upon his spirit, Steinbeck finds himself reflecting, "Can it be that we do not love to be reminded that we are very young and callow in a world that was old when we came into it? And can there be a strong resistance to the certainty that a living world will continue its stately way when we no longer inhabit it?" (193). In such a way the land reminds us, and in heeding the reminder humanity learns to live in harmony with the land, finding a place at one time in the timeless.

That discovery colors, in one way or another, all the following events of *Travels with Charley*. Whether arising amid the colored rocks and terrifying delicacy of the Arizona desert or in the midst of turbulent social strife in New Orleans, the essential message endures. The heart of an environmental ethic, as also in an ethical guide toward human understanding and living, resides in a deep commitment to harmonious living, respecting the life of the land itself and respecting oneself in relationship to that land.

Something of that same discovery may be seen in his fiction also. In fact, the argument here is that while his ethic of the environment received rational elucidation rather late in his career, it achieved formulation and validation much earlier in his fiction.

The evidence for that claim could be supplied from his earliest works but at considerable risk. Joseph Wayne's grappling with seasons of discontent, his druidic embrace of the dying oak tree, his frantic religion of rain, show a man deeply involved with the land but also one who loses himself for the land. No harmony arises from his madness, which seems propelled only by an insistence that all is wrong, that it should be different, but with little rational or emotional clarity of things being set right. Joseph steps from his porch, studies the dead oak, and laments, "If only it were alive . . . I would know what to do. I have no counsel anymore" (*TGU* 183). Indeed, he does not. *To a God Unknown* bitterly inscribes the circle of helplessness and disharmony, its spiral leading to the sacrifice of oneself. To claim, as deluded Joseph does, that "I am the land . . . and I am the rain" (261) seems like anything but an environmental ethic. Yes, someone might point out, but it *does* rain. And the peasants celebrate the efficacy of Wayne's sacrifice, despite the priest's scorn and threats of penance.

The real hero of the novel, as Jackson Benson points out in *The True Adventures of John Steinbeck, Writer*, "is nature, an organic whole, which has its own being apart from man's vain attempts to control, influence, or understand it deductively" (1984, 239). In effect, the novel shows humanity and nature at odds with each other and depicts a negative ethical attitude toward nature as something to be used for individual self-interest. In his discussion of the novel and Steinbeck's thinking about nature at this stage of his life, Benson demonstrates how Steinbeck extrapolated a holistic view of nature from his study under C. V. Taylor, a disciple of William Emerson Ritter. Basically, Ritter argued a necessary harmony of parts, including humanity, in the natural whole, a view that very much defined Steinbeck's lifelong environmental ethics.

Despite the labored mysticism of the novel, then, one detects a seminal attitude of Steinbeck that grew, deepened, and matured in later years. Undeniable is the fact that Wayne's sacrifice was for the land. Even the priest recognizes this: "He thought of Joseph Wayne, and he saw the pale eyes suffering because of the land's want. 'That man must be very happy now,' Father Angelo said to himself" (264). And at the end of his life, Wayne's thinking has changed, as he sees human life as a part of a whole, natural pattern. The failure of the ethic, if it may even be called such at this stage, is that Wayne himself fails to achieve the harmonious relationship with the land—unless one points to the ironic symmetry of his corpse stretched out upon the rock. All such talk about Wayne's absorption into the cosmic flow means very little when Wayne lies dead. Ethics, finally, are the actions and attitudes of living people in a living environment. In a sense, then, *To a God Unknown* shows a negative view in regard to an environmental ethic.

To step from the demon-haunted landscape of *To a God Unknown* to the sun-washed hills of *The Pastures of Heaven* is a journey between worlds that show similarities but are finally different. This point is particularly clear in Steinbeck's attitude toward humanity and the environment. The similarity appears first, for the notorious curse of the Battle Farm seems to afflict the very earth, to live and breed in it. While different characters are content to resign the curse to demons, and to avoid the Battle land, it seems that the curse will not leave them alone.

In the words of T. B. Allen, "Maybe your curse and the farm's curse has mated and gone into a gopher hole like a pair of rattlesnakes. Maybe there'll be a lot of baby curses crawling around the pastures the first thing we know" (*PH* 19).

With the increasing interest in Steinbeck's short stories during recent years, and the revelation through those stories both of Steinbeck's developing artistry and also of his thematic directions, the nature of the curse has been amply discussed. It has, in the critical views set forth, both biblical analogues to the Edenic curse and implications for Steinbeck's view of humanity in contention with the destructive forces of modern civilization. It is in relation to that thematic pattern, however, that the similarities with *To a God Unknown* end, for *The Pastures of Heaven* is ultimately a testimony to the triumph of human nature as it learns to live in harmony with the land. Paradoxically, the battle may remain, engaged upon different fronts, but the conflict may achieve amelioration, even resolution, as individuals learn their own quiet patterns of living with the land.

The pattern of person and land in a state of discord or dominion prevails throughout the stories. One can tell a great deal about the characters by how they manage the land: whether they let it grow coarse and wild, as does Junius Maltby; whether they impose a kind of tyrannical order, as do Helen Van Deventer and Raymond Banks; or whether they achieve a degree of harmony, as does John Whiteside. The pastures are full of gardens and orchards. Often they are twisted and grotesque, signifying this crooked and confusing world. At times the land responds bountifully to the human touch. In either case, the curse lies buried just out of sight. While *The Pastures of Heaven* is littered—as a place and as a novel—with the detritus of shattered dreams and broken lives, it also remains as a powerful force that reshapes those lives. Herein lies the harmony: the discovery of the land as a powerful, living thing, having intrinsic self-worth.

The epilogue of *Pastures of Heaven* serves as a kind of propaedeutics to Steinbeck's environmental ethic as he worked it out in his fiction over the course of the following two decades. Here in the epilogue, modern pilgrims arrive at the rim of the valley and feel the disconcerting tug of its allure upon their spirits. That tug is disconcerting, for it at once invites them and challenges them. Here, each one believes, things might be different. But each pilgrim comes with a sense of how he or she would use the land to make things different. It is the Edenic paradox played out all over again: does one exercise dominion over the land by thrashing it into submission to fit some concept of usefulness or by discovering its usefulness through harmonious integration with it? None of these pilgrims, at least, discovers the harmony—giving of oneself wholly in order to experience fully the beneficence and power of the land. Each tramps back aboard the tour bus slightly dismayed but packed off to a former self.

That conflict between use of the land and living at harmony with the land intensifies in later fiction. *The Grapes of Wrath*, for example, complicates the pattern dramatically, for the sun-blasted plains of Oklahoma seem unforgiving of humanity. Even here, however, the historical information given in the interchapters explains the case; the relentless scraping of the tractors so scarified the topsoil as to damage it nearly beyond repair. The unfortunate homesteaders reap the whirlwind. When these same homesteaders migrate to the land of milk and honey, they find the cycle repeated in a more treacherous way, for in the lush valleys of California rapacious use by the landowners insists upon destroying even the plenty. Humans are set against humans in times of bounty as in time of need. In interchapter 25, Steinbeck names this greed as "a crime . . . that goes beyond denunciation. A sorrow . . . that weeping cannot symbolize" (385).

Interchapter 25 shapes one of Steinbeck's sharpest social commentaries and most carefully develops a concept of what one might call the "land-use ethic" of this period. The chapter begins with a lyrical celebration of spring in the California valleys, when the land bursts with promise. The descriptive sentence "The full green hills are round and soft as breasts" suggests connections with the life-giving act of Rose of

Sharon. The lushness of the country invokes a vast promise of plenitude, until Steinbeck introduces the men "of understanding and knowledge and skill" who shape the promise to the desires of the landowners. The description of these men is carefully rendered—the images tender, the tone appreciative. "They have," he writes, "transformed the world with their knowledge" (383).

But knowledge, as in Eden, serves as a curse here when it is used to satisfy personal pride and to reap personal gain from the earth at the expense of others. Midway through the chapter, the bounty of fruit, nourished by a sea of chemicals, proliferates to the fullness of decay, which is also the decay of human responsibilities to fellow humans. The decay acquires a macabre life of its own, symbolizing a cloud of greed that covers the land: "The decay spreads over the State, and the sweet smell is a great sorrow on the land" (384). The smell of rot, Steinbeck writes, "fills the country" (385). In this case, nature's abundance is perverted to a kind of grotesque life form, manipulated by and in order to satisfy human greed. With the decay of the fruit, human values, concerns for the well-being of others, similarly rot away in disuse.

In the *Cannery Row* novels this mechanical ruin of nature's riches sharpens intensely. While *Cannery Row* takes place in the very throbbing blast of the fishing boilers, thereby creating from the start a metaphor for the "hot taste of life," *Sweet Thursday* opens with a melancholic description of the effects of that hot taste:

The canneries themselves fought the war by getting the limit taken off fish and catching them all. It was done for patriotic reasons, but that didn't bring the fish back. As with the oysters in *Alice*, "They'd eaten every one." It was the same noble impulse that stripped the forests of the West and right now is pumping water out of California's earth faster than it can rain back in. When the desert comes, people will be sad; just as Cannery Row was sad when all the pilchards were caught and canned and eaten. The pearl-gray canneries of corrugated iron were silent and a pacing watchman was their only life. The street that once roared with trucks was quiet and empty. (*ST* 3)

By this time, of course, Steinbeck had tried, tested, and finally found wanting his marine-biology analogy for human life, the notorious Group Man who is finally little more than a naturalistic particle in a random universe. However flawed the philosophical apparatus of the Group Man theory, it does pose an intriguing explanation of, and support for, Steinbeck's mandate to live in harmony with the land. As he argues in *The Log from the Sea of Cortez*:

> There is tied up at the most primitive and powerful racial or collective instinct a rhythm sense or "memory" which affects everything and which in the past was probably more potent than it is now. It would at least be more plausible to attribute these profound effects to devastating and instinct-searing tidal influences active during the formative times of the early race history of organisms. The fact remains that the imprint is there. . . . The imprint lies heavily on our dreams and on the delicate threads of our nerves. . . . The harvest of symbols in our minds seems to have been planted in the soft rich soil of our prehumanity. (*LSC* 39)

Steinbeck's Group Man theory enforces that sense of humanity's link to the environment; its ethical implications during this period were shaped more particularly, however, by his accompanying theory of nonteleological thinking.

Nonteleological thinking also forms a sort of premise for Steinbeck's environmental ethic, since it requires that one see the thing as it is, disinterestedly, rather than through the framework of personal, or interested, use: "The truest reason for anything's being so is that it is. This is actually and truly a reason, more valid and clearer than all the other separate reasons, or than any group of them short of the whole. Anything less than the whole forms part of the picture only, and the infinite whole is unknowable except by *being* it, by living into it" (*LSC* 176). Such expressions of Steinbeck's attitude toward the environment testify to a persistent concern and collectively form the outlines of an ethical view guiding human responsibility toward an appreciation of the environment. Perhaps it receives some entelechy in a novel where the environmental concern is least overt, through the character of Samuel Hamilton in *East of Eden*.

Adam Trask's initial perception of Samuel Hamilton as a biblical patriarch is appropriate, for Hamilton's is the elder voice in the novel, full of tested wisdom and ancient knowledge. Especially important to Steinbeck's maturing view of the environment is the fact that this patriarchal figure knows the land from the past to the present. Hamilton holds a patriarchal view of the land itself, imbued by an acute understanding of how the land was formed and what its secret resources are. Hamilton draws a verbal map of the land for Adam Trask, explaining the forces that have so shaped it. That intensive knowledge, that suprarational intimacy, is fundamental to living with the land as opposed to merely using or abusing the land.

It is an irony in the novel that Samuel Hamilton, more pointedly than anyone, lives East of Eden, working upon the sun-baked soil of his farm quite literally by the sweat of his brow. His life's quest is for sufficient water to replenish his stony soil. But the point of the irony is not easily missed. Hamilton is the good man making the best of his way in harmony with a bad place. More so than Joseph Wayne ever dreamed, Samuel Hamilton "is the land."

When Adam Trask, now successful on his valley farm, asks Hamilton why he has stayed upon his desert hill, Hamilton professes that he never had the courage to dare greatness but instead contented himself with mediocrity. The desert farm, it seems, ensures this. But Hamilton also qualifies *mediocrity*, and by it he means precisely a harmonious living with all living things, as opposed to the aloof arrogance that is the temptation of greatness: "On one side you have warmth and companionship and sweet understanding, and on the other—cold, lonely greatness. There you make your choice" (347-48). Thus defined, mediocrity proves heroic in the novel, and Samuel Hamilton's relationship with the land—a strange mixture of contentment and contention— proves metaphorical also for his ethics of human living.

In the end, of course, Samuel is not to be apotheosized. He may be patriarchal in bearing, but he is no saint. His primary flaw, as the narrator suggests, is his denial of death as a necessary part of the fabric of living:

> Samuel may have thought and played and philosophized about death, but he did not really believe in it. His world did not have death as a member. He, and all around him, was immortal. When real death came it was an outrage, a denial of the immortality he deeply felt, and the one crack in his wall caused the whole structure to crash, I think he had always thought he could argue himself out of death. It was a personal opponent and one he could lick. (383)

In this matter, and as Abra tutors Aron, Liza is the necessary tutor or counterpart to Samuel. She is a realist, the temper to his fancy. Even heaven, in her view, is a place marked first of all by realistic comforts—clean clothes and dishes, for example. She tutors Samuel, and nowhere is the effect of her tutoring more evident than in Samuel's attitude toward that contrary horse, Doxology. Of this animal, Samuel says: "I have never in thirty-three years found one good thing about him. He even has an ugly disposition. He is selfish and quarrelsome and mean and disobedient. To this day I don't dare walk behind him because he will surely take a kick at me. When I feed him mash he tries to bite my hand. And I love him" (400). And that sums up his ethic also. Whether in contention with an ornery land, a wayward child, or a recalcitrant horse, Samuel's contention is charged with love.

Perhaps we are misled by the sometimes strident tones of Steinbeck's later nonfiction to demarcate his final years as a "moral phase." Certainly an attitude of urgency infiltrates his letters during the 1960s, and certainly the raveled moral fabric of the nation appears as a major theme in such works as *Travels with Charley* and *America and Americans*. We are misled if we see those pronouncements and that attitude as something oddly apart from all his former life. Rather, they emerge out of a developing but fairly consistent ethic located in his fiction throughout his life.

This is particularly true in Steinbeck's ethic of the environment. From his earliest years he was exploring an ethical attitude—a pattern of right living—based upon a belief in the possibility of a harmonious relationship between humanity and the environment. If one approaches the land in a self-interested way, the result will inevitably be despoliation and depletion of what it means to be human. Humanity and the environment are linked in a delicate interplay. It is inevitably so in the fiction. Respect for this linkage, seeing the land as it is in its own right, as a living and delicate thing, not only ennobles humanity and ultimately liberates humanity but also grants self-knowledge and validation through a loving and harmonious relationship between humanity and the land. While Steinbeck may have had his "moral phase," while his moral voice may even have turned shrill at times, it was only because of his deepening sense of urgency about environmental matters. But an ethic about the land, a sense of how and why one ought to live with the land, was a part of his personal nature and his public work from his earliest years. In that sense, it would be fair to say that Steinbeck engaged a moral phase from his first lines.

From *Steinbeck and the Environment: Interdisciplinary Approaches*, edited by Susan F. Beegel, Susan Shillinglaw, and Wesley N. Tiffney, Jr. (1997), pp. 310-322. Copyright © 1997 by University of Alabama Press. Reprinted with permission of University of Alabama Press.

Works Cited

Benson, Jackson J. *The True Adventures of John Steinbeck, Writer*. New York: Viking, 1984; Penguin, 1990.

Ritter, William Emerson. "The Marine Biological Station of San Diego: Its History, Present Conditions, Achievements, and Aims." *University of California Publications in Zoology* 9.4 (1912): 137-248.

_____. *The Unity of the Organism; or, The Organismal Conception of Life*. Vol. 1. Boston: Gorham, 1919.

Steinbeck, John. *America and Americans*. New York: Viking Press, 1966.

_____. *Cannery Row*. 1945. New York: Penguin, 1994.

_____. *East of Eden*. 1952. New York: Penguin Books, 1987.

_____. *The Grapes of Wrath*. 1939. New York: Penguin Books, 1981.

_____. [With Edward F. Ricketts, Jr.] *The Log from the Sea of Cortez*. 1951. New York: Penguin Books, 1986.

_____. *Of Mice and Men* [1937]/*Cannery Row* [1945]. New York: Penguin Books, 1987.

_____. *The Pastures of Heaven*. 1932. New York: Penguin Books, 1986.

_____. *Steinbeck: A Life in Letters*. Edited by Elaine Steinbeck and Robert Wallsten. New York: Viking Press, 1975.

_____. *Sweet Thursday*. 1954. New York: Penguin Books, 1984.

_____. *To a God Unknown*. 1933. New York: Penguin Books, 1986.

_____. *Travels with Charley in Search of America*. 1962. New York: Penguin Books, 1986.

_____. *The Winter of Our Discontent*. 1961. New York: Penguin Books, 1988.

Steinbeck and the Woman Question:
A Never-Ending Puzzle

Mimi Gladstein

It is some thirty years since the problem of John Steinbeck's depiction of women in his fiction first crossed my critical radar screen. It has remained a provocative puzzle, one that provides rich resources for continuing analysis and exploration. In those days, before we had the benefit of Jackson Benson's massive biography, there was a tendency to decode the life by reading the fiction. There were few women in the fiction, a fact that had been noted by early readers such as Claude Edmonde Magny, who pointed out that as male couples played such a predominant role in Steinbeck's fiction, it acted to create a sense of the exclusion of women from the human community. Or there was Peter Lisca's observation about the prevalence of male relationships, with the added caveat that Steinbeck relegated such women as did appear in his fiction to the limited roles of either housewife or prostitute. A 1974 dissertation by Angela Patterson analyzed Steinbeck's depictions of and attitudes toward women. Finding few women of worth in their own right, she concluded that Steinbeck was reflecting his own life and times. My own dissertation of the previous year (1973) acknowledged the dearth of women but argued the consequent significance of the few who were accorded some narrative stature. Patterson's unsubstantiated position that Steinbeck was portraying reality as he knew it was replicated as late as 1988 by Beth Everest and Judy Wedeles, who excused Steinbeck for his limited portrayal of women by asserting that the historical realities of his life and of the times he is writing about limited "the roles he could assign them" (23).

Once Jackson Benson had published his massive and painstakingly researched biography in 1984, it became difficult to sustain the exculpatory explanations for the short supply of women in Steinbeck's fiction. Benson provided such an abundance of information about the many women in Steinbeck's life that I was moved to question the strange disconnect between the life and the fiction in a presentation at the 1989 conference "The Steinbeck Question." This initial exploration presented some possible reasons for the inexplicable disparity between the many women who played key roles in Steinbeck's life and the paucity and limited possibilities of those in his fiction.[1] The subject was so intriguing that I began to study the historical context for two of his key novels: *In Dubious Battle* and *The Grapes of Wrath*.

The facts of Steinbeck's life easily refute the idea that he was simply reflecting his personal reality and the social and political situation of his time when he presented no evidence of women professionals, activists, or public figures in his narratives. Women were key players in the drama of his life and in the resources for his fiction. Most recently, at the 2001 Steinbeck Festival that kicked off the celebrations and conferences of the centennial year, I presented information about the women instructors, not the least of whom was his schoolteacher mother, who were instrumental in the formation of the man and the writer. These include Edith Brunoni, his piano teacher who nurtured in the budding writer a strong appreciation for music, and Ora M. Cupp, who did likewise for his writing talent. But no greater tribute can be paid to a teacher's influence than Steinbeck's own acknowledgment of Emma Hawkins: "I suppose that to a large extent I am the unsigned manuscript of that high school teacher" (". . . . like" 7). Teachers such as this do not appear in the fiction. I've always wondered why.

Another factor that has complicated the issue of Steinbeck's depiction of women is the contradictory nature of that depiction. There are many apparently misogynistic characterizations; indeed, I credit him with the most vicious female villain in American fiction—the amoral Kate Trask of *East of Eden*. Yet at the same time Steinbeck is the creator of some of the most positive female characters who ever graced the pages of twentieth-century literature. Certainly Ma Joad has few equals in terms of a characterization of woman. The portrait the narrator draws of her is a paean to woman as mother, a source of strength and love for her family—assertive, steadfast, and compassionate. Steinbeck's narrator portrays her as goddess, judge, and citadel; one could not ask for a more durable role model of endurance and indestructibility.

Also weighing in on the side of Steinbeck's positive depiction of women is the resolute and enduring Juana of *The Pearl*. Juana is made all the more significant in that fable because she is purely a manifestation of Steinbeck's creative resources. The parable of the Indian boy who found the pearl of great worth that serves as the inspiration for the novelette is recounted first in *Sea of Cortez*. That version does not include a wife and a child. In it, after the boy experiences the greed and violence incited by the pearl, he curses it and throws it back into the water. A freer and wiser man, "he laughed a great deal about it." In Steinbeck's retelling of the tale, he adds a wife whom he invests with the wisdom of the boy in the original parable.

Add to Ma Joad, Juana Abra from *East of Eden*, a character Steinbeck constructs because he needs a "strong female principle of good." Abra has few, if any, analogs in Steinbeck's fiction. She is a young woman characterized as "a fighter and an effective human being" (*Journal* 195). Her function in the novel is as a force for good, an incarnation of Steinbeck's *timshel* principle. Whereas Adam cannot find an appropriate Eve for his dream of a garden, Abra represents the new Eve who, together with Cal, will be the mother for new generations.

There are other inspirational female characters—ones who approach the status of heroines. Certainly Suzy, the spunky whore who wins Doc's heart in *Sweet Thursday*, is a character drawn with compassion and caring. Steinbeck uses her to show how resilient not just women but all humans can be, speaking through Doc: "My God, what a brave thing is the human!" (248). There are more women who seem to transcend the ordinary rules of morality with their creator's approval, such as Mordeen in *Burning Bright* and Rama in *To a God Unknown*.

But just as one gets ready to categorize Steinbeck's women as positively depicted, their appearance is equaled or outweighed by a cacophony of sometimes monstrous, sometimes vapid women. For example, what are readers to make of the women in *East of Eden* other than Abra? (I exclude here the female characters that are based on real-life members of Steinbeck's family.) *East of Eden* adds to the puzzling evidence of the strange disconnect between the women in Steinbeck's life and those he creates for his stories—the tension between women in his reality and his imaginative reconstruction of woman. His portrayals of the women in his mother's family, the Hamiltons, are drawn with a pen of pride, humor, and nostalgia. But, save for Abra, every woman who is Steinbeck-manufactured, the woman he could create "from the ground up," is pallid, hysterical, mean, and/or stupid. The first Mrs. Trask is a religious, suicidal hysteric; her successor is too dumb to know her own son, callous to his near murder of his stepbrother; Faye though a whorehouse madam, is easily duped by Kate; Kate's mother is sadistic and clueless about her daughter. The best mother in the novel is a man, Lee.

And how are women supposed to read *The Wayward Bus*? Bobbi Gonzales, who first read it in order to make a report for a Steinbeck seminar, was so appalled by the misogyny rife in the female character-izations that we ended up writing an article together about that novel as Steinbeck's misogynistic manifesto. Steinbeck begins the book with an inscription of lines from *Everyman*. If he also has "Everywoman" in mind, she presents a pitiful picture, running the gamut from hopelessly naive waitresses to manipulative wives who suppress their husbands' sexual desires. And while the women are drawn with misogynistic venom, the men, including the protagonist, present and voice an ap-palling array of sexist thinking. However, there is pointed textual evi-dence that Steinbeck is satirizing aspects of male behavior and double standards. In one instance, when describing Pritchard, the narrator points out that while Pritchard considered the dancers at stag parties depraved, "it would never have occurred to him that he who watched and applauded and paid the girls was in any way associated with de-pravity" (40). Steinbeck's perceptions here are very much in keeping with feminist critiques that would be put forth a decade later.

Yet despite an occasional enlightened perspective, it is not only in the serious works that Steinbeck exhibits these sexist and misogynistic attitudes. *Cannery Row* is a wonderfully funny narrative—if you read it like a man. The humor is decidedly phallocentric, often at the expense of women. With few exceptions, the only good women are prostitutes. Wives are anathema. Again, though he uses memories of Ed Ricketts and life on Old Ocean Avenue as sources for the story, he leaves out the many women who worked in the canneries, the many active and professional women who were part of the group that partied and shared ideas at the lab.

There is a school of Steinbeck critics who respond to the castigations of Steinbeck's limited and repellent portrayals of women by explaining that Steinbeck's purpose in doing so is to critique woman-less or woman-oppressive culture. Chief among these are Abby Werlock, Jean Emery, and Charlotte Hadella. Werlock argues that the character I dismiss as baby-laden Lisa in *In Dubious Battle* is a Madonna figure, whose presence in the novel represents morality, caring, and conscience in opposition to the violent and often "cold-blooded" men. "If hope exists in this novel, it lies in the different world and different voice of the female embodied in Lisa," contends Werlock, using my own *Indestructible Woman* to buttress her arguments (63). Emery convincingly argues that *Of Mice and Men* is not a poignant, sentimental drama, but rather the achievement of a dream of male fraternity that represses and eliminates women and femininity. However, in her reading Steinbeck's tale is a critique of that sterility and lack of diversity, "a scathing commentary on misplaced values." She contends that "Steinbeck's sympathy clearly lies with the feminine" (41). Hadella, noting all the "guarded, fenced, and repressed" women in *The Pastures of Heaven* and *The Long Valley*, concludes: "Ultimately, cloistering women to prevent the human race from falling into sin proves to be a major cause for unhappiness in Steinbeck's disturbed 'valley of the world'" (69).

Of Mice and Men and its *one* unnamed woman has drawn a wondrously diverse set of readings about what it all means in terms of gender issues and feminist critique. Leland Person examines the novel "within a pluralized discourse of masculinity—as a novel about men's relationships to other men" (1), a homosexual reading in the sense that the term means intimate, but not necessarily same-sex, relationships. In his analysis, Curley's wife operates as a kind of outlaw virgin because by crossing "the carefully drawn lines between the ranch house and the bunkhouse, the owners and workers . . . she exaggerates the fault lines between homosocial and heterosexual desires" (2). Killing her imperils the "utopian homosexual dream" (4). Mark Spilka reads the same work with a different outcome. For him, there is something "painfully adolescent" about the dream of the female-less cooperative farm Lennie and George dream about. In his view Steinbeck "projects his own hostilities through George and Lennie" (64), and he sees a connection between Cathy Ames and Curley's wife. In the creation of Cathy, over a decade later, Spilka observes "a monstrous projection of his old hostility toward women as exploiters of the sex impulse" (70).

Complicating the matter of what to make of Curley's wife is the fact that she has evolved since her first manifestation in the novelette. Steinbeck enlarged her role for the play and tried to "explain" her to Claire Luce, who played the character on Broadway. Charlotte Hadella explores the "dialogic tension" of Steinbeck's portrait, citing Steinbeck's paradoxical explanation that you would love her if you knew her, but that you could never know her. Hadella theorizes that the differing analyses of the character may be attributed to the "levels of discourse in the story that compete for definition." In her estimation, the fiction "does not offer an authoritative or absolute statement on the woman's character" (73). My own study ("*Of Mice and Men*: Creating and Recreating Curley's Wife"), via three of her cinematic re-creations, concludes that how Curley's wife is portrayed on film often owes as much to the time of the film production as it does to Steinbeck's text. Betty Field's 1939 bejeweled, made-up, dark-stockinged vamp morphs over the decades into Sheryl Lynn Fenn's 1992 simple, sweet-faced, and bare-legged lost girl, the sexuality of each coded to the audience's semiotic expectations rather than Steinbeck's narrative descriptions. That she can change so much and yet remain an interpretive puzzle for succeeding generations is tribute to the universality of Steinbeck's creation.

My review of the various analyses of how Steinbeck depicts women is not meant to be exhaustive. Many critics whose work I admire are left out. Those I have mentioned are but some of the astute readers who have provoked my thinking and influenced my reading and teaching. The diversity and often-contradictory interpretations they present are also testament to the complexity and levels of interpretation Steinbeck's works inspire. For example, John Ditsky's reading (at the Third International Steinbeck Congress) of Steinbeck's work as itself being an "elusive and remarkable Woman" raises insightful issues about the gender coding of his creative process. What has been unendingly stimulating for me is that the question of how Steinbeck views women continues to inspire such disparate readings. Once all the readers settle on a single view, the issue ceases to be provocative, its mystery resolved. Not the case here.

Over the years I have received both verifications and refutations of my theories about Steinbeck's women. Particularly interesting have been responses from those who knew the man. After delivering my conclusions about the negative portrayal of women in *East of Eden* that resulted when Steinbeck had the opportunity to build a female character from the ground up in comparison to his portraitures of the women in his family, I was greeted by the outstretched hand of John Steinbeck IV, who introduced himself and let me know how much he liked my paper, how valid he found my conclusions. Virginia Scardigli and Jean Ariss were generally supportive of my ideas that Steinbeck had problems in relating to women. Margery Lloyd, on the other hand, found him quite gallant and responsive to women. She told me a charming story about how Steinbeck sympathized with her, holding her while she threw up and telling her that a pretty girl like her should not be sick. John Kenneth Galbraith, upon hearing my conclusions about misogyny in *The Wayward Bus*, insisted that Steinbeck loved women. Both the major biographies chronicle at once his dependence on and sometimes callous treatment of women.

After some twenty years of puzzling out the problem of women in Steinbeck, I decided to turn my attention to other approaches. For the 1990 Third International Congress, I explored the universality of the immigrant paradigm in *The Grapes of Wrath*. Though the Okies are migrants, rather than immigrants, Steinbeck presents their situation in terms of time-coded patterns of the treatment of foreigners. My students verified this conclusion in subsequent years, particularly when I taught in Venezuela and Spain. For Venezuelans, the Okies were analogous to the Colombians, who were swarming legally and illegally into their country, taking all the low-paying jobs. My students in Madrid saw the Okies as Moroccans and Algerians who used the poorly guarded Gibraltar border as a pathway to Spain. A German student related the attitude of the Californians toward the Okies to the response many Germans have toward the Turks who have come in large numbers to avail themselves of economic opportunities not present in their country.[2]

Each new generation rereads Steinbeck through the lens of its own interests. The "Steinbeck and the Environment" conference—the brainchild of Susan Shillinglaw, Susan Beegel, and Wes Tiffany—inspired a second look at many of his works, a look that reveals Steinbeck's prescient environmentalism. *Sea of Cortez*, which has long since achieved mythic status with naturalists, yields further insights when subjected to a "green perspective." From the new approach of environmentalism to the time-tested exploration of how Steinbeck used the Arthurian myths as an underlying archetype, Steinbeck's works, both fiction and nonfiction, provide a never-ending treasure trove for study. Following the Arthurian theme from the early novels to its consummation in *America and Americans* was another revelation of the depths and levels of the man's endlessly questing mind.

In the 1956 film production of the Rodgers and Hammerstein musical *Anna and the King of Siam*, the king, memorably portrayed by Yul

Brynner, sings a delightful song about his worries about what to do, whom to believe, how to lead his country.[3] Recently, as I replayed it on video, I thought the words quite apropos to the issue of Steinbeck and women. "Very often find confusion in conclusion," sings the king, a sentiment not unlike the one I feel when trying to unravel the many threads of John Steinbeck's tapestry of humanity. No sooner do I make my mind up about the woman issue when someone's astute reading convinces me to rethink my position. That is much of what has made the study of Steinbeck such a joy. In the song, after analyzing each issue and not being able to come to a conclusion, the king repeats the refrain: "Is a Puzzlement." That is the statement that ends his song. That is my conclusion after decades of studying Steinbeck and the woman question. Indeed, it is a puzzlement.

Notes

1. Once, after the presentation of one of my feminist critiques of Steinbeck's limited and often negative depictions of women, Jack Benson chided me for being "hard" on Steinbeck. I jokingly reminded him that he was the one who provided me with all the ammunition, as much of my evidence came from his biography.

2. A number of my students at the Complutense in Madrid were with ERASMUS, a European Union student exchange program. Therefore, I was able to get the input from students in a number of European countries.

3. Steinbeck was familiar with the song. He refers to it in one of the "Letters from John Steinbeck" published in the *Salinas Californian* on February 18, 1967. He quotes the line, "Is a Puzzlement," in referring to the difficulty of explaining New York City politics to students in Bangkok.

Works Cited

Benson, Jackson J. *The True Adventures of John Steinbeck, Writer*. New York: Viking, 1984.

Ditsky, John. "Your Own Mind Coming Out in the Garden: Steinbeck's Elusive Woman." *John Steinbeck: The Years of Greatness, 1936-1939*. Ed. Tetsumaro Hayashi. Tuscaloosa: U of Alabama P, 1993. 3-19.

Emery, Jean. "Manhood Beset: Misogyny in Steinbeck's *Of Mice and Men*." *San Jose Studies* 18.1 (1992): 33-42.

Everest, Beth, and Judy Wedeles. "The Neglected Rib: Women in *East of Eden*." *Steinbeck Quarterly* 21.1-2 (1988): 13-23.

Galbraith, John Kenneth. "John Steinbeck: Footnote for a Memoir." *The Atlantic* 224.5 (1969): 65-67.

Gladstein, Mimi R. "Deletions from the *Battle*; Gaps in the *Grapes*." *San Jose Studies* 18.1 (1992): 43-51.

_____. *The Indestructible Woman in Faulkner, Hemingway, and Steinbeck*. Ann Arbor: UMI Research Press, 1986.

_____. "*Of Mice and Men*: Creating and Recreating Curley's Wife." *Beyond Boundaries*. Ed. Susan Shillinglaw and Kevin Hearle. Tuscaloosa: U of Alabama P, 2002. 205-220.

Hadella, Charlotte Cook. "The Dialogic Tension in Steinbeck's Portrait of Curley's Wife." *John Steinbeck: The Years of Greatness, 1936-1939*. Ed. Tetsumaro Hayashi. Tuscaloosa: U of Alabama P, 1993. 64-74.

Noble, Donald, ed. *The Steinbeck Question: New Essays in Criticism*. Troy, NY: Whitston, 1993.

Pritchard, H. A. "Does Moral Philosophy Rest on a Mistake?" *Moral Obligation* by H. A. Pritchard. Oxford: Oxford UP, 1950.

Scardigli, Virginia. Telephone interview with Stephen George. 28 July 2001.

Spilka, Mark. "Of George and Lennie and Curley's Wife: Sweet Violence in Steinbeck's Eden." *The Short Novels of John Steinbeck*. Ed. Jackson J. Benson. Durham: Duke UP, 1990. 59-70.

Steinbeck, John. *America and Americans*. New York: Viking, 1966.

_____. *Cannery Row*. 1945. New York: Penguin, 1994.

_____. "Dear Alicia: Letter from John Steinbeck." *Salinas Californian* 20 May 1967: 4.

_____. *East of Eden*. 1952. New York: Penguin, 1992.

_____. *The Grapes of Wrath*. 1939. New York: Penguin, 1986.

_____. *In Dubious Battle*. 1936. New York: Penguin, 1992.

_____. *Journal of a Novel: The* East of Eden *Letters*. New York: Viking, 1969.

_____. ". . . . like captured fireflies." *CTA Journal* (Nov. 1955): 7.

_____. *The Long Valley*. 1938. New York: Penguin, 1986. 41-66.

_____. *Of Mice and Men*. 1937. New York: Penguin, 1994.

_____. *The Pastures of Heaven*. 1932. New York: Penguin, 1995.

_____. *Sea of Cortez*. New York: Viking, 1941.

_____. *Sweet Thursday*. New York: Viking, 1954.

_____. *The Wayward Bus*. New York: Viking, 1947.

Werlock, Abby H. P. "Looking at Lisa: The Function of the Feminine in Steinbeck's *In Dubious Battle*." *John Steinbeck: The Years of Greatness, 1936-1939*. Ed. Tetsumaro Hayashi. Tuscaloosa: U of Alabama P, 1993. 46-63.

Steinbeck and Ethnicity_____

Susan Shillinglaw

In the spring of 1992, *Nude Zapata* was performed by El Teatro de la Esperanza in San Francisco. The play featured an impassioned Latina conceptual artist, Connie, whose work deconstructs what she sees as the racist 1952 film *Viva Zapata!* Her goal in *Nude Zapata* is to "redeem Zapata from his celluloid prison," where he was bound by the white male establishment—read Steinbeck and Kazan. In the play, writes a lukewarm reviewer, "Steinbeck and his cronies slurp margaritas and conclude they couldn't possibly make 'Viva Zapata!' in Mexico, where they'd be surrounded by Mexicans" (Winn).

In February 1992, I sat on a panel called "Expanding the Canon" at a California Studies conference in Sacramento. My role was to argue that Steinbeck should be reconsidered, not excised, from a multicultural perspective. After all, I began, *In Dubious Battle* (1936) earned Steinbeck a place on a much-touted "Multicultural Reading list for America" compiled a few months earlier by the *San Jose Mercury News* (notably absent was Faulkner). In response to this presentation, an ethnic studies professor from Southern California reported that he had stopped teaching *Tortilla Flat*—a book he liked—because he grew tired of defending Steinbeck. Chicano students, he said, objected to images of lazy, lustful, and drunken paisanos.

That same spring, my students were discussing *To a God Unknown*, and one Chicana, heretofore silent, read the following passage describing a festival hosted by the hero, Joseph Wayne:

> At the pits the Indians moved up and thanklessly took the bread and meat
> that was offered. They moved closer to the dancers, then, and gnawed the
> meat and tore at the hard bread with their teeth. As the rhythm grew heavy
> and insistent, the Indians shuffled their feet in time and their faces re-
> mained blank. (130)

They sound like animals, she noted softly.

During the 1992 Steinbeck Festival, *The Californian* ran articles on "Reading Steinbeck," where Louis Owens notes that the author "doesn't offer a great deal to multiculturalism. His treatment of women and what today would be called people of color leaves a lot to be desired. He was a white, middle class male from Salinas. He was a product of his times" (Neary).

These examples summarize the criticism leveled against Steinbeck's treatment of ethnics, particularly Mexicans. But a reconsideration is surely in order for an author who wrote so frequently and searingly about race and ethnicity. One third of his work either is set in Mexico or treats Mexican subjects. And it is of no small significance that his first published story—"Fingers of Cloud," which ran in *The Stanford Spectator* in 1924—treats an ethnic confrontation and his last published book—*America and Americans*—begins with a chapter on race in America. In that late text he writes: "From the first we have treated our minorities abominably, the way the old boys do the new kids in school. All that was required to release this mechanism of oppression and sadism was that the newcomers be meek, poor, weak in numbers, and unprotected . . ." (15). That statement holds one key to Steinbeck's concern with this country's attitude toward ethnics, for since childhood he had abhorred bullies and developed a quick sympathy for outcasts: a handicapped neighbor, foreign laborers. He visited often and spoke Spanish at the Wagners, a Salinas family that had lived in Mexico for three years. Throughout high school and college he worked with Mexicans at the Spreckles sugar plant and on the company's vast farms, hearing stories, sharing jokes. When he finally had a substantial advance from his publisher, his first trip with Carol Steinbeck in 1935 was a three-month stay in Mexico, a country he had long wished to visit and one to which he repeatedly returned.

In short, he wrote about Mexican-Americans, in particular, because they, like his weary dreamers and gritty laborers, lived outside the dominant culture. He wrote about them because the energy and joy of their culture cut against the rigid middle-class morality that he long scorned, and because their lives and values critiqued the prevailing cultural mythos. As California writer and critic Gerald Haslam has noted, Steinbeck must be recognized for *seeing* the diversity of the state's population, for writing about the paisanos of Monterey, for example, at a time when the majority of Californians did not acknowledge the importance or even the existence of mixed-blood Mexicans. Not only did Steinbeck create a voice for these paisanos, but he also invoked prevailing patterns of the American mythos in giving them form.

Another statement made in the introductory essay in *America and Americans* suggests a second reason for Steinbeck's abiding interest in ethnicity. He tells a story about a native American he met when working at Lake Tahoe in the late 1920s:

Many white people, after association with the tribesmen, have been struck with the dual life—the reality and super-reality—that the Indians seem to be able to penetrate at will. The stories of travelers in the early days are filled with these incidents of another life separated from this one by a penetrable veil; and such is the power of the Indians' belief in this other life that the traveler usually comes out believing in it too and only fearing that he won't be believed. (18)

Compare this vision with one of Steinbeck's own, outlined in a 1930 letter to his Stanford classmate Carl Wilhelmson:

Modern sanity and religion are a curious delusion. Yesterday I went out in a fishing boat—out in the ocean. By looking over the side into the blue water, I could quite easily see the shell of the turtle who supports the world. I am getting more prone to madness. What a ridiculous letter this is; full of vaguenesses and unrealities. I for one and you to some extent have a great many of the basic impulses of an African witch doctor. (*Life* 31)

The playful tone masks the letter's real significance. Steinbeck was no mere realist, either in art or life. Metaphysics intrigued him. Although many of his works have a realistic texture, a journalistic precision, they also contain layers of meaning beneath the surface, a point he often noted in correspondence when he referred to the various "levels" of his books. (*Cannery Row*, for instance, was "written on several levels of understanding and people can take out of it what they can bring to it.")[1] One way that he suggests alternative meaning is through marginal characters, ethnics with radically different perspectives: the Indian Tularecito in *The Pastures of Heaven* (1932), whose face holds "ancient wisdom"; Gitano in "The Great Mountains" (1953), behind whose eyes was "some unknown thing"; Pepe in "Flight" (1938), who acknowledges the dark watchers of Big Sur; the "old Chinaman," who "flap-flapped" mysteriously to the beach at dusk in *Cannery Row*; and the Chinese Lee, who, as one of Steinbeck's self-reliant and wise "self" characters, speaks for the author and plays complex roles in *East of Eden* (1952). These ethnics fascinated Steinbeck in part because they represented a vision that he longed to grasp, that he often suggested in his fiction through their ritualistic significance. Steinbeck was in large part attracted to "others" because of their exoticism and mysticism.[2] A key question, of course, is whether or not he diminishes them by his treatment or if, as symbol or prophet or seer, these ethnics help blend ritual and realism, and thus help reconstruct a vision of wholeness.

Far from exhaustive, this essay will examine representative and sometimes problematic texts about the ethnic presence in America. It will focus on two strains plucked from *America and Americans*: first, Steinbeck's treatment of ethnicity as cultural saga; second, his fascination with the primitive as intriguing and often unfathomable other.

I

That first published story, "Fingers of Cloud," sets up a significant paradigm for much of Steinbeck's work. As the story opens, Gertie, the restless heroine, flees her home to nearby mountains because she feels a visceral craving for mountaintops, clouds, and beauty. A rainstorm, however, sends her down into a migrant camp, where bleak reality banishes her visionary aspirations. Subsequently the white Gertie marries the "black" Filipino worker, Pedro. He is a violent, sexually charged man, who demands that both Gertie and the reader confront the grim underside of the American experience, the insistent violence that shatters visionary quests. Like so many of Steinbeck's central characters, Gertie is an idealist, and her quest, like Joseph Wayne's or the Joads' or Adam Trask's, is also America's—the hope for a new beginning. Her disillusionment and dark knowledge is also theirs.

For embedded both in the American experience and in Steinbeck's retelling of the nation's Edenic impulse are other stories, ones of racial conflict, sexual excesses, tainted deeds. "Fingers of Cloud" articulates boldly—and with no little artistic uncertainty as to exactly what the 22-year-old author wanted to say—that America's story includes, but often suppresses, ethnic confrontations. For Steinbeck, the saga of continental conquest in broad sweep is a tale of Edenic expectation and consequent disillusionment; and that inevitable fall means, in part, that character and (more insistently) reader glimpse what so often taints the dream: racial and ethnic suppression and violence. The brief first chapter of *The Pastures of Heaven*, for example, ironically deflates the notion of paradisiacal America announced by the title: the archetypal American here is a white corporal chasing renegade Indians, a man who, upon locating them, beats the lot and then ultimately dies of the pox after somewhat more intimate contact with an Indian woman. What Steinbeck acknowledges is that racial and sexual violence is as much a part of the American saga as is the Edenic mythos that the visionaries in the book blithely seek.

That parable of America's dark destiny represents a defining moment in much of Steinbeck's fiction. Repeatedly he undercuts sagas of idealism, dynastic control, or social harmony with less insistent voices and stories of racial and ethnic turmoil. Examples are numerous. In his first epic treatment of Westward expansion, *To a God Unknown*, the hero Joseph Wayne's Mexican friend Juanito discovers brother Benjy's sexual infidelity and kills him, thus enduring as punishment a self-imposed exile. The loss of Juanito, Joseph's most trusted confidant, signals the beginning of his spiral downward. Alone, Joseph falters. Alone, he ignores Juanito's warning to avoid the mysterious rock. The rollicking tale of contractual social harmony, *Tortilla Flat*, is punctured by one tale of sexual infidelity and death—the corporal's—and one of desperation and suicide—Grandfather Ravanno's. And at the conclusion Danny spins into a maelstrom of unbridled destruction and sexual conquest that dismantles the fragile fraternal order. In the short story "Johnny Bear," what must be suppressed in the Buffalo Bar are not Johnny's fragmented words telling of Amy's pregnancy and suicide, but that one phrase that reveals her liaison with a Chinese man. To silence Johnny Bear, Alex smashes his face. A black man is lynched in "The Vigilante," and the violence of that moment is compared, at the conclusion, to a sexual liaison. Curley's wife in *Of Mice and Men* (1937), her own dream of Hollywood stardom snuffed by her marriage, threatens the black man Crook's thin security by giving voice to the lynching threat. By far the darkest vision in the multilayered *Cannery Row* is early glimpsed in the Chinaman's eyes, "the desolate cold aloneness of the landscape . . . [where] there wasn't anybody at all in the world and he was left" (24). In *East of Eden* Adam Trask's vision of fecund California acres is shattered as fully by his wife Cathy's betrayal as it is qualified by the Chinese Lee's interpolated tale of his parents' arrival in California, their own story of migration and hope cut short by Lee's mother's rape and subsequent death.

In short, throughout Steinbeck's work, fragmentary voices of ethnic Americans suggest, like an insistent discordant note, America's violent and oppressive past. Sexuality and violence are implosive in these texts. The stories and episodes convey, I think, not Steinbeck's racism—far from that—but rather his sensitivity to the contradictions at the heart of the American character and experience. Idealism, superficial structures of belief, confidence in American pragmatism, Edenic quests—all are altered or destroyed when touched by subversive violence, repressed knowledge, sexual energy.

More can be said, however, about Steinbeck's sensitivity to the ethnic presence in the West. Tales of California's settlement repeatedly show how intertwined are dominant and marginal voices. In each of his western epics—*To a God Unknown*, *The Grapes of Wrath*, and *East of Eden*—the patriarch is dethroned, his ties to the land severed, and family bonds strained. With the loss of certainty in cultural and familial coherence, voices other than those of the dominant culture emerge and carry the burden of meaning in each text. In the first novel it is the Indians' wisdom and acceptance. In *The Grapes of Wrath* it is Ma Joad's iron will. And in *East of Eden* it is the Chinese Lee's intuitive grasp of *timshel*, the doctrine that he so fluidly accepts and Adam so trenchantly resists. In terms that Werner Sollors uses in *Beyond Ethnicity*, the tension between lines of descent, or inherited privilege and culture, and "a forward-looking culture of consent" (4) is an essential national drama and one that Steinbeck draws upon in his most ambitious accounts of California settlement.

In his first novel set in California, *To a God Unknown*, for example, Joseph Wayne is the archetypal patriarch, tracing lines of descent. He's also a magnificently wrongheaded visionary, and as such a kind of American fictional icon. He would rule the land, his three brothers, and his wife absolutely; even the self-possession of his sister-in-law falters before Joseph's physical presence. This ungodly god-like man—to apply Ahab's tag to the hero modeled after him—countermands the cycles of nature, first believing that a drought will not return, a foolhardy notion, and then defying the drought when it comes, a wickedly defiant stance. But as hereditary ties and inherited willfulness fail him, other voices are tentatively acknowledged and fragile bonds are forged.

Steinbeck complicates the story of Joseph's dynastic ambitions through rough contrasts between white and Indian characters. Each of Joseph's three brothers is, in his way, as monomaniacal as he: Benjy lusts for women, Thomas craves animal contact, Burton is a religious fanatic. Each brother fixes on a teleological purpose, and if Joseph's vision is the most grandiose, his is nonetheless as confining as their "gods"—women, animals, religious fundamentalism. But Joseph is also engaged with three Indians whose words and actions have symbolic bearing on his life. Each Indian in the book represents knowledge that the hero would suppress. Joseph is linked to Indian alter-egos. Romas gives him practical advice, most pointedly, not to build his dynastic seat under an oak tree; Romas also tells him about drought years. His son, Willie, embodies a vision Joseph ignores: Willie's nightmares of defeat and death become, at last, Joseph's own. Finally, Juanito, his friend and worker, tells him of the mysterious rocks that are both his sanctuary and his tomb. "My mother brought me here, señor," Juanito tells Joseph. "My mother was Indian . . . the Indian in me made me come, señor" (45). The symbolic place intrigues Joseph, and his need to know it—in a word to conquer the ineffable—proves futile. The intangible resists his domination, and he perishes because he does not heed the Indian voice signifying an alternate truth. The Indians in *To a God Unknown* form a kind of chorus that imparts significant and telling information that Joseph does not and, in his myopia, cannot absorb.

The structure of the text also qualifies Joseph's story. Not unlike *The Pastures of Heaven*, this novel is framed by passages that undercut Joseph's dynastic impulses. This is Joseph's first sight of the town of Our Lady, as he enters into the valley he will call his own:

> The huts of Indians clustered about the mud walls of the church, and although the church was often vacant now and its saints were worn and part of its tile roof lay in a shattered heap on the ground, and although the bells were broken, the Mexican Indians still lived near about and held their festivals, danced La Jota on the packed earth and slept in the sun. (4-5)

This sentence suggests a long history of Spanish conquest, and yet what survives here—as in the book's conclusion—are the Indians and their pagan ways. In the final chapter, the Indians celebrate the end of the drought with orgies of pleasure, as their throbbing music blends with the sounds of rain and their naked bodies roll in the mud. Indians and nature seem as one. If their resilience as well as their acceptance of cycles of drought and rain offer one foil to Joseph's monomaniacal quest, the Catholic Church—surprisingly—offers another. Father Angelo, who can be as doctrinaire as Joseph is single-minded, nonetheless compromises his faith. It is surely significant that this text ends not with Joseph's solitary death in a parched land but with Father Angelo's gesture of acceptance in the midst of a drenched community. As he listens to the rain in the final chapter, he belatedly remembers that he had, indeed, prayed for rain. No fanatic, he. And in the closing paragraphs, as the sound of the people's pagan rites blend with the life-giving rain, he checks his doctrinaire need to stop their blasphemy. Penance can be administered later, he tells himself. Because the priest accommodates himself to the Indians' paganism, he assures his survival and that of his church. In contrast, although Joseph consults the priest and notes Juanito's warning about the drought, he cannot meaningfully contemplate change or heed warnings. His teleological purpose defines and dooms him.

The wisdom of the Indians' holistic vision thus undercuts Joseph's monomaniacal quest, and their world view ultimately defines meaning in this text, acceptance of what is. Mexicans are as thematically important in *To a God Unknown* as is the exotic Lee in *East of Eden* and as are marginalized women's voices that emerge at the conclusion of important books: *In Dubious Battle*, *Of Mice and Men*, *The Grapes of Wrath*, and *The Winter of Our Discontent* (1961). In each, the female character—like the ethnic—is largely discounted throughout the book, seen only through the eyes of males, silenced. But Curley's wife, the whining Rose of Sharon, the meek Lisa, and the winsome Ellen Hawley find voices or assume a symbolic role at the end of each novel and articulate values that the author endorses. In a "passion of communication," the lonely wife of furious Curley pours out her life's "story" of missed chances to the only audience she's ever had, Lennie, an innocent who cannot hear her (but the reader can). As Rose of Sharon evolves from self-centered girl to empathetic woman, she stops whining and smiles, becoming the text's symbolic center. Lisa's vision of domestic pleasure is what organizer Jim so pointedly and fatally resists. And only Ellen fully recognizes Ethan's desperation: "Take me with you," she pleads. "You're not coming back" (278), words that will save Ethan in the final chapter because he "had to return the talisman to its new owner" (281). Male characters may resist or dismiss the fragmented female voice, but the reader should not. Steinbeck has been accused of creating one-dimensional female characters as often as he has been said to create ethnic stereotypes. Both charges, I would argue, must be qualified by the thematic and cultural significance given alternative perspectives, both female and ethnic. That vision is, in many texts, only haltingly and belatedly acknowledged by central male characters who cannot abandon inherited notions of patriarchal control of family, fate and nature. But the very fragmentation of women and ethnics is precisely the point. Steinbeck's patriarchs cannot heed the words appealing to contractual bonds and readers often discount their import.

II

How can we conceive of difference without fetishizing it by a separatist and ultimately hedonistic, self-canceling politics of identity?

(E. San Juan Jr. 4)

If, in part, Steinbeck's ethnic characters play key roles in his settlement dramas, they also enact significant parts in a personal and writerly drama. He cast himself early on as an outsider, and for much of his life he identified with marginal groups. His most sympathetic characters don't belong. "For American intellectuals," writes Fred Matthews,

[F]olk romanticism tended to lead not to hatred of "outsiders" and a lust to purge them from the nation, but rather to a sense of guilt about their own society's exploitation of the strangers, and to the desire to protect them from the aggressive majority. In the American context, alienated romanticism created not xenophobia but xenophilia. (qtd. in Sollors 29)

With other modernists, Steinbeck found in the untutored a vital source of artistic expression. Throughout his career Mexican subjects in particular intrigued him because he identified with their otherness—a zest for life, scorn for a dominant culture, and an inherent exoticism and often mysticism. When he was writing *Tortilla Flat*, he wrote to critic and book reviewer Joseph Henry Jackson: "The work has been the means of making me feel that I am living richly, diversely, and, in a few cases and for a few moments, even heroically" (*Life* 119). In 1948, depressed and lonely, he wrote to friends that he needed to go to Mexico, for, he said, there's an "illogic there that I need" (Letter to Lovejoys). Steinbeck discovered a transforming power in ethnicity. He kept returning to Mexico and Mexican subjects as a way to live and he translated that personal need into a cultural need.

In contemporary discussions of ethnicity, however, Steinbeck's impulse is problematic. To attach even compelling qualities to the primitive encodes ethnic stereotypes: the Mexican is perpetually the "other," essentially exotic and strange. This argument is, from one point of view, unassailable, since Steinbeck, a writer of the dominant culture, drew portraits of mystical, untutored, and spontaneous primitives. Louis Owens, for one, recently has argued that Steinbeck's Indians are "purely symbols, walking shadows illustrating the kind of intuitive, nonrational state he and Ricketts celebrate in the *Log*." Passages like this are, in this view, representative:

[Indians] seemed to live on remembered things, to be so related to the seashore and the rocky hills and the loneliness that they are these things. To ask about the country is like asking about themselves. "How many toes have you?" "What, toes? Let's see—of course, ten. I have known them all my life, I never thought to count them. Of course it will rain tonight, I don't know why. Something in me tells me I will rain tonight. Of course, I am the whole thing, now that I think about it. I ought to know when I will rain." (*Log* 78)

Here, as in *To a God Unknown*, the Indians are one with the land, bound to a vision that has perished in the modern world. But when assessing Steinbeck's acknowledged and frank impulse toward primitivism, I believe that several points must be kept in mind—points that do not, finally, counter the argument that this sympathetic white male, more than any other, avoids encoding identities or that he, more than others, writes fully and deeply in any one book about the Mexican culture. A few observations may, however, qualify the resistance to Steinbeck's ethnic portraits.

First, a holistic vision of character and environment is as essential to Steinbeck's ecological vision in *Sea of Cortez* as it is in *To a God Unknown* or in *Cannery Row*. His biological holism, a conviction that humans must be seen in the context of their environment, often finds an objective correlative in the primitive. For Steinbeck, marginal groups, not the dominant culture, lived non-teleologically and thus accepted "what is." Second, an assessment of Steinbeck's primitivism must acknowledge his range. In his works simplicity and spontaneity cut across racial and ethnic lines: Mack and the boys are as untrammeled as the lusty paisanos in *Tortilla Flat*. Casy in *The Grapes of Wrath* and Doc in *Cannery Row*, both of whom live non-teleologically and holistically, can be as mystical as the Indians in *Sea of Cortez*. Values associated with the Mexican are applied to other characters who live non-teleologically and thus seem "simple" (Dr. Winter), "childlike" (Lennie), or "sentimental" (Doc Burton). Naivete is not, in short, ethnically determined. Finally, Steinbeck is, in fact, as sensitive to the Indians' economic and social plight as he is fascinated by their spiritualism, holism, and zest. It must not be forgotten that as he was working out ideas for *Sea of Cortez* in 1940, he was simultaneously writing a controversial script for *The Forgotten Village*, a documentary set in an isolated Mexican village which contrasts traditional mores—particularly an unquestioned faith in a healer or curandera—with the village's need for modern medicine to combat cholera: the script poses knotty questions about modernity and progress.[3] Nor must the many foils to Steinbeck's intuitive Indians be discounted when measuring his ethnic sensitivity: wily Zapata, artful Pilon, and hardheaded Juan Chicoy are, in the main, vividly realized and incisive portraits. And critics of Steinbeck's primitivism must also acknowledge his firm insights about social reality:

> It is said so often and in such ignorance that Mexicans are contented, happy people. "They don't want anything." This, of course, is not a description of the happiness of Mexicans, but of the unhappiness of the person who says it. (*Log* 99-100)

> To us, a little weary of the complication and senselessness of a familiar picture, the Indian seems a rested, simple man. If we should permit ourselves to remain in ignorance of his complications, then we might long for his condition, thinking it superior to ours. The Indian on the other hand, subject to constant hunger and cold, mourning a grandfather and set of uncles in Purgatory, pained by the aching teeth and sore eyes of malnutrition, may well envy us our luxury. (*Log* 248)

In short, Steinbeck would have readers as fully sympathetic to ethnics as to Okies, working stiffs, bums, and villagers locked in resistance with Nazi oppressors. "In every bit of honest writing in the world," he wrote in a 1938 journal entry,

> there is a base theme. Try to understand men, if you understand each other you will be kind to each other. Knowing a man well never leads to hate and nearly always leads to love. There are shorter means, many of them. There

is writing promoting social change, writing punishing injustice, writing in celebration of heroism, but always that base theme. Try to understand each other. ("*Long Valley* Ledger")

That could well serve as an epigraph to his writing on ethnicity.

All of the author's types and anti-types are sketched fully in *Tortilla Flat*, an engaging account of the adrift in Monterey. *Tortilla Flat*, notes Charles R. Metzger in a sympathetic discussion of the author's diverse portraits of Mexican-Americans, "does not purport to do more than present one kind of Mexican-American, the *paisano* errant, in one place, Monterey, and at one time, just after World War I" (149). To respond further to charges of essentialism in Steinbeck, I wish to examine this most problematic text where, I will posit, Steinbeck deliberately avoids characterizations that depend on an ethnic component.

Chicano critic Philip Ortega, among others, finds Steinbeck's paisanos objectionably flat. "The romanticized stereotype and caricature of the Chicano," he notes,

> is nowhere more evident in *Tortilla Flat* than when Steinbeck wrote that the Chicanos are "clean of commercialism, free of the complicated systems of American business, and, having nothing that can be stolen, exploited, or mortgaged, that system has not attacked them very vigorously. (41)

The passage Ortega cites is, I would agree, a crucial one in a text so centrally concerned with identity—but crucial not because it caricatures the paisano. It appears on the second page of the novel, where Steinbeck pointedly defines a paisano by what he is not; he is not a part of the dominant culture and so avoids the most objectionable qualities of that culture. When, in the following paragraph, Steinbeck poses the obvious next question, "What is a paisano?" the response avoids reference to character, to any essentialist premises. The paisano, a name Steinbeck may have used because it lacks a racist context and because its meaning is indeterminate,

. . . is a mixture of Spanish, Indian, Mexican, and assorted Caucasian bloods. His ancestors have lived in California for a hundred or two years. He speaks English with a paisano accent and Spanish with a paisano accent. . . . His color, like that of a well-browned meerschaum pipe, he ascribes to sunburn. He is a paisano, and he lives in that uphill district. . . . (2)

Although Ortega objects to ethnic distortion in this passage as well, in essence Steinbeck describes externals, not innate qualities of a Mexican. Throughout these tales, in fact, it is the characters, not the author, who paint with broad strokes. The paisanos show little reluctance to make essentialist distinctions. "Race antipathy" toward Italians "overcame Danny's good sense" (5). Torelli had, Pilon knew, "The Italian's exaggerated and wholly quixotic ideal of marital relations" (42). Portagees "always want to marry, and they love money" (28). To heartily insult a stingy friend is to call him a Jew. Women are best, as Danny and his friends know well, when "lively." Often women are grasping. "That Rosa will want new dresses. All women do. I know them," asserts Pilon (28). He weeps with Danny "over the perfidy of women" (19). It is precisely this rigidity—however comic in context—that Steinbeck avoids in his depictions. Only the paisanos' personalities, not their ethnic identifies, are tagged: "Their campaign [against Sweets] had called into play and taxed to the limit the pitiless logic of Pilon, the artistic ingenuousness of Pablo, and the gentleness and humanity of Jesus Maria Corcoran. Big Joe had contributed nothing" (105). Logic, ingenuousness, humanity and Big Joe's uncouthness are the essentialist characteristics of Steinbeck's paisanos.

Steinbeck avoids reductionist attitudes toward ethnics in part because, as is clear from the two paragraphs quoted above, he focuses the reader's attention not on fixed norms but on *questions* of identity. What Danny's house is becomes the central concern in a book that takes as its model *Le Morte d'Arthur*, tales of knightly prowess where heroes earn for the round table its identity. *Tortilla Flat*, like Malory's epic, is about process. Indeed, although Danny, Pilon, Pablo, and Pirate have distinct and rather complex personalities, they enter the book with indeterminate identities, each in a kind of liminal state. As first introduced, Danny and Pilon are no longer soldiers, nor was Danny a "mule skinner" before the war, as he had confidently labeled himself. Heretofore Danny has not been a homeowner, and when he acknowledges ownership "one cry of pain escaped him before he left for all time his old and simple existence" (13). Pablo is on parole, the months ahead a test of his resolve. Pirate is initially a shadowy presence, for "no one knew him very well, and no one interfered with him" (57), but his character deepens as his pile of quarters mounts. As individuals, each paisano is adrift. In the early chapters, they are occasionally lonely and dissatisfied because obligations—being a tenant or a homeowner—cramp their freedom. Only when all move in with Danny, only as a "unit of which the parts were men" (1) does their identity jell. They become Danny's men. The first sentence of the novel, in fact, articulates Steinbeck's central concern in the text, group identity. "This is the story of Danny and of Danny's friends and of Danny's house. It is a story of how these three became one thing . . ." (1). The book is not about drunken sots, but as many critics have noted, it is about Steinbeck's theoretical concerns with group man: how a unit functions as a whole and how the identity of that whole is distinct from that of individuals composing the group.

In fact, Steinbeck's paisanos are defined most precisely by the codes they develop as comrades, codes of survival. Together the paisanos exhibit endurance, pluck, and skill; together they are generous to Pirate; together they listen solemnly to the corporal's story; together they are loyal and respect the rhythms of nature and the privacy of friends. The qualities that he identifies with the paisano clan are far from objectionable or, in fact, ethnically determined. Demands of communal living and the paisanos' economic isolation establish identity with far more conviction than "paisano" norms—whatever they may be. As a mutually dependent unit, the paisanos share traits with Steinbeck's Okies and the *Cannery Row* bums who are similarly marginalized by their economic status. The paisanos' virtues are theirs—endurance, pluck, communal spirit. Their plights are similar—the need of a home and space for shared experience. And central to all three books is ecological holism in a community, human interdependence. In each novel Steinbeck works with the part of reality he knew and translates that known truth into the contours of art.

There is also a mimetic defense to be made for the text: these were real figures around Monterey in the 1930s. Steinbeck heard many of the stories first from Sue Gregory, a popular Monterey High School Spanish teacher, president of the Spanish club, and mentor, friend, and counselor to Monterey's paisanos. A couple he heard when he worked with Mexicans in the Spreckles sugar plant during summers in high school and college. And, as demonstrated by countless newspaper accounts in the *Monterey Peninsula Herald*, their exploits were famous around town. This is Edward Martin's story of himself, told to a reporter, Dudley Towe, when he was 97:

> "Absolutely, Pilon and me, we was just like brothers. . . . We were always together. When you see one, you wait a few seconds, and then you see the other one. . . . We had a whole lot of fun." Doing what? "We pretty well drinking wine. In Iris Canyon, across the highway from the cemetery. We lived in a box in Iris Canyon behind the willows. A big box. Like a coffin. Made out of tin. We used to get in there to drink wine. Especially when raining. . . . Just drinking, that's all we did. . . . We used to sell bottles, beer bottles, sody bottles. Enough to get more wine. We would get in underneath the box and sleep there. Next morning we would figure what we are going to do to get another bottle of wine. We had a little dog. 'Borracha.' You know what that means in Spanish? 'Drunkard!' Everybody know him here in town. He used to pick him up bottle of wine. We put the bottle of wine on the floor, and he would pick him up and bring it over to us." (14)

In short, Steinbeck's interest in these paisanos is in part psychological—the study of group man—and in part realistic—the "history" of a subculture—and finally in part aesthetic—wrestling with the contours of artistic expression. As a writer who declared with some frequency throughout the 1930s and 1940s that the novel was dead, he restlessly sought alternate forms for expression and self-consciously, in most of his books, wrote about the process of creation. *Tortilla Flat* is as much about the tradition of the oral story telling as it is about a culture that recounts the stories. Cast in a consciously artistic language that captures the rhythms of Spanish (a device that to some ears sounds artificial, to others charming), Steinbeck records the tales he heard as an "outsider." In the first paragraph of the novel, the word "story" appears five times. And the book's "plot" is concerned always with stories: making them (hatching schemes), listening to them, or allowing the reader to watch the paisanos tell them. The *caporal*'s sad tale of lost love, for example, is a "drama that made the experiments of Cornelia Ruiz seem uninteresting and vain. Here was a situation which demanded the action of the friends" (118). A good story engages the paisanos in "action," just as the "story" told by the artist engages the reader in understanding. And engagement in the narrative is, in fact, the book's method, as Pilon reveals when he listens to Jesus Maria's account of the soldiers and Arabella: "The story was gradually taking shape. Pilon liked it this way. It ruined a story to have it all come out quickly. The good story lay in half-told things which must be filled in out of the hearer's own experience" (45). That may well be Steinbeck's artistic credo; certainly it is Pilon's. As the book's most vivid character, Pilon is the consummate artist, creating romantic visions and artful constructs with equal facility. Pilon is the Artful Dodger, the confidence man. He is as fully a study of the possibilities of art as are Steinbeck's other artist figures of the same period: Johnny Bear, whose stories record life with absolute fidelity, stripped of empathy; Elisa Allen or Mary Teller, whose gardens reflect their artistic compulsions; the boy Jody, whose youthful romanticism must be tempered with life's hardest lesson, the reality of death. Steinbeck repeatedly wrote self-consciously about art: the roles artists play, the forms they seek, the plots they create. So, Arthur

Pettit's objection to the texture of *Tortilla Flat* may, in fact, be Steinbeck's very point: that the art of story telling is a mixed bag. "Alternately tender and tasteless, subtle and simple, comical and crude, the novel is handicapped by a baffling mixture of moods and motifs which collide rather than meet. The mock-heroic elements conflict with the theme of paradise lost, and we are left uncertain as to which is more important" (195). The uncertainty of art, of many stories told by many personalities, mirrors the instability of the paisanos' culture. And life on the edge—charmingly told, raucous and doomed—is far preferable, in Steinbeck's vision, to entrenched ease—teleologically focused, predictable, and no doubt the subject for an intricately plotted novel that he couldn't write.

III

The Latina artist in *Nude Zapata* is "so mad about a 40-year-old film she's going on strike as a gesture of her rage." For Connie, Steinbeck's *Viva Zapata!* "represents white male domination" (Winn). Indeed, a root cause of Steinbeck's perceived insensitivity to ethnics may be traced to films of Steinbeck's works. There is seepage from popular translations of the novels back to the texts themselves. As a result, an uncritical regard of both may be synonymous. I close with two examples.

On January 10, 1944, bitterly disappointed with *Lifeboat*, the Hitchcock film he had scripted, Steinbeck wrote a letter of complaint to Twentieth Century-Fox Film Corporation:

> While it is certainly true that I wrote a script for Lifeboat [*sic*], it is not true that in that script as in the film there were any slurs against organized labor nor was there a stock comedy Negro. On the contrary there was an intelligent and thoughtful seaman who knew realistically what he was about. And instead of the usual colored travesty of the half comic and half pathetic Negro there was a Negro of dignity, purpose and personality. (*Life* 266)

Steinbeck wanted his name withdrawn from the film.

When Jack Kirkland began writing a script of *Tortilla Flat* for Broadway, Steinbeck was enthusiastic. In September, 1937, he told a reporter for the *Los Gatos Mail-News*, "We are going to have something new in an all-Mexican company. Then we won't have to bother about accent, and all that. The actors won't be able to talk in any other way. We expect to pick up our cast in and around LA." But his concern for authenticity evaporated when he read Kirkland's final script. "[W]e read the thing out loud and it sounded so bad that I got to feeling low . . . ," he wrote his agent.

> There are so many little undertones that he has got wrong. I don't want to maintain my book but I would like to maintain the people as I know them. Let me give you an example. Jack makes them want wine and need wine and suffer for wine whereas they want the thing wine does. They are not drunkards at all. They like the love and fights that come with wine, rather than the wine itself. (*Life* 150)

"'I think it will flop,' Steinbeck predicted calmly" to reporter Louis Walther a few days before the New York opening (Walther 11).

In his best work Steinbeck achieved what Hitchcock and Kirkland did not—a balance between fidelity to fact and fidelity to art, between empathy for marginalized Americans and the inescapability of his perspective as an outsider. But artistic balance is a fragile construction. From *Tortilla Flat* on, Steinbeck was engaged in a lifelong debate with critics over the fidelity of his ethnic portraits, over his use of dialect, folklore, and historical sources. Contemporary reviews of *Sea of Cortez* and *The Forgotten Village* throw the debate into focus. Writing for the Springfield, Massachusetts, *Republican*, Eileen Carlson notes that in *Sea of Cortez* one sees "the value of meeting each new experience unfettered by prejudices from previous experiences, to the value of different ideals of civilization—ours and that of the Mexican Indian. . . . Best of all it is splendidly tolerant." Reviewing *The Forgotten Village*, the author's good friend, fellow traveler to Mexico in 1935, novelist and book reviewer, Joseph Henry Jackson, found troubling Steinbeck's implied superiority to the peasants:

> Some day a critic will take time to analyze the curious, fatherly-godlike love that Steinbeck manifests for his characters, to examine the chastiseth-whom-he-loveth attitude implicit in so much of Steinbeck's work, the insistent diminishment of his human characters (no not his turtles) by which the author-creator unconsciously magnifies himself in relation to them. (17)

Jackson, with Connie the Latina conceptual artist, faults the outsider's vision. Outsider Steinbeck most definitely was. And "splendidly tolerant" as well. The truth about his art probably lies between the two, but tipping the balance, to my mind, is his intention, his "base theme. . . . Try to understand each other" (Steinbeck, "*Long Valley* Ledger").

From *After "The Grapes of Wrath": Essays on John Steinbeck in Honor of Tetsumaro Hayashi*, edited by Donald V. Coers, Paul D. Ruffin, and Robert DeMott (1995), pp. 40-57. Copyright © 1995 by Ohio University Press. Reprinted with permission of Ohio University Press, Athens, Ohio (www.ohioswallow.com).

Notes

1. Letter to Joseph Henry Jackson.

2. See Lewis and Britch, who argue that Steinbeck "characterizes his Indian figures as members of a particular race, who act as they do because of some subconscious predisposition, and who, in like manner, are so identified as Indians by members of Western culture" (128). While I agree that Steinbeck's Indians are associated with a powerful but vanishing culture, I also think that, first, he associates the mystery of the "other" with several ethnic groups, not only Indians; second, that although the figure of the Indian is doomed (most perish) his voice, in its very insistence, survives in the consciousness of the central character and the reader. The fragmentation of the ethnic voice is, I believe, the author's critique of the dominant culture. Therefore, I disagree with Lewis and Britch's conclusion that "Steinbeck has managed to reveal Indian suffering without indicting the white majority as in any willful way the cause of it" (152). Steinbeck's critique of white imperialism is clear enough in the opening pages of *The Pastures of Heaven*.

3. Steinbeck's closest friend, Edward Ricketts, visited Steinbeck during filming in Mexico, and he strongly opposed Steinbeck's tacit support of progress in the film: medicine is seen as the cure for the cholera epidemic. Education is endorsed as corrective to a bad water supply. Ricketts, in contrast, thought that any outside influence undermined traditional beliefs, and that Steinbeck should simply study and accept what is. Ricketts wrote an anti-script to Steinbeck's own.

Works Cited

Carlson, Eileen. "Steinbeck in a Boat: 'Sea of Cortez' Is Marine Biology, Philosophy and Sea Narrative Mixed in Splendid Prose." *Springfield Republican* 21 Dec. 1941: 12.

Haslam, Gerald. "Travels with John," Keynote Address. Steinbeck Festival XII. Salinas, 1 Aug. 1991.

Hearle, Kevin. "Regions of Discourse: Steinbeck, Cather, Jewett, and the Pastoral Tradition of American Regionalism." Diss. UC Santa Cruz, 1991: 136-41.

Jackson, Joseph Henry. "The Bookman's Daily Notebook: Steinbeck Goes All Simple and Just Overdoes It." *San Francisco Chronicle* 1 June 1941: 17.

Lewis, Cliff, and Carroll Britch. "Shadow of the Indian in the Fiction of John Steinbeck." *Rediscovering Steinbeck—Revisionist Views of His Art, Politics and Intellect*. Ed. Cliff Lewis and Carroll Britch. Lewiston: Mellen, 1989. 125-54.

Metzger, Charles R. "Steinbeck's Mexican-Americans". *Steinbeck: The Man and His Work*. Ed. Richard Astro and Tetsumaro Hayashi. Corvallis: Oregon State UP, 1971. 141-55.

Neary, Walter. "Students Drawn to Human Themes of Hope, Equality," *The Californian* 10 Aug. 1992: 1.

Ortega, Philip D. "Fables of Identity: Stereotype and Caricature of Chicanos in Steinbeck's *Tortilla Flat*." *The Journal of Ethnic Studies* 1 (1973): 39-43.

Owens, Louis. "Grandpa Killed Indians, Pa Killed Snakes: Steinbeck and the American Indian." *Melus* 15 (1988): 85-92.

Peck, Llewellyn B. "Noted Author Returns from European Trip." *Los Gatos Mail-News and Saratoga Star* 16 Sept. 1937: 1, 4.

Pettit, Arthur G. *Images of the Mexican-American in Fiction and Film*. College Station: Texas A&M UP, 1980.

San Juan, E. Jr. *Racial Formations/Critical Transformations*. Atlantic Highlands: Humanities, 1992.

Sollors, Werner. *Beyond Ethnicity: Consent and Descent in American Culture*. New York: Oxford UP, 1986.

Steinbeck, John. *America and Americans*. New York: Viking, 1966.

_____. *Cannery Row*. New York: Viking, 1945.

_____. "Fingers of Cloud: A Satire on College Protervity." *The Stanford Spectator* 2 (February 1924): [149], 161-64.

_____. Letter to Joseph Henry Jackson. Aug. 1944. The Bancroft Library. University of California, Berkeley.

_____. Letter to Ritch and Tal Lovejoy. 27 May 1948. John Steinbeck Library. Salinas, CA.

_____. *The Log from the Sea of Cortez*. New York: Penguin, 1951.

_____. "*Long Valley* Ledger." Steinbeck Research Center. San Jose State University, San Jose, CA.

_____. *Steinbeck: A Life in Letters*. Ed. Elaine Steinbeck and Robert Wallsten. New York: Viking, 1975.

_____. *To a God Unknown*. 1933. New York: Penguin, 1976.

_____. *Tortilla Flat*. 1935. New York: Penguin, 1986.

_____. *The Winter of Our Discontent*. New York: Viking, 1961.

Towe, Dudley. "Pilon and Me." *Game and Gossip* 20 Jan. 1957: 14-15.

Walther, Louis. "Oklahomans Steinbeck's Theme: Author Says Migrants Altering California." *San Jose Mercury Herald* 8 Jan. 1938: 11, 13.

Winn, Steven. "Curtain Calls." *San Francisco Chronicle* 14 Feb. 1992: D11.

Steinbeck's War

Robert E. Morsberger

Mention war and modern writers, and it is Hemingway rather than Steinbeck who comes to mind. We tend to associate Steinbeck with migrant farm workers or happy-go-lucky bums around the Monterey peninsula or with the Salinas Valley. When the United States entered World War II, Hemingway had already been in just about every war of the century; three of his four novels, many of his short stories, and his one play dealt with war, and he was the natural choice to edit an anthology of *Men at War*. We therefore expected that Hemingway would write the major novel about World War II. Instead, he wrote nothing for ten years but a minimal amount of war reporting, got sidetracked into his androgynous and unwieldy *Garden of Eden*, and his war novel, when it finally appeared, was his weakest, *Across the River and into the Trees*, which deals more with love and death in Venice than it does with the war. On the other hand, the war galvanized Steinbeck into action; before we even entered the war, he wrote a novel/play, *The Moon Is Down*, and within the next nine months he wrote *Bombs Away*, a book for the Army Air Force on the training of a bomber crew. The next year he wrote in the form of a novel a treatment for a film about the merchant marine that Alfred Hitchcock filmed as *Lifeboat*. Another film, *A Medal for Benny*, based upon a story by Steinbeck and Jack Wagner, shows the war from the Chicano perspective on the home front. As a war correspondent, Steinbeck wrote enough dispatches to be collected in a substantial book, *Once There Was a War*. Thus by contrast to Hemingway's one disappointing novel, a bit of war correspondence included in *By-Line*, and one episode of *Islands in the Stream*, Steinbeck's war writing consists of one novel, a play, three movies, two complete books of nonfiction, and parts of *The Wayward Bus* and *A Russian Journal*. No major American author wrote as much about the war.

Let us now examine what he had to say about the war and how he said it. Steinbeck became involved even before Pearl Harbor. In the fall

Steinbeck's War **275**

of 1941, he was writing broadcasts for what became the Office of War Information (*SLL* 237). He did not broadcast himself; he wrote to Webster F. Street that his voice tested badly: "My enunciation is so bad and the boom in my voice is so bad that I can't be understood. I am glad too because now they will never ask me again" (243-44).

That fall 1941, he began writing *The Moon Is Down* at the request of William J. Donovan's Coordinator of Information office that shortly became the Office of Strategic Services (OSS). Outraged at the Nazi invasion and occupation of Norway and punitive acts against patriots who resisted, Steinbeck had already become involved with resistance movements and with fugitives from occupied countries attempting to aid the underground at home. Thus when Donovan asked him to write something that would encourage such resistance movements, he had his subject ready at hand. To prevent "each separate people" from having "to learn an identical lesson, each for itself and starting from scratch," he thought that ". . . if I could write the experiences of the occupied . . . such an account might even be a blueprint, setting forth what might be expected and what could be done about it" ("Reflections on a Lunar Eclipse" 3).

He started the work as a play, set at first in an American town to show, as in Sinclair Lewis's *It Can't Happen Here*, that it can happen here. But the Foreign Information Service rejected this premise, arguing that even a fictional story of our possible invasion and occupation might harm morale (Benson 489-90). Steinbeck therefore "placed the story in an unnamed country, cold and stern like Norway, cunning and implacable like Denmark, reasonable like France" ("Reflections" 3). He made the names of the characters as international as he could and did not even identify the invaders, though from the fact that they are fighting England and Russia, there is no doubt that they are Germans. The play might be set in any country, but the novel version, with much more detail about terrain and weather, clearly takes place in Norway. The film throws aside any ambiguity by opening with a shot of Hitler's hands moving possessively over a map of Norway.

To Webster F. Street, Steinbeck wrote about the play that "It isn't any country and there is no dialect and it's about how the invaders feel about it too" (*SLL* 237). On December 7, Pearl Harbor Day, he, completed the play and titled it *The Moon Is Down*. Then, reversing his procedure with *Of Mice and Men*, he quickly turned it into a novel, which was rushed into print by March, 1942. On April 8, the play opened in New York, under the direction of Chester Erskin, with Otto Kruger as Colonel Lanser, Ralph Morgan as Mayor Orden, and Whitford Kane as Dr. Winter. As the novel was initially outselling *The Grapes of Wrath* by two to one, hopes for the play ran high, but Steinbeck was prophetic when he wrote to Webster Street that "the critics will crack down on the play" (243). Two days later, he informed Street that the reviews were "almost uniformly bad," that the play was in fact dull (244). But critics of both the play and the novel objected not to the dullness but to the way in which Steinbeck dealt with the feelings of the invaders. Dorothy Thompson and James Thurber (then undergoing a series of eye operations for oncoming blindness) were intensely hostile, going almost so far as to accuse Steinbeck of treason because he treated the Nazis as human beings, capable of lethal brutality but also lonely and homesick. When the widow of an executed villager kills a basically decent German who was lonely enough to seek her companionship in a Platonic way, our sympathies are certainly mixed. Critics also charged that Steinbeck's thesis that a people cannot be conquered unless they want to be and that the resistance movement will inevitably triumph was bland and wishful thinking. Later, Alfred Kazin and Stanley Edgar Hyman complained of Steinbeck's propaganda and used *The Moon Is Down* as a reason to dismiss Steinbeck as a serious writer (Kazin 1; Hyman 10). But such sweeping judgments must be challenged. Of course, *The Moon Is Down* is not in the same league with *The Grapes of Wrath*. Steinbeck did not intend it to be. He wrote it quickly, on assignment, and it fulfilled his objective—to encourage underground resistance and to show how it can demoralize and ultimately destroy the invaders. The resistance movements applauded the novel, and the underground distributed mimeographed copies (Benson 499). I would argue that it is the best novel about the war written during the war. But putting aside aesthetic considerations and focusing only on the war, one factor that hostile critics overlook is that while Steinbeck was writing the play, we were not even in the war, and when the novel and play appeared in the spring of 1942, the Axis powers still seemed to be winning everywhere. Yet Steinbeck was prophetically accurate in picturing the nature of the ultimate defeat. In his portrayal of the supposed conquerors admitting that in essence they have already been defeated by the relentless resistance of the supposedly conquered, there is considerable subtlety. Scene/Chapter 5 is particularly effective as Steinbeck shows the invasion force terrified "by death in the air, hovering and waiting" (*Moon* 101), by the persistent sabotage, assassinations, the sullen hatred of the villagers, by their inability to relax and lower their guard for a moment, by the nervous tension growing uncontrollably, intensified by homesickness and loneliness, by their suspicion that everywhere else where victory has been officially proclaimed, a similar sense of hopeless futility prevails, by the knowledge that if given the chance, the conquered will kill them all and that punitive measures bring not submission but only more hatred and defiance.

With the hysteria of war long passed, we can now see that *The Moon Is Down* is unquestionably anti-Nazi. Steinbeck deserves credit for the very quality that caused him to be denounced in 1943—for his awareness that not all members of the Wehrmacht were intrinsically evil, that some may have been decent people deceived by their own propaganda or forced by military discipline to participate in actions that they too found revolting. But while Colonel Lanser realizes that the Führer is a madman and that his orders to execute more hostages only intensify the hatred and resistance, he carries out those orders nevertheless, starving the families of miners who refuse to cooperate and shooting hostages. Richard Lockridge's protest that Steinbeck's invaders are "more sinned against than sinning" (Mantle 72) is wholly unjustified. Lanser prides himself on being a civilized man who wants to minimize casualties, but he commits the fatal error of war criminals, trying to exonerate himself by just obeying orders, rather than engaging in civil disobedience. He admits he has no faith in those orders, but he says that they are unambiguous and that he will carry them out "no matter what they are" (*Moon* 186). In the play he adds, "I can act apart from my knowledge. I will shoot the Mayor . . . I will not break the rules. I will shoot the doctor. I will help tear and burn the world" (Mantle 104-05). Steinbeck's characterization of the Germans is, however, far subtler than those in wartime movies, which generally portrayed them all as sadistic butchers. Obviously some, perpetrating the atrocities of the death camps, were so, but the worst of these horrors had not yet happened in 1941 or had not yet come to light. In any case, with his belief that people are not "very different in essentials" ("Reflections" 3), Steinbeck portrayed even the Nazis as human beings. It was this portrayal that caused hostile critics to call Steinbeck's humane approach sentimental at best, at worst, close to treasonable. To Webster Street, Steinbeck observed, "The controversy that has started as to whether we should not hate blindly is all to the good and is doing no harm. What does the harm is that it is not a dramatically interesting play" (*SLL* 244).

Though the play ran only nine weeks in New York, it had a successful tour on the road, came in second in the New York Drama Critics' vote for the best play of the year, and was a smash hit in London and Stockholm. While Steinbeck was in Moscow in 1963, the play was revived there and reviewed favorably in *Tass* (Tuttleton 89). As for the novel, Steinbeck noted that "The little book was smuggled into the occupied countries. It was copied, mimeographed, printed on hand presses in cellars, and I have seen a copy laboriously hand written on scrap paper and tied together with twine. The Germans did not consider it unrealistic optimism. They made it a capital crime to possess it, and sadly to my knowledge this sentence was carried out a number of times. It seemed that the closer it got to action, the less romantic it seemed" ("Reflections" 3). In 1957 Steinbeck wrote to Covici: "At a cocktail party I met an Italian man from the underground, a fugitive not only from Mussolini but Hitler. He told me that during the war he came on a little thin book printed on onion skin paper which so exactly described Italy that he translated and ran off five hundred copies on a mimeograph. It was *The Moon Is Down*. He said it went everywhere in the resistance and requests came in for it from all over even though possession was an automatic death sentence. And do you remember the attacks on it at home from our bellicose critics?" (*SLL* 590). Thus, while *The Moon Is Down* may have fewer intellectual and aesthetic complexities than fiction and drama more admired in graduate schools, it made more of an impact in real life and fulfilled the purpose for which Donovan requested it. Certainly Norway appreciated Steinbeck's work, awarding him the Haakon VII cross for the support he gave in *The Moon Is Down* (*SLL* 767).

Despite the play's brief run in New York, the novel's sale of nearly a million copies in its first year (*Time* 41: 54) encouraged Twentieth Century-Fox to pay an unprecedented $300,000 for the film rights, by comparison to $75,000 for *The Grapes of Wrath* (*Time* 39: 84). The book was the most expensive aspect of the film. To economize on the production, Fox used no big-name players and redressed the sets from the Welsh mining village of *How Green Was My Valley* to use for Norway. Nunnally Johnson, who had scripted *The Grapes of Wrath*, wrote an adaptation and produced the film. When he asked Steinbeck for suggestions, the novelist replied, "Tamper with it." Actually, Johnson did very little tampering, retaining much of Steinbeck's dialogue and remaining faithful to the plot. His chief contribution was to open up the action and dramatize episodes that are offstage in the play and only summarized in the novel. The movie shows the Nazi capture of the town, the storm troopers massacring a handful of Norwegian soldiers, the details of German brutality that (as in *The Grapes of Wrath* and later in *Viva Zapata!*) provokes the spontaneous anger of the oppressed and turns resentment into resistance. *Time*'s reviewer found the Nazis much harsher in the film and the story more effective as it used "the sharp language of action rather than introspective comment" to "describe the villagers' growing hatred and resentment, the Nazis' growing fear" (*Time* 41: 54). Steinbeck acknowledged, "There is no question that pictures are a better medium for this story than the stage ever was. It was impossible to bring the whole countryside and the feeling of it onto the stage, with the result that the audience saw only one side of the picture" ("Brighter Moon" 86).

With controversy over the book still fresh, reviewers were primed to see whether the film made the Nazis in any way sympathetic. Bosley Crowther was gratified to find that Nunnally Johnson "has carefully corrected the most censurable features of the work" by making Colonel Lanser "a cold and ruthless tyrant. . . . He has wrung out such traces of defeatism as were apparent in the book and has sharpened with vivid incidents the horror of being enslaved" ("The Moon Is Down" 8). (Actually the book's resistance thesis is a denial of defeatism.) According to Crowther, Sir Cedric Hardwicke turned Lanser into a cold contemptuous intellectual. Likewise, *Newsweek*'s reviewer praised the "cold, impersonal intelligence" that Hardwicke gave Lanser ("Brighter Moon" 86). Yet the scenario is faithful to Steinbeck's characterization of the Nazi commander; calling Hardwicke's performance "magnificent," Philip T. Hartung described the film's Lanser as "a wise, experienced officer who learned in the last war not only how a conquered people behaves but also the futility of expecting a complete vanquishment" (Hartung 617). Above all, the film retained Steinbeck's psychology; and while *Time*'s reviewer considered this "an extraordinarily naive view of the facts of Nazi life" (*Time* 41: 54), Hermine Rich Isaacs wrote in *Theatre Arts* that Johnson's adaptation was "faithful to the author's almost revolutionary concept of the Nazis as credible human beings, invested with intelligence as well as sheer brute strength and subject to the fallibility of mortals. They have a three-dimensional quality that stands out in bold relief against the usual run of Nazi villain, Hollywood style. . . . In Lanser's sense of the futility of the Nazi brutalities is the most convincing promise of their eventual nemesis" (Isaacs 289-90).

Two other films on the Norwegian resistance movement were released at the same time as *The Moon Is Down*: Columbia's *The Commandos Strike at Dawn*, with Paul Muni, directed by John Farrow, and
Warners' *The Edge of Darkness*, starring Errol Flynn, Ann Sheridan,
and Walter Huston, directed by Lewis Milestone from a screenplay by
Robert Rossen. All three had a positive reception, but critics were
unanimous in preferring the low-budget *The Moon Is Down*, observing
that even the lack of star performers was an asset because the unfamiliar faces aided the film's realism. Irving Pichel's direction received
universal acclaim. Above all, *The Moon Is Down* stood out from the
usual war films of violent adventure as "essentially a conflict of ideas"
(Isaacs 289). Bosley Crowther found it too Socratic and dispassionately intellectual yet concluded that it is the "most persuasive philosophical indictment of the 'new order' that the screen is ever likely
to contain" ("Moon" 8). If it had more words than action, Hermine
Rich Isaacs found that "the speeches that rang out most gloriously
from the pages of the novel sound a clarion call once more upon the
screen . . . eloquent reminders that in talking pictures there is a seat up
near the throne for talk that is worth hearing" (Isaacs 289). It seems that
as a movie *The Moon Is Down* found the proper medium for its message.

During the spring of 1942, Steinbeck did some temporary and un-
paid work for Robert E. Sherwood's Foreign Information Service.
When it was to be moved into the Office of War Information, the
O.W.I. offered Steinbeck a job, which he declined because he would
have to have a security check, and his friends wanted to use him as a
test case for all those who had been accused of subversion because of
their liberal sympathies, and he did not want to be a "clay pigeon"
(Benson 503).

Instead, General "Hap" Arnold, of the Army Air Force, proposed
that Steinbeck write a book about the selection and training of bomber
crews. Steinbeck was reluctant at first, not because he objected to writing journalism but because he did not want the responsibility for any-

one's being injured or killed (Benson 504). But when President Roosevelt invited him to the White House and asked him to take on the project, he was unable to refuse. Having agreed, he entered wholeheartedly into the project, writing to Gwyndolyn Conger, "It's a tremendous job I've taken on and I have to do it well" (Benson 504). At a briefing in Washington, he was told that he would spend about a month visiting twenty air fields in nine states, where he would study every aspect of the flying fortress. Though some kinds of bomber crew members had three or four months of intense training, Steinbeck had to cram all of their various experiences into thirty days, during which he sampled their classes and exercises, took some of their tests, practised with some of their equipment, crawled into their positions in the bombers to experience their hands-on operations and their viewpoint, and relaxed with them after work at diners, bars, and dance halls. This firsthand experience was supplemented by material sent to him by the Air Force, which was not provided on time, though the Air Force was pressuring him to meet his deadline. By June, he was dictating about 4000 words a day and was worried that he was writing too rapidly (Benson 506). Late in the month, he sent some introductory pages to Pascal Covici with the complaint that the promised material had not yet come from Washington and expressed frustration with "the army game of doing nothing and passing the buck" (Fensch 33). When prodded to hurry with the project, he insisted that he would not do slipshod work. Though he missed his August 1 deadline, he finished the manuscript by the end of the summer. A few weeks later, Covici informed him that the Air Force wanted him to add a final chapter describing a bomber crew on a real combat mission. But Steinbeck had not gone on such a mission and refused to write something not authentic (Benson 506-07). Viking rushed to publish a first printing of 20,000 copies on November 27, 1942 (Fensch 33). *Bombs Away* was a book of 185 pages, roughly 43 of them taken up with sixty photographs by John Swope to accompany 130 pages of closely detailed text by Steinbeck.

Though written on assignment and under pressure, *Bombs Away* is by no means a piece of hackwork journalism. Perhaps Steinbeck's most neglected book today, and one of the few out of print, it is well worth reading and has a number of elements significant to Steinbeck studies. In particular, it is the most elaborate treatment of Steinbeck's so-called phalanx theory, his interest in what happens when people work together as a group. The focus of *Bombs Away* is "the training of the individual members of the bomber crew and its final assembling into a close-knit team" (*Bombs* 32). Repeatedly, Steinbeck stresses the point that the successful operation of a bomber does not depend just on a hot-shot pilot but on a bomber team functioning as a unit in which each member is essential and all are dependent on the others. He even cites the motto of Dumas' three musketeers, "All for one, and one for all." He writes at length about the advantages American boys enjoy in having played team sports, in which fullbacks, quarterbacks, and block-ers, pitchers, catchers, infielders and outfielders all make essential contributions to the team. Writing in part to encourage qualified young men to apply for bomber crew training, Steinbeck stresses the indis-pensability of each member and the fact that each must command as well as obey. Though the pilots seem in control, they must take direc-tions from the navigator and, once over the target, from the bombar-dier, while the radio man keeps the plane in contact with its squadron and home base, the engineer keeps things functioning, and the gunners defend them from enemy fighter planes. "Here is no commander with subordinates, but a group of responsible individuals functioning as a unit while each member exercises individual judgment and foresight and care" (23). Steinbeck found such a team exciting, a genuinely dem-ocratic organization in which each person plays the role for which he is best suited after undergoing elaborate testing to determine his qualifi-cations. In his chapters on the training of each member, Steinbeck tried to make them no longer frustrated that they are not all pilots and to help them take pride in their roles and in the team as a whole. Identifying himself with the raw recruits, tired, disheveled, apprehensive, lonely, and homesick, Steinbeck wrote his book in part to brief them on each step that they would experience in training that would turn them into effective members of the bomber crew.

Steinbeck was never a gung-ho military type, and he contrasts the responsibility that each member of the Air Force must take to the "old iron discipline" of the regular army, with its too frequent martinets (153). Ridiculing the old-time soldier's argument that discipline can be maintained only through blind obedience, Steinbeck admired the concept that in the Air Force, discipline comes from respect and trust, that "the Air Force cannot have bad officers or the ships do not fly" (153). One thing that appealed to him about the bomber crews was the fact that the success of their operations depends on individual judgment, that each crew member develops leadership instead of being subordinated by fear or "stultified by unquestioned orders and commands. For it is the principle of the Air Force that men shall know the reasons for orders rather than that they shall obey blindly and perhaps stupidly. Discipline is in no way injured by such an approach. In fact, it is made more complete, for a man can eventually trust orders he understands" (46). In this way, *Bombs Away* relates not only to Steinbeck's studies of group man but also to his studies of leadership in *In Dubious Battle*, *The Leader of the People*, *The Grapes of Wrath*, *The Moon Is Down*, and *Viva Zapata!*

Steinbeck found that as the men got to know, like, and trust each other, they developed a good feeling about the "concerted action of a group of men," even taking pride in the precise unison of close-order drill (49). The effective teamwork of a bomber crew contrasts to the near-fatal disunity of the survivors in Steinbeck's script for *Lifeboat*, an allegory about the need for the quarrelsome Allies to put aside their differences and pull together. Repeatedly Steinbeck stresses the point that "Air Force tactics have definitely become group tactics where men and machines work together toward an objective" and in which the pilot, instead of being the knight errant of World War I dogfights, "is only one part of the functioning unit . . ." (114).

Besides aiming at building morale and esprit de corps for potential members of a bombing crew, *Bombs Away* has something of the quality of Studs Terkel's *Working*, as it helps the reader experience vicariously the various roles of the bombardier, aerial gunner, navigator, pilot, engineer or crew chief, and radio engineer. Devoting a chapter to each, in that order (note that the pilot comes not first but fourth), Steinbeck introduces us to a representative cross-section of American life: Bill the bombardier was a trumpet player from Idaho; Al the gunner was a tough little man from a Midwestern small town where he was an amateur boxer, a hunter, and a soda jerk until the war; Allan the navigator, from central Indiana, had a degree in civil engineering; Joe the pilot was a farm boy from South Carolina; Abner the engineer or crew chief was a wizard car mechanic from a small town in California; Harris the radio engineer was a ham radio operator who worked in a chain grocery store. In keeping with Steinbeck's interest in proletarian protagonists, most of them are blue-collar types. Steinbeck gives idealized portraits of them but at the same time presents realistic details about their backgrounds and makes them well-rounded character studies, getting into their minds, providing dialogue for dramatized episodes, and considering the way in which the Air Force will help them in their postwar careers. We do not know if they are actual individuals or imaginary composite figures. But in describing the training that welds them together as a team, in as much precise detail as wartime security could permit, Steinbeck imparts the flavor of an epic, like the recruiting of the Argonauts, the knights of the Round Table, Robin Hood's band, or the Seven Samurai.

In giving their backgrounds, Steinbeck dwells at length on the advantages American boys have in experience with team sports, their love of tinkering with jalopies and other machinery, and their familiarity with guns. In 1942, the latter would not have seemed controversial, but in today's era of violence, murder, and random shootings, he sounds like a zealous lobbyist for the NRA, as he writes that "we may be thankful that frightened civil authorities and specific Ladies Clubs have not managed to eradicate from the country the tradition of the possession and use of firearms, that profound and almost instinctive tradition of Americans" (29). Steinbeck's picture of the supposedly typical American boy's experience with guns sounds like the boyhood of Ernest Hemingway. He concludes that "Luckily for us, our tradition of bearing arms has not gone from the country, and the tradition is so deep and so dear to us that it is one of the most treasured parts of the Bill of Rights—the right of all Americans to bear arms, with the implication that they will know how to use them" (30). Perhaps echoing the movie *Sergeant York*, for which Gary Cooper won the Oscar in 1941 as a twentieth-century Daniel Boone, Steinbeck portrays the aerial gunners as natural descendants of frontier marksmen.

Although dedicated to helping us win the war, Steinbeck was no hawk or militarist. Criticizing the tradition of blind obedience—whereby the men in arms are not to reason why but only to do and die—he insists that the Air Force recruit "should not enter the Service with any martyrish complex about dying for his country. . . . The best soldier in the world is not the one who anticipates death with pleasure or with the ecstatic anticipation of Valhalla, honor, and glory, but the one who fights to win and to survive" (32). Just as *The Moon Is Down* presents the Germans as human beings, misled by a murderous führer, Steinbeck argues in *Bombs Away* against flag-waving propaganda that encourages "frothy hatred"; "There is only time for hatred among civilians. Hatred does not operate a bombsight" (66). Yet Steinbeck once indulges in racial stereotypes, writing about "the dark Aryans of Italy and the yellow Aryans of Japan" (20) and he is at times insensitive about the suffering caused by war; he calls it a great game in which the gunners and bombardiers "could not ask for better sport" and "will be hunting the biggest game in the world" (74, 76). Obviously, the heavy bombers wreaked havoc not only upon military targets but upon the civilian population as well. Yet Steinbeck cannot be considered an accomplice in such later actions as the bombing of Dresden and of Hiroshima and Nagasaki.

In his introduction, Steinbeck portrays the nation as floundering without a direction during the Depression of the 1930s and finds that the war restores a sense of national purpose and draws together the nation's energy, ability, and vitality, directing them towards a common purpose. Thus the Axis powers, by attacking us, "destroyed their greatest ally, our sluggishness, our selfishness, and our disunity" (14). These are the weaknesses that must be overcome by the Allied survivors in *Lifeboat*. Steinbeck's account of the building of the American war machine sounds like a wartime newsreel. When it was written, *Bombs Away* was designed to inform and encourage the bomber crew trainees, but today its value is its vivid recreation of the atmosphere of the war years. It also contains some of Steinbeck's best narrative and descriptive prose, lean, precise, cinematic, and full of sensory detail as he dramatizes planes warming up, taking off, flying in formation, maneuvering, and returning from practice missions.

The book sold well and was purchased by Hollywood for the formidable figure of $250,000 (Lisca 184-85). (Margaret Mitchell got only $50,000 for *Gone with the Wind*.) When Steinbeck was not allowed to donate his royalties to the government, he gave them to the Air Forces Aid Society, a gift all the more generous because he had to pay income taxes on them (Benson 509). Despite paying an immense sum for film rights, Hollywood did not use Steinbeck or his material.

While waiting for the studio to make up its mind about filming *Bombs Away*, Steinbeck proposed another picture, reversing *The Moon Is Down* by having a Japanese invasion force parachute into a Middle Western town so that he could expose "the kind of greed and apathy of the country inside the mountains" that he had seen while crossing the country (Benson 507).

Though Twentieth Century-Fox and Nunnally Johnson liked the concept, the head of the film division of the Office of War Intelligence vetoed it, asking Steinbeck instead to write about our defenses in Alaska but then procrastinating on giving him clearance to do so. A sequel to *Bombs Away* about bombers in combat failed to materialize. In December, 1942, Jack Wagner approached Steinbeck with an idea for a film and asked him to collaborate on the script. Together, they wrote in a few weekends the scenario for *A Medal for Benny*.

Steinbeck was expecting to be released from the O.W.I. and commissioned in the Air Force as an intelligence officer, but the plans bogged down in bureaucratic red tape. While he was waiting, Kenneth MacGowan of Twentieth Century-Fox informed him that the Maritime Commission had asked Alfred Hitchcock to make a picture about the merchant marine, and MacGowan invited Steinbeck to write the story. Steinbeck was receptive, saying that he had many ideas for such a story and that he would like to go East with Hitchcock and interview seamen who had been torpedoed. He would write it as a novella that he would be free to publish if he wished (*SLL* 249).

He never did publish the novella, which remains in the archives at Twentieth Century-Fox. Those who know *Lifeboat* only from the film that was released in 1944 as "Alfred Hitchcock's Production of *Lifeboat* by John Steinbeck" will be considerably misled as to what Steinbeck actually wrote, for the scenario is by Jo Swerling, who considerably distorted Steinbeck's treatment. Swerling was a competent screenwriter who had collaborated on Gary Cooper's *The Westerner* and *Pride of the Yankees* for Samuel Goldwyn, but unfortunately, he altered Steinbeck's material, perhaps with Hitchcock's encouragement, to make it more slick and melodramatic. Most of the dialogue and many of the details of plot and characterizations are Swerling's and Hitchcock's, not Steinbeck's. Hitchcock's own explanation is as confusing as it is enlightening.

> I had assigned John Steinbeck to the screenplay, but his treatment was incomplete and so I brought in MacKinlay Kantor, who worked on it for two weeks. I didn't care for what he had written at all . . . and hired another writer, Jo Swerling, who had worked on several films for Frank Capra. When the screenplay was completed and I was ready to shoot, I discovered that the narrative was rather shapeless. So I went over it again, trying to give a dramatic form to each of the sequences. (Truffaut 113)

The result is an uneven mixture of Hitchcock suspense, Swerling situation and dialogue, and Steinbeck philosophy. Enough of Steinbeck's ideas and structure survive that there is a discernable resemblance to some of his novels. As in *The Wayward Bus*, Steinbeck isolates a group of representative individuals and then has them interact. In *Lifeboat*, we have adrift in the ship's launch eight survivors of an American freighter that has been sunk by a German submarine, plus the commander of the U-boat, also sunk in the encounter. Except for the ending, when an Allied destroyer sinks a German supply ship, all the action is confined to the lifeboat, which becomes a microcosm.

In Swerling's scenario, the survivors are Connie Porter (Tallulah Bankhead), a wealthy and bitchy reporter; Rittenhouse (Henry Hull), a conservative millionaire; Gus (William Bendix), a seaman with an injured leg; Kovac the oiler (John Hodiak), an embittered leftist whom Connie considers a Communist or at least a fellow traveller; Stanley Garrett (Hume Cronyn), a British radio operator; Alice MacKenzie (Mary Anderson), an American Red Cross nurse; Charcoal (Canada Lee), a Black steward; an English woman with her dead baby; and the Nazi (Walter Slezak).

In *Lifeboat*'s allegory, the representatives of democracy are drifting aimlessly at sea, quarrelsome and ineffectual, while the Nazi is dynamic, resourceful, and virtually assumes command. He navigates, keeps the boat from capsizing, rows alone when the others are too weak, maintains morale with his wit and cheerfulness, amputates Gus's gangrenous leg, and displays such self-confidence that the others generally look to him for leadership. Overlooking the fact that he is also consistently treacherous, reviewers who had accused *The Moon Is Down* of being "soft" on Nazis now charged Steinbeck with perpetuating the myth of the Aryan superman. Bosley Crowther thought that though Hitchcock and Steinbeck "certainly had no intention of elevating the 'superman ideal,' . . . we have a sneaking suspicion that the Nazis, with some cutting here and there, could turn 'Lifeboat' into a whiplash against the 'decadent democracies'" ("Lifeboat" 17). Dorothy Thompson gave *Lifeboat* "ten days to get out of town," though what she would do after that deadline, she did not say, and the movie had a long and successful New York run (Lardner 65). According to a review in *Life*, most of the blame was put on Steinbeck, who "disclaimed any responsibility for Director Hitchcock's and Scenarist Jo Swerling's treatment of his material" (*Life* 16: 77). Apparently Steinbeck agreed with those critics who thought that the picture might encourage the Nazis, for he sent two protests to Twentieth Century-Fox, telegraphing in the second one: ". . . in view of the fact that my script for the picture Life Boat has been distorted in production so that its line and intention has been changed and because the picture seems to me to be dangerous to the American war effort I request my name be removed from any connection with any showing of this film" (*SLL* 267).

Certainly neither Steinbeck, Hitchcock, nor Swerling was pro-Nazi, but in any case the nearly superhuman Nazi is Swerling's and Hitchcock's portrait, not Steinbeck's. In the original novella, the Nazi nurses a broken arm, never rows the boat, is not a surgeon, is not an intellectual, cannot even speak English, and does not take command. But even in the film, he is sinister. While the others suffer from hunger and thirst, he has a secret supply of food tablets, energy pills, and water. With a hidden compass, he steers the boat towards a German supply ship, and when Gus discovers his deceit, the Nazi drowns him. Realizing his treachery, the others turn on the Nazi in a murderous hysteria, beat him, and drown him as he had drowned Gus. Hitchcock explained that *Lifeboat*'s allegory signified that "while the democracies were completely disorganized, all of the Germans were clearly headed in the same direction. So here was a statement telling the democracies to put their differences aside temporarily and to gather their forces to concentrate on the common enemy, whose strength was precisely derived from a spirit of unity and of determination" (Truffaut 1134). Lewis Jacobs agreed, finding that "*Lifeboat* was a grim reminder against underestimating the resourcefulness and power of the enemy" (Jacobs 38). *Time*'s reviewer concurred, calling *Lifeboat* "an adroit allegory of world shipwreck," paralleling e. e. cummings'

> King Christ this world is all aleak;
> and life preservers there are none . . .
> ("Cinema," *Time*, p. 94)

James Agee considered *Lifeboat* "more a Steinbeck picture than a Hitchcock" (Agee 108), but the reverse is the case. Steinbeck's novella is narrated in the first person by a seaman curiously named Bud Abbott at the time when Bud Abbott and Lou Costello were Hollywood's most popular comedy team. Abbott is a not-too-bright high school graduate whose language is realistically slack, run-on, and repetitive to the point where it becomes monotonous. He is not particularly interesting in himself, but he represents the ordinary man's commonsense attitudes towards politics and economics, and Steinbeck gives him extensive meditations on these subjects, all of which are missing from Swerling's screenplay. He complains of wartime propaganda and news commentators trying to stir up Americans to mindless hysteria by polarizing them into heroic allies and bestial enemies, manipulating them into losing their individuality.

> It seemed to me that most people were kind of comfortable with war, because they didn't have to think any more. We were all good and the enemy was all bad. And it made it kind of simple. When they bombed us they were murderers and when we bombed them, why we were winning for some good reason. And if they sunk our ships, they were stabbers in the back, and if we sunk their ships we were winning a war. You have to put a good name on a thing in a war, and I haven't seen any papers from Germany or heard any speeches, but I'd like to take a small bet that everything we say, they say, only it's the other way around . . . and I bet they believe it just as much as we do. (*Lifeboat* 75)

Perhaps this passage is Steinbeck's response to the critics who called him "soft on Nazis" when he portrayed the German soldiers as three-dimensional, occasionally sympathetic human beings instead of stereotypical Huns in *The Moon Is Down*. In any case, his attack on self-righteously mindless propaganda resembles George Orwell's statement that "Actions are held to be good or bad, not on their own merits but according to who does them, and there is almost no kind of outrage . . . which does not change its moral colour when it is committed by 'our' side. . . . The nationalist not only does not disapprove of atrocities by his own side, but he has a remarkable capacity for not even hearing about them" (Orwell 165-66).

Abbott goes on to observe that he doesn't know much about the enemy, "But when they tell us we're all noble and white, that's just a bunch of horse manure." He goes on to recall crooked contractors and self-serving, flag-waving politicians at home, but "Now you can't say it because you're interfering with the war effort. Those chiselers are absolutely protected for the duration of the war. I think that's bothering us as much as anything else, but I think all of us know that's just part of the big stick, just a part of the dirt of war. And we'll fight this war . . . and we'll win it but we hate to be kidded all the time and we hate to be yelled at and told what we ought to think and what we ought to do." He especially objects to hate-mongering commentators who say how they'd love to be in combat so "they could get in there with a bayonet and slaughter up a few Germans." Abbott knows "that war is a dirty business . . . every part of it. When you've got to clean out a cesspool you do it quick. . . . You don't have to get fighting mad to do it" (*Lifeboat* 75-79).

The film not only eliminates Abbott but cuts most of his political consciousness. It makes some superficial attempts at political controversy but fails to develop them. There is an initial conflict between Kovak, the leftist oiler (who in Steinbeck's treatment is Albert Shienkowitz, a Pole from around Chicago, who is not a fellow traveller and who falls in love with the nurse rather than having a love-hate romance with Mrs. Porter) versus the high-society Mrs. Porter and the right-wing Rittenhouse, but the film renders them as cartoon characters (Rittenhouse even smokes cigars throughout the film, whereas Steinbeck's character has salvaged nothing but the clothes on his back) and turns them all into buddies, making a pitch for wartime solidarity and suggesting that under the surface, all Americans are pretty good guys. "We're all sort of fellow travellers here, in a mighty small boat on a mighty big ocean," says Rittenhouse (Swerling 45).

Steinbeck's novel makes the opposite point—that at home there is a lot of economic exploitation, profiteering, and corruption, and that when the GIs return, there must be radical reformation. In its attacks on propagandistic paranoia and in its comments on the less than utopian postwar world to which the veterans will return, Steinbeck's script resembles criticism of the Vietnamese War, its aftermath, and political and corporate crimes of the Watergate era. Abbott, the narrator, reflects,

> Albert, he says that some of the fellows that're yelling the loudest about protecting Democracy against Germany are the same guys that were using machine-guns on labor unions before the war. Albert, he says, well maybe the war changed those fellows and they aren't like that any more. . . . We'll find out when the war is over. What I hope is that those commentators don't think that if we get good and fighting mad the way they want us to that we won't do any thinking any more, 'cause that's not the way it is. (*Lifeboat* 79-80)

Reminiscing about the Depression, in which those who lost their jobs were accused of laziness, Abbott observes that there are 10 million men in the Armed Forces, and when they come home as veterans,

> they're going to be tough guys, and they'd better come back to something besides relief because they're not going to like that. I don't think anybody in the Army or out of it is so dumb to think that there is nothing wrong with this country. But it seems to me . . . they're all fighting because . . . the one

thing that's best of all is that in this country if enough of you don't like a thing—you can go about and change it. Well, all those fellows are going to come back from the Army, and they're going to find a lot of people elected to office, that were elected by people who weren't in the Army, and they're not going to be the kind of people who'd . . . see that the Army didn't go back on relief. You see I remember when a bunch of Congressmen got up and said if they voted two billion dollars to feed starving people in this country it would bankrupt the nation and then a little later those same Congressmen they voted a hundred billion dollars for the war. . . . Maybe all this kind of thing isn't a good thing to think about and talk about in a time of war, but I never could get the idea the best thing to do wasn't to tell people the truth. (*Lifeboat* 81-82)

Mrs. Porter, the spokesman for laissez-faire, tells Abbott "she wants to free the American workingman from a dictatorship of labor unions," but he reflects that "the people who were most anxious to free us laboring men from dictatorship and the unions were the same people that the unions made raise wages a little bit. Maybe what they wanted to free us from was good wages." He recalls a shipmate's saying that "we got one great right in the United States . . . poor people and rich people they got the right to starve to death. But he said rich people don't very often exercise that privilege" (*Lifeboat* 91-92). When Mrs. Porter talks "about how the unions were full of labor racketeers," Abbott thinks that "If there's one racketeer in a labor union why the whole country's all upset about it. But if a board member of a corporation goes west with the treasure, nobody thinks very much about it; they kind of expect it of him" (*Lifeboat* 93).

Steinbeck's novella makes a detailed case for the liberal position on economics and warfare. Unfortunately, most of his ideas, being part of Abbott's interior monologue, are not translatable to the screen. Swerling's dialogue fails to pick them up and turn them into conflict among the cast—probably sensibly so in cinematic terms, but a loss in terms of social consciousness.

One feature of the film that critics found particularly objectionable is the racist stereotype of the Black steward. This characterization is entirely Swerling's, not Steinbeck's. Steinbeck protested to Twentieth Century-Fox against the film's "stock comedy Negro," pointing out that in his script, "instead of the usual colored travesty of the half comic and half pathetic Negro, there was a Negro of dignity, purpose and personality. Since this film occurs over my name, it is painful to me that these strange, sly obliquities should be ascribed to me" (*SLL* 266). In the film, the steward, called Charcoal, is a pickpocket and minstrel-show type; in Steinbeck's novella, where he is called Joe, he is a sensitive individual who plays the flute with a classical chamber music group. In addition, he saves several people from drowning, and Abbott says, "I think Joe was about the bravest man I ever saw" (*Lifeboat* 243). Far from being racist, Steinbeck attacked racism, having Abbott observe "how hard it must be for him [Joe] to be in this boat, even harder than it was for the German. Nobody had anything against Joe except his color. We hated the German because he was an enemy" (203).

The movie ends on yet another racist note. When the German supply ship is sunk, the lifeboat survivors rescue a 17-year-old boy, who proceeds to pull a pistol on them. Rittenhouse says, "You see? You can't treat them like human beings. You've got to exterminate them" (Swerling 161-62). By contrast, Steinbeck takes a broad humanitarian outlook that would not have pleased the superpatriots any more than Swerling's superNazi did. His original narrative argues against the insanity of war, as the nurse says, "When you've helped take the arms and legs off young men, you heard them raving in the night, then maybe it wouldn't make any sense to you either." To her, the German is "just a man with a broken arm" (*Lifeboat* 32). When the German first comes aboard, Albert wants to throw him overboard, but after he helps set the arm, he is ready to fight to save him. "Albert said he could still hate Germans, but he said once you laid your hand on a man why you couldn't hate him the same anymore" (39-40). Nevertheless, Steinbeck has Albert throw the Nazi overboard when the others discover that he has been betraying them. Swerling's and Hitchcock's version ends with what Swerling calls an "orgasm of murder," in which the main attackers are the nurse and Mrs. Porter, who "are more unbridled and primitive in their attack than the men" (Swerling 139-40). Audiences were apt to applaud, as they do the slaughter in *Rambo* movies. Afterwards, Abbott feels "as though we murdered that German, just murdered him in cold blood." The nurse, who had not been involved, says, "I don't understand about people hurting each other and killing each other. . . . I'm doing the only thing I can, trying to put them together again when they get hurt. . . . That's the only way I can keep from going crazy, because the whole thing is crazy to me . . ." (*Lifeboat* 231).

But though it is far more commercialized and melodramatic than Steinbeck's treatment, the film is unusual, without the customary Hollywood heroics of *Action in the North Atlantic*, the other wartime film about the Merchant Marine. It retains some of Steinbeck's ambiguity and his allegory about the need for the confused and disorganized Allies to unite against a common enemy, and its climax, in which the Allied survivors turn upon the Nazi like a pack of savage animals and kill him in an act of group hysteria, is startling; though altered by Swerling, it recalls Steinbeck's story "The Vigilante" and the animal imagery of *In Dubious Battle*, where "when the crowd saw the blood they went nuts . . . it was just one big—animal" (*In Dubious Battle* 316-17).

Between the time that he finished his novella in February 1943 and the time that the film was released in January 1944, Steinbeck himself went to war. Fed up with waiting for the government to give him either a commission or an assignment, he decided to become a war correspondent for "a big reactionary paper like the Herald-Tribune because I think I could get places that way that I couldn't otherwise" (*SLL* 250). At the beginning of April 1943, he was accredited a war correspondent with the New York *Herald-Tribune* for the European theater (251). Early in June, he sailed for England aboard a troopship. In London, the only war was in the air, as German planes were still trying to keep up a blitz. Steinbeck found no hot war news to report; instead, he focused on the human factor among both the Americans and British, sending home dispatches that in their self-effacing way are more interesting than the first-person heroics in Hemingway's war correspondence. But Steinbeck too wanted to get where the action was, and in the second week of August, he got permission to go to North Africa. In Algeria, he observed the preparations for the invasion of Italy. At this point, he got himself assigned to a commando unit of Lord Louis Mountbatten's Anglo-American Combined Operations department of strategic and tactical deception, for which Douglas Fairbanks, Jr., had organized amphibious operations nicknamed the "beachjumpers." Steinbeck and Fairbanks were old acquaintances from Hollywood; Fairbanks recalls that they discussed Steinbeck's doing screenplays for prospective Fairbanks swashbucklers based on Scottish history—*The Armstrong* and *Bonnie Prince Charlie*—but as Fairbanks was unable to raise the money for them, neither materialized. Fairbanks suspects that Steinbeck may have asked to be attached to his unit, though how he knew about the highly secret operation remains a mystery.

Fairbanks is one of the few actors who was an authentic war hero; for gallantry in combat, he was awarded the Silver Star, the Distinguished Service Cross, the *Croix de guerre*, membership in the *Légion d'honneur*, and a British knighthood. Though a civilian, Steinbeck conducted himself like one of the beachjumpers, taking off his foreign correspondent identification and carrying a tommy gun when he climbed into a PT boat and went ashore on their hit-and-run night raids to create diversions, carry out rescue operations, or capture islands (Benson 532; phone conversation with Fairbanks). (Fairbanks does not recall that Steinbeck ever used the tommy gun.) Steinbeck joined the beachjumpers when they were trying to deceive the Germans into thinking there would be an invasion in the north, while the actual invasion of Sicily was under way. In fact Fairbanks succeeded in tricking the Germans into holding an entire division north of Naples (Benson 529). When the Allies landed at Salerno, Steinbeck left Fairbanks' commandos and spent a week under fire at the front. Then he rejoined the beachjumpers for several more weeks and took part in capturing the island of Ventotene, when Fairbanks, with five fellow commandos and Steinbeck, went ashore under fire and took prisoner some 250 Italians and then, reinforced by 43 paratroopers, captured at least twice as many Germans as the landing party (87 according to Steinbeck; some 400 according to Fairbanks' biographer), entrenched on a hill, with machine guns and artillery. Steinbeck called it "A real Dick Tracy stunt. They had told us that there were no Germans on the island, so we landed with flashlights lit and yelling to one another and they thought we had an army with us. Hell, the captain and Douglas Fairbanks had nothing but tommy guns and, so help me, they took the whole island. Two very tough citizens they are" (Connell 164).

On September 24, Steinbeck was back in London. A few weeks later, he was in New York, where he sorted out his notes and turned them into further dispatches, so that the dates of the later ones do not correspond to the actual events. Though he had spent only three months in Europe and about six weeks in combat, the experience had been very intense, and the dispatches he collected in *Once There Was a War* (not published until 1958) remain fresh and vivid, perhaps his best work of nonfiction.

The first section of 34 dispatches, written between June 20 and August 12, 1943, is labeled "England," though in fact the first six take place aboard a troopship, from embarkation to docking. During the voyage, Steinbeck's account of rumors, fear, courage, anxiety, crap games and USO shows, with voices from a motley crew of representative and composite soldiers, resembles his treatment of migrant camps in *The Grapes of Wrath*, whose members are also journeying from the known to the unknown. There is prose poetry in his evocative descriptions of the ship casting off after midnight, being nudged out of the harbor past the darkened city and into a misty sea prowled by enemy submarines.

Once ashore in England, his first six dispatches, about a bomber station, are like a continuation of *Bombs Away*, with scraps of dialogue from crew members, remarks on the jivey names of aircraft, like *Bomb Boogie* or *Volga Virgin* rather than dignified ones like St. Louis or other cities that would injure the ship and damage morale, observations on the men's nerves on the night before a mission and a description of their careful and complicated dressing for a high altitude flight, and the suspense of waiting for the planes to return from their raid. Throughout the book, Steinbeck focuses on the human interest rather than dramatic news items. Many of the dispatches have a cinematic quality, with shifting angles of perspective and quick cuts from one person or scene to another.

Leaving the flying fortress base, Steinbeck moves in and out of London, not so much reporting as dramatizing episodes and people of interest. He contrasts the homesickness of GIs in London on the Fourth of July with images of the Fourth at home; imagines stories the veterans will tell after the war; admires the indomitable spirit of the common people of Dover under daily bombardment; tells how women operating a coastal battery work, live and play; and chronicles the comic transformation of a billy goat mascot to the alcoholic Wing Commander William Goat, DSO. His style is relaxed, conversational, often with the low-keyed humor of *Cannery Row*, though he can leave indelible images such as "St. Paul's against a lead-colored sky and the barrage balloons hanging over it. Waterloo Station, the sandbags piled high against the Wren churches . . ." (*Once There Was a War* 45). A chapter on the spreading popularity of the German song "Lili Marlene" has a folkloristic quality. Some dispatches are almost short stories, such as one about a soldier's disbelief that he saw a ghostly cottage, well-lit and comfortably inhabited, when it was in fact a bombed-out ruin, the apocryphal account of how Eddie's masterful crap-shooting on Sundays went haywire because he failed to account for the international date line; two dispatches on the artistry of Private Big Train Mulligan, an amiable and easygoing con man who would be at home in Tortilla Flat or Cannery Row; a wounded soldier beginning to regain the use of his crippled left hand. Steinbeck admires the English as well, with their victory gardens, and despite their shockingly bad cooking and brutality with vegetables, and shows how English and Americans have to overcome generalities about each other.

But his reporting is not all comic. Admiring Bob Hope's dedication and energy, he shows how difficult it was to be funny in a hospital, "the long aisles of pain" (90). He pictures a group of children laughing gleefully at a comic movie just before a bomb makes a direct hit on the theater, leaving the building "torn and shredded" and the children "broken," dead or "screaming . . . in pain and fear" (79). He portrays the Blitz with scraps of conversation, recalling the sound of "broken glass being swept up, the vicious flat tinkle," the sight of an evening slipper protruding from a pile of rubble, a pair of stockings hanging from the topmost fireplace of a bombed-out building, birds being killed by concussion, the curious things people save from the ruins, a blind man tapping to cross the street with everything in flames around him. He observes that "In all of the little stories it is the ordinary, the commonplace thing or incident . . . that leaves the indelible picture" (62), and it is these stories that he relates, so that his war correspondence consists of sketches rather than conventional dispatches.

Just as in *The Moon Is Down* and *Lifeboat* he objects to blind propagandized hatred, so he now observes that "civilian ferocity disappears from the soldier or the sailor close to action or in action" (65). And as in *Lifeboat* and *The Wayward Bus*, he is concerned about how the veterans will be treated after the war and their fear of the war's aftermath. Most of them, he thinks, are less afraid of the enemy than of returning home to unemployment and depression, of coming back to find "the cards stacked against them" by the same special interests that exploited them during the 1930s; for "They remember that every plan for general good life is dashed to pieces on the wall of necessary profits" (77). Steinbeck makes a passionate plea that the Four Freedoms be not just empty words but be practically extended to the veterans, who know they can win the war but are terrified of losing the peace.

Following the dispatches from England is a section of six from

North Africa, mainly Algiers, "a mad, bright dreamlike place . . . a whorl of color and a polyglot babble" (125). The African dispatches are more fragmentary, though two of them make good short stories— one about the capture of a gang bootlegging GI watches and another about a kid from New York who succeeds in going home by drifting into a group of Italian prisoners of war about to be shipped to the States.

From North Africa, Steinbeck observed preparations for the invasion of Italy—the final training, the armada of ships and lighters, the night attacks by enemy planes, the tension, suspense and anxiety of untested men waiting to see how they will conduct themselves in combat. Always focusing on the human factor rather than the spectacle, he brings the actual invasion to life in one soldier's first-person account. From his own experience of battle, he recalls dust, shell bursts, slit trenches, ants crawling by his nose as he lay on his stomach under fire, groups of men "scuttling like crabs" under machine gun fire (157), dead and mangled mules, wrecked houses torn open with beds hanging out of holes in the walls, stretcher-bearers carrying bleeding casualties, the walking wounded "with shattered arms and bandaged heads," the smell of cordite and dust, the stench of dead men and animals and his own sweat, and the shocking sight of "a small Italian girl in the street with her stomach blown out" (158). Out at sea, bombed by German planes, the ships bombard enemy positions, while landing craft transport supplies to shore. Later, he recalls walking through the deserted streets of Palermo and being spooked by their dark emptiness.

Ordinarily, according to Douglas Fairbanks, Jr., Steinbeck was quite fearless, though horrified at the atrocities and mutilations on every hand. Attached to Fairbanks' commando Task Group 80.4, Steinbeck blended in with the group and became simply one of the beachjumpers. In his accounts of their activities, written later in London or New York, Steinbeck sometimes concealed identities, scrambled dates and combined details of different operations, both for artistic and security purposes. Fairbanks is never named, though he is the "commodore" at

Ventotene and the captain of an MTB who goes ashore on a small island near Naples to rescue an Italian admiral and his wife. He may have been the commodore who indirectly orders an officer to rescue a worried bartender's pregnant daughter while supposedly forbidden to do so. Some of the episodes would make good films, especially Steinbeck's final six dispatches about the capture of Ventotene, which read like a Horatio Hornblower adventure, but Fairbanks does not know if Steinbeck contemplated any fiction or screenplays based upon their war experiences, though they did discuss the possibility of collaborating on a movie about the knights of the Round Table. (It was an introduction from Fairbanks that enabled Steinbeck and Eugène Vinaver to explore the Duke of Northumberland's Alnwick Castle, where they actually discovered a lost Arthurian manuscript of Sir Thomas Malory.) When Steinbeck and Fairbanks got together after the war, they mainly reminisced about times when and asked what happened to old so and so.

Back home, after writing the dispatches from his notes in Italy, Steinbeck wrote *Cannery Row* to enable both himself and his readers to escape from the war for a while. His final war movie dealt with the home front. *A Medal for Benny*, based on the story that Steinbeck and Jack Wagner had written at the end of 1942, was finally filmed by Paramount and released early in 1945. The original story has never been published, but Frank Butler's screenplay was included in *Best Film Plays*, 1945, edited by John Gassner and Dudley Nichols. Cut from the same cloth as *Tortilla Flat*, it returns to the paisanos, this time in a town called Pantera. Benny, who never appears in the film, is so legendary for his roistering and amours that he has been run out of town. During his absence, an amiable scamp named Joe Morales (Arturo de Cordova), who considers himself a better man than Benny any day, woos Benny's girl, Lolita Sierra (Dorothy Lamour). Benny has been (in the words of *Time*'s reviewer) "a five-star heel," and Lolita clearly prefers Joe but feels it her patriotic duty to be faithful to Benny because he is now in the Army. Joe's comic courtship is so irresistible that Lolita admits her real feelings. But when news arrives that Benny has been killed in action and is to be awarded a posthumous Congressional Medal of Honor, the community expects her to remain forever faithful to his memory.

Meanwhile, the mayor and chamber of commerce try to exploit for all it is worth the publicity that Benny's medal will bring. Like Abbott's reflections in *Lifeboat*, the film is sharply satirical of civic boosterism and wartime profiteering. The town's politicians and businessmen know so little of Benny that they think his name is Martin. When they discover that it is Martín and that he is a Chicano from the barrio, they try to move his grieving father (J. Carrol Naish) from the family shack to a new house, just long enough to make a good impression on the media and the military. When the father realizes what they are up to, he walks out in disgust, and the medal is awarded in the scruffy surroundings of the barrio. Benny may have been a heel, but he was also a hero, and the film defends the dignity of Chicanos against the snobbery, hypocrisy, and racism of the ruling class. In 1945, this was not a message that everyone wanted to hear, nor is it even today, but under Irving Pichel's direction, the film got rave reviews, and Steinbeck and Wagner were nominated for an Oscar for best original story.

In *The Wayward Bus*, his first full-length novel after the war, Steinbeck touched again on the idea which Abbott discussed in *Lifeboat*, that the veterans would not want to return to business as usual and be thrown back on the economic slag heap by exploitative right-wing profiteers and politicians. Among the bus's passengers are Ernest Horton, a veteran who is now a traveling salesman, and Mr. Pritchard, a vacationing Babbitt-type businessman who has become a cold war warrior, fearing and hating as Red anything vaguely threatening his profits, even while he calls business "the most democratic thing in the world" (*The Wayward Bus* 147). When conversing with Horton, Pritchard says patronizingly that the veterans are "a fine bunch of boys . . . and I only hope we can put in an administration that will take care of them." "Like after the last war?" asks Horton cynically (154). Horton's father had believed in the puritan ethic of hard work and thrift only to see the corruption of the Harding administration and lose his shirt in the Depression. Now Pritchard says he worries that the returning soldiers "don't want to settle down and go to work. They think the government owes them a living for life and we can't afford it" (277). Horton looks sick at Pritchard's reactionary bias (Pritchard wants another president like Coolidge who will let business do whatever it wants) and protests that some of his friends, who would seem like bums to Pritchard, make more sense than members of the Cabinet, but he can't make a dent in Pritchard's right-wing ideology and finally says, in despair, that if there were another war, the most awful thing is that he would go fight again (278).

The war was not over when hostilities ended, for many of the survivors were maimed or mutilated, and all grieved for the dead. Bombed and shelled cities were in ruins. Steinbeck was acutely aware of the aftermath of the war. When in the summer of 1947, he and photographer Robert Capa went together to Russia, reminders of the war were everywhere, and Steinbeck noted them in *A Russian Journal*, their record of the trip. They found that the Russians were particularly reluctant to let Capa loose with his camera. Steinbeck's explanation was that the camera is especially frightening to people who have been bombed and shelled in war, "for at the back of a bombing run is invariably a photograph. In back of ruined towns, and cities, and factories, there is aerial mapping, or spy mapping, usually with a camera" (*A Russian Journal* 5). He found Helsinki "considerably shot up" but not too badly bombed. The planes in which they flew around Russia were C-47s left over from lend-lease. From the air, Steinbeck could see the scars of the siege of Leningrad—in addition to trenches and machine gun nests, "The burned farmhouses with black and standing walls littered the landscape. Some areas where strong fights had taken place were pitted and scabbed like the face of the moon" (12). Moscow, because of its formidable anti-aircraft defense, was less damaged, though there were some signs of the war. At the Lenin Museum, Steinbeck encountered a group of war orphans. Throughout the Ukraine, Steinbeck noted shell holes, trenches, roofless and burned buildings. He noted that the destruction was comparable to that "if the United States were completely destroyed from New York to Kansas" and if it lost fifteen percent of the population, for the Ukrainians lost six of their forty-five million civilians as well as military casualties (60). The destruction was particularly bad at Kiev, which was half in ruins, "Every public building, every library, every theater, even the permanent circus, destroyed, not with gunfire, not through fighting, but with fire and dynamite. Its university is burned and tumbled, its schools in ruins . . . this was the crazy destruction of every cultural facility the city had, and nearly every beautiful building that had been put up during a thousand years" (53). Steinbeck was incensed at this work of German "culture" and found a poetic justice in the fact that German prisoners were helping to clean up the debris. He did not register concern that the Russians still kept prisoners of war two years after the peace treaty. Instead, he reflected on "the stupid, calculated cruelties of the Germans" and understood why the Ukrainians would not look at the columns of prisoners, still in their uniforms (64). In the city park, he noted the graves of the city's defenders.

The Russians had been traumatized by the invasion and expressed fear and concern that the United States might attack them. Steinbeck tried to reassure them that the news stories about Americans calling for a preventive war reflected the views of the radical right, not of Americans as a whole. At the same time, Americans feared an attack from the Soviet Union, a mutual paranoia that grew during the Cold War. Steinbeck, on the spot, tried to allay the fears.

Meanwhile, the Ukrainians were trying to rebuild, but since the Germans had destroyed all the machinery, the reconstruction had to be done by hand until new machinery could be made. Steinbeck was impressed by the resilience of the Russian spirit, by the people's ability to live on hope. But many of the Russians were the walking wounded—

veterans with amputated limbs, a half-crazed woman lying in the ruins of a bombed chapel, children legless and missing an eye, a beautiful young girl living in a hole in the ground, scavenging for garbage, and snarling savagely, her eyes inhuman, at someone who offered her bread. Steinbeck noted that there were very few artificial limbs, that the survivors made do with the stump of an arm or leg. Veterans told him of the horrors of combat in the "dreadful cold," when one man warmed his hands in the blood of a friend just killed so that he could still pull his trigger. In the countryside, whole forests were ravaged by machine-gun fire, and everywhere were wrecked pieces of rusting military equipment. On some farms, the Germans killed all the animals, and if there was time, they destroyed the villages as well.

The worst devastation was at Stalingrad, around which the debris of war spread for miles. The city had been ravaged not so much by bombing as by shell and rocket fire, and its remaining walls were pocked by machine-gun bullets. Some of the survivors were living underground.

Back in Moscow, Steinbeck saw a display of war trophies near Gorki Park, with captured plans, tanks, artillery, and a variety of guns and vehicles, and observed the children looking with wonder as their fathers told what the equipment was and how they captured it.

Though Steinbeck and Capa spent much of their time in the Soviet Union being wined, dined, entertained with circuses, theatre, and ballet, the evidences of the war were unavoidable and unforgettable, and *A Russian Journal* is an eloquent *memento mori*, a fitting conclusion to Steinbeck's treatment of World War II and a warning against all future wars.

From *The Steinbeck Question: New Essays in Criticism*, edited by Donald R. Noble (1993), pp. 183-212. Copyright © 1993 by Whitston Publishing. Reprinted with permission of Whitston Publishing.

Works Cited

Agee, James. "Films." *The Nation* 158 (22 January 1944): 108.

Benson, Jackson J. *The True Adventures of John Steinbeck, Writer*. New York: Viking Press, 1984.

"Brighter Moon." *Newsweek* 21 (5 April 1943): 86.

"Cinema." *Time* 43 (31 January 1944): 94.

Connell, Brian. *Knight Errant: A Biography of Douglas Fairbanks, Jr*. Garden City, NY: Doubleday, 1955.

Crowther, Bosley. "Lifeboat." *New York Times* 13 January 1944: 17.

_____. "The Moon Is Down." *New York Times* 27 March 1943: 8.

Dick, Bernard F. *The Star-Spangled Screen: The American World War II Film*. Lexington: University Press of Kentucky, 1985.

Fensch, Thomas. *Steinbeck and Covici: The Story of a Friendship*. Middlebury, VT: P. S. Eriksson, 1979.

Hartung, Philip T. "The Moon Is Down." *Commonweal* 27 (9 April 1943): 617.

Hyman, Stanley Edgar. *The New Leader* 10 December 1962: 10.

Isaacs, Hermine Rich. "The Films in Review." *Theater Arts* 27 (May, 1943): 289-90.

Jacobs, Lewis. "World War II and the American Film." *Film Culture* 47 (Summer 1969): 38.

Kazin, Alfred. "The Unhappy Man from Unhappy Valley." *The New York Times Book Review* 4 May 1958: 1.

Lardner, David. "The Current Cinema." *The New Yorker* 19 (4 February 1944): 65.

Life, 16 (31 January 1944): 77.

Lisca, Peter. *The Wide World of John Steinbeck*. New Brunswick, NJ: Rutgers University Press, 1958.

Mantle, Burns, ed. *The Best Plays of 1941-42 and the Year Book of the Drama in America*. New York: Dodd, Mead, 1942.

Orwell, George. "Notes on Nationalism." *Decline of the English Murder and Other Essays*. Harmondsworth: Penguin Books, 1965.

Steinbeck, Elaine, and Robert Wallsten, eds. *Steinbeck: A Life in Letters*. New York: Viking Press, 1975.

Steinbeck, John. *Bombs Away: The Story of a Bomber Team*. New York: Viking Press, 1942.

_____. *In Dubious Battle*. New York: Random Modern Library, n.d.

_____. *Lifeboat*. Unpublished manuscript, Twentieth Century-Fox Corporation, revised March 26, 1943.

_____. *The Moon Is Down*. New York: Viking Press, 1942.

_____. *Once There Was a War*. New York: Viking Press, 1958.

_____. "Reflections on a Lunar Eclipse." *San Francisco Examiner* 6 October 1963:3.

_____. *A Russian Journal*. New York: Viking Press, 1948.

_____. *The Wayward Bus*. New York: Viking Press, 1947.

Swerling, Jo. *Lifeboat*. Revised Final Screenplay, July 29, 1943, Twentieth Century-Fox Film Corporation.

Time 39 (18 May 1942): 84.

Time 41 (5 April 1943): 54.

Truffaut, François. *Hitchcock*, with the collaboration of Helen G. Scott. New York: Simon & Schuster, 1967.

Tuttleton, James W. "Steinbeck in Russia: The Rhetoric of Praise and Blame." *Modern Fiction Studies* 11 (Spring 1965): 82.

Beyond Evil:
Cathy and Cal in *East of Eden*_____

Carol L. Hansen

How can one defend a female character who, at the age of ten, lures boys into sexual experimentation; at age sixteen, drives her Latin teacher to suicide and then incinerates her parents; runs away to become mistress to a brothel owner and, after being brutally beaten by him, marries another man for protection; shoots her husband and deserts her twin sons (one of whom was fathered by her husband's brother on her wedding night); returns to prostitution and murders the madam in order to become madam herself of the most infamous brothel in the west; and commits suicide by drinking poison?

From the beginning, Cathy does not appear to fit into the novel's patriarchal structure postulating free will; rather she eschews a choice between good and evil because she appears driven to defy 19th century conventions which involve binary oppositions between good and evil, specifically the *timshel* theme which, on one level, centers the book. Set outside this framework, Cathy/Kate exists as an amoral monster who brings into question the validity of this theme. She falls into a triploid of familiar associations: an amoral monster, a satirical fantasy, and a genetic mutation, all of which suggest the subterranean mystery at the heart of *East of Eden*.

In his article "The Mirror and the Vamp: Invention, Reflection, and Bad, Bad Cathy Trask in *East of Eden*," Louis Owens raises critical questions about Cathy's character:

> A consideration of *East of Eden* as a self-conscious fiction may also allow
> us to come to terms with one of the major problems often cited by critics:
> Cathy Ames Trask. Is Cathy the C. A. T., a genetically misshapen monster
> who simply is predetermined to be evil because of something she lacks? (Is
> she, as Benson suggests, a product of Steinbeck's pondering upon the evils
> of his second wife?) Or is she more psychologically complex than this, as

her early and late obsessions with the Wonderland Alice seem to suggest? Why, if *timshel* must apply to all of us, does it seem not to apply to Cathy or Adam, or even Charles, who is incapable of feeling sorry? If this novel is designed to mark the end of an era—naturalism with its emphasis upon pessimistic determinism—as Ditsky has persuasively suggested, why does Steinbeck create absolutists such as Adam and Cathy, who seem, for most of the novel, incapable of free will? (253)

Cathy is beyond evil; she is a monster to those of conventional morals and mores, but, from her perspective, those who judge her are monsters. Steinbeck writes early in the novel:

> to a monster the norm must seem monstrous, since everyone is normal to himself. To the inner monster it must be even more obscure, since he has no visible thing to compare with others. . . . It is my belief that Cathy Ames was born with the tendencies, or lack of them, which drove and forced her all of her life. Some balance wheel was misweighted, some gear out of ratio. She was not like other people, never was from birth. (72)

Here Steinbeck's comments sound more like those of a clinical psychologist than those of an overt moralist, and in his *Journal of a Novel: The* East of Eden *Letters*, he writes that he, too, in a way, is a monster like Cathy and details fluctuating shifts in her characterization. Moreover, he also describes her enigmatic contradictions in the novel.

> Cathy always had a child's figure even after she was grown, slender, delicate arms and hands—tiny hands. Her breasts never developed very much. Before her puberty the nipples turned inward. Her mother had to manipulate them out when they became painful in Cathy's tenth year. Her body was a boy's body. . . . Her feet were small and round and stubby, with fat insteps almost like little hoofs. . . .
>
> Even as a child she had some quality that made people look at her, then look away, then look back at her, troubled at something foreign. Something looked out of her eyes, and was never there when one looked again. (73)

From the beginning, Cathy is seen as the "other," "a girl set apart," and, according to Jackson Benson, is "Steinbeck's nonteleological white whale. Like so many other Steinbeck characters, she is a sport born out of nature who simply does what she does . . ." (167).[1] In her denial of conventional morality, Cathy questions the binary opposition between good and evil; she exists outside the norm of the biblical sym-bolism which structures the novel. In her phantasmagoria, she lives as an alien who refuses to fit into the conventional code of the good woman. But in her perversity she remains eerily fascinating, an enigma who cannot be contained. Cathy defies classification in a male-dominated world. From her viewpoint, she is an observer of the true monsters of masculine control as seen in Mr. Ames, her father; Mr. Edwards, her master; and Adam Trask, her husband. Therefore, she is beyond the boundaries of conventional family life as exemplified by the roles of daughter, wife, and mother. Instead she emerges as a force beyond good and evil, a force of perverse freedom. Yet she is more alive than any other character in the novel.[2]

As Mark Schorer notes in his review of the book:

With Adam Trask we move, too, into the core story, if we accept at all, we accept at the level of folklore, the abstract fiction of the Social Threat, of a Witch beyond women. This account may suggest a kind of eclectic irreso-lution of view, which is, in fact, not at all the quality of the book. I have hoped to suggest, instead, a wide-ranging imaginative freedom that might save the life of many an American Novelist. (22)

Strangely enough, Cathy is linked not so much to the biblical sym-bolism of the book's superimposed patriarchal ideologies, but rather to a seemingly innocuous children's fantasy: Lewis Carroll's *Alice in Wonderland*. When Cathy's mother asks, "What's the book you are hiding?" Cathy retorts, "Here! I'm not hiding it." Her mother rejoins, "Oh, *Alice in Wonderland*. You're too big for that." And Cathy replies, "I can get to be so little you can't even see me. . . . Nobody can find me"

(82). This image of willing herself to become small, this telescoping of self in order to escape the restrictions of control, are repeated near the end of the book when she, like Alice, recalls the literary injunction to "eat me," and "drink me," and she swallows the poisoned tea.

> She thrust her mind back to Alice. In the gray wall opposite there was a nail hole. Alice . . . would put her arm around Cathy's waist, and Cathy would put her arm around Alice's waist, and they would walk away—best friends—and tiny as the head of a pin. (554)

Steinbeck's association of Cathy with Alice is significant in that this fantasy—with its correlation with free imagination and satire—again places Cathy outside the biblical symbolism in the novel. In a sense, the other characters may be seen, from her point of view, as puppets on a string. In an inversion of the norm, she may also be viewed as a bewildered Alice caught in a nightmare world. For, in her mind, she is not culpable but is instead an observer of the true monsters—the mad hatters, the queens and kings of hearts, or as Richard Wallace suggests in a decoding of the word "hearts," *haters* (39).

In a letter to his friend, Carlton Sheffield, written 16 October 1952, Steinbeck says of Cathy's character:

> You won't believe her, many people don't. I don't know whether I believe her either but I know she exists. I don't believe in Napoleon, Joan of Arc, Jack the Ripper, the man who stands on one finger in the circus. I don't believe Jesus Christ, Alexander the Great, Leonardo. I don't believe them but they exist. I don't believe them because they aren't like me. You say you only believe her at the end. Ah! but that's when, through fear, she became like us. This was very carefully planned. All the book was very carefully planned. (*SLL* 459)

Indeed, in a sense *East of Eden* may be viewed as an intricately plotted mystery as well as a morality tale. At the heart of the mystery lies the enigmatic Cathy/Kate—a shift in name signifying an ever-shifting characterization—and a split personality. Paradoxically, Cathy appears to develop and change from defiance to fear in the course of the novel. After being brutally beaten by Mr. Edwards, Cathy is next introduced in Chapter 11 as a non-human species:

> A dirty bundle of rags and mud was trying to worm its way up the steps. One skinny hand clawed slowly at the stairs. The other dragged helplessly. There was a caked face with cracked lips and eyes peering out of swollen, blackened lids. The forehead was laid open, oozing blood back into the matted hair. (110)

While Charles instinctively gleans the truth about Cathy's character in this scene, Adam benevolently ministers to her every need and sees in Cathy the purpose for his life, a dream built upon the illusion of his own needs. After Adam's proposal to Cathy, we are given a rare glimpse into her motivation for marriage.

> She had not only made up her mind to marry Adam but she had so decided before he had asked her. She was afraid. She needed protection and money. . . . And Mr. Edwards had really frightened her. That had been the only time in her life she had lost control of a situation. She determined never to let it happen again. (121)

But it does happen again. Late in the novel Joe Valery convinces Kate that a witness with circumstantial evidence related to the murder of Faye is still alive, and Kate reacts to the news with "almost hopeless fear and weariness."

But Kate is seen not only as powerful or fearful. In a brief reversal from a life of sin, after confronting her twin sons in the brothel, Kate wills her fortune to Aron. After her death, we learn that she has stored her marriage certificate in a safe deposit box, a rather conventional gesture. Earlier, she fantasizes about moving to New York and attending concerts with her fair-haired son Aron. Nearer home, she attends the Episcopal Church in Salinas so that she may view her favorite son Aron. These shades of chiaroscuro in Kate's character, however, mask a sociopathic personality. Alternating between a wish for respectability and a new life with her "angelic" son Aron and a fear of discovery by Cal "the smart one—the dark one—" Kate muses:

> mother of two sons—and she looked like a child. And if anyone had seen her with the blond one—could they have any doubt? She thought how it would be to stand beside him in a crowd and let people find out for themselves. What would—Aron, that was the name—what would he do if he knew? His brother knew. That smart little son of a bitch—wrong word—must not call him that. Might be too true. Some people believed it. And not smart bastard either—born in holy wedlock. Kate laughed aloud. She felt good. She was having a good time.
>
> The smart one—the dark one—bothered her. He was like Charles. (512)

This inner debate is immediately followed by a new dark plan of attack—"a comical murder" of Ethel, the aging prostitute who divines the truth about Kate's murder of Faye. Although changes in her character appear, Kate ultimately runs on parallel tracks that end nowhere. She commits suicide, never achieving a resolution of her self-willed sense of superiority and Cal's unspoken affront. "The glint in his eyes said, 'You missed something. They had something and you missed it'" (554).

In swallowing the final draft of poison, the "drink me" potion, Kate returns to the fantasy world of *Alice in Wonderland*, perceiving herself as a victim surrounded by towering trees of enemies, but never fully confronting her involvement in a life gone awry. She seeks Alice as an innocent feminine icon, but finds herself desolate and isolated from even that fantasy. Steinbeck captures her whirling perceptions: "She thought or said or thought, 'Alice doesn't know. I'm going on past.'" Kate goes on her last adventure alone.

Her eyes closed and a dizzy nausea shook her. She opened her eyes and stared about in terror. The gray room darkened and the cone of light flowed and rippled like water. And then her eyes closed again and her fingers curled as though they held small breasts. And her heart beat solemnly and her breathing slowed as she grew smaller and smaller and then disappeared—(554)

Steinbeck brilliantly concludes this passage with the dismissal "and she had never been," the total annihilation of her character. The next reference he makes to Kate is clinical:

Already Kate was on the table at Muller's with the formalin running into her veins, and her stomach was in a jar in the coroner's office. (559)

However, the riddle of Cathy/Kate remains. In willing her fortune to Aron and leaving her marriage certificate behind, she may be subtly reinforcing the *timshel* theme; yet, in Kate's case, the timing suggests a shadow theme: her choice for good may be seen as a kind of epiphany when the reader is dealt a final shock: We remember her not only as the serpentine Eve (or more precisely Lilith) of the beginning, but as a kind of avenging angel at the end.

The mystery of Kate's complex characterization comes full circle. After incinerating her parents and staging a mysterious disappearance, the young "Cathy left a scent of sweetness about her"; the aged Kate leaves a final shock of apparent conversion—until we remember the ugly photographs of her customers—and her determination to blackmail them. Certainly the fearful, tormented Kate at the end is a kaleidoscopic reversal from the defiant and desolate Kate we find in Chapter 25 when she confronts Adam with the fact that perhaps Charles fathered one son. Although Kate prefers Aron, who physically resembles her and, like Adam, represents all she is not, it appears that Cal is the probable son of Charles, the man Kate "could have loved." As Louis Owens notes:

Caleb and Aron, the twin sons born to Cathy, pick up the Cain and Abel theme introduced in the characters of Charles and Adam and carry it through to the end of the novel. The twins are each "born separate in his own sack" (194), and it is impossible to determine their respective paternity. Again, determinism and psychological realism are confused in the characters of the boys—Is Cal bad because he may be descended from Charles or is he bad because, like Charles, he feels rejected? Is it the "channel in the blood" that makes Cal different from the good Aron, or is it the father's response that determines each son's character? Steinbeck makes it impossible to determine who the boys' respective fathers may be. (*JS's Re-Vision of America* 152)

The multiple ironies of this dilemma both undercut and strengthen the *timshel* theme. If Cal is not Adam's son, his genetic roots lie with Cathy and Charles and hence the question of choosing good over evil becomes more problematic, although, admittedly, he has found his mother out and rejects her. "'I was afraid I had you in me.' 'You have,' said Kate. 'No, I haven't. I'm my own. I don't have to be you'" (466). If Cal is not Adam's son, Adam raises himself to a level of spiritual transcendence when he offers Cal the opportunity to choose between good and evil. Like Joe Saul in *Burning Bright*, Adam acknowledges a spiritual paternity which transcends and reconciles the rivalry of three generations of Trasks.

And yet we don't know what choice Cal will make after the final scene; he appears strangely passive and the ending is open-ended, enigmatic, and ambiguous. After all, it is Lee's energy which propels the action at the end of the novel when he delivers his Daedalus-like analogy of a craftsman who had refined his cup with "all impurities burned out," leading to Adam's climactic offering of *timshel*.

Steinbeck notes his exhaustion near the completion of the book in a letter to Covici:

So we go into the last week and I must say I am very much frightened. I guess it would be hard to be otherwise—all of these months and years aimed in one direction and suddenly it is over and it seems that the thunder has produced a mouse. Last week there was complete exhaustion and very near collapse. (*JN* 171)

In a sense, then, the ending of *East of Eden* is as problematic as the characterizations of Cathy and Cal: both bring into question 19th and 20th century attempts to define morality by conventional norms. Indeed, both may be seen as precursors of Generation X's skepticism of conventions, an evolutionary cycle. Almost like *X-Files* detectives, they peer, with x-ray vision, into the raw truth of human behavior and lift the veil of pretense behind hypocrisy. Cal's cry near the end of the novel—"I've got her blood"—questions the predictability of an optimistic, moralistic ending, although Lee and Abra's words offer hope, as does, finally, Adam's labored whisper of *timshel*, which applies to Cal, and today still, to Everyman and Everywoman.

From *Beyond Boundaries: Rereading John Steinbeck*, edited by Susan Shillinglaw and Kevin Hearle (2002), pp. 221-229. Copyright © 2002 by University of Alabama Press. Reprinted with permission of University of Alabama Press.

Notes
1. According to Richard Lee Hayman, of the National Steinbeck Center in Salinas, California, the character of Cathy/Kate is modeled after a combination of someone Steinbeck knew in Salinas at one time, and his second wife, Gwyndolyn Conger Steinbeck. Robert DeMott writes, "Through another imaginative, linguistic investiture that compensated for his real-life experience, Steinbeck reprised his tumultuous marriage to Gwyn in the pathetic *Burning Bright* and went a long way toward exorcising his memory of her in the devastating portrait of the evil, conscienceless Cathy Ames in *East of Eden*" (Hayashi, *JS: The Years of Greatness* 44-45).
2. In an article entitled "The Neglected Rib: Women in *East of Eden*," Beth Everest and Judy Wedeles conclude that Kate's bitterness comes from her dealing with men like Mr. Edwards, who somehow manages to manipulate her. She punishes men simply for their maleness and finds them most vulnerable when sexually aroused. She is able to manipulate men because she sees their weaknesses (20).

Works Cited

Benson, Jackson. *The True Adventures of John Steinbeck, Writer.* New York: Viking, 1984.

Owens, Louis. *John Steinbeck's Re-Vision of America.* Athens: U of Georgia P, 1985.

_____. "The Mirror and the Vamp: Invention, Reflection and Bad, Bad Cathy Trask in *East of Eden.*" *Writing the American Classics.* Eds. James Barbour and Tom Quirk. Chapel Hill: U of North Carolina P, 1990. 235-57.

Schorer, Mark. "*A Dark and Violent Steinbeck Novel.*" *The New York Times Book Review* 21 Sept. 1952: 22.

Steinbeck, John. *East of Eden.* 1952. New York: Penguin, 1992.

_____. *Journal of a Novel: The* East of Eden *Letters.* 1969. New York: Penguin, 1990.

_____. *Steinbeck: A Life in Letters.* 1975. Eds. Elaine Steinbeck and Robert Wallsten. New York: Viking, 1989.

Wallace, Richard. "Malice in Wonderland." *Harper's Magazine* Nov. 1996: 37-39.

Sweet Thursday Revisited:
An Excursion in Suggestiveness_____

Robert DeMott

I am not a great writer but I am a competent one. And I am an experimental one.

—Steinbeck, in an unpublished 1946 diary

It's quite a performance. I bet some of it is even true, and if it wasn't, it is now.

—Steinbeck's encomium for Gypsy Rose Lee's memoir, *Gypsy* (1957)

I

In the fall of 1969, Ted Hayashi wrote from Muncie, Indiana, inviting me to participate in a Steinbeck conference he was co-organizing with Richard Astro at Oregon State University. Slated for April, 1970, it would be only the second Steinbeck conference ever convened (the first, which both Ted and I attended, was a thirtieth anniversary celebration of *The Grapes of Wrath* organized by John Seelye a year earlier at the University of Connecticut). Fresh out of graduate school, I was trying to turn my dissertation on the creative process in Thoreau's major writings into a book. At the same time, I was trying to suppress the growing realization that, except for being a well-intentioned and nominally intriguing topic, the dissertation was straight-laced and pedantic, and would probably be a boring read. When the summons came from Hayashi, toward the end of my first quarter of full-time teaching at Ohio University, I put down Thoreau (for good as it turned out) and picked up Steinbeck's just-published *Journal of a Novel: The* East of Eden *Letters*. Borrowing from Steinbeck's writing journal, as well as from some of my Thoreau *cum* Georges Poulet/Gaston Bachelard inspired theories, and armed with a recent reading of Richard Brautigan's avant-garde fiction and Allen Ginsberg's poetry and prose (part of my eventual title came from his essay on legalizing marijuana), I opened a hermeneutic path into *Sweet Thursday*, a novel I felt had taken undeservedly hard knocks from formalist critics who held sway in academic circles during the 1950s and 1960s.

The result was "Steinbeck and the Creative Process: First Manifesto to End the Bringdown Against *Sweet Thursday*," a meta-critical divagation temperamentally at home in that age of rampant iconoclasm, and which—true to its era—raised more questions than it answered. The essay's tenuousness and irreverent tone—its breezy affectivity and hip talk of *Sweet Thursday* being a parable of the artist, a "novel about the writing of a novel"—owes partly to the fact that I labored on it in the dead of an unusually cold Appalachian winter in a rented house that, I learned too late, had a faulty furnace—a coal burner ineptly converted to burn fuel oil. Between dives into the cellar to coax the ancient beast back to life, I worked in the owner's window-lined study laboriously writing and typing in woolen gloves and heavy clothes. Like Doc in the novel I was attending to, I couldn't sustain my concentration long enough to develop my argument in a more systematic manner, and so the essay became susceptible to its context, but was not wholly constructed by it (the legitimacy of some post-structuralist beliefs aside, common sense tells us that such makings never are wholly unmixed, a point I believe Steinbeck's disposition toward writerly habits supports). As a result, I abandoned many pretenses of objectivity while the essay became a performative piece about a self-displaying text, a way of "using something to cover up something else," in Mack's definition of "substitution," which appears in chapter 9 of *Sweet Thursday* (64).

There are few more excruciating events than rereading one's own early writing, but as I realize now (without, I hope, being shamelessly vain) the informal voice of "Steinbeck and the Creative Process" fit the conversational format and ebullient dialogue of the Corvallis conference, though since being printed in Astro and Hayashi's *Steinbeck: The Man and His Work* its silences, rifts, and lacunae seemed to have grown more—rather than less—blatant. It would be impossible to re-dress all its shortcomings—nor, at this late date, would I care to (ab-sences have a way of becoming part of the permanent record, and both objectivity and dispassion remain, for me, anyway, elusive and dubi-ous goals). Yet I am grateful for this second chance not only to elabo-rate a few old points about Steinbeck's controversial little book, *Sweet Thursday*, but to resurrect briefly a forgotten public debate on its merits (a 1954 television broadcast), suggest an important vector of popular culture influence (Al Capp's *Li'l Abner* comic strip), and arrive, with-out being too fanciful or precious, at a new trope of relevancy (Stein-beck's portable typewriter) in the following circuitous revisitation to his still underrated fable of the life in art.

While this essay performs a personal function by forestalling the closure of my lifelong professional friendship with Professor Hayashi, it also proves, as Thoreau knew, that it's possible to catch two fish with one hook. Indeed, returning to this novel after such a long hiatus strikes me as fitting, because doing so has once again been occasioned by Ted Hayashi. That alone creates a happy gesture of personal Pietas. But re-visiting also constitutes a renewed arc of connection, which both re-fines and postpones an inevitable end that began in the later 1960s when we hit it off as graduate students at Kent State University, where I first glimpsed through Ted (and through my mentor, Howard Vin-cent) the intriguing possibility that critical discourse could be en-hanced by personal engagement and appreciative intervention. In that it also circles toward a meeting many years later with Steinbeck's el-der son, Thom, from whom I received, temporarily at least, his father's favorite typewriter (which became a metaphor for a way of looking at the senior Steinbeck's creative drive), the landscape of this essay in-scribes an intersubjective ground (Hawthorn 85), a moving geography of inner and outer voices, private and public presences, selves and texts.

II

From the outset, the conversation surrounding *Sweet Thursday* was heated and antagonistic, as the following account by Pascal Covici demonstrates. One evening in early August, 1954, Covici, John Steinbeck's loyal friend and his editor at Viking Press, turned on the television set at his brother-in-law's house in New Rochelle, New York, to watch a show called "The Author Meets the Critics." The topic that night was Steinbeck's *Sweet Thursday*, published in June and already selling by the box load. Steinbeck was living in Paris with his wife, Elaine, and his two sons, Thom and John IV, that summer, and so could not appear on the program. The critics, however, according to Covici's previously unpublished August 9, 1954, letter to Steinbeck, were represented by chief discussants Lewis Gannett and Joseph Bennett.

Gannett, the book critic for the venerable New York *Herald-Tribune*, and a longtime friend and supporter of Steinbeck's, took an affirmative position toward the novel. Bennett, a founding editor of the upstart *Hudson Review*, argued negatively. Bennett's "salubrious" opinion that *Sweet Thursday* was "dull, repetitious and phony" met with extreme resistance from Gannett and the other panelists, who defended the novel for its "delightful" wit and humor. The moderator, perhaps sympathetic to Bennett's plight, broadened the topic to include the overall importance of Steinbeck's contribution to contemporary American literature. According to Covici, Bennett asserted that Steinbeck had managed to produce some "worthwhile" fiction only when he was "angry," as in *In Dubious Battle* and *The Grapes of Wrath*. Steinbeck, however, was not one of the truly significant American novelists, but was merely a commercially successful writer who had skillfully learned how to "appeal to the largest public" audience possible. Gannett took the long view, arguing that Steinbeck had earned his recent success by virtue of his initial obscurity, his long years of hard work, and his willingness to experiment with the novel genre. Apparently, his persuasiveness carried the day, for at the end of his correspondence,

Covici reassured Steinbeck that Bennett's "harangues" were unconvincing, and would do nothing to injure the novel's reputation: ". . . the book keeps on selling!"

There is truth on each side of this debate, just as there is misapprehension and intolerance. Bennett's rigorous intellectualism and Covici's glib commercialism both represent passionate positions, but reductive ones, too, which impede understanding. Covici never was a consistently brilliant appreciator of fiction's technical properties, and may even have done Steinbeck a disservice during his career by pushing the marketable aspects of the novelist's work above all else. On the other hand, Steinbeck was a professional writer, a man who supported his family and earned his living by writing, so his being financially successful at his chosen vocation need not automatically have qualified as a cause for shame. Ironically, Bennett, quick to wave the avant-garde flag, seems to have missed the contemporaneity of *Sweet Thursday*, especially its artistic playfulness and self-reflexivity, its internalization of the American frontier theme, and its fabular dimensions. Steinbeck's text seems to have appeared too soon in our critical history to have been amply tolerated; in some ways, it belongs more comfortably to the nineties than to the fifties. At the very least, even though Bennett, Gannett, and Covici were unable to recognize it, Steinbeck exposed the American reading public to an early example of experimental metafiction, on the order of what Linda Hutcheon has called a "self-referring or autorepresentational" text (xii).

Historically—as the Bennett-Gannett fiasco symbolizes—*Sweet Thursday*'s reputation has always been unsettled. Even though many newspaper and magazine reviews were extremely critical, the book sold prodigiously: on one day alone—June 15, 1954—Viking sold 2000 copies; in another letter to Steinbeck written the following day (this also heretofore unpublished), Covici predicted it would top 100,000 for the year. Unimpressed by such abundance, *Time*'s anonymous reviewer castigated *Sweet Thursday* as "a turkey with visibly Saroyanesque stuffings. But where Saroyan might have clothed the book's characters and incidents with comic reality, Steinbeck merely comic-strips them of all reality and even of much interest" (121). In *The New Yorker*, Brendan Gill called the novel "labored" (71). And in the *New York Times*, Carlos Baker judged *Sweet Thursday* as "gaily inconsequential" (4), while Robert H. Boyle told *Commonweal* readers it was "a grade-B potboiler" (351).

A few contemporary notices, however, reached a moderately balanced assessment, leavening disapproval, bewilderment, or reservation with optimism. Milton Rugoff covered *Sweet Thursday* for the *Herald-Tribune*'s Book Review, situating it in the "ancient and honorable tradition" of "low comedy"; Steinbeck saves the book from corniness, he says, by the "up-bubbling notes of rowdy humor, and the occasional broad satiric thrusts . . ." (1). *Saturday Review*'s Harvey Curtis Webster announced that ". . . Steinbeck can become as great an American writer as we've had in our century (I thought so when I read 'East of Eden'); at other times, it appears that he is a gifted writer who can never control his fiction sufficiently to write a first-rate book. 'Sweet Thursday' makes one feel betwixt and between" (11). Hugh Holman, writing in *The New Republic*, struck a rarely heard revisionary note:

> I think we have been wrong about Steinbeck. We have let his social indignation, his verisimilitude of language, his interest in marine biology lead us to judge him as a naturalist. . . . Steinbeck is . . . a social critic . . . occasionally angry but more often delighted with the joys that life on its lowest levels presents. I think *Sweet Thursday* implicitly asks its readers to take its author on such terms. If these terms are less than we thought we had reason to hope for from *The Grapes of Wrath*, they are still worthy of respect. (20)

Despite Holman's prophetic warning, however, with few exceptions scholarly opinion of *Sweet Thursday* is, Roy Simmonds claims, "unfavorable and at best lukewarm" (141). Everyone agrees that *Thursday* is not among Steinbeck's premier efforts, but there has been so much disagreement over the locus of the book's apparent flaws, its numerous aporia (does it fail in technique, characterization, gender coding, philosophy, or tone?), that even that minority cadre, including Astro, Holman, Howard Levant, Charles Metzger, and myself, who have found the book worth attention, cannot agree on the basis of our attraction. Moreover, during the past fifteen years, since Roy Simmonds surveyed the scene, serious interest in *Sweet Thursday* has been nearly nonexistent. Brian St. Pierre and David Wyatt say nothing of it in their books on the California aspects of Steinbeck's career. Paul McCarthy's monograph mentions the novel only in passing (19, 21, 24, 125), and even Jackson Benson's scrupulously detailed biography, *The True Adventures of John Steinbeck*, has little on *Thursday* itself, though it does provide a factual context for the book's background and its inception as a musical comedy in 1953 called "Bear Flag" (740-45). Louis Owens's 1985 thematic study of Steinbeck's *Western Fiction: John Steinbeck's Re-Vision of America*, perpetuates a line of objection to the novel that extends all the way from Joseph Bennett, through critical monographs by Peter Lisca, Warren French, Joseph Fontenrose, and on to Stoddard Martin. Owens finds the novel contemptuous and dismisses it out of hand. His judgment is founded on his belief that the novel rejects "the most meaningful symbol in Steinbeck's fiction and Western culture: the Christian sacrifice" (196), though it is hard to imagine how such a caveat can be considered a universally applicable norm for judging twentieth-century fiction. More intriguing—but no less caustic—is the recent political argument on male authority/female portrayal in *Sweet Thursday* raised by feminist critic Mimi Reisel Gladstein, who exposes Steinbeck's "time-worn sexist cliches" ("Missing" 92).

Amid such looming dissensus, John Timmerman went against the grain. In *John Steinbeck's Fiction*, he advanced a positive view of *Sweet Thursday* based squarely on Wylie Sypher's theory of comedy, and offered a convincing analysis of the novel as a literary "farce" (174-80). Meantime, what goes around, comes around: in an essay written for Jackson Benson's collection, *The Short Novels of John Steinbeck*, Louis Owens apparently rethought *Sweet Thursday*, and now considers it "an investigation into the role of the artist as author" (200). His tune has a suspiciously familiar ring to it, but makes good reading anyway when paired with another chapter in Benson's anthology, Mimi Gladstein's considered attempt—partly gender-driven, partly formalistic—to explain *Thursday*'s "enjoyable" but manipulative enigmas ("Straining" 244-48).

So if the opinions of Bennett and Covici represent mutually exclusive positions on *Thursday*, then perhaps Gannett's synthesism is the one to recommend. Criticism, his view suggests, is an act of understanding, a tolerance for what actually exists in a work of fiction, rather than a lament for what it lacks. This perspectival stance jibed with Steinbeck's own theories on writerly texts and readerly participation at this juncture of his career. Steinbeck's announcement in "Critics, Critics, Burning Bright" that an "experiment, which at first seems outrageous to the critic and the reader who have not been through the process of its development, may become interesting and valid when it is inspected a second and third time" (47), and his "wish" in *East of Eden*—"that when my reader has finished . . . he will have a sense of belonging . . ." (*Journal* 61), by which he invited his reader to actively enter the process of fictionality—carried over to "Mack's Contribution," the original 156-line Introduction to *Sweet Thursday*. Mack, reacting to some unflattering reviews of *Cannery Row* and sounding much like a modern Huck Finn, claims to "have laid out a lot of time on critics," and wonders whether they all read the same book: "Some of them don't listen while they read, I guess," he states, because they are more interested in assigning handy catchwords to a work—"overambitious," "romantic," "naturalistic doggavation"—than in "understanding" (Galley I). In the truncated forty-seven-line version which became *Sweet Thursday*'s published Prologue, Mack's pointed suggestions about chapter headings, character descriptions, and loose-limbed hooptedoodle (ix-x) are laid out as matters of personal preference, not as punitive markers, and they are eventually incorporated in the novel to undercut aesthetic distance and to initiate the audience's "belonging."

Most importantly, Steinbeck is in on the con game, part of its web of decentered intrigue. *Sweet Thursday*'s affective and constitutive implications—its multiple layers of meaning, its "reality below reality" (133), its rambunctious tone, and its wilful blurring of historical reality/ actual persons with invented scenarios/made-up actions (marginalized characters in an earlier *roman-à-clef* discuss a novel they appeared in; its real-life author follows their advice in a fictional sequel in which they once again appear as dramatic participants)—took precedence over traditional, directed representational means. At this juncture, before looking more closely at *Sweet Thursday* in the next section, it is worth recalling Steinbeck's 1959 letter to Elia Kazan, for it summarizes his radical epistemological project of the 1950s: "Externality is a mirror that reflects back to our mind the world our mind has created of the raw materials. But a mirror is a piece of silvered glass. There is a back to it. If you scratch off the silvering, you can see through the mirror to the other worlds on the other side. I know that many people do not want to break through. I do, passionately, hungrily" (*Life* 625).

III

Although his critics and literary historians do not agree on much else, nearly all concur that John Steinbeck staked out two major themes in his fictional career: the California experience, including the westering process and the ironic vision of Eden; and the phalanx, or group-man, theory of social and familial organization. Just about everything Steinbeck wrote touches one or both of these compelling concepts; they run so deep in the first twenty years of his career that one or the other (or both) inform his conceptions of character, setting, plot, style, and theme. When allied with his non-teleological philosophy and omniscient narrative technique, these aspects became recognizable signatures of the Steinbeck novel from the early 1930s through the late 1940s. Steinbeck's harshest critics (Edmund Wilson and Arthur Mizener, for instance) expected Steinbeck to play some variation of this music over and over again, an expectation he refused to fulfill because of his periodic dissatisfaction with the "clumsy" novel form (*Life* 194).

But if Steinbeck's proletarian narratives have a social necessity and documentary integrity that urges us to think of them as whole-cloth fabric, his late fictions can equally profit from being grouped as products of necessity and integrity, too, though of an aesthetic order and literary sensibility removed from documentary realism. Steinbeck's shift radiates from a confession in his June 8,1949, letter to novelist John O'Hara, in which he relinquishes his earlier mode: "I believe one thing powerfully—that the only creative thing our species has is the individual, lonely mind. . . . The group ungoverned by individual thinking is a horrible destructive principle" (*Life* 359). Following this breakthrough, Steinbeck composed four experiments: the play-novelette *Burning Bright* (1950), the filmscript *Viva Zapata!* (1952), the epic *East of Eden* (1952), and the comic *Sweet Thursday* (1954). While these intensely personal books still carry elements of Edenic mythos and phalanx organization, and while they also evince a moral quality which can be said to perform a social or cultural function, overall they comprise a different order of fictionality from their predecessors. By calling attention to their own literariness through allusions, language play, scriptable referentiality, and artful framing devices, they demonstrate Steinbeck's turn toward an incipient postmodernism, a condition of openness where the act of writing in all its paradoxical manifestations becomes its own valid end (Clayton 10). "If a writer likes to write," he claimed in 1950,

> he will find satisfaction in endless experiment with his medium. He will improvise techniques, arrangements of scenes, rhythms of words, and rhythms of thought. He will constantly investigate and try combinations new to him, sometimes utilizing an old method for a new idea and vice versa. Some of his experiments will inevitably be unsuccessful but he must try them anyway if his interest be alive. This experimentation is not criminal . . . but it is necessary if the writer be not moribund. ("Critics" 47)

The result of Steinbeck's (r)evolution has been the source of much notorious and uncompromising critical reaction to his work after *Cannery Row*. However, the canonical critical ground rules of formalism do not always apply to the later Steinbeck, whose writing moved farther away from naturalism and closer toward fabulation, parable (Jones 3), and magical realism; with his new-found prerogative, Steinbeck veered from the documentary novel toward a self-revealing scriptive art. In light of this dramatic swerve, I propose that in his late career he discovered nothing less than a third major theme, which I call "The Creative." This set of values was motivated by autobiographical consciousness, individual choice, redemptive love, domestic themes, and, of course, artistic experimentation, all of which enabled Steinbeck to explore a new narratological world after 1950.

Sweet Thursday was consciously proposed as a tonal, thematic counterbalance to the "weight" of *East of Eden* (*Life* 472). It is a boisterous sequel (with the same geographical location and many of the same characters) to Steinbeck's more famous *Cannery Row*, which appeared nine years earlier (treating Monterey's pre-War era). *Thursday* takes up the post-World War II life of Doc (based on Steinbeck's soul mate, Edward F. Ricketts, who had died in a car-train crash on Drake Avenue in May, 1948); it emphasizes Doc's difficulties in reestablishing his Western Biological Laboratory on Monterey's Cannery Row, including his vicissitudes with a scholarly treatise, his rocky off-again, on-again relationship with a tough-talking, golden-hearted hooker-turned-waitress named Suzy. It also features the burlesque-like antics of the Row's Palace Flophouse denizens (Mack, Hazel, and others) and Fauna, the madame of the Bear Flag, who—playing Cupid for Doc and Suzy—want to insure a happy romantic ending.

As this brief precis suggests, when approached from a rigid analytical position, *Sweet Thursday* can be considered sentimental (like most other hookers at Fauna's Bear Flag brothel, Suzy's indelible goodness erases her stigma as a prostitute), reductive (Doc imagines he cannot be happy without a woman to complete his identity), slapstick (events and characterizations have a cartoon-like quality), and improbable (the plot hinges on coincidences and convenient superficialities). Such flaws have made the book an easy target for snipers. But to arrive at the deeper significance of this fiction, questions of character motivation, realism, agency, and gender portrayal need to be willingly suspended here (and may even be beside the point). Rather, *Sweet Thursday* is important for what it reveals of Steinbeck's aesthetic and philosophical sea-changes, and for his attitude toward the necessity of fictive experimentation in the unsettling wake of a postwar depletion that affected all levels of the Row's socio-economic, philosophical, aesthetic, personal, and linguistic existence. Old ways of doing business no longer obtain for Doc, for inhabitants of the Row, or for the narrator and author (implied or otherwise): "discontent," he writes, is "the lever of change" (21). *Sweet Thursday*, then, is Steinbeck's effort at accomplishing what "has not been done a million times before" (23) in American writing.

Steinbeck understood the corrosive nature of disaffection. There was a span in his career, beginning in mid-1948, when he was cut adrift from accustomed moorings by the death of Ed Ricketts and by his divorce from Gwyn (his second wife and the mother of his two children). On and off for over a year, mired in his own enervation, misogyny, and self-pity, Steinbeck's self-identity as a writer seemed splintered, fragmented, even fraudulent. After *The Pearl* and *The Wayward Bus*, both published in 1947, this customarily resilient writer found it increasingly difficult to settle on his next project (the many versions of *Zapata*, for instance, the false starts on *East of Eden*, as well as the several unwritten plays he planned during this period). Steinbeck's personal disarray and emotional discontentedness, coupled with his awakening reaction to America's Cold War intellectual climate, which called into question the currency of social(ist) visions (Schaub 25-26), set him willy-nilly on a road toward an end he could not yet envision, but whose allurements he could not refuse. In the feverish and sometimes blind searches of that period he underwent deep readjustments toward many things, not the least of them his own fictive art. In his relationship with his third wife, Elaine, whom he met in May, 1949, and married in December, 1950, Steinbeck discovered healing powers in love and domestic attachment which in turn had a direct, exponential bearing on his work energy and anticipation (*Life* 397) and, by his own admission, may have saved him from suicide (Personal Diary 1951). Eventually, as if to validate that recovery by repeating it, Steinbeck raised his own emotional and creative processes to the level of subject, at once self-generating and historically determined. Once he entered that thorny realm he probably realized he knew it as well as anything else, which is perhaps why he considered *Sweet Thursday* "a little self-indulgent" (*Life* 473). In writing Doc trying to write, Steinbeck turned out to be narrating nothing less than the symbolic story of his own emotional rescue and artistic refashioning. In the process Steinbeck did not destroy Doc (Lisca 282) but replaced him with himself; in recasting his portrait of the artist, he did so on an entirely personal scale.

That Steinbeck took so much pleasure in writing this blissful, ludic novel should not, I think, be held against him. As a person who labored with words day in and day out, year after year, he often spoke of his need for his task to be "fun." "There is a school of thought among writers which says that if you enjoy writing something it is automatically no good and should be thrown out. I can't agree with this," he told Elizabeth Otis, his agent, and the dedicatee of *Sweet Thursday*, on September 14, 1953 (*Life* 472). If *Cannery Row* represented the way things were, he explained two months later, then *Sweet Thursday* became the way things "might have" been (474). The two propositions ("[t]he one can be as true as the other") are necessary for a holistic view of the novelist's mind, and for an understanding of what the spirit of Ed Ricketts meant to Steinbeck, who didn't "seem . . . able to get over his death" (474). Thus, only by embracing comedy and tragedy, realism and fabulation, the inarticulate "transcendental sadness" of *Cannery Row* and the "frabjous" expression of joy of *Sweet Thursday*, could Steinbeck lay to rest the ghost of Ed Ricketts, which, by this time, had become the ghost of Steinbeck himself. In giving himself to revisionary impulses, Steinbeck presented his new Doc not as an unapproachable mythic hero, a practitioner of rigorous non-teleology, or an enigmatic isolato, but as a man—like the newly renovated Steinbeck—who was once again connected to quotidian life, to the local human community, and to author and readers, by common links—the search for meaningfulness, the potentially saving grace of love, and the ongoing struggle of the creative consciousness toward articulation:

> For hours on end he [Doc] sat at his desk with a yellow pad before him and his needle-sharp pencils lined up. Sometimes his wastebasket was full of crushed, scribbled pages, and at others not even a doodle went down. Then he would move to the aquarium and stare into it. And his voices howled and cried and moaned. "Write!" said his top voice, and "Search!" sang his middle voice, and his lowest voice sighed, "Lonesome! Lonesome!" He did not go down without a struggle. He resurrected old love affairs, he swam deep in music, he read the *Sorrows of Werther*; but the voices would not leave him. The beckoning yellow pages became his enemies. (*Sweet* 58)

Though I obviously still endorse the premise that *Sweet Thursday* is a novel about the creative process, because it foregrounds the struggle of individual consciousness in (and through) language, I am inclined to regard Steinbeck's attitude toward the key artist figure in a less totalizing way than I did twenty-five years ago; that is, less as a result of Doc's masterful, isolated genius (his figurative role in *Cannery Row*) than as a workaday, representative negotiator between public and private realms: "When trouble came to Doc," Steinbeck notes, "it was everybody's trouble" (58). In chapter 6, "The Creative Cross," Doc's tribulations in researching and writing his proposed scholarly essay, "Symptoms in Some Cephalopods Approximating Apoplexy" (32), mirror aspects of Steinbeck's preparatory stages in his own creative regime and his usual pre-writing jitters and inability to concentrate, and reflect as well Steinbeck's wrenching artistic and personal upheavals of the late 1940s. Embedded in Steinbeck's comic treatment of Doc's trials of mind and heart is a felt psychological validity and sense of emotional immediacy. Steinbeck's new artistry lay in striking a balance between the old desire for the sovereignty of the imagination and the new awareness of contextual facticity, the ineluctability of quotidian demands. In *Sweet Thursday* this pragmatic balance took the form of a comedic stance toward the artist's traditionally elitist position. Steinbeck does not entertain the death of the author (that would erase his own reason for being), but he does give us a restrained view of Doc's performance, suggesting that success lies as much in the marshalling of conjunctive forces and ambient fortune as it does in the completion of the writing project. Paradoxically, even though Doc is freighted with Steinbeck's self-projection and autobiographical angst, there is also a telling difference in ends, because the form Steinbeck adopts for *Sweet Thursday* takes on a life of its own, "gives form to its own curiosities," as he said of André Gide's *The Counterfeiters*, and veers away from the kind of objective, autonomous document a practicing scientist would be expected to produce.

Revising, Steinbeck must have realized as he reread and reprocessed the Doc of *Cannery Row* and "About Ed Ricketts," was not a tidy allegorical process; rather, it was a way of re-entering a slippery emotional place that was no less a part of the makeup of "reality" than the physicality of his present moment. Thus "Sweet Thursday" functions as a double signifier, at once private and public utterance, reference and object, process and product, text and work. The name refers to a "magic kind of day" (122) when all manner of unanticipated, fissionable, random events occur on Cannery Row (to which Steinbeck devotes three contiguous, titled chapters—19, 20, 21—at the midpoint of his novel, and one—39—at the very end). Then, refracted, *Sweet Thursday* becomes the title of the book Steinbeck brings into being, which operates in turn as a textual looking glass that reflects, distorts, enlarges, and/or magnifies the implicit ethereality and quantum activities of the "magic day" by borrowing a sense of its own disruptive form from the carnival quality of life on the Row.

That inherent duality, that fluid interchangeability, which is encoded in the title, also functions as a symbol for Steinbeck's imaginative concerns. When Fauna tells Joe Elegant, "'When a man says words he believes them, even if he thinks he is lying'" (134), she is suggesting that language (not only experience) is a reality, and a seductive one at that. Philosophically and aesthetically, after 1949 Steinbeck wrote out of a belief in the preeminence of individual—rather than group—creativity, but he did so in such a way that his expressivism was also a critique of realism, and the issue of origination was open to authorial skepticism. The moral center he wrote toward in his late works was, like Cannery Row itself, not so much a sacred ground as it was a negotiable site of contingency and indeterminacy. For good reason, then, Steinbeck names chapter 10 "There's a Hole in Reality Through Which We Can Look if We Wish," for in its pointed artificiality, in its intertextuality, his fiction partially dismantles (but does not completely explode) the authority implicit or embedded in traditional authorship and in narrative propriety. It demonstrates that in the random, seesaw poetic form of *Sweet Thursday*, he was able to bring both the narrative plot and the process of reflexive commentary into a single work, which has the spontaneity of appearing to be made up on the spot, to undercut its own profound pretensions, and to deconstruct the rules and format of its own invention and ontology: "There are people who will say that this whole account is a lie, but a thing isn't necessarily a lie even if it didn't necessarily happen" (57). In such instances as various characters' use of malapropisms, and in Mack's humorous use of Latin phrases and exalted language, *Sweet Thursday* interrogates the representational qualities of language (and class) at the same time it validates the fluctuating process by which such mysteries emerge without ever being fully concluded. That characters as diverse as Doc, Joe Elegant, the Bear Flag's cook, who is writing a Freudian novel called The Pi Root of Oedipus, and Fauna, who not only writes horoscopes but authors Suzy's conduct and manners ("I should write a book. . . ." "If She Could, I Could" [143]), all wrestle with compositional acts and problems of inscription invites us to consider seriously Steinbeck's perception that the tangled wilderness of language (whether of speech, writing, body gesture, or masquerade dress) is one of the few frontiers left to us in a discontented, apocalyptic age.

IV

To the degree that the divorced Steinbeck was often an absentee parent to his boys, his writing in *East of Eden* (the original manuscript was addressed explicitly to his sons) and in *Sweet Thursday* represents surrogate ways of being a father, alternate means of assuaging his guilt and easing their dislocation by making them participants in his fictional landscape. (Two short stories from this era, "His Father" and "The Affair at 7, Rue de M—," are drawn directly from Steinbeck's family life.) While young boys could hardly be expected to read, much less understand, the philosophical *East of Eden* (Thom was 8, John IV was 6 when it appeared), *Sweet Thursday* was another matter, for with it he wrote a humorous book that not only profited from being read aloud to children, but also explained in a comedic and self-deprecating manner what it was that their father did every day with sharpened pencils and yellow note pads.

In enacting this mysterious concept of "work," *Sweet Thursday* gains its exaggerated propriety from self-conscious adaptations of fictive reality, including Steinbeck's own prior writings (*Tortilla Flat* and especially *Cannery Row*), and from parallel, engendering artifices. As I have detailed in *Steinbeck's Reading*, Steinbeck often read to write. *Sweet Thursday* is no exception. In the populist echoes, and in the literary parodies, mimicries, puns, wordplays and allusions to The Bible, *The Little Flowers of Saint Francis*, the Welsh *Mabinogian*, Coleridge's "Kubla Khan," Lewis Carroll's "Jabberwocky" and "The Walrus and the Carpenter" from *Through the Looking Glass*, Robert Louis

Stevenson's *Child's Garden of Verses*, to list but a few, *Sweet Thursday* is enriched by Steinbeck's eclectic browsing in favorite works. Perhaps more than anything else, however, Steinbeck's avowed reading of Al Capp's enormously popular, extremely inventive *Li'l Abner* comic strip, which he and his family followed assiduously in newspapers at home and abroad, propelled *Sweet Thursday* toward what New Historicists might consider its contextual thickness and tonality (Hawthorn 118-19). "Yes, comic strips," he told Sydney Fields in 1955. "I read them avidly. Especially Li'l Abner. Al Capp is a great social satirist. Comic strips might be the real literature of our time. We'll never know what literature is until we're gone" (*Conversations* 59). New Historicism and cultural materialism aside, what more natural way to find common ground between a stoic father and his rambunctious sons than by employing the familiar language and gestures of their milieu—comic books?

I have long been an advocate of Steinbeck's ephemeral writings ("Introduction" 3-4). Far from being marginal documents, his introductions, prefaces, dust jacket blurbs, and testimonials actually illuminate his own art. In 1953, the same year he was working on "Bear Flag," the musical precursor of *Sweet Thursday*, Steinbeck introduced Capp's book-length collection, *The World of Li'l Abner*. Steinbeck did not habitually provide encomia or introductions to the work of other writers, but when he did it was for a strong reason (*Your Only Weapon* [v]). As with many of Steinbeck's lesser-known or fugitive items, this six-page brief reveals much about his creative bearings, influences, and purposes. Beneath his jaunty, tongue-in-cheek tone there are numerous revelations which bear directly on *Sweet Thursday*'s zany style and technique. To state it simply, *Sweet Thursday* is Steinbeck's attempt at writing a literary comic book, his conscious attempt "to get into Capp's act" ([ii]).

Steinbeck theorizes that Al Capp "May very possibly be the best writer in the world today . . . the best satirist since Laurence Sterne." From a patrician point of view Steinbeck's reasoning might not at first seem convincing, and yet, while his proofs reveal some very large leaps of faith, given Steinbeck's interest in pictorialism, his populist beliefs, and his aggressively non-academic disposition, this argument is not entirely fallacious either and should not be dismissed out of hand. Steinbeck asserts that, like Dante, who redefined the established traditions of literature in his time by writing in Italian rather than in Latin, Capp, too, is a pioneer, perhaps even a visionary. The literature of the future, he claims, might eventually depart from the "stuffy" adherence to "the written and printed word in poetry, drama, and the novel," and eventually include popular forms of cultural discourse such as the comic book, Capp's *métier*. Steinbeck asks:

> How in hell do we know what literature is? Well, one of the . . . diagnostics of literature should be, it seems to me, that it is read, that it amuses, moves, instructs, changes and criticizes people. And who in the world does that more than Capp? . . . Who knows what literature is? The literature of the Cro Magnon is painted on the walls of the caves of Altamira. Who knows but that the literature of the future will be projected on clouds? Our present argument that literature is the written and printed word . . . has no very eternal basis in fact. Such literature has not been with us very long, and there is nothing to indicate that it will continue. . . . . If people don't read it, it just isn't going to be literature. ([i; iv])

The key point of Steinbeck's prophetic thesis is less shocking to a reader in the mid-1990s—accustomed as we are to issues of contingency and indeterminacy caused by recent theoretical debates over the existence of a uniform canon, shared texts, and the autonomy of representation—than it was forty years ago (Eagleton 1-4). Indeed, in an age that has ushered in interactive media forms, including virtual reality and hypertexts, the comic book as a literary form appears now to be rather tame.

Nevertheless, in Capp's ability to "invent" an entire world in Dogpatch, to give it memorable characters, recognizable form, and unique spoken language, he created just that quality of aesthetic "participation" Steinbeck aimed for in all his fictions, in which the reader completed his or her own arc of a subjective transaction. The unbridled license to make up in any way that fits the artist's or the medium's immediate, compulsive demands—not those of a critical blueprint—are what Capp and Steinbeck share. Indeed, Steinbeck's description of the key elements of the *Li'l Abner* strip can be applied to *Sweet Thursday*: its plot has a "fine crazy consistency" of (il)logic, it satirizes the "entrenched nonsense" of blind human striving, respectable middle-class life, and normal male/female courting rituals; it constructs an entire fictive world in the Palace Flophouse and its larger domain, Cannery Row itself (where, like Capp's Dogpatch, realistic outside rules of aesthetics and morality do not necessarily apply); and it contains suitably exaggerated situations (Capp's Sadie Hawkins Day and Steinbeck's annual return of monarch butterflies to Pacific Grove, and The Great Roque War), as well as characters whose names are distinctive, colorful, and unique (Steinbeck's Whitey No. 1, Whitey No. 2, and Jesus and Mary Rivas; Capp's Hairless Joe, and Moonbeam McSwine, for example). In Hazel's absurd run for the presidency of the United States, we catch Steinbeck's echoes of Zoot Suit Yokum's improbable presidential nomination in 1944 (Capp 47).

Moreover, in its optimistic, life-affirming treatment of the roller-coaster love affair between Doc and Suzy, Steinbeck playfully echoes not only his own affair with Elaine, but the courtship and marriage of the recalcitrant Li'l Abner and bountiful Daisy Mae. There are numerous examples of passages, such as the one in chapter 16, where Mack believes he can heal the psychosomatic diseases of rich women, that not only pay homage to Capp (there are echoes in Mack's proposal of Marryin' Sam's "perspectus" for expensive weddings), but that also underscore Steinbeck's own self-mimicking method, his application of Capp's satiric "tweak with equal pressure on all classes, all groups," and his appreciation for the "resounding prose" of Capp's folk dialogue. Mack boasts:

". . . first I'd hire me a deaf-and-dumb assistant. His job is just to set and listen and look worried. Then I'd get me a bottle of Epsom salts and I'd put in
a pretty little screwcap thing and I'd call it Moondust. I'd charge about
thirty dollars a teaspoonful, and you got to come to my office to get it. Then
I'd invent me a machine you strap the dame in. It's all chrome and it lights
colored lights every minute or so. It costs the dame twelve dollars a half-
hour and it puts her through the motions she'd do over a scrub board. I'd
cure them! And I'd make a fortune too. Of course they'd get sick right
away again, so I'd have something else, like mixed sleeping pills and
wake-up pills that keeps you right where you was when you started." (102)

Perhaps more than anything else, however, there is a scene in chapter 28 that I think serves as a synecdoche in language, execution, and
purpose for Capp's influence. In "Where Alfred the Sacred River Ran"
(all *Sweet Thursday*'s chapters have similarly parodic or incongruent
titles, very much like Capp's bold-faced commentary and frame headings in his comic strip; the chapters themselves are short and easily ap-
prehended, like cartoon strip panels, which is one of the features Mack
called for in his Prologue), Steinbeck describes the action of a wild
party, and Doc's reaction to it, in a way that can best be understood if
we imagine ourselves to be reading a comic strip or cartoon, blissfully
participating in its "preposterous" archi-text-ure. It is necessary to
quote at length from the following scene, a masquerade on the theme of
"Snow White and The Seven Dwarfs," to suggest the flavor and dimensions of Steinbeck's recitation:

A fog of unreality like a dream feeling was not in him but all around him.
He went inside the Palace and saw the dwarfs and monsters and the prepos-
terous Hazel all lighted by the flickering lanterns. None of it seemed the
fabric of sweet reality. . . .
    Anyone untrained in tom-wallagers might well have been startled. . . .
Eddie waltzed to the rumba music, his arms embracing an invisible partner.
Wide Ida lay on the floor Indian wrestling with Whitey No. 2, at each try

displaying acres of pink panties, while a wild conga line of dwarfs and animals milled about. . . .

Mack and Doc were swept into the conga line. To Doc the room began to revolve slowly and then to rise and fall like the deck of a stately ship in a groundswell. The music roared and tinkled. Hazel beat out rhythm on the stove with his sword until Johnny, aiming carefully, got a bull's eye on Hazel. Hazel leaped in the air and came down on the oven door, scattering crushed ice all over the floor. One of the guests had got wedged in the grandfather clock. From the outside the Palace Flophouse seemed to swell and subside like rising bread. (196-97)

This festive carnival passage (Ames 21-25), which occurs in what Mack calls a "veritable fairyland" (189), is one of Steinbeck's most pleasurable fictive moments. It revels in a sense of fancifulness, in a luxurious staging and fluid movement that joins sacred and profane experience in startling ways. Steinbeck's reversals of gender expectations, and his conscious abdication of the "fabric of sweet reality" account for the bizarre, ridiculous swelling house, the instances of cross-dressing and masquerade impersonation, the unpredictable loops and digressions of the novel's structure, his abandonment of overtly linear, "literary," progression in favor of a quantum randomness, and for his one-dimensional (but not necessarily simplistic) characterizations. All in all, it is an example of his belief that "Technique should grow out of theme" (*Life* 521).

Furthermore, Steinbeck's postwar change of aesthetic sensibility made an enormous difference between his treatment of Doc, whose "transcendent sadness" and essential loneliness closed *Cannery Row*, and this portrayal which ends with the partially incapacitated, but romantically redeemed, Doc riding off with Suzy (she is driving) into the sunset of a day that was "of purple and gold, the proud colors of the Salinas High School." Steinbeck continues: "A squadron of baby angels maneuvered at twelve hundred feet, holding a pink cloud on which the word J-O-Y flashed on and off. A seagull with a broken wing took off and flew straight up into the air, squawking, 'Joy! Joy!'" (268). It is a moment that lends *Sweet Thursday* the same quality Steinbeck found in *The World of Li'l Abner*: "such effective good nature that we seem to have thought of it ourselves" ([ii]). Love, considered both seriously and as a form of play, Steinbeck suggests, heals the split between language and life, self and world, parent and children, text and audience.

Recognizing the supremacy of such playful fictive invention underscores that for the late Steinbeck authoring was not a thoroughly mimetic task, a representational rendering of shared social reality; it was the creation of a reality all its own, a reality once set down in or arising from language that created its own set of interpretative valuations, and whose norms, values, and ground rules changed from work to work, so that even to speak of the novelist's fictive task of creating a world in *East of Eden* would not be to describe the same created world in *Sweet Thursday*, published only two years after *Eden*, and also set in a remembered California. Far from being a tired failure because he abandoned critical realism after *The Grapes of Wrath*, Steinbeck was a prophetic Postmodernist, a journeyer in the literary fun house, a traveler in the land behind the mirror of art, a mirror which in *Sweet Thursday* had become nearly silverless, so that we see his hand at work, calling attention to the house he is building, insistently redeeming it from "mechanical convention" by "unmasking" the originating system (Hutcheon 24). Thus the old thinking, with its imposition of preordained critical hegemonies of harmony, unity, distance, mimesis, for instance, simply will not work with a textual construct like *Sweet Thursday*, or for that matter, much of what Steinbeck wrote in the last phase of his career. Authoring these texts, he authored himself anew, and vice-versa.

The pejorative *Time* magazine review, which I quoted earlier, was only partly—and unintentionally—correct in its assessment of *Sweet Thursday*. Indeed, Steinbeck did "comic-strip" his characters of reality, but that, I suggest, was his desire; far from being proof of his decline into an undifferentiated Saroyanesque landscape, his appropriation of

Al Capp's free-form inventiveness, vivid technique, exaggerated scenarios, and "dreadful folk poetry" helped further in the novel what Steinbeck saw in *Li'l Abner*—a "hilarious picture of our ridiculous selves" ([ii]). Even that most significant of late Steinbeckian topics—the role of the artist—came in for its share of satire; rather than elevating it to a vaunted, culturally unassailable position, Steinbeck demystifies it by emphasizing the pre-writing process, the elusive valences of language, and the necessity for human bonding, rather than the austere finished result (Doc has yet to write his essay as the book ends). In lifting the veil to expose the process of fictionalizing the fictionalizing process, Steinbeck saves *Sweet Thursday* from being masturbatory or egregiously narcissistic by its parodic tone and functionally inspired purpose. "Don't think of literary form," he advised famous humorist Fred Allen. "Let it get out as it wants to. . . . The form will develop in the telling. Don't make the telling follow a form" (Foreword n.p.). In seeking its own trajectory, *Sweet Thursday* turns out to be, on closer inspection, not an overstuffed turkey, but more like that gull which presides over the conclusion—earthbound on occasion, but still capable of some startling flights of fancy. Pascal Covici was correct—the novel sold with abandon—and while its commercial success justified Covici's smug faith in Steinbeck, just as it fueled Bennett's scorn, there is, as with all Steinbeck's late work, a mediating ground, an aesthetic/emotional context, a cultural current, a text behind the text that provides an enabling evaluative presence.

V

"You fix the day and hour," Steinbeck says in *Sweet Thursday*, "by some incident that happened to yourself" (121). In the fall of 1984, midway in the second semester of my visiting appointment at San Jose State University as Director of the Steinbeck Research Center, I called on Thom Steinbeck, the novelist's elder son, in Carmel Highlands. I meant only to deliver a Xeroxed mock-up of *Your Only Weapon Is Your*

Work, a limited edition pamphlet publication of a 1957 letter Steinbeck had written to Dennis Murphy, the son of a longtime Steinbeck family friend, and himself author of a highly acclaimed novel, *The Sergeant* (which Steinbeck had directed first toward Elizabeth Otis, who in turn successfully placed it with Viking Press). The day, however, quickly turned into something more. We spent that afternoon lounging on the deck of his splendid rented house, taking in its view of sheltering pines, craggy bluffs, and beyond them the sparkle and flash of the Pacific Ocean north of Big Sur. For a transplanted easterner the locale provided a spectacular glimpse of a remnant of the old Pacific coast frontier, the intimidating unpeopled landscape of Robinson Jeffers's poems and Steinbeck's "Flight," and, on a different scale, "the foreign and fancy purlieus" where, in *Sweet Thursday*, Whitey No. 1 peddled raffle tickets for the Palace Flophouse sale. For several hours Thom and I talked and drank wine—much wine, as I recall—which undoubtedly helped create the glow of camaraderie in that luminous time and place. We were contemporaries—a year apart in age—and our sense of having shared generational experiences and opinions seemed pronounced that afternoon.

Of course, we spoke often of his father and I remember vividly how Thom talked in that specially tinged, offhand and amazed way that children of the celebrated and famous have of communicating their conflicted sense of acceptance and estrangement, honor and renunciation, pride and embarrassment in their legacy. The afternoon was interrupted by at least two long-distance telephone calls from Thom's younger brother, John IV, and while these hiatuses stopped the flow of our talk for a while, each time Thom came back he was fueled with new energy, new reminiscences, often circling around tales of his father reading aloud to them, and his exasperation at their short attention spans. While I was not actively seeking gossip, I admit I was not averse to such inside news, though I was also leery of its implications, and the burden of complicity or degree of co-option it might create in the future. But such knowledge is always double-edged and serves unanticipated ends: listening to stories of Thom's childhood following his parents' divorce, I glimpsed something of the cause of his father's paternal attachment to Dennis Murphy, who became, for a while anyway, a surrogate son for what might not have been the best of reasons.

As much as anything else that afternoon I was painfully aware that even with firsthand information I was being offered in moments of spirited fellow-feeling, I could not know this man's father, John Steinbeck, whom I had spent so many years studying, in anything but a partial way, refracted through the bias of my own sensibility, the lens of my own being. Perhaps, I thought, I really had failed the test of perspectival criticism after all, and had fallen a long way from the level of a Lewis Gannett, or, in my own time, a Jackson Benson, who had more than anyone else I knew given Steinbeck's life and career the fairest assessment. And yet if such musings made Steinbeck less a monument, less a cultural icon, to me, I wasn't sure that I was willing to trade places with my host either, who, with his brother, knew even more than I the burden of shadows cast by the dead. Sometimes, I figured, it is better to be an everlasting outsider, inventing reasons for the reasons, rather than having to live them.

In the course of that afternoon, though, in addition to regaling me with raucous tales and anecdotes, Thom showed me Steinbeck family memorabilia, and we briefly entertained the possibility of my purchasing some items for the Steinbeck Center at a later date. (Almost a year later I bought a number of 8 mm home movies for the Center, including rare footage of Steinbeck and Ricketts's Sea of Cortez collecting trip.) As I was about to leave for Los Gatos, Thom said he had something he wanted me to have. I told him I was representing the Research Center and could not accept a gift for myself, though I could and would— gladly—receive one on behalf of San Jose State. He agreed, then hauled out a 1950s vintage portable typewriter, which he opened for my inspection. It was a Hermes, aptly named for the messenger of the gods, and himself a deity who embodied plural functions—god of invention, god of thievery, and god of roads and travel—in short, the god of process. "This was my father's," he said. "I want you to have it."

But only after reaching home that night did I notice the most intriguing part of the gift: on the back of the typewriter's grey cover Steinbeck had scratched indelibly with a pin, or knife, or maybe a nail, these words: "The Beast Within." I think that it was his way—part humorous, part deadly serious—of personalizing an otherwise somber-looking mechanical device, giving a name and an identity to one of those technological gadgets that the inventor side of him dearly loved and remained fascinated by throughout his life. In its ideal state the typewriter (and its kin) abetted the writer's imagination, processed his arc of reality, helped turn emergent material, whatever its source, into fictive form, and—not to put too purple a shade on this—gave shape, weight, palpability to experience in/of language: "The discipline of the written word punishes both stupidity and dishonesty," he told Pascal Covici, Jr. "A writer lives in awe of words for they can be cruel or kind, and they can change their meanings right in front of you" (*Life* 523). As a mediating trope, so to speak, for transmission of shifting words, the typewriter paradoxically distorts, transforms, and modifies in order to clarify and illumine; although it is not an "appendage," an "umbilical connection" like the more comfortable pencil Steinbeck often preferred, it still operates in the same way as a focussing "tool" (*Life* 624), like his later use of the dictaphone, that tends outward as well as inward, facilitating (and in some cases creating) his view of the world. The important thing, however, is the process of looking and of immersion implied in writing—the pen(cil) or knife or nail or typewriter key scratch on the surface of a papery medium—that records what it means to have been alive in the magnificent constellation of inner and outer experience. "After all," Doc says, "I guess it doesn't matter whether you look down or up—as long as you look" (*Sweet* 273).

In my moment of obsessive identification, the tiny machine came alive as a cumulative metaphor for the entire complex of Steinbeck's working life, an artifice situated on a horizon somewhere between expressivism and determined construction. On one hand, it represents process: the constant tyranny of being driven by "ancient" human compulsions toward expression (*Life* 523) and the daily, obsessive financial need to write (which made him frequently moody, selfish, inward-looking in a way no doubt only those who lived in his life—his wives, children, and stepchild, for instance—could fully ascertain and in a perverse way were fully qualified to judge). On the other hand, it symbolizes product: the indescribable and fleeting moments of success when a work was published and commercially viable, and then nominally at least put behind him as he went on restlessly to the next project. "To finish is sadness to a writer—a little death. He puts the last word down and it is done. But it isn't really done. The story goes on and leaves the writer behind, for no story is ever done" (*Life* 523).

The unfinished story surfaces in unforeseen ways, even when you think it is done, including its intrusion into this fragmentary attempt at synthesis and integration, when Steinbeck rewrites Ed Ricketts by reimagining Doc as himself, when he revises Capp's act by reinventing the comic book for his children, when I revisit the scene of my revisionism, and all of us—fathers and sons, current lovers and ex-spouses, past mentors and abiding friends—drive, so to speak, toward La Jolla, where all things seem to resolve into metaphoric simplicity and intuitive clarity: "This is the greatest mystery of the human mind—the inductive leap. Everything falls into place, irrelevancies relate, dissonance becomes harmony, and nonsense wears a crown of meaning. But the clarifying leap springs from the rich soil of confusion, and the leaper is not unfamiliar with pain" (*Sweet* 28). It is a moment when the machinery, the inventions, the necessary metaphors and tropes of leaping and journeying which so fixed and fascinated Steinbeck during his career—the Joads' Hudson Super Six, the Western Flyer, The Word, Juan Chicoy's broken-down bus, Olive Hamilton's airplane ride, the telescope that Mack and the boys present Doc at the conclusion of *Sweet Thursday* (he actually needed a microscope), his Hermes typewriter, his truck camper Rocinante, even the hieroglyphic *timshel*, and the surreal, topsy-turvy architecture of Al Capp's Dogpatch—all begin moving evocatively in roughly the same direction to fuel the transforming "drama of magic and alchemy" by which Steinbeck entered fascinating worlds of resonant language and rich experience, where, because the old strictures no longer applied, he felt obliged to make "new rules" of artistic conduct, propriety, and deportment (*Life* 532). Steinbeck's gift—much underrated in the final phase of his career—was his ability to make each book a different kind of "life experience" (*Journal* 61) by sending back reports from all the creative venues he entered—whether it was the tidepool, human speech and language, or the conflicted labyrinth of the heart. Maybe after all critical commentary subsides, after the process and nature of writing itself has been redefined yet again according to whatever the future current fashion will be, then what has gone around will come around, and John Steinbeck will prove to have been on the right road all along, the rest of us dust swirls in the spokes of his wheels.

Works Cited

Ames, Christopher. *The Life of the Party: Festive Vision in Modern Fiction*. Athens: U of Georgia P, 1991.

Astro, Richard. "Steinbeck's Bitter Sweet Thursday." *Steinbeck Quarterly* 4 (1971): 36-47. Rpt. in Benson, ed. 204-15.

_____, and Tetsumaro Hayashi, eds. *Steinbeck: The Man and His Work*. Corvallis: Oregon State UP, 1971.

"Back to the Riffraff." *Time* 14 June 1954: 120-21.

Baker, Carlos. "After Lousy Wednesday." *New York Times Book Review* 13 June 1954:4.

Benson, Jackson J. *The True Adventures of John Steinbeck, Writer*. New York: Viking, 1984.

_____, ed. *The Short Novels of John Steinbeck: Critical Essays with a Checklist to Steinbeck Criticism*. Durham: Duke UP, 1990.

Boyle, Robert H. "Boozy Wisdom." *Commonweal* 9 July 1954: 351.

Capp, Al. *The World of Li'l Abner*. Introd. John Steinbeck. Foreword by Charles Chaplin. New York: Ballantine, 1953.

Clayton, Jay. *The Pleasures of Babel: Contemporary American Literature and Theory*. New York: Oxford UP, 1993.

Covici, Pascal. *Letter to John Steinbeck*. 16 June 1954. Harry Ransom Humanities Research Center, Austin, Texas.

_____. *Letter to John Steinbeck*. 9 August 1954. Harry Ransom Humanities Research Center, Austin, Texas.

DeMott, Robert. "Introduction." *A New Steinbeck Bibliography: 1971-1981*. By Tetsumaro Hayashi. Metuchen: Scarecrow, 1983. 1-4.

_____. "Steinbeck and the Creative Process: First Manifesto to End the Bringdown against *Sweet Thursday*." Astro and Hayashi 157-78.

_____. *Steinbeck's Reading: A Catalogue of Books Owned and Borrowed*. New York: Garland, 1984.

Eagleton, Terry. *Literary Theory: An Introduction*. Minneapolis: U of Minnesota P, 1983.

Fontenrose, Joseph. *John Steinbeck: An Introduction and Interpretation*. New York: Barnes, 1963.

French, Warren. *John Steinbeck*. New York: Twayne, 1961.

_____. *John Steinbeck*. 2nd ed. rev. Boston: Hall, 1975.

Gill, Brendan. *New Yorker* 10 July 1954: 71.

Gladstein, Mimi Reisel. "Straining for Profundity: Steinbeck's *Burning Bright* and *Sweet Thursday*." Benson, ed. 234-48.

_____. "Missing Women: The Inexplicable Disparity Between Women in Steinbeck's Life and Those in His Fiction." *The Steinbeck Question: New Essays in Criticism*. Ed. Donald R. Noble. Troy: Whitston, 1993. 84-98.

Hawthorn, Jeremy. *A Concise Glossary of Contemporary Literary Theory*. London: Arnold, 1992.

Holman, Hugh. "A Narrow-gauge Dickens". *New Republic* 7 June 1954: 18-20.

Hutcheon, Linda. *Narcissistic Narrative: The Metafictional Paradox*. 1980. London: Methuen, 1984.

Jones, Lawrence William. *John Steinbeck as Fabulist*. Ed. Marston LaFrance. Steinbeck Monograph Series, No. 3. Muncie: Steinbeck Society, 1973.

Levant, Howard. *The Novels of John Steinbeck: A Critical Study*. Columbia: U of Missouri P, 1974.

Lisca, Peter. *The Wide World of John Steinbeck*. New Brunswick: Rutgers UP, 1958. Rpt. with new Afterword. New York: Gordian, 1981.

McCarthy, Paul. *John Steinbeck*. New York: Ungar, 1980.

Martin, Stoddard. *California Writers: Jack London, John Steinbeck, The Tough Guys*. 1983. Boston: St. Martin's, 1984. 67-122.

Metzger, Charles. "Steinbeck's Version of the Pastoral." *Modern Fiction Studies* 6 (1960): 115-24. Rpt. in Benson, ed. 185-95.

Murphy, Dennis. *The Sergeant*. New York: Viking, 1958.

Owens, Louis. *John Steinbeck's Re-Vision of America*. Athens: U of Georgia P, 1985.

_____. "Critics and Common Denominators." Benson, ed. 195-203.

Rugoff, Milton. "Business as Usual, and Fun, Too, on John Steinbeck's *Cannery Row*". *New York Herald-Tribune Books* 13 June 1954: 1.

St. Pierre, Brian. *John Steinbeck: The California Years*. San Francisco: Chronicle, 1983.

Schaub, Thomas Hill. *American Fiction in the Cold War*. Madison: U of Wisconsin P, 1991.

Simmonds, Roy S. "Steinbeck's *Sweet Thursday*". *A Study Guide to Steinbeck, Part II*. Ed. Tetsumaro Hayashi. Metuchen: Scarecrow, 1979. 139-64.

Steinbeck, John. *Burning Bright*. New York: Viking, 1950.

_____. *Cannery Row*. New York: Viking, 1945.

_____. *Conversations with John Steinbeck*. Ed. Thomas Fensch. Jackson: UP of Mississippi, 1988.

_____. "Critics, Critics, Burning Bright." *Saturday Review* 11 November 1950: 20-21. Rpt. in *Steinbeck and His Critics: A Record of Twenty-five Years*. Ed. E. W. Tedlock and C. V. Wicker. Albuquerque: U of New Mexico P, 1957. 43-47.

_____. Dust Jacket Encomium. *Gypsy: A Memoir*. By Gypsy Rose Lee. New York: Harper, 1957.

_____. *East of Eden*. New York: Viking, 1952.

_____. "His Father." *Reader's Digest* 55. 329 (1949): 19-21.

_____. Introduction. *The World of Li'l Abner*. By Al Capp. [i-vi].

_____. Introduction. Mack Contribution. Unrevised galley proofs of *Sweet Thursday*. MS. 776642. Harry Ransom Humanities Research Center, Austin, Texas.

_____. *Journal of a Novel: The* East of Eden *Letters*. New York: Viking, 1969.

_____. Letter to Fred Allen. Qtd. in Foreword. *Much Ado About Me*. By Fred Allen. Boston: Little, 1956. n.p.

_____. *Personal Diary*, 1946. MA 4685. The Pierpont Morgan Library, New York.

_____. *Personal Diary*, 1951. MA 4689. The Pierpont Morgan Library, New York.

_____. *Steinbeck: A Life in Letters*. Ed. Elaine Steinbeck and Robert Wallsten. New York: Viking, 1975.

_____. *Sweet Thursday*. New York: Viking, 1954.

_____. "The Affair at 7, Rue de M—." *Harper's Bazaar* 2921 (1955): 112, 202, 213.

_____. "*Un Grand Romancier de Notre Temps*." "Hommage à André Gide 1869-1951." Spec. issue of *La Nouvelle Revue Francaise* (Nov. 1951): [30].

_____. *Your Only Weapon Is Your Work: A Letter by John Steinbeck to*

Dennis Murphy. Ed. Robert DeMott. San Jose: Steinbeck Research Center, 1985.

Timmerman, John. *John Steinbeck's Fiction: The Aesthetics of the Road Taken.* Norman: U of Oklahoma P, 1986.

Webster, Harvey Curtis. "'Cannery Row' Continued." *Saturday Review* 12 June 1953: 11.

Wyatt, David. *The Fall into Eden: Landscape and Imagination in California.* New York: Cambridge UP, 1986. 124-57.

"John Believed in *Man*":
An Interview with Mrs. John Steinbeck_____

Donald V. Coers

On the 23rd and 24th of April, 1993, Donald Coers, accompanied by his wife, Mary Jeanne, interviewed Elaine Steinbeck in the Manhattan apartment on East Seventy-Second Street that she and John Steinbeck moved into in 1963. The interview began with the Coers giving Mrs. Steinbeck a box of Godiva chocolates.

DC: Do you like the white or dark chocolate?
ES: Any chocolate, and Godiva is my favorite. You know who that lady Godiva was, don't you? She rode naked through the streets.

DC: Eating chocolates.
ES: Eating chocolates! Did you ever read that poem in *Life in Letters* that John wrote in calypso [style] about Elaine, comparing old style Elaine, the Tennyson "Elaine the fair, the loveable, Elaine the lily maid of Astolat," to new style Elaine? "New style Elaine, she walked real proud. Got a b-flat baritone c-sharp loud." He always used to laugh at me because I would get real excited and talk loud. He talked very softly and mumbled. I said, "Nobody can understand a word you're saying." Once we found ourselves at a big party— people, people, people. I was out on the edges and I looked over in the middle of the room and saw that John had been caught somewhere. He was big-shouldered so you could always see him, and he looked like he was sick or mad or something so I thought, I've got to get to him, get over there and get him out. And I worked my way, wormed my way through the crowd, and he wasn't sick or mad; he was talking to Truman Capote! You see, they were so close together, there was such a crowd, that they couldn't put any distance between them. Truman was talking *up* to John, and John was talking *down* to Truman!

DC: Let's talk about your Texas background.

ES: Well, I'm a Texan and even though I've lived in New York fifty-three years, I still think of myself as a Texan. And I go back once a year, always. And this I'm very proud of: When I go to Fort Worth I still see all of my chums I went to school with from the second grade on. They're mostly widows now. We're going to meet in Mexico in the fall. Anyway, I have a lot of Texas friends. I was born in Austin, but I never lived there as a child. My father was connected with the University of Texas.

DC: Didn't you tell me once he was an Assistant Professor of English? Was he there when J. Frank Dobie was teaching?

ES: I think this was earlier. I'll be seventy-nine this August [1993], and I don't care who knows it. Anyway, my mother lived in Stephenville, and my father first was a principal of the high school there. Then he went into the independent oil business when Texas was discovering all of the great oil fields. It was a thing that a lot of young Texans did to make their fortunes. It was like going to the Gold Rush, you know. I lived in Stephenville through the first grade and then we moved to Fort Worth. I acted in all the shows; I was very interested in theater. I had a wonderful teacher who opened my life to me with Shakespeare. My father used to imitate me when I would walk around carrying a Shakespeare book and they couldn't get me to come to the table. I lived in Fort Worth until I graduated, and then I left for the University of Texas. My first husband was Zachary Scott. Texans know him; he had a theater named for him in Austin. Zack and I came to New York together in 1939 after he got his degree. Even though many years later Zack and I were divorced, his family and I are still very close. I always go to the Zachary Scott Theater when I go to Austin. One of my sisters is married to an Austinite and I go to see them every year. I show them Europe and they show me America—it's a good deal. We drive in Arizona, and we drive in Texas, and we drive in Colorado.

DC: *You also go to Santa Fe fairly frequently, don't you?*

ES: I love Santa Fe! In fact, I like the Southwest, and Fort Worth is part of the Southwest so that's why I've got it in my bones. It's still a part of my heart. While we're talking about my life in Texas, let me tell you a funny story. During the Vietnam War President Johnson asked John to go to Vietnam to do some reporting, and John said, "I'll go if I can take Elaine." And so the President gave me a press pass and I got around a lot over there, sometimes with John, sometimes not. On one occasion we were at the top of Laos, and I said to John one evening, knowing he was busy the next day with the military or with literary people or whatever, "Would you mind terribly if I got in a jeep and drove over to the jungle with some Marines to a village where they've never seen a white woman before? And he said, "No, if you're not afraid to, that's o.k." And then he said, "Honey, you won't go fifteen minutes until you've run into somebody that you went to the University of Texas with."

MJC: *Funny you should say that. Just a few days ago I was in Austin to hear Hillary Clinton speak and I met a woman who said she knew you at the University. Her name was Colleen Grant.*

ES: Sure, sure, Colleen Grant. I remember her. Did you like Hillary?

MJC: *I loved her.*

ES: Me too. I was in Santa Fe last year when the presidential campaign was going on. One morning I got up early to walk by myself and as I went into the plaza, I saw that there was no traffic there, and a lot of people, so I said to a cop, "What's happening?" He said, "Hillary Clinton is having breakfast with the Governor and his wife and various people and they are going to walk through the plaza." Now, I had not met her. I had been invited to a breakfast here in New York for her, in her honor, and had bought my ticket and then I decided to go West. While I was standing there in the plaza, I noticed a group of women, so I went up and said, "Are you women for Clinton? Can I join you?" And they said, "Sure, come on." I worked my way to the front, toward the street, so that I could get a good look, because I'd never met her, you see. She came along soon and was graciously saying hello to people, and then she got near me and I said, "Was the breakfast in New York fun last week?" And she stopped cold and said, "It was the best political party we've had in the whole campaign so far." I said, "I would have been there except I'm here, but my sister and I helped plan it." Well, she stopped and discussed it. Then she shook hands with all of us. She was just wonderful! I think she's going to do a good job. I've always been political. Zack was also political and very liberated although his family was strictly right wing. Then I married John, and, of course you know from reading *The Grapes of Wrath* where he stood! One of the most interesting things that John and I did while we were married was try twice to get Adlai Stevenson elected. John went to both conventions, and I went with him. He always took me with him, which was wonderful for me. And that's why I know so much about John in all directions, because he always said, "I'll go if Elaine can go." We went to the Democratic Convention when Adlai was nominated. I've always worked with politics in New York, and so I was working for Adlai. I'd phone John from one of the Democratic headquarters and he would be at the house working, and I'd say, "Write a five-minute speech for Hank Fonda to give in Minneapolis." And he'd say, "Yeah, o.k., right now." And I'd say, "Get it done within the hour, so somebody can pick it up." He was always writing speeches.

DC: Tell us what you mentioned in our phone conversation this morning about the speech Steinbeck wrote for the Nobel Prize.
ES: Well, that's something funny. John was thrilled to death to win the Nobel Prize, but then he suddenly realized he would have to give a speech in Stockholm. Some writers can speak, and some can't. John just couldn't, and he mumbled, anyway. And he said, "Oh my

Lord, I've got to make a speech in Stockholm." So John wrote Adlai a funny letter, saying, "Adlai, you're indebted to me. I've done a lot for you. I've tried to get you elected" and so forth. "Now all you've got to do is go to Stockholm and make a speech for me." Unfortunately some critics read what he said and took it seriously. That's why you scholars have to be careful about these things. John didn't have to be careful at all, you see. He adored the press when they were being smart. John would say to them, "I have a request for you. I don't request that you give me good write-ups; I request that you be as interesting to me as I am to you." Sometimes I would listen to John talk with the press in foreign countries, and by the time the interview was over he would have found out more about the country we were visiting than they would have found out from him. He was pretty clever, and that's what he enjoyed—the give and take. And sometimes, it was quite true, a lot of people would miss John's humor, and also I've heard John swear at the press. But John was never really mean to the press, although sometimes they provoked him. The British press is the most persistent. When we moved to Bruton, that year we lived in Somerset, the press at first nearly drove us crazy. And the village would help us out. The postmaster would say, "Steinbeck? Oh, yes, that chap did come near here. Whether he's stayed or not, we don't know."

DC: *A village conspiracy.*

ES: They protected him with a village conspiracy that was wonderful. One day I found a reporter outside of our cottage, and I said, "Get out of our meadow!" And the guy said, "It's all right, Mrs. Steinbeck. I'm *American* press." And I said, "O.k., I can really tell *you* what I think. Get the *hell* out of our meadow!"

DC: *Tell us more about your days as a drama major at the University of Texas.*

ES: Is this interview about *me*?

DC: We might slip this into a prologue or something.

ES: Well, I had acted in Fort Worth while I was in high school. I played the lead in the senior class play. You may be sure if I hadn't I would have laid myself on the floor and held my breath until my face turned purple! And then I acted all the time I was at the university. Lady Bird Johnson used to say, "Oh, you will just never know what a great actress Elaine was."

DC: Were you and Lady Bird in the same class?

ES: No, she was two years older.

DC: Wasn't Nellie Connally [wife of the late Texas Governor John Connally] there at that time?

ES: Nellie is a little younger than I, but Nellie and John and I are still friends. In fact, Nellie and I acted together. You see, one of the things that was so great about the drama department at the University of Texas was that it was so rich. The university had the best drama faculty, and then they built the auditorium and we had all the best facilities and equipment. And now when I go there to visit—I went to my fiftieth class reunion a few years ago—I see the most glorious places to rehearse theater, and to do theater, and to audition, and I say to the students, "Think of all you young actors; a few of you will get to New York after acting in this magnificent theater. You'll go to a scrubby theater on West Forty-Fourth Street where the toilets don't work and there's not enough light to put on make-up. And the only thing you'll have is that you'll walk onto a stage on Broadway." Anyway, we really had a superior faculty there [at the University of Texas]. A lot of them were from Yale. That was a great, great university for people going into the theater, drama, playwriting, and acting. Zack and I did a lot of plays together. And then we married while he was still in school. I went back to school and took some courses, some art history, and those things. And we also acted in the Austin theater, and in the university theater. In those days, all Broadway shows trouped. So we'd meet all the actors. We'd see them in Austin, then we'd drive to San Antonio and see them again in the same play the next night. We met the Lunts, Alfred Lunt and Lynn Fontanne, just after we had done one of their plays. I had played Miss Fontanne's part. I practically worshipped her, so I was never as embarrassed as one night at a party, in Austin, when Miss Fontanne said, "Where's the little girl who's supposed to be so much better than me?" I nearly died. Anyway, the Lunts had heard so much about Zack and me that they wrote the Theater Guild and said, "There's a very talented young couple down here and they're coming to New York and we think you should see them and give them a chance." We were the only actors I knew who already had jobs when we got to New York. The Theater Guild was one of the big producers at that time, and they also ran the Westport Country Playhouse, which is one of the best of the country summer stock playhouses, and Zack and I decided that one of us should have a salaried job so that our families wouldn't have to support us. We discussed the matter, and I finally said, "Look, Zack, it doesn't mean that I think you are a better actor than I am, but I think that I'm more interested in production than you are, so I'll work twelve months of every year in production." That's where I got my training, and so I was one of the first—one of the very first—women stage managers on Broadway. They just didn't let women do that in those days. I had such good teachers there. My bosses taught me so well. The ones who are alive are still my great friends. Zack had sense enough to take bit parts—any parts. He worked himself up quickly and got sent to Hollywood. So it worked out beautifully for us.

DC: So you were living in Hollywood, then, in the late 1940s?
ES: After I'd been working on *Oklahoma!* for about a year and a half—it was an enormous smash, of course—Zack wanted to see me and Waverly, our daughter. I went out just to see if we could make a go and I stayed awhile. I met John there, as a matter of fact. Anyway, I loved my work in production. I was in casting, and I always had a

job. Theater was having a bad time then, but I did some interesting ones. I worked on the Paul Robeson *Othello* [1942-43] with Jose Ferrer as Iago and Uta Hagen as Desdemona. Robeson was a big star then on the concert stage. He's one of my most unforgettable characters. I didn't go on the American Tour with *Othello* because I was already doing *Oklahoma!* by then. I just went on the preliminary and part of the Broadway [run]. And this great star, Robeson—they had trouble getting him a hotel room. Can you believe it? No wonder he went to Russia. He was the most wonderful man in the world to work with. He spoke beautiful English. Once, though, he started a rehearsal of *Othello* and began calling Desdemona: [drawling] "Oh Desmonia!" and all that. I said, "What are you doing?" And he said, "I decided to rehearse today with a Texas accent just for you." He was playing *Othello* with a Texas accent! And I said, "Well, stop at once. We ain't getting nowhere!" Don't you love it! We did our first tryouts with it. The Harvard theater was in Brattle Hall, and this was in the summer because Paul had some concerts he had to do in the fall before we opened on Broadway. So we were traveling by train from the Brattle Hall Theater at Harvard to the McCarter Theatre at Princeton. We stopped for an hour in a station in New York before we moved, and Paul said as I started to get off the car, "Where are you going?" And I said, "I'm going down to check on the car to see if our costumes and scenery are o.k." And he said, "By yourself?" And I said, "Yes, by myself." And he said, "Will it be safe? I'll go with you." And I said, "Now look here, you are the star of this show and I, a woman, have tried very hard to get this job, and if you come I will kill you. I have to prove that I can do anything by myself." So he said, "O.k., all right, o.k. Damn you women!" He was a wonderful man.

DC: Didn't you come back to live here in New York right before you married Steinbeck?
ES: Yes. When John and I fell in love I said to him, "I've not moved here to California permanently. I'm going back to New York. That's

where my work and my life is—and my friends." And I wasn't trained to do anything in the movies, so I was bored the whole time I was there because I didn't have any work. John said, "Well, I'm going back to New York, too." So he came on here, and I then came with my maid, my daughter, and my dog! And we stayed at the Algonquin [Hotel] till I found an apartment. Since 1951 I have lived in this "village" right here [East Seventy-Second Street]. The house John and I lived in is right over there. I lived there for nearly fourteen years and here [in this apartment] for thirty, so I know all of these people who have shops around here. You know them in your "village."

DC: As you know, this interview will be published in a book of essays on Steinbeck's middle and later period—the works written after **The Grapes of Wrath.** *You were married to him, of course, during most of that time.*
ES: Yes, I lived the last twenty years of John's life with him. I met him early in 1949 and he died late in 1968. He was really very famous when I was married to him. I met him in Pacific Grove. People there more or less left him alone, so I don't think I realized how famous John was until I came to New York. And then when we started travelling, the press met every plane that John was on or every train.

DC: That bothered him, didn't it?
ES: He said until the day he died, "The best thing that Elaine ever did for me was not to be shy and to know how to handle this." Anybody who knows me knows that I'm not shy. I would talk to everybody and get everything warmed up. Then I could just disappear, go out and mind my own business, and he could take it up from there, whether we were standing in the open somewhere or in a hotel room. John could handle it here in New York, but when we were travelling, I always did the warm-up. He was very shy at the beginning.

DC: Let me ask you about one of the frequently voiced ideas of critics and scholars about John Steinbeck: that his writing changed fundamentally several years after **The Grapes of Wrath.** *Jackson Benson puts that change ten years or so after* **The Grapes of Wrath,** *about the time Steinbeck met you in California. Benson says the nature of the change, at least in the major works he would write during the remainder of his career, was from a focus on group behavior to a focus on the social and ethical problems of the individual. What are your views on the perceived change? Was the move from California to New York significant? Was he just wanting to get on with something new?*

ES: Oh, I have very definite views about that. When I met him in Pacific Grove, John said, "I can't live here. Why in the hell did I think I could come home? You can't go home again. I've lived in New York. I can't live here." And he said to me, "I'm here because I've got a job writing *Viva Zapata!* and I want to write it near the studio so I can help them put it into screen form." But he also said, "One reason I'm here now is that I'm going to write a book. I've been doing research for it a long time. I've been living under such unhappy circumstances in New York that I haven't been able to write." As Jay Parini [author of an upcoming biography on John Steinbeck] said the other day, "He didn't write well with Gwyn because they were so unhappy all the time, because they were fighting all the time." Anyway, John said, "I still have some research to do out here with the newspaper, in history, about when I was a little boy. I'm going to write a book and put everything in it that I know. I'm going to tell everything I know about my family." Well, I think when he had done that [finished his work on *Zapata!* and the research for his book], even if he hadn't met me . . . I don't think John moved back to New York because of me. I think he may have moved *when* he moved because of me, but he had already said he wasn't going to stay, that he couldn't stay anymore [even though] he was delighted with his house in Pacific Grove on Eleventh Street. Once while he was living there he told me, "I felt so good this morning. That old man next door looked across and saw me in the garden, and he said, 'You Ernst Steinbeck's son?' 'Yes sir, I am.' 'Been away?'" He just loved it. That old man only knew him as Ernst Steinbeck's son. Anyway, I know that he was going to move back here [to New York]. How long can you stay and write about Cannery Row? I don't see why anyone is startled that he moved around. One of the first things I asked John when I first met him was, "When Fitzgerald and Hemingway were abroad, why didn't you go?" And he said, "I didn't have the price of a ticket." And he said, "I'm very glad now that I didn't because I stayed at home and wrote about my own people."

DC: Would you agree with those scholars who say that Steinbeck always insisted on doing what he wanted to do, that he maintained his individualism and didn't look at the critics?

ES: Yes, he did not do what the critics wanted, ever. He never wrote to anybody's formula. Critics faulted him, but he never paid attention to them. He wrote whatever he wanted to write. And I would like to say that I know that's why John did not do more on the Arthurian legend—it's all right to say it now because the people involved are dead. In the first place, John had no idea he was going to die so young. He wouldn't have had a spinal operation the year before if he had known he was going to die. That's one of the hardest things anyone could have gone through, learning to walk again and all that. He had no idea his heart system was going to go out and his heart was going to fail. He certainly meant to finish the Arthurian cycle. His agent, Elizabeth Otis, whom he adored, had never interfered in his writing and neither had his editor, Pascal Covici. The man Elizabeth Otis loved and lived with for many years, Chase Horton, owned the bookstore that supplied John with all of those books, so many books, that he used for Middle English. And suddenly John said to me once when we came back from the year in Somerset, "Elizabeth and Chase have gotten so involved in this. How did I let this happen? I can't work like this. I'm going to stop for awhile." I think he stopped and wrote *The Winter of Our Discontent*. John always meant to go back and finish the Arthurian book. I studied Middle English with him just for fun, and he loved the fact that I did. When we would go to London and visit the British Museum, while he was doing research I'd be reading letters in the display case. And he would pass by me getting a book and he would say, "Having fun?" and I'd say, "I'm reading Queen Elizabeth writing to Queen Mary of Scotland; of course I'm having fun." Anyway, what John had meant to do was this: he had meant to translate the Malory straight as Malory wrote it and then to go back and to fictionalize it, write the Steinbeck version of it. But he simply didn't get around to it. He died; that's the only reason. But he just said, "The people who work with me are getting too involved and they are driving me crazy and I will stop for awhile and write something else and then I'll go back to it quietly and not tell anybody I've gone back to it." That's the truth. These are the things that nobody knows but me, because I lived with him. Then about two years after John died, Elizabeth Otis said, "Let's publish it." She said, "I'd like to publish it and publish his letters to Chase there in the back of the book." I wasn't too with it at the time. I had had a terrible time adjusting to John's death.

DC: So, you're not sure you would make that same decision again?

ES: I'm not sorry; every once in a while somebody loves the book, and it gets better as it goes. Towards the last third of the book John is beginning to have fun and to embroider a little. We had gone down to the coast . . . Southampton . . . no, I can't remember where now, and he begins to write about that because he and I had walked there. And he begins to put his characters into that landscape, and, I think, to have fun. It would have been wonderful.

DC: *He certainly has fun with those private jokes he puts in the book—the one, for instance, about Toby Street [Steinbeck's long-time friend], who appears as Sir Tobinus Streat de Montroy.*

ES: Oh yes, he was happiest . . . if John had finished that book, nobody could have said that he had gone downhill. Because that's what he wanted to do and that's what I regret more than anything for his sake—that he never got that done. Remember the story I told you about when he was dying?

DC: *About the time you spent in Somerset?*

ES: He was in bed and I was sitting beside him. I was reading to him—he had the oxygen tubes in his nostrils—and he suddenly said, "What was the best time we had in our twenty years together?" I started to answer, but then I said, "You tell me first." And he said, "No, I'm dying and you'll agree with me." And I kind of laughed and he laughed. I said, "I'll write it on a piece of paper and put it in your hand." And I did. Then I asked him, "What's the best time we've had?" And he said, "The year we spent in Somerset." And I said, "Open your hand." And I had written "Somerset." It's an incredible story for me to remember during the last hours with John. I also remember one day when we were alone in the cottage [in Somerset] and he said, "Elaine, can you hear me?" I said, "Yes, I'm on the stairway." He said, "Can you look out the window toward the garden?" And I said, "I'll go quietly and look out." He said, "I'm writing about Morgan le Fay and I want you to see what's in the garden." There was a raven sitting in the garden and he said, "Maybe that raven knows what I'm writing about. That raven is looking for Morgan le Fay." She always rode with a raven on her wrist, you know. The Arthurian legend was all magic to him. Camelot was just a few miles from us; that's why we were there. Once John took Adlai Stevenson up there around midnight and they thought they heard King Arthur's horses riding by. The best two Americans to be out at Camelot to hear King Arthur's horses riding by are John Steinbeck and Adlai Stevenson. Don't you love it!

DC: [Indicating on a desk a small sword stuck in a glass replica of a stone] Where did that come from?

ES: That's the last present I gave John. Tiffany had it—no, Baccarat. It's "The Sword in the Stone." I got it not long before John died and I said, "Here, this is for your desk." Isn't it beautiful? It's a paper opener. And they only made a few of them. It's very heavy crystal.

DC: It looked like something you might have given him when he was working on The Acts of King Arthur.

ES: Well, he was always writing it in his head. But yes, that's why I gave it to him, of course. Out hanging on the wall at Sag Harbor is a sword he always had with which he made his sister Mary "Sir Mary." That's in *Life in Letters*, incidentally. Sometimes I wonder how he anointed her, because he and Mary played all these games. He had two sisters much older than he, and the sister Mary who died a few years before him.

DC: Didn't another sister die just recently?

ES: Beth died just the other day at ninety-eight. She died in October while I was in London.

DC: I remember she was still living when we were out in Salinas [for the Steinbeck Festival] last August.

ES: Beth and John were not much alike [but] they were very much family people. Oh my God, everybody is so surprised I'm very caught up in the Steinbecks. When they marry I go there; when they die, I go. The reason I didn't go to Beth's funeral was that I was in London because of *Kiss of the Spider Woman*. But I had said to John's niece, "If she dies while I'm away, here's the hotel number and phone me." John's sister, Mary, was four years younger than John. Her husband was an officer in the American Air Force, and he had been killed as [the Allies] came up the Italian peninsula taking it back. He was killed by friendly fire. By the time I met John, Mary was a widow and she travelled. She and I were very close. She was nearer my age. You see, John was about thirteen and a half years older than I. And Mary was nearer me in age. We were very compatible. And if we were going abroad, she would meet us somewhere and be with us part of the time and then go on her way. I adored her. She died in the year Churchill died, 1965. We happened to be in Paris then. John was very close to her. They always read the Arthurian legends together and acted them out. John, of course, always thought he was Lancelot. When he built me a little swimming pool in Sag Harbor—he never could keep a secret—and before Christmas and my birthday, by the time it got there, I always knew what he was giving me. One day he said to me, I guess it was in July, "Elaine, for your birthday—" And I said, "I'm not listening. I don't care." And he said, "I have to tell you something about your birthday." And I said, "I'm not going to listen. I'm going to run; I'm going to stop my ears up." He said, "Elaine, there's a bulldozer coming up the street, damn it! Up the road to make you a pool!" So anyway, while they were pouring the cement for the pool, he said, "Pour a little cement right over here on the ground." They did, and he wrote in it, following Lancelot, "Ladye, I take reccorde of God, in thee I have myn erthly joye." And so I looked up and said, "I'd rather have that than the pool."

DC: *What problems do you have as both literary executor and the widow of a literary institution?*
ES: Oh, I say all the time, "Gosh, wasn't he smart to leave the copyrights to me?" Because I work at it all the time. I literally have had four chances to remarry, three near his death, one about two or three years ago. Once I thought about it for awhile. But in the first place, I guess I'm still in love with John. And then I've learned to live alone and like it, and I'm just too busy with Steinbeck. I'm just so lucky. I can talk about him. I can't write. It makes me angry that people ask me to write things. Just because I lived with a writer doesn't mean I can write. Sometimes someone will say, "Pretend it's a letter." Well,

you can't do that. The point is, I can talk about him endlessly as you know, and I can go on the air and do those morning shows, T.V. shows, that I did. When *The Grapes of Wrath* [the 1990 dramatic production at the Cort Theater] was opening here, they had no stars, so they had to use anyone they could get to talk and go on the air, and they had me. I can always talk about him in any vein anybody wants. I want to be perfectly frank with you. I'm having a great deal of fun, but I can't do it too often because I don't want to live in the past that much. I live for John and I live for continuation in my life. I'm so happy I didn't have to move to new surroundings that had no relationship with John. And yet, I would no more talk all day long about John or read all day long about John . . . I couldn't live in the past. That's not normal. So I try to balance it. I go to the theater all the time and I read lots of modern fiction.

DC: Who do you like particularly in modern fiction?
ES: I like [Gabriel] García Márquez very much. I also like Toni Morrison, David McCullough, Anne Tyler, Muriel Spark, and Julian Barnes. But let me finish this: I live a life of a modern woman of my age. I travel a lot. I have a lot of friends, but I'm always available for my job as John's widow. I'd never lived alone before in my life, ever. When I went away to college I lived in a sorority house. I'd never lived alone and at first it was horrible, but I've gotten used to it now. John will always be with me in a certain way, but not in the spooky, ridiculous way. I have one thing that bugs me the most. No matter where I am in this city, when it's around six o'clock I think I ought to rush and get home. I have to remind myself that John's not here waiting for me, which is very strange isn't it? I still say, "Oh, it's six o'clock. He's surely finished his work and he wants a drink and he wants some conversation, and I want it, too." But when people think they can't criticize John and his work, I think that's ridiculous. Of course, some of it isn't as good as it ought to be. When the *New York Times* said that John shouldn't have won the Nobel Prize, I

still think that's absolutely the most miserable thing I've ever heard. And by God, it's one of the reasons I'm so glad he's proving them— they said, "Oh, he's just a regional writer." We were in Sag Harbor when that article came out, and I felt so bad. It was pouring rain and I went out and worked in the garden, and John would stand at the door and say, "Elaine, please come in. It's all right. We'll live through it." He had found it and read it. He said, "You can't treat me like a child. I've had criticism before." So now I always answer back, and I always say, "Yes, I'm sure you're right; some of the works are not good." But guess who's reading *The Grapes of Wrath*? People in forty languages.

DC: Those critics who lashed out in 1942 at **The Moon Is Down,** *claiming that it was counterproductive propaganda, that it would hurt the Allied war effort . . . I'm talking mainly about Clifton Fadiman and James Thurber and Stanley Edgar Hyman—*
ES: Oh boy! John said bad things about *them.*

DC: Did he ever have any kind of contact at all with any of them after their attacks?
ES: I don't think so.

DC: I was just curious whether Steinbeck ever discussed the contro-versy with any of them later, because they never retracted anything.
ES: Oh, no. They never retracted anything even after the war when there were many indications that they had been wrong. All of that was stupid. They called him a traitor. John never had a kind word to say for them. I always loved Thurber's writing. But I've never said a good thing about Thurber since I found out about his attack on John. I think it [the attack] was the stupidest thing in the world. Even when they found out how important the book was, how valuable it was to the underground [in Nazi-occupied Europe during World War II], they never retracted a thing, no, not at all.

DC: The odd thing about the attacks was that they were so mean-spirited.

ES: There are a lot of people who didn't like John. I first thought in the back of my head that John must be paranoid when he began to tell me why he went to the war as a correspondent instead of in the service. He started telling me how he kept trying to get in the service. J. Edgar Hoover was behind all this. When the Freedom of Information Act was passed, I immediately sent away for all the papers on John. Everything John suspected was exactly true. J. Edgar Hoover kept saying, "You cannot let him go in any service. He's a communist. He wrote *The Grapes of Wrath*." And everything John tried Hoover stopped him. I wish to God I could tell John that Hoover also wore a black taffeta dress! Nobody would have had more fun with that! The stories about Roy Cohn [legal counsel to Senator Joseph McCarthy]—and John had many gay friends; that wouldn't have been a problem—but J. Edgar Hoover and Roy Cohn . . . he would have just loved to know that Hoover wore that dress. Anyway, John was telling the absolute truth about why he couldn't get in the service. They wouldn't let him in. So he had to go as a war correspondent to get abroad. He went to all the dangerous spots; he didn't try to protect himself at all.

DC: Something I've been wanting to ask you about is a comment Bo Beskow [Steinbeck's friend, the Swedish artist] made to me in an interview I did with him in 1981. Bo said that he always had the impression you discouraged Steinbeck's lighthearted pieces because you wanted him to write serious novels.

ES: That is absolutely untrue. I never wanted John to write anything like that. That is the most ridiculous thing I have ever heard. Bo and John stayed the greatest friends until the Nobel Prize. Bo tried to take over everything when we got to Sweden, and they had a falling out.

DC: Didn't Bo sort of take the two of you in hand when you arrived at the airport in Stockholm?

ES: Guess who was the elbow to everybody and all the [Nobel] committee and everyone around to meet John at the plane, and who elbowed me out of the pictures? They all showed John arriving in Stockholm and with Bo Beskow instead of me. Except for one picture.

DC: He met you at the plane then?

ES: I'll say he did. When you are a laureate in chemistry, physics or literature, you are assigned an aide [upon arrival in Sweden], and John and I had the nicest aide. He eventually became the President of the Nobel Committee. Every day before you go out he tells you where you're going, what the protocol is, exactly what to do, whom you will meet, how to address certain members of the royal family and members of the committee. He's *your* aide. And this young man—we couldn't have lived without him; we just adored him. About the third day, John's aide said to John, "I'm going to have to tell you I'm having a dreadful time. I'm having to fight off Bo Beskow because he wants to take charge of everything." Bo didn't have to do that. John and he were friends. But in every photograph with the king and the queen, you know, you had Bo right there with his arm around John. Have you ever heard the charming story about the last evening of the Nobel Prize festivities? The aide said to John and me, "Tonight you'll be going to the Royal Ball. I've watched you, and you know how to handle yourselves with anybody." One night at one banquet I had been with the prime minister and John had been with one of the princesses. Another time I was with Bertil, one of the princes, and James Watson, who was getting the award for discovering DNA, he and Crick. Anyway, the aide said to John and me, "Now, in Sweden it's not the way it is at the White House where the guests walk around and the hosts, the president and his wife, stay still. Here, the guests form a semicircle and the royal family go by and then they go stand in the middle of the floor and someone is chosen to accompany them in to dinner. But no literature laureate has ever been chosen for that, so you're all right. You'll probably get someone else in the royal family." We said, "Fine." Well, we were standing in a line, everybody's dressed in gown and white tie and so forth, when a man in a wig carrying a long staff and dressed in medieval clothes came and stood in front of John and me and he stamped the floor with his staff and he said, "Madam, would you advance to the middle of the floor and take the arm of the king and lead the dinner party in? Sir, would you please take the arm of the queen and lead in?" That was the first time a literature laureate had ever been chosen. Our aide was standing over there dying. John says that I said, "I sure will, Honey," but I didn't.

DC: *What did you say?*

ES: I said, "Thank you, yes." Then I looked at John and he was bursting with pleasure, and pride. John was selected for that because he was such a popular choice [for the Nobel Prize]. So I advanced and took the king's arm and John advanced and took the queen's arm and we led everyone. Here were all these *famous* laureates, and Steinbeck was leading them. I had never had more fun than with the king. John had never had more fun than with the queen. She was Louie Mountbatten's sister, Queen Louise. They had a marvelous time; I had a marvelous time. During the dinner the king said to me, "Look around the table. Anywhere you see this placemat is a member of the royal family." And I said, "Yes, sir, I noticed it." He said, "One of our forefathers was a messy eater. Now it means we're royalty." Then he said, "Where do you live?" And I said, "In the summer, in Sag Harbor." And he said, "You know I was crown prince for so long that I travelled around the world. I've even been out and seen the Hamptons." I said, "Sir, I know all these flowers are grown in your gardens, and I know you're a great gardener." And he said, "Let me think about the climate in Sag Harbor. I'll write you down some things that will grow well there." We had the time of our lives. Bertil, the prince, was sitting on one side of me; I was sitting with the king on the other. I turned to talk to Bertil a minute, and he said, "I've been watching you have a good time for five days, and I've never known anybody to talk so much." We became close friends.

DC: Bertil is the present King's brother?

ES: Bertil was the son of the king [at that time, Gustaf VI Adolf]. He did not inherit the throne. The grandson did [Bertil's nephew, Carl XVI Gustaf]. Bertil said to me that night, "What plane are you going to use? Aren't you going to London?" And I said, "Yes." Alice Guinzburg was with John and me. Her husband, who had been John's publisher, had died just a few months before, and Alice was about to die because her husband had died—they'd been married for fifty years. John had phoned her when he won the Nobel Prize and said, "You're going to Stockholm." And Alice said, "I'll never travel again with Harold dead." And John said, "You're going to represent him, Alice. You have to come." And she went and it was wonderful. She knew so many people all over the world. She and her husband were very cosmopolitan. Anyway, Prince Bertil said to me, "Aren't you and Mrs. Guinzburg and your husband going to London?" And I said, "Yes, we're going to go there and have some parties before we go home for Christmas." He said, "You've met the woman I'm going to eventually marry." She was a commoner. "She's going to London and she's riding in steerage. Are you riding first class?" I said, "Yes, we are." And he said, "Will you invite her up for a drink?" I said, "We'd love to." So later I said to the stewardess, "Tell Mrs.—I've forgotten her name now, but they all knew who she was—I want to see her up in first class." And she came and sat in first class with us and had a ball. She said, "I've never had so much fun! Bertil and I just don't have the money to afford for me to go first-class." Now, one thing I want to say here: Whenever John is called a drunk, or an alcoholic, nothing makes me any madder. We did grow up in a time of hard drinking. We all did. I did at Texas, at the University. Zack and I did. John and I drank a lot here. I think John drank an extra lot with Gwyn because of the kind of society they lived in. But John could go anytime he wanted without a drink. And what he said to me, oh, weeks before we went to Stockholm, was, "When we go to Stockholm, will you do something with me?" And I said, "Sure, what?" He said, "Will you go there and party those five days without taking a drop of booze?" And I said, "Why, certainly." And he said (and I love the wording), "With the possible exception of Pearl Buck, every American literature laureate who went to Stockholm has been drunk those five days." Sinclair Lewis said he was; Faulkner told in my presence that he was, and Eugene O'Neill. John said, "I'm going to represent myself, my profession, my country, and I'm not going to do it drunk." And we had not one drop. When we went to a public place I would find a waiter and say, "See that man out there? Tell the waiters to pour him nothing but water."

DC: Water looks just like aquavit anyway.
ES: Well, nobody even noticed it. The point about John is, the Austin paper had one of those gossip columns several years ago. Fran, my sister, sent one to me that said something about John's drinking, so I just sat down and wrote this story to [the columnist] and he published it. I don't think he published the letter; he just said that Elaine Steinbeck says that her husband spent five days in Stockholm going to five parties a day and never had a drop of liquor.

DC: Speaking of other American Nobel literature laureates and their wives, did you know any of them well?
ES: I got to know Mary Hemingway. We were at a big birthday party for Carl Sandburg here in New York right after Hemingway's death, and somebody at the party said to John, "Mary Hemingway is here and she's having such a hard time. Do you know her?" And

John said, "I've never met her, but I would like to meet her." So John sent a note over to her table saying, "My wife and I are here. Would you care to join us for a nightcap downstairs?" We were at the Waldorf. And she did, and John was so wonderful with her. We saw her often after that. We would have a party, and if we had anybody interesting from England, or had Adlai [Stevenson], or had various people, we would always include Mary. We had a wonderful time with her.

DC: So you got to know her well?
ES: Oh, after John died, she was wonderful to me, and she and I got to be good friends. It was so funny . . . when *Steinbeck: A Life in Letters* was published [in 1975], Mary had her own book coming out. She was really not very good with an audience and got shy, I understand. Her agent called me one day and said, "I've been talking to John Steinbeck's agent, I know you're going to do a program in Connecticut that's going to be televised." I said, "Yes, I am." He said, "Would you object at all if Mary touted her book while you're touting yours?" Of course, I didn't write mine; I just edited mine. And I said, "I think it will be the greatest fun in the world." Well, we went out and Mary was scared to death. And when we got in front of the audience, I said, "Mary, tell about such and such." She started to talk. I found that during the entire show I never got to say anything about Steinbeck or my book. I was just interviewing Mary, and she was having a ball. The ladies in the audience were laughing. It was so marvelous! When it was over, Mary said, "That was fun, wasn't it?" and left. I went on to lunch with all the ladies. Mary couldn't go. And then the agent phoned the next day and said, "Mary wants to know if you'd like to do that all over the country." And I said, "Oh, Honey, I'm so sorry; I can't do that." I was so busy interviewing her and feeding her cues that I wasn't saying anything about my own book. But I would go and have dinner with her alone and would walk to her apartment, you know, filled with animal heads and all that, and the doorman would say through the button, "Mrs. Stein-

beck to see Mrs. Hemingway." Once I whispered and said, "The only person who's missing is Mrs. Faulkner." And Mary said, "We don't want her. She's a party pooper."

DC: *Did you ever meet Mrs. Faulkner?*
ES: No. But I loved Mary. She lived over here on Sixty-Fourth Street, I think, not very far from me. She moved home when she got very sick. Anyway, she and I got along just marvelously. She did the cleverest thing, this woman, when Castro took over in Cuba. She told me this herself. She heard that Castro's government was going to take over their property. What did they call that place?

DC: *The Finca?*
ES: The Finca. She realized that their things left in it were everything she and Ernest valued, and so she did the following thing—Ernest was dead by then. She invited Castro to tea. She said it could be tea or coffee or whatever he chose. She said to him, "I want to present the Finca to you. I know you will give me plenty of time to get all of my possessions and all of my husband's possessions out. Don't rush me. I know you will let me do it; just give me time." What could he say? And she got all those personal things she wanted.

DC: *She went back to visit the Finca right before she died, didn't she?*
ES: Yes, she did.

DC: *And said Castro's government had left everything exactly the way it was, right down to Hemingway's cigar butts in the ashtray.*
ES: Sure they did. It was a tourist attraction. I'm sorry I never met Hemingway. John knew him when he and Gwyn were living in New York, I believe, but he never knew him well. John mourned him when he died; John really mourned him. John said, "This is the most imitated American writer of the century. All young writers want to

be like him." I don't know whether John and he would have been very close friends or anything like that, but I know John loved his work. You know the first time we met Faulkner?

DC: Tell me.
ES: Jean Stein, who was Faulkner's friend in New York, phoned me and said, "Bill's coming into town and wants to meet John." And I said, "Let me talk to John." And John said, "Oh, wouldn't that be marvelous? Go on and arrange it." Jean said, "We'll come over to your house for drinks, and then we'll go out to a little bistro or somewhere." I never saw John so pleased, because he was crazy about Faulkner. Anyway, we had a library over there [house on East Seventy-Second Street] which was very informal, with a fireplace and two easy chairs on each side of it, just a very comfortable room. We were dressed very informally and so forth, and John was all excited. They came in, Jean Stein, Faulkner, and his editor, Saxe Commins, and Faulkner was blind drunk, a walking zombie. The first thing John said was, "I rarely ever give up my chair to anybody, but it would be my honor if you would sit in my chair." And Faulkner walked straight across to the other chair. Now they had asked to come, mind you, and I have never in my life seen anyone as astonished as Jean and the editor. We had the most miserable time. John never lost his composure because he knew Faulkner was drunk, and he said, "What can I make you to drink?" Faulkner said, "Whiskey and branch water." John said, "I've heard that a lot in Texas. My wife's from Texas, so I've heard that." Everybody would try to talk, and he would either not answer or would answer rudely. Somebody said, "Where should we go for dinner tonight?" And I said, "Mr. Faulkner, I've understood from Tennessee Williams and the [Elia] Kazans that they love to go to your house because you have the old Southern food." And he said, "Don't know what they ate. I eat what's put before me." And I wanted to say, "Well, why the hell don't you . . ." It was absolutely awful. We went to a little pub over

here where we've gone a million times, and instead of ordering in English—all the waiters spoke English—Faulkner decided to order in French, in that Southern French. It was an evening . . .

DC: **Southern *French?***
ES: Yes, Oxford, Mississippi, French! By the time we got home, John and I were so exhausted we were just wrecks. Trying to be civil, and, why, we were sick at our stomachs. The next morning Jean phoned me and said, "Elaine, he was so nervous about meeting John that he got drunk." About a week later John got a letter from Faulkner saying he was so sorry and asking John's forgiveness, and they became good friends. But oh, what an experience.

DC: What year was that Faulkner visit?
ES: Let's see, [it was before] we moved into this apartment in '63. I couldn't find those letters [the ones from Faulkner].

DC: So when you came back home from Stockholm, you came back to this apartment?
ES: No, when John and I heard that he had won the Nobel Prize we were in Sag Harbor and the announcement from the committee that he had won was sent to the house [on East Seventy-Second Street]. He won in the autumn of '62 and we moved here in March of '63 right after we returned from Stockholm. The prize was announced the day after we were almost blown up by the Russians—the Cuban Missile Crisis. John and I never listened to daytime television, certainly not at Sag Harbor. And neither did John have breakfast with me, ever, because he would go down to the village. But that morning—we had stayed up so late listening to the television because we felt that things were so bad—I was cooking bacon and eggs in the kitchen, and I said, "John, I think we ought to turn on the television to see if the world is still turning."

And he turned, click, and it said, "This morning John Steinbeck won the Nobel Prize for Literature." Those were the words we heard. Our kitchen and sitting room open together, and I turned around from cooking bacon and looked at John and we just started screaming. You see, the announcement, a telegram that had been sent to him, was in the mailbox at the house back here in the city. And there was nobody at the house. I put the pan with the bacon in it in the refrigerator. Three days later we came back and it was sitting there. Anyway, I said, "What do we do? What shall I do?" And he said, "First of all, I'm going to tell the boys" [Steinbeck's two sons who were away at boarding school]. So I called each school and I had such fun. I got through first to Thom's school, and I said, "Can I speak with my son, Thom?" And she said, "Now, Mrs. Steinbeck, you know he's in his first class." And I said, "Oh, never mind. Just send someone when you get a chance to tell him his father just won the Nobel Prize." And then I called Johnny's school and did the same thing. Then our phone started ringing and it rang off the wall. Viking [Press] got on the line and said, "Elaine, get him into town some way, because in spite of the Cuban Missile Crisis we'll have to have a press conference this afternoon. We've already been flooded with calls." I said to John, "Shall we fly in?" Every once in a while we fly these little planes in from Long Island because it's about 100 miles. And John said, "No, let's just drive in the car because we can talk about it and have fun and turn on the radio and listen to it being announced over the radio." He would have never said that to anybody but me, but he did say it. And it was such fun. I have wonderful pictures of us at Viking when they had the press conference—Elizabeth [Otis, Steinbeck's literary agent], and John and me. You've seen them. So that was a big thrill. But then the mail was so overwhelming from all over the world. I said to John, "We can't handle this." And he said, "Yes, let's get secretaries, but out here." So we got secretaries for Sag Harbor. All the really personal letters John would answer himself at his little house. And I just turned the big room at the house into an office and got secretaries to help. We had known

Princess Grace through Tom Guinzburg [son of Steinbeck's publisher] before she became princess. John got an early telegram from her saying, "I'm so proud to be an American today." And he wrote her a letter. Then he came to me and said, "Elaine, do you know Princess Grace's address?" And I said, "Oh, I can find out." He had written, "Dear Princess Grace, Honey . . ." Later on when I saw her she said, "That's the best letter I ever got being a princess."

[Earlier that year], we were in Athens with Terrence [McNally] and the boys when Crown Prince Juan Carlos, who is now the King of Spain, married the Greek princess. And we made sure our hotel room had a balcony because we knew that during the week they were going in a procession from one church to another and we wanted to sit out there and have our breakfast and watch. And we did and it was such fun because right behind [the bride and groom] were a lot of other royalty, some of whom we knew, including Princess Grace, Honey. I leaned out and said, "Princess Grace, Honey!" And she looked up and said, "Who in the world would call me Princess Grace, Honey, from a balcony except Steinbeck?"

DC: You were talking to me yesterday about the role that you had in the dramatic productions of two of Steinbeck's plays, Burning Bright *and* Pipe Dream.
ES: Yes, I thought a lot about all of this during the night. I do not believe for one minute that anybody told John what to write, ever. I think the biggest influence of anybody would have been Ed Ricketts, definitely. John always said his other passion was marine biology. Every year we went to the Caribbean John always went over to the marine station and went out with the guys and talked about what was under the water. He did that any place we went in the Caribbean and he did it at Nantucket. Ed Ricketts influenced him in many ways and I think that influence lasted all of John's life, not only while he was writing about Cannery Row. I never knew what he was going to write until he told me. I never influenced what he wrote.

DC: What about the plays he wrote after you were married? With your theatrical background, did you ever act as liaison between him and those responsible for the performances?

ES: Oh, I was always a liaison, but I didn't tell him what to write. I remember—it was very interesting—the year before we married we took a trip to Mexico. He had written *Burning Bright* and had dedicated it to me and he was turning it into a play. He would read aloud to me because he was making dialogue. And the only time that he ever accepted influence from me I would say, "Wait a minute; your scene has just ended," because, you know, a scene or an act has to end on a certain beat. Something is said and that's the curtain or the blackout. And John, as a novelist, would sometimes add two or three more lines. John's preparation for writing was thinking. That's why he rewrote so seldom. Believe me, I would know when he was beginning to think about something he was going to write because he would become very distant. And I would say, "Do you have something in mind?" And he would say, "I really do." Just before he sat down to write, nothing got through to him, nothing anybody said got through to him. He was very kind and polite, but he was just thinking what he was going to do when he sat down to write. But at that point, I never knew what he was going to write. He might say to Gadg [Elia] Kazan or Frank Loesser or some of his friends, "I think I'll write a play about such and such." But he never discussed it with me as some writers do with their wives—or their husbands. And I'm pretty sure he didn't with Gwyn. How much Carol did, I don't know. Susan Shillinglaw [editor of the *Steinbeck Newsletter*] would be able to tell you more about that. [Jackson] Benson says how helpful Carol was. She did all the typing. She worked like a *fiend*. Now whether Carol said anything to John about writing, I have no way of knowing. John never told me.

DC: But in the case of the play version of **Burning Bright**...

ES: When the producers would say, "Elaine, what do you think about so and so playing that part?" and when John would say, "Elaine what do you think?" I would tell them because it would have been somebody I worked with or that I had seen act a lot. I think one of the reasons John wrote *Burning Bright* was that we were coming to New York together. Remember, he had come here earlier [in 1937] with George Kaufmann and had turned *Of Mice and Men* into a play, and he had worked on various movie scripts. But the only one that I had any suggestions about was for *Burning Bright*.

DC: What about after rehearsals started? Did you have any suggestions then?

ES: Oh sure; of course, but they always had their own stage manager. I did not go on a salary and work on the play. But John would say, "How do you think such and such a scene is playing now?" And I would answer. John and I stayed together constantly, at every rehearsal and everything.

DC: What was your professional sense as a theater person of what Rodgers and Hammerstein did with **Sweet Thursday** *in* **Pipe Dream***?*

ES: We all realized later they were the wrong ones to choose. Anybody in the world would have given a million dollars to have them, but as Billy Hammerstein said, neither one of them had ever been to a whorehouse! And then Helen Traubel had left the Metropolitan Opera and nobody had told us that she didn't have a voice any more. They never asked her to sing out in rehearsal. She was a great, great opera singer, but Rudolph Bing [then General Director of the Metropolitan Opera] had fired her and he was too much of a gentleman to say he had fired her because she had lost her voice. We got to New Haven to rehearse with the full orchestra and you couldn't hear her on the first row. And she had a run of the play contract. They should have bought her off. Everything went wrong. The second day of rehearsal, Richard Rodgers had half of his face cut away because of cancer. We knew the play was going wrong. But we kept hoping—you know when you get in those situations you keep hoping something can pull it out of the fire. But nothing ever did. It got bad reviews in Boston. But [even today] people still want to do it. Every once in a while it's done somewhere just because it's Rodgers and Hammerstein and Steinbeck. But the force of John's wonderful story, the intellectual falling in love with a whore, was lost. When it was being performed in Boston, we were all living at the Ritz, and every night after every performance, Dick and Oscar would write John notes and John would write them notes. Oscar would say, "Would you add a couple of lines in such and such a scene?" That's the way you work. Then one day, John just said to me, "I'll have to tell you what I've written Oscar: 'You've turned my whore into a visiting nurse!'" So *Pipe Dream* was Rodgers and Hammerstein's only real flop. When we were celebrating the fiftieth anniversary of *Oklahoma!* and the fiftieth anniversary of the beginning of the collaboration of Rodgers and Hammerstein, we all said, "Well, it was the only one that flopped." Linda Rodgers Emory, Dick's daughter, said to me, "Elaine, I put money myself into *Pipe Dream*. Wouldn't you know the only one you and I invested in would flop?"

DC: We were talking yesterday about a part of Steinbeck that general readers and even scholars sometimes miss, his humor.
ES: People who knew him knew his humor. And people in California knew his humor and everybody around here knew it. It's just some of the scholars now. They think he's the Great Steinbeck and that everything he wrote has to be taken seriously. I find that a lot of young people or very pompous people or people who are teaching will pick up something that John meant to be ridiculous and think that he was being profound.

DC: Let me ask you about John Steinbeck the man as opposed to Steinbeck the writer. One of my memorable experiences while I was doing research in Europe in 1981 for my book on **The Moon Is Down** *was an interview in Copenhagen with Otto Lindhardt, who of course you know had been Steinbeck's Danish publisher. It was late in the afternoon, and I had been throwing questions at him for two and a half hours. He was surely weary of me, but he had remained kind and patient and responsive, if a little formal. At the end of the interview when I turned off my tape recorder and put down my pen, he asked how my research had been going, and I told him how helpful and sympathetic the Europeans I had already interviewed had been, and I said something like, "You know, the most remarkable thing I've picked up from Steinbeck's European readers whom I've interviewed so far is how profoundly John Steinbeck really touched people—all kinds of people. They speak of him almost as if they knew him personally." Then I said to Mr. Lindhardt, "You did know him personally. You had a long-standing professional relationship with him, and you were also a friend. What was he like?" I still remember his response. His face relaxed, and he told me that Steinbeck was different from most geniuses because he was so interested in other people, and so thoughtful and personal in his dealings with them, and he finished by saying, "I never met anyone like him." That last comment particularly struck me because Otto Lindhardt had had dealings over the years with many well-known authors. Obviously Steinbeck had a common touch for those who knew him personally as well as for his readers . . .*

ES: But you see John was not always able to do that in person. He was only able to do that . . . that's why he liked to write. When we first started seeing each other—I didn't know it at the time but we were falling in love—he took me over to show me his house, and he said, "I started to write in that room." I said, "When was that?" And he said, "I don't remember a time I didn't write." You see, he just did not remember a time that he didn't put words on paper. His common touch came from that. I can't tell you how shy John was. Sumner Locke-Elliott, the Australian writer whom I love, once said to me, "Elaine, I had one opportunity to meet John, and he talked solemnly and I understood about every tenth word. I was too shy to say, 'I can't understand you.'" John *really* mumbled. I would say to him, "Honey, please speak up." And all of his friends would say, "Stop mumbling!" He was *genuinely* shy with new people, but not with his old friends like Otto. But his common touch was in his writing. John expressed himself well in words [when he talked]; I'm not saying that he did not. He expressed himself in the most interesting way. He was very witty and very funny. I'm a big crossword puzzler, and I used to ask him for a synonym but I would have to say, "I don't want the history of the word, John; I want the synonym." He loved words and I learned to love words from him. John was the most fun to travel with of anyone I've ever known. Somebody said to me the other day, "We're going to be in Rome a short time. Should we go out to Hadrian's Villa?" I said, "Oh my God, that is the most important and most interesting—" But then I said, "I don't know whether you should go or not. You won't be with John." When I was there with John we took a bottle of wine and some cheese and some ham and bread and went out and spent the day. The ruins are very sparse and low, and John just filled in the whole scene, right in front of my eyes. And we spent the day there, and I was *in* Hadrian's Villa. And although there was just a little of it standing, we would sit and walk in the garden and then sit and drink our wine and have a picnic. Travelling with him was simply wonderful. He always knew what to tell me to read. I always read about what I'm going to see and read about it while I'm there and then read about it more when I leave. He was a marvelous man to travel with. But—and now I'm trying to think of things about him—he was a man who wanted privacy. He didn't want to go out as much as I did. Once when we were getting ready to go abroad for several months and we were living here, he said, "Why are we going out so much?" Then he said, "We're saying good-bye to people I scarcely ever say hello to." He was very funny—and fun to live with—but also very moody. At first when he went through those terrible black moods when he was writing—I found out those were writer's block—I would think, What have I done, what have I done? He was very hard to live with in many ways. But I think most writers probably would be.

DC: You said something yesterday about his being the most complicated person you ever knew.
ES: Oh, his mind went in so many directions. He was very political. He knew world history very well indeed. He was very opinionated, which I liked, and he was very liberal.

DC: When you read the comments he made in the 1950s about how the Soviet empire would collapse . . . he also had amazing foresight.
ES: Where did you read that? Because he said to me, "Elaine, you have been with me this last trip"—this was just before he died—and he said, "You will live to see the downfall." And I said, "That is the most ridiculous thing I ever heard, John, that the wall in Berlin with everything I've seen—nobody is going to see it fall." And he said, "People will not stay cooped up and cut off from the rest of the world. I predict that you will see it in your lifetime." When the wall started to crumble and fall, I said to [my sister] Jean, "You remember he told us."

DC: That prediction I was talking about regarding the collapse of the Soviet empire is in the journal he kept while he was writing **East of Eden**—*the* **Journal of a Novel.** *Do you have a copy of it here?*
ES: I think so. [Walks to bookshelves and returns with *Journal of a Novel.*]

DC: Let me see if I can find it.

ES: While you're looking, I want you to hear this marvelous story. We went to the Soviet Union during Khrushchev's last years. John wanted to meet young writers. And we did meet them, a lot of young writers, and they stayed our friends. There was a Russian man who had been in trouble, a Soviet writer who had been in prison, and who was then in hiding. The Soviets had said to John, "He's gone. You won't see him. He's not writing anymore." And John kept saying, "Maybe we'll see him someplace." Anyway, we were sitting at a long table and the press was all behind us. There were all kinds of people there; there must have been three hundred people. And suddenly the door opened and everybody went "Ah," and then a man, rather bedraggled, walked square into the room and he put his hands in front of John and said, "Nekrasov!" And John put his hands on top of his and said, "Steinbeck!" And John said, "Sit down. I want to see you. That's one of the reasons I came to Russia." And the man came and spent the night with us at the hotel. John and he sat and talked all night and then he went back into hiding.

DC: This was in 1963?

ES: Yes. And the hotel . . . of course, there were spies, and we were bugged constantly. When we first arrived there, I wouldn't talk, and then I'd say things to John such as, "What this room needs is a few more ashtrays and another chair or two." And, of course, the next day I'd have them. I would tell this at parties, and they would all laugh because they weren't used to people doing like this. John and I were just perfectly open. But there were certain things that John said we must remember: "Anything that is secret, we must be very careful about." We had the most fascinating things happen. Before we left on our trip we went by the White House to see the President.

DC: This was Kennedy?

ES: Yes, Kennedy. And I said to the President, "Can I kick up a little dust?" And he said, "I'd like you to be debriefed when John comes to be debriefed. I want to hear everything you have to tell the State Department about the women." So when I got comfortable there—we were there three months—we'd be at a party with all these men, and they'd have wonderful food—six courses—and I would say, "Just a minute. I have something I want to say." "Oh, yes, madam; yes, madam." I'd say, "Where are the wonderful women who made all this food?" And they would say, "Oh, they're off in the kitchen." And I would say, "Well, I won't have another bite or drink until I meet them." The women adored me. They'd bring them all out, and John and Ed[ward] Albee and I would toast them. And then I would get up and talk with them and go out with them. So when I came home, I had a lot to say. I had a wonderful time. John adored the fact that I did that. Let me tell you another funny story. You know the Russian toast, *za vashe zdorovie* ("to your health")? And everytime you have a forkful of food you're starting to eat, you have to put it down and say, *za vashe zdorovie!* and you have to drink. So we had been over there a long time by now, and we were sick of that. And we were down in Tbilisi, and we are at a long table again with all those men in those black suits with the vests, and some women. John's down here, and I'm here and Edward's over here. And John's very shy. He never made toasts or anything; he was strictly cordial and polite with the talk. So I was looking down and watching him, and he was getting pretty tired of trying to eat and having to toast everything, and suddenly he stood up—Edward and I were absolutely mesmerized—and he said in a loud voice, "Natchez to Mobile," and I stood up and said, "Memphis to St. Jo." And everybody stood up and drank except for Edward Albee, who fell under the table laughing. "Wherever the four winds blow." They thought it was a toast! John said to me afterwards, "Oh Honey, I knew you would pick it up for me." "Natchez to Mobile." Sounds foreign, doesn't it? They didn't know what the hell "Natchez to Mobile" meant! Now you see, if you wrote that and somebody picked it up and made something political out of it, that would be pretty silly. And one of these days, somebody will.

DC: Will see it as political commentary?
ES: Yes, somebody will say, "It's political reporting to Russia on the South." But I want to tell you, I'll never forget Edward Albee's reaction. He said, "That was the funniest thing. Imagine Steinbeck doing that." And I said, "He just got pissed off!"

DC: Speaking of political commentary, I can see what you mean when you say he was very opinionated. Here's what he says about General MacArthur in Journal of a Novel: "April 19 . . . Today is MacArthur Day, and [he] will be filling the air with his horrid platitudes. I get such a sense of dishonesty from this man. Wonder what his wife thinks of him?"
ES: We went to the theater one night. We sat down in the center near the aisle. The curtain hadn't gone up yet when John said, "Look who just came in." It was General MacArthur with his wife. He was sitting on the aisle, and as he took off his hat and put it upside down on his lap, the hair dye was all the way around the band. John looked at me and said, "I wouldn't have missed this for the world!" John was fun like that; it was fun to be with him, because anybody else would have missed that, but not John. But you know what he did, Don? This was his whole philosophy: Whenever we were abroad and something bad was happening at home, for instance, during the McCarthy period, he always said, very seriously of course, "These are things every country has done. I discuss these things at home, but I don't discuss them away from home." And I thought it was so wonderful that he could handle that. He was always outspoken here and always wrote about such matters and discussed them, but he was not about to sit there [abroad] and slander his country in any way.

DC: Here, I've found the passage where Steinbeck predicts how the Soviet empire will unravel. It's in the entry for March 20, 1951, in Journal of a Novel: *"This morning the Schuman Plan started its route for signature. This, I think, is the beginning of the pattern of the future—the opening of the supra-state. Our businessmen in particular and people in general are very much in fear of communism. Now mark my prophecy—The so-called communist system will break up and destroy itself in horrible civil wars because it is not a permanent workable system. It will fly apart from its own flaws. On the other hand the Schuman Plan is a workable system. The businessmen so anxious about the status quo have little to fear from communism. The Schuman Plan is the thing that will change the world. I do not believe that America can compete with this new form of sponsored and controlled cartel. We will be forced either to fight it or to join it . . . (End of prediction)." He's predicting not only the breakup of the Soviet Union and the demise of communism, but also the new European order. The Schuman Plan led to the European Common Market and to all that we're seeing unfold in Europe even as we speak—an even more united Europe with a common currency. And, of course, the [Berlin] Wall fell in 1989.*

ES: When John and I stood at Checkpoint Charlie, the press said, "What do you think, Mr. Steinbeck?" And he said, "It's the most obscene sight I've ever seen." And I thought that was a great way to describe it, "obscene." And they said, "Would you like to go over and visit East Germany?" And he said, "Certainly not." That passage you read, I don't remember that at all. We ought to use that in your book somewhere. Now, please, turn that page down.

DC: Don't you want me to mark it with a slip of paper?
ES: No, just turn it down. John taught me to turn down pages. I said to him once, "Do you think it's awful to turn down pages?" He said, "Honey, mark it anyway you want, but don't put a slice of bacon be-

tween the pages. The fat would go through!" He was always saying something like that that you didn't expect him to.

DC: You know, those predictions about the collapse of communism—he was making them at the height of the cold war. And they show the same fundamental faith in democracy and human decency he proclaimed in **The Moon Is Down** *during the darkest days of the Second World War.*

ES: You see, John believed in *man*. That's what his Nobel Prize speech says. He said, "You believe in the perfectibility of man. Man will never be perfect, but he has to strive for it." That's the whole point. That was his whole point about life. And religion to John was very interesting. He was religious. He didn't believe in any church creeds, but he said to me when he was dying, "Don't you let a bunch of people get together and tell yarns about me. Make sure it's the Episcopal burial service." And I said to him, "Do you believe?" And he said, "I'm like Socrates before he drank the hemlock: I don't know if there are gods or not, but in case there are . . . ."

From *After "The Grapes of Wrath": Essays on John Steinbeck in Honor of Tetsumaro Hayashi*, edited by Donald V. Coers, Paul D. Ruffin, and Robert DeMott (1995), pp. 214-271. Copyright © 1995 by Ohio University Press. Reprinted with permission of Ohio University Press, Athens, Ohio (www.ohioswallow.com).

RESOURCES

Chronology of John Steinbeck's Life_____

1902	John Ernst Steinbeck is born on February 27 in Salinas, California, to John Ernst Steinbeck II and Olive Hamilton Steinbeck.
1919	Steinbeck graduates from Salinas High School.
1920-1925	Steinbeck attends Stanford University while working on and off as a laborer on ranches. His first short stories are published in the *Stanford Spectator.*
1925	Steinbeck drops out of Stanford and moves to New York City, where he works as a construction laborer for Madison Square Garden and reports for the *American* newspaper.
1926	Steinbeck returns to California, where he writes stories and novels.
1929	Steinbeck's first novel, *Cup of Gold*, is published.
1930	Steinbeck marries Carol Henning and moves to the family home in Pacific Grove, in California's Monterey County. He meets Edward F. Ricketts, with whom he begins an important lifelong friendship.
1932	*The Pastures of Heaven* is published. Steinbeck moves to Los Angeles.
1933	*To a God Unknown* is published. Steinbeck returns to Monterey, California. Parts of what will become *The Red Pony* appear in *North American Review*.
1934	Steinbeck's mother dies. His short story "The Murder" is selected as an O. Henry Prize story.
1935	*Tortilla Flat* is published. Steinbeck's father dies.
1936	*In Dubious Battle* is published. Steinbeck travels to Mexico.
1937	*Of Mice and Men* is published and is chosen as a Book-of-the-Month Club selection. The novella *The Red Pony* is published. Steinbeck travels to Europe, then from Oklahoma to California with migrants.

1938	*Their Blood Is Strong*, a collection of articles, is published. A collection of short stories, *The Long Valley*, is published. Steinbeck receives the New York Drama Critics' Circle Award for his stage adaptation of *Of Mice and Men*.
1939	*The Grapes of Wrath* is published and attracts nationwide attention. Steinbeck is elected to the National Institute of Arts and Letters.
1940	*The Grapes of Wrath* wins the Pulitzer Prize. *The Forgotten Village*, a documentary film, is produced. Steinbeck goes on a research trip with Edward Ricketts to the Gulf of Mexico. The film version of *The Grapes of Wrath* is released.
1941	*Sea of Cortez*, a collaboration between Steinbeck and Ricketts, is published.
1942	*The Moon Is Down* is published. Steinbeck and his wife divorce. The nonfiction *Bombs Away*, written for the U.S. Air Force, is published.
1943	Steinbeck moves to New York City and marries Gwyndolyn Conger. He serves as a war correspondent in Europe for the *New York Herald Tribune*.
1944	Director Alfred Hitchcock's film *Lifeboat*, written by Steinbeck, is released. Steinbeck buys his childhood dream house in Monterey, and his first son, Thom, is born.
1945	*Cannery Row* is published. Steinbeck moves to New York.
1946	Steinbeck's second son, John IV, is born.
1947	*The Wayward Bus* and *The Pearl* are published. Steinbeck travels through Russia with photographer Robert Capa.
1948	*A Russian Journal*, an account of Steinbeck's 1947 tour of Russia, is published. Steinbeck and Gwyndolyn Conger divorce. Steinbeck moves from New York to Pacific Grove.
1950	*Burning Bright* is published. Steinbeck marries Elaine Anderson Scott. He writes the script for *Viva Zapata!*

1951	*The Log from the Sea of Cortez*, the narrative part of *Sea of Cortez*, is published.
1952	*East of Eden* is published.
1954	*Sweet Thursday*, a sequel to *Cannery Row*, is published.
1957	*The Short Reign of Pippin IV* is published.
1958	*Once There Was a War,* a collection of Steinbeck's wartime dispatches, is published.
1960	Steinbeck travels around the United States for three months with his dog, Charley.
1961	*The Winter of Our Discontent* is published.
1962	*Travels with Charley*, the journal of Steinbeck's 1960 tour, is published. Steinbeck is awarded the Nobel Prize in Literature.
1963	Steinbeck travels to Scandinavia, Eastern Europe, and Russia on a cultural tour for the U.S. Information Agency.
1964	Steinbeck is awarded the Presidential Medal of Freedom.
1966	Steinbeck becomes a member of the National Arts Council. *America and Americans*, a collection of reflections on contemporary America, is published.
1966-67	Steinbeck reports from Vietnam for *Newsday*.
1968	Steinbeck dies of a heart attack in New York City on December 20. His ashes are buried in the Garden of Memories cemetery in Salinas, California.

Works by John Steinbeck

Long Fiction

Cup of Gold, 1929
The Pastures of Heaven, 1932
To a God Unknown, 1933
Tortilla Flat, 1935
In Dubious Battle, 1936
Of Mice and Men, 1937
The Red Pony, 1937
The Grapes of Wrath, 1939
The Moon Is Down, 1942
Cannery Row, 1945
The Pearl, 1945 (serial), 1947 (book)
The Wayward Bus, 1947
Burning Bright, 1950
East of Eden, 1952
Sweet Thursday, 1954
The Short Reign of Pippin IV, 1957
The Winter of Our Discontent, 1961

Short Fiction

Saint Katy the Virgin, 1936
The Long Valley, 1938

Nonfiction

Their Blood Is Strong, 1938
The Forgotten Village, 1941
Sea of Cortez: A Leisurely Journal of Travel and Research, 1941 (with Edward F. Ricketts)
Bombs Away, 1942
A Russian Journal, 1948 (with Robert Capa)
Once There Was a War, 1958
Travels with Charley: In Search of America, 1962
Letters to Alicia, 1965
America and Americans, 1966
Journal of a Novel: The "East of Eden" Letters, 1969
Steinbeck: A Life in Letters, 1975 (Elaine Steinbeck and Robert Wallsten, editors)

Steinbeck and Covici: The Story of a Friendship, 1979 (Thomas Fensch, editor)
Working Days: The Journals of "The Grapes of Wrath," 1938-1941, 1989 (Robert DeMott, editor)
America and Americans, and Selected Nonfiction, 2002 (Susan Shillinglaw and Jackson J. Benson, editors)

Screenplays
The Forgotten Village, 1941
Lifeboat, 1944
The Pearl, 1945
A Medal for Benny, 1945
The Red Pony, 1949
Viva Zapata!, 1952

Drama
Of Mice and Men, pr., pb. 1937
The Moon Is Down, pr. 1942
Burning Bright, pb. 1951

Translation
The Acts of King Arthur and His Noble Knights, 1976

Bibliography

Astro, Richard. *John Steinbeck and Edward F. Ricketts: The Shaping of a Novelist*. Minneapolis: University of Minnesota Press, 1973.

Astro, Richard, and Tetsumaro Hayashi, eds. *Steinbeck: The Man and His Work*. Corvallis: Oregon State University Press, 1971.

Beegel, Susan F., Susan Shillinglaw, and Wesley N. Tiffney, Jr., eds. *Steinbeck and the Environment: Interdisciplinary Approaches*. Tuscaloosa: University of Alabama Press, 1997.

Benson, Jackson J. *Looking for Steinbeck's Ghost*. 1988. Reno: University of Nevada Press, 2002.

_____. *The True Adventures of John Steinbeck, Writer*. New York: Viking Press, 1984.

_____, ed. *The Short Novels of John Steinbeck: Critical Essays with a Checklist to Steinbeck Criticism*. Durham, NC: Duke University Press, 1990.

Bloom, Harold, ed. *John Steinbeck*. New York: Chelsea House, 1987.

Burkhead, Cynthia. *Student Companion to John Steinbeck*. Westport, CT: Greenwood Press, 2002.

Coers, Donald V. *John Steinbeck Goes to War: "The Moon Is Down" as Propaganda*. 1991. Tuscaloosa: University of Alabama Press, 2006.

Davis, Robert Con, ed. *"The Grapes of Wrath": A Collection of Critical Essays*. Englewood Cliffs, NJ: Prentice Hall, 1982.

DeMott, Robert. *Steinbeck's Typewriter: Essays on His Art*. Troy, NY: Whitston, 1996.

Ditsky, John. *Critical Essays on Steinbeck's "The Grapes of Wrath."* Boston: G. K. Hall, 1989.

_____. *John Steinbeck and the Critics*. Rochester, NY: Camden House, 2000.

Fiedler, Leslie. "Looking Back After 50 Years." *San Jose Studies* 16.1 (1990): 54-64.

Fontenrose, Joseph. *John Steinbeck: An Introduction and Interpretation*. New York: Holt, Rinehart and Winston, 1963.

French, Warren. *John Steinbeck*. Boston: Twayne, 1975.

_____. *John Steinbeck's Fiction Revisited*. New York: Twayne, 1994.

George, Stephen K. *John Steinbeck and His Contemporaries*. Lanham, MD: Scarecrow Press, 2007.

_____, ed. *John Steinbeck: A Centennial Tribute*. New York: Praeger, 2002.

_____, ed. *The Moral Philosophy of John Steinbeck*. Lantham, MD: Scarecrow Press, 2005.

Gray, James. *John Steinbeck*. St. Paul: University of Minnesota Press, 1971.

Hayashi, Tetsumaro, ed. *John Steinbeck: The Years of Greatness, 1936-1939*. Tuscaloosa: University of Alabama Press, 1993.

_____, ed. *A New Study Guide to Steinbeck's Major Works, with Critical Explications*. Metuchen, NJ: Scarecrow, 1993.

_____, ed. *Steinbeck's Literary Dimension: A Guide to Comparative Studies*. Metuchen, NJ: Scarecrow Press, 1973.

_____, ed. *Steinbeck's Short Stories in "The Long Valley": Essays in Criticism*. Muncie, IN: Steinbeck Research Institution, 1991.

Heavlin, Barbara A., ed. *The Critical Responses to John Steinbeck's "The Grapes of Wrath."* Westport, CT: Greenwood Press, 2000.

Hughes, R. S. *John Steinbeck: A Study of the Short Fiction*. New York: Twayne, 1989.

Johnson, Claudia Durst, ed. *Understanding "Of Mice and Men," "The Red Pony," and "The Pearl": A Student Casebook to Issues, Sources, and Historical Documents*. Westport, CT: Greenwood Press, 1997.

Levant, Howard. *The Novels of John Steinbeck: A Critical Study*. Columbia: University of Missouri Press, 1974.

Lewis, Cliff, and Carrol Britch, eds. *Rediscovering John Steinbeck: Revisionist Views of His Art, Politics, and Intellect*. Lewiston, NY: Edwin Mellen, 1989.

Lisca, Peter. *John Steinbeck: Nature and Myth*. New York: Crowell, 1978.

_____. *The Wide World of John Steinbeck*. New Brunswick, NJ: Rutgers University Press, 1958.

McCarthy, Paul. *John Steinbeck*. New York: Frederick Ungar, 1980.

McElrath, Joseph R., Jr., Jesse S. Crisler, and Susan Shillinglaw, eds. *John Steinbeck: The Contemporary Reviews*. New York: Cambridge University Press, 1996.

Millichap, Joseph R. *Steinbeck and Film*. New York: Frederick Ungar, 1983.

Noble, Donald R., ed. *The Steinbeck Question: New Essays in Criticism*. Troy, NY: Whitston, 1993.

Owens, Louis. *Steinbeck's Re-Vision of America*. Athens: University of Georgia Press, 1985.

Parini, Jay. *John Steinbeck: A Biography*. New York: Henry Holt, 1995.

Railsback, Brian. *Parallel Expeditions: Charles Darwin and the Art of John Steinbeck*. Moscow: University of Idaho Press, 1995.

Railsback, Brian, and Michael J. Meyer, eds. *A Steinbeck Encyclopedia*. Westport, CT: Greenwood Press, 2006.

Schultz, Jeffrey, and Luchen Li. *A Critical Companion to John Steinbeck: A Literary Reference to His Life and Work*. New York: Facts On File, 2005.

Shillinglaw, Susan, and Kevin Hearle, eds. *Beyond Boundaries: Rereading John Steinbeck*. Tuscaloosa: University of Alabama Press, 2002.

Tedlock, E. W., Jr., and C. V. Wicker, eds. *Steinbeck and His Critics: A Record of Twenty-five Years*. Albuquerque: University of New Mexico Press, 1957.

Timmerman, John H. *The Dramatic Landscape of Steinbeck's Short Stories*. Norman: University of Oklahoma Press, 1990.

_____. *John Steinbeck's Fiction: The Aesthetics of the Road Taken*. Norman: University of Oklahoma Press, 1986.

Wilson, Edmund. "The Boys in the Backroom: Notes on California Novelists." *Classics and Commercials: A Literary Chronicle of the Forties*. New York: Farrar, Straus and Giroux, 1962.

CRITICAL INSIGHTS

About the Editor

Don Noble has been the host of the Emmy-nominated Alabama Public Television literary interview show *Bookmark* since 1988. Since 2002 his weekly reviews of fiction and nonfiction, mainly southern, have been broadcast on Alabama Public Radio. His most recent edited books include Salem Press's Critical Insights volumes on *To Kill a Mockingbird*, by Harper Lee (2010), and on F. Scott Fitzgerald; *A State of Laughter: Comic Fiction from Alabama* (2008); *Climbing Mt. Cheaha: Emerging Alabama Writers* (2004); and *Zelda and Scott/Scott and Zelda: New Writings on Their Works, Lives, and Times* (2005). He is also the editor of *Hemingway: A Revaluation* (1983), *The Steinbeck Question: New Essays in Criticism* (1993), *The Rising South* (with Joab L. Thomas; 1976), and *A Century Hence*, by George Tucker (1977). His reviews, essays, and interviews have appeared in numerous periodicals over the past forty years, and he has written introductions to several books, most recently a reissue of William Cobb's *Coming of Age at the Y* (2008). He serves on the board of directors of the Alabama Humanities Foundation and is an honorary lifetime member of the Alabama Writers' Forum. He holds a B.A. and an M.A. from the State University of New York-Albany. After receiving a Ph.D. from the University of North Carolina, Chapel Hill, Noble joined the English Department at the University of Alabama in 1969 and is now Professor Emeritus of English. He has been a Senior Fulbright Lecturer in the former Yugoslavia (1983-1984) and Romania (1991-1992) and has been a faculty member and director of the Alabama in Oxford Program and director of the Alabama in Ireland Program. He has been inducted into the international scholars' society Phi Beta Delta. In 2000, Noble received the Eugene Current-Garcia Award for Alabama's Distinguished Literary Scholar. With Brent Davis, he received a regional Emmy in 1996 for Excellence in Screenwriting for the documentary *I'm in the Truth Business: William Bradford Huie*.

About The Paris Review

The Paris Review is America's preeminent literary quarterly, dedicated to discovering and publishing the best new voices in fiction, nonfiction, and poetry. The magazine was founded in Paris in 1953 by the young American writers Peter Matthiessen and Doc Humes, and edited there and in New York for its first fifty years by George Plimpton. Over the decades, the *Review* has introduced readers to the earliest writings of Jack Kerouac, Philip Roth, T. C. Boyle, V. S. Naipaul, Ha Jin, Ann Patchett, Jay McInerney, Mona Simpson, and Edward P. Jones, and published numerous now classic works, including Roth's *Goodbye, Columbus*, Donald Barthelme's *Alice*, Jim Carroll's

Basketball Diaries, and selections from Samuel Beckett's *Molloy* (his first publication in English). The first chapter of Jeffrey Eugenides's *The Virgin Suicides* appeared in the *Review*'s pages, as well as stories by Rick Moody, David Foster Wallace, Denis Johnson, Jim Crace, Lorrie Moore, and Jeanette Winterson.

The Paris Review's renowned Writers at Work series of interviews, whose early installments include legendary conversations with E. M. Forster, William Faulkner, and Ernest Hemingway, is one of the landmarks of world literature. The interviews received a George Polk Award and were nominated for a Pulitzer Prize. Among the more than three hundred interviewees are Robert Frost, Marianne Moore, W. II. Auden, Elizabeth Bishop, Susan Sontag, and Toni Morrison. Recent issues feature conversations with Salman Rushdie, Joan Didion, Norman Mailer, Kazuo Ishiguro, Marilynne Robinson, Umberto Eco, Annie Proulx, and Gay Talese. In November 2009, Picador published the final volume of a four-volume series of anthologies of *Paris Review* interviews. *The New York Times* called the Writers at Work series "the most remarkable and extensive interviewing project we possess."

The Paris Review is edited by Philip Gourevitch, who was named to the post in 2005, following the death of George Plimpton two years earlier. A new editorial team has published fiction by André Aciman, Colum McCann, Damon Galgut, Mohsin Hamid, Uzodinma Iweala, Gish Jen, Stephen King, James Lasdun, Padgett Powell, Richard Price, and Sam Shepard. Poetry editors Charles Simic, Meghan O'Rourke, and Dan Chiasson have selected works by John Ashbery, Kay Ryan, Billy Collins, Tomaž Šalamun, Mary Jo Bang, Sharon Olds, Charles Wright, and Mary Karr. Writing published in the magazine has been anthologized in *Best American Short Stories* (2006, 2007, and 2008), *Best American Poetry*, *Best Creative Non-Fiction*, the Pushcart Prize anthology, and *O. Henry Prize Stories*.

The magazine presents two annual awards. The Hadada Award for lifelong contribution to literature has recently been given to Joan Didion, Norman Mailer, Peter Matthiessen, and, in 2009, John Ashbery. The Plimpton Prize for Fiction, awarded to a debut or emerging writer brought to national attention in the pages of *The Paris Review*, was presented in 2007 to Benjamin Percy, to Jesse Ball in 2008, and to Alistair Morgan in 2009.

The Paris Review was a finalist for the 2008 and 2009 National Magazine Awards in fiction, and it won the 2007 National Magazine Award in photojournalism. The *Los Angeles Times* recently called *The Paris Review* "an American treasure with true international reach."

Since 1999 *The Paris Review* has been published by The Paris Review Foundation, Inc., a not-for-profit 501(c)(3) organization.

The Paris Review is available in digital form to libraries worldwide in selected academic databases exclusively from EBSCO Publishing. Libraries can contact EBSCO at 1-800-653-2726 for details. For more information on *The Paris Review* or to subscribe, please visit: www.theparisreview.org.

Contributors

Don Noble has been the host of the Emmy-nominated Alabama Public Television literary interview show *Bookmark* since 1988. His most recent edited books are *A State of Laughter: Comic Fiction from Alabama* (2008), *Climbing Mt. Cheaha: Emerging Alabama Writers* (2004), and *Zelda and Scott/Scott and Zelda: New Writings on Their Works, Lives, and Times* (2005). He is also the editor of *Hemingway: A Revaluation* (1983), *The Steinbeck Question: New Essays in Criticism* (1993), *The Rising South* (with Joab L. Thomas; 1976), and *A Century Hence*, by George Tucker (1977).

Gordon Bergquist was Professor of English at Creighton University in Omaha, Nebraska.

Hua Hsu teaches in the English Department at Vassar College. His work has appeared in *The Atlantic*, the *New York Times*, *Bookforum*, *Slate*, the *Village Voice*, the *Boston Globe* "Ideas" section, and *The Wire* (for which he writes a bimonthly column). He has served on the editorial board for the *New Literary History of America*.

Matthew J. Bolton is Professor of English at Loyola School in New York City, where he also serves as Dean of Students. He received his doctor of philosophy degree in English from the Graduate Center of the City University of New York (CUNY) in 2005. His dissertation at the university was titled "Transcending the Self in Robert Browning and T. S. Eliot." Prior to attaining his Ph.D. at CUNY, he also earned a master of philosophy degree in English (2004) and a master of science degree in English education (2001). His undergraduate work was done at the State University of New York at Binghamton, where he studied English literature.

Jennifer Banach has served as the Contributing Editor of *Bloom's Guides: Heart of Darkness* (2009) and *Bloom's Guides: The Glass Menagerie* (2007) and is the author of *Bloom's How to Write About Tennessee Williams* (2009) and *Understanding Norman Mailer* (2010). She has also composed teaching guides to international literature for Random House's Academic Resources division and has contributed to numerous literary reference books for academic publishers such as Facts On File, Inc., and Oxford University Press on topics ranging from Romanticism to contemporary literature. Her work has appeared in academic and popular venues alike; her fiction and nonfiction have appeared under the *Esquire* banner. She is a member of the Association of Literary Scholars and Critics.

Gurdip Panesar earned her M.A. and Ph.D. degrees in English literature from the University of Glasgow, Scotland. She has contributed various entries to recent literary reference works and is at present teaching in the Department of Adult Education at the University of Glasgow.

Cynthia A. Bily teaches in the English Department at Macomb Community College in Michigan. She has written hundreds of essays for reference publications on literary topics ranging from Chinua Achebe to Zora Neale Hurston.

Jackson J. Benson is Professor Emeritus of English and Comparative Literature at San Diego State University. He has published nine books on modern American literature, including *John Steinbeck, Writer: A Biography* (1990) and *The True Adventures of John Steinbeck, Writer* (1984). He is also the author of *Wallace Stegner: His Life and Work* (1996), which won the David Woolley and Beatrice Cannon Evans Biography award from Utah State University.

Joseph Fontenrose was a classical scholar and Professor Emeritus of Classics at the University of California, Berkeley. An expert on John Steinbeck, he published *John Steinbeck: An Introduction and Interpretation* (1963) and often researched the role of California settings in Steinbeck's literature. His other books include *Didyma: Apollo's Oracle, Cult and Companions* (1988), *Classics at Berkeley: The First Century (1869-1970)* (1982), and *Steinbeck's Unhappy Valley: A Study of the Pastures of Heaven* (1981).

Thomas M. Tammaro is Professor of English at Minnesota State University Moorhead. As a Steinbeck critic, he is the author of two chapters included in Tetsumaro Hayashi's *John Steinbeck: The Years of Greatness, 1936-1939* (1993).

Anne Loftis is a journalist, freelance writer, and author. Her publications include *A Long Time Coming: The Struggle to Unionize America's Farm Worker* (1977), *California, Where the Twain Did Meet* (1973), and *The Great Betrayal: The Evacuation of Japanese-Americans During World War II* (1969).

Louis Owens was a novelist and scholar who contributed greatly to the mystery genre and to Native American studies. His Native American-themed mystery novels include *Dark River* (1999), *Nightland* (1996), and *Bone Game* (1996). He also published three books of literary criticism: *Mixedblood Messages: Literature, Film, Family, Place* (2001), *Other Destinies: Understanding the Native American Novel* (1992), and *John Steinbeck's Re-Vision of America* (1985).

John Seelye is Graduate Research Professor of American Literature at the University of Florida. Among his numerous publications are *Beautiful Machine: Rivers and the Republican Plan* (1991), *Prophetic Waters: The River in Early American Life and Literature* (1990), and *The True Adventures of Huckleberry Finn* (1970). He is the recipient of a Guggenheim Fellowship and two fellowships from the National Endowment for the Humanities for his continuous work on the river in American culture.

Warren G. French is Professor Emeritus of English at Indiana University-Purdue University in Indianapolis. His research interests include American studies, American literature, and social history. He received the doctor of humane letters degree from Ohio University in 1985. His publications include *John Steinbeck's Nonfiction Revisited* (1996), *John Steinbeck's Fiction Revisited* (1994), and *The "Lostness" of a Joyless Generation* (1993).

James C. Kelley, currently an expedition leader and naturalist, is former Dean of the College of Science and Engineering at San Francisco State University. He has written extensively on John Steinbeck's works and how they relate to the environment. His publications include "John Steinbeck and Ed Ricketts: Understanding Life in the Great Tide Pool" in *Steinbeck and the Environment* (1997) and "The Geoecology of Steinbeck Country" and "Ed Ricketts, Ecologist, on *Cannery Row*," both of which appeared in *The Steinbeck Newsletter.*

John H. Timmerman is Professor of English at Calvin College. His recent publications include *Woman, Why Are You Weeping? Daily Meditations for Lent* (2007) and *Light of the World: Daily Meditations for Advent* (2007). His scholarly writings focus on the works of Robert Frost, T. S. Eliot, John Steinbeck, and others.

Mimi Gladstein is Professor and Department Chair of Theatre, Film, and Literature at the University of Texas at El Paso. Her lectures center on contemporary American literature, Steinbeck, women's studies, and theater arts. She is the author of *The Indestructible Woman in Faulkner, Hemingway, and Steinbeck* (1986) and has published articles in such scholarly journals as *The Steinbeck Quarterly* and *College English*. Her most recent publication is *The Last Supper of Chicano Heroes: Selected Works of José Antonio Burciaga* (2008).

Susan Shillinglaw is Professor of English at San Jose State University and Scholar-in-Residence at the National Steinbeck Center in Salinas, California. A distinguished Steinbeck scholar, she is former director of the Center for Steinbeck Studies at San Jose State University and editor of the award-winning journal *Steinbeck Studies*. She is currently working on a biography of John Steinbeck and his first wife, Carol Steinbeck.

Robert E. Morsberger is Professor Emeritus of English at California State Polytechnic University. In addition to serving on the editorial board of *The Steinbeck Quarterly*, he is the editor of John Steinbeck's screenplay *Viva Zapata!* and author of *Lew Wallace: Militant Romantic* (1980), *Commonsense Grammar and Style* (1975), *Swordplay on the Elizabethan and Jacobean Stage* (1974), and *James Thurber* (1964).

Carol L. Hansen is an English Instructor at the City College of San Francisco. She has contributed essays to *Beyond Boundaries: Rereading John Steinbeck* (2002), and she is the author of the paper "The New Man in Hemingway and Steinbeck," which was presented at the Steinbeck and His Contemporaries conference held in 2006, where she was chosen to be part of the conference's panel.

Robert DeMott is the Edwin and Ruth Kennedy Distinguished Professor of American Literature and Writing at Ohio University. He has published more than a dozen books, including *Steinbeck's Typewriter: Essays on His Art* (1996), and has edited John Steinbeck's *Working Days: The Journals of "The Grapes of Wrath," 1938-1941* (1989). His essays have appeared in such literary journals as *The Georgia Review, The Southern Review*, and *Studies in American Fiction and American Literature*.

Donald V. Coers is Provost and Vice President for Academic and Student Affairs at Angelo State University and former Professor of English at Sam Houston State University, where he taught for thirty years. He is the author of *John Steinbeck as Propagandist: "The Moon Is Down" Goes to War* (1991) and coeditor of *After "The Grapes of Wrath": Essays on John Steinbeck in Honor of Tetsumaro Hayashi* (1994).

Acknowledgments_____

"John Steinbeck" by Gordon Bergquist. From *Dictionary of World Biography: The 20th Century.* Copyright © 1999 by Salem Press, Inc. Reprinted with permission of Salem Press.

"The *Paris Review* Perspective" by Hua Hsu. Copyright © 2011 by Hua Hsu. Special appreciation goes to Christopher Cox, Nathaniel Rich, and David Wallace-Wells, editors at *The Paris Review.*

"John Steinbeck: The Favorite Author We Love to Hate" by Jackson J. Benson. From *The Steinbeck Question: New Essays in Criticism*, edited by Donald R. Noble (1993), pp. 8-22. Copyright © 1993 by Whitston Publishing. Reprinted with permission of Whitston Publishing.

"*Tortilla Flat* and the Creation of a Legend" by Joseph Fontenrose. From *The Short Novels of John Steinbeck*, edited by Jackson J. Benson (1990), pp. 19-30. Copyright © 1990 by Duke University Press. All rights reserved. Used by permission of the publisher.

"Sharing Creation: Steinbeck, *In Dubious Battle*, and the Working-Class Novel in American Literature" by Thomas M. Tammaro. From *John Steinbeck: The Years of Greatness, 1936-1939*, edited by Tetsumaro Hayashi (1993), pp. 95-105. Copyright © 1993 by University of Alabama Press. Reprinted with permission of University of Alabama Press.

"A Historical Introduction to *Of Mice and Men*" by Anne Loftis. From *The Short Novels of John Steinbeck*, edited by Jackson J. Benson (1990), pp. 39-47. Copyright © 1990 by Duke University Press. All rights reserved. Used by permission of the publisher.

"*Of Mice and Men*: The Dream of Commitment" by Louis Owens. From *John Steinbeck's Re-Vision of America* (1985), pp. 100-106. Copyright © 1985 by Louis Owens. Reprinted with permission of Polly Owens.

"Come Back to the Boxcar, Leslie Honey: Or, Don't Cry for Me, Madonna, Just Pass the Milk: Steinbeck and Sentimentality" by John Seelye. From *Beyond Boundaries: Rereading John Steinbeck*, edited by Susan Shillinglaw and Kevin Hearle (2002), pp. 11-33. Copyright © 2002 by University of Alabama Press. Reprinted with permission of University of Alabama Press.

"California Answers *The Grapes of Wrath*" by Susan Shillinglaw. From *John Steinbeck: The Years of Greatness, 1936-1939*, edited by Tetsumaro Hayashi (1993), pp. 145-164. Copyright © 1993 by University of Alabama Press. Reprinted with permission of University of Alabama Press.

"Steinbeck's 'Self-Characters' as 1930s Underdogs" by Warren G. French. From *Beyond Boundaries: Rereading John Steinbeck*, edited by Susan Shillinglaw and Kevin Hearle (2002), pp. 66-76. Copyright © 2002 by University of Alabama Press. Reprinted with permission of University of Alabama Press.

Index

career, 8, 17, 22; education, 7, 17, 22, 136; and FBI investigation, 29, 52; journals and letters, 35, 320; and politics, 21, 39, 45, 104, 355, 385; and self-characters, 197, 332; speechwriting, 10, 53, 355; and theater, 32, 140, 271, 279, 381; travels abroad, 10, 31, 305, 385; war correspondent, 9, 31, 50, 56, 275, 297, 354, 369

Steinbeck, John Ernst (father), 40

Steinbeck Research Center. *See* Martha Heasly Cox Center for Steinbeck Studies

Stevenson, Adlai, 53, 355

Stewart, Randall, 97

Street, Toby, 25

Street, Webster F., 277

Sturges, Preston, 15

Sullivan's Travels (film), 15

Sweet Thursday (Steinbeck), 32, 100, 236, 320, 381

Taylor, Frank J., 178, 184

"Teague of California" (Taylor), 185

Teller, Mary ("The White Quail"), 81

Themes; Arthurian, 116; commitment, 147, 149; death and dying, 66, 148, 200, 257, 310; hunger, 84; loneliness, 138, 145; male-female relationships, 76, 245, 310; poverty, 66; *timshel*, 310; violence, 66, 87, 244, 256-257, 310; woman as nurturer, 65, 78

Thompson, Dorothy, 291

Thompson, Ralph, 140

Thurber, James, 368

Timmerman, John H., 88, 130, 326

To a God Unknown (Steinbeck), 8, 24, 43, 63, 232, 252

Tom Joad. *See* Joad, Tom

Tompkins, Jane, 155

Tortilla Flat (Steinbeck), 3, 8, 25, 101, 110, 198, 257, 265, 269

Trask, Adam (*East of Eden*), 238, 312

Travels with Charley (Steinbeck), 34, 55, 229

Uncle Tom's Cabin (Stowe), 153

Van Doren, Mark, 26, 31

Vietnam War, 10, 34, 56, 106

Viva Zapata! (Steinbeck), 252, 270, 331, 361

Wagner-Martin, Linda, 49, 51

Warner, Susan, 156

Wayne, Joseph (*To a God Unknown*), 43, 232, 252, 257-258; as Jesus Christ, 44

Wayward Bus, The (Steinbeck), 32, 51, 245, 304

Webster, Harvey Curtis, 325

Wedeles, Judy, 242, 318

Werlock, Abby, 246

"White Quail, The" (Steinbeck), 81

"Wife of Chino, The" (Norris), 66

Wilson, E. O., 5

Wilson, Edmund, 24, 29-31, 99, 142, 328

Winter of Our Discontent, The (Steinbeck), 33, 54, 98

Working-class novels, 125, 127

Working Days (Steinbeck), 35

World War II, 50, 275

Young, Sanborn, 179, 194

Zihlman, Adrienne, 216

Zola, Émile, 60